Global Sociology

Introducing Five Contemporary Societies

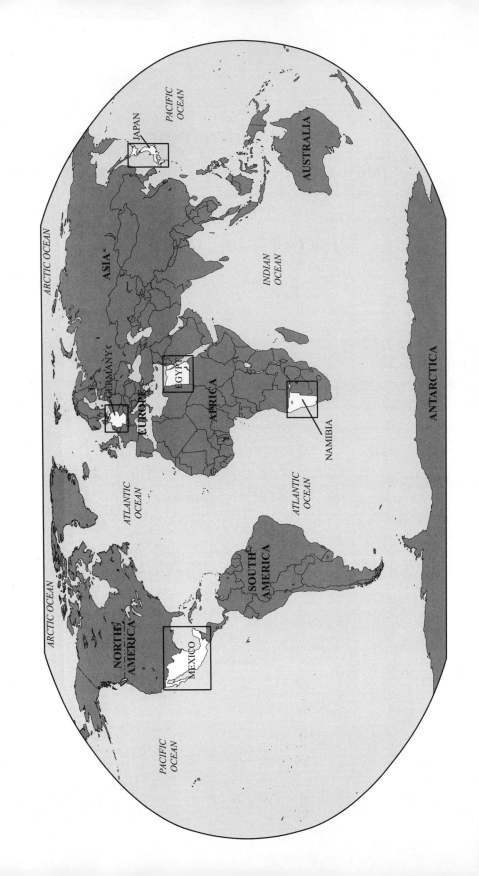

Global Sociology

Introducing Five
Contemporary Societies

FIFTH EDITION

Linda Schneider

Arnold Silverman

 **Higher Education**

Boston   Burr Ridge, IL   Dubuque, IA   New York   San Francisco   St. Louis
Bangkok   Bogotá   Caracas   Kuala Lumpur   Lisbon   London   Madrid   Mexico City
Milan   Montreal   New Delhi   Santiago   Seoul   Singapore   Sydney   Taipei   Toronto

The **McGraw·Hill** Companies

Mc Graw Hill Higher Education

Published by McGraw-Hill, an imprint of The McGraw-Hill Companies, Inc., 1221 Avenue of the Americas, New York, NY 10020. Copyright © 2010, 2006, 2003, 2000, 1997. All rights reserved. No part of this publication may be reproduced or distributed in any form or by any means, or stored in a database or retrieval system, without the prior written consent of The McGraw-Hill Companies, Inc., including, but not limited to, in any network or other electronic storage or transmission, or broadcast for distance learning.

This book is printed on acid-free paper.

3 4 5 6 7 8 9 0 DOC/DOC 0 9

ISBN 978-0-07-340418-9
MHID 0-07-340418-7

Editor in Chief: *Michael Ryan*
Editorial Director: *Beth Mejia*
Publisher: *Frank Mortimer*
Sponsoring Editor: *Gina Boedeker*
Managing Editor: *Nicole Bridge*
Marketing Manager: *Pam Cooper*
Developmental Editor: *Phil Butcher*
Project Manager: *Amanda Peabody*
Cover Designer: *Ashley Bedell*
Photo Research: *Brian Pecko*
Production Supervisor: *Louis Swaim*
Composition: *10.5/12 Times Roman by Laserwords Pvt. Ltd*
Printing: *45# New Era Matte Plus, R. R. Donnelley*

Photo Credits: p. 14, © Kaori Kamei and the Maruzen Company; p. 16, © Royalty-Free/Corbis; p. 23, © Joshua Handler; p. 25, © Kaori Kamei and the Maruzen Company; p. 48, © Joshua Handler; p. 79, © David Zurick; pp. 104, 105, © Copyright 1997 IMS Communications Ltd/Capstone Design. All Rights Reserved.; p. 119, © Royalty-Free/Corbis; p. 143, © Irven DeVore/Anthro-Photo; p. 152, © R. Lee/Anthro-Photo; p. 170, © Anthony Bannister/Gallo Images/Corbis; p. 171, © Digital Vision Ltd.; pp. 206, 212, 218, 221, 226, 239, © Jerry Kugler; p. 261, © Royalty-Free/Corbis; p. 267, Andrew Ward/Life File/Getty Images; p. 270, © Edeltraut Patterson; p. 278, © James Gibbon; p. 302, From D. Jenkins, et al. *Manual of the Causes & Control of Activated Sludge Bulking & Forming,* 1986. U.S. Environmental Protection Agency

Cover: Courtesy of Jerry Kugler

Library of Congress Cataloging-in-Publication Data
Schneider, Linda.
    Global sociology: introducing five contemporary societies / Linda Schneider. Arnold
  Silverman.— 5th ed.
    Includes bibliographical references and index.
    ISBN-13: 978-0-07-340418-9
    ISBN-10: 0-07-340418-7
    1. Sociology. 2. Sociology—Cross-cultural studies. I. Silverman, Arnold R., 1940- II. Title.

HM585.S36 2008
301—dc22   2008039053

The Internet addresses listed in the text were accurate at the time of publication. The inclusion of a Web site does not indicate an endorsement by the authors or McGraw-Hill, and McGraw-Hill does not guarantee the accuracy of the information presented at these sites.

www.mhhe.com

Contents

List of Tables

Introduction: To the Student

Global Sociology

Today, no one can afford to ignore the variety of the world's societies. If you go to work in the business world, it is very likely that in selling your products, or buying supplies, or managing your company's factories, you will need to deal with people from other societies. If you join your country's military forces, understanding local cultures will be critical to the success of your mission and may save your life. When you go on vacation or listen to music, you may come into contact with unfamiliar cultures. You will enjoy yourself more if you are comfortable with diversity. *Global Sociology* is a sociological introduction to the diversity of the world's societies.

Sociology has an important message for you: There are many ways to arrange human lives—many different kinds of families, economies, and governments, and endlessly varied values, beliefs, attitudes, and customs. Until very recently in human history, most people lived quite isolated lives, seldom meeting people from other societies. People readily believed that their own way of life was the only way, or the best way, and that other societies were strange or evil. In today's global world, condemning other societies leads to misunderstanding and violence. The world's peoples need to learn about one another. We believe that the more you know about different ways of life, the more profoundly you will appreciate how much all humans have in common.

We chose five societies to include in this book:

Japan: The Importance of Belonging

Mexico: Conflict and Cooperation

The San Peoples of Namibia: Ancient Culture in a New Nation

Egypt: Faith, Gender, and Class

Germany: Diversity in a Modern Nation-State

It was hard to choose just five societies from all the hundreds in the world today. First of all, we chose societies from different parts of the world and different cultural traditions. One society in this book is in Asia, one in Latin America, one in

Europe, and two in Africa (although one of these, Egypt, is culturally part of the Middle East). Japan and Germany are rich, industrialized nations. Mexico, Namibia, and Egypt are "developing" nations that are struggling with poverty.

We looked for societies very different from your own to illustrate the range of the world's social diversity. Egypt is an Islamic society, where five times a day the call to prayer penetrates every street and house. Many people pray at every call and strive to follow the laws of Islam. In Japan, people enjoy celebrating the holidays of many religions. At Christmas, Japanese people give one another presents and eat takeout fried chicken. Afterward, they attend a ceremony in a Buddhist temple. But only 10% of Japanese people consider themselves religious.

The Germans and the San people of Namibia could not be more different peoples, but they have in common the experience of rapid social change. The San are one of the last peoples on earth who have lived by gathering wild food. They are now losing their land and their way of life, marking the end of a major chapter in the story of humanity. In the past two decades, Germans have struggled to adjust to an increasingly diverse society, first as the former East Germany was reunified with the west, and then as Germany's immigrant population grew dramatically.

Egypt and Mexico are both relatively poor countries experiencing rapid economic growth. In both societies there are tremendous disparities between the rich and the poor. Rich Egyptians have made their country one of the world's largest importers of German luxury cars, but poor Egyptians, desperate for housing, have taken to living in cemeteries. A decade ago, impoverished Indian peasants in Chiapas, Mexico, took up arms against local landowners and the government. Today, farmers, Indians, and poor Mexicans still protest government policies.

Learning Sociology from Diversity

Learning about many different societies will help you deepen your understanding of sociological concepts. Sociology textbooks teach concepts like values, norms, roles, socialization, deviance, social stratification, modernization, and so forth. The five societies in this book were chosen to illustrate these and other important sociological concepts. When you understand how sociological concepts can be applied to differing societies, you will understand the concepts much better.

Let's take an example: the concept of social inequality. For this book, we have chosen societies with highly varied forms of social inequality. In Namibia the San lived for centuries with almost complete equality. No one had any more possessions or any more power than anyone else. Learning about the San will sharpen your ability to see inequalities in other societies, including your own. In Egypt, there are sharp inequalities between men and women. In Japan, people pay close attention to status differences in age, gender, education, and occupation, but income inequalities are quite minimal. In Mexico, millions of people earn the minimum wage of under $4 a day, while the richest Mexicans have imported cars and air-conditioned houses and send their children to colleges and universities abroad. When you learn about many different systems of social stratification, you will understand the concept better.

To help you understand what life is like in different societies, we have included in each chapter a number of *vignettes:* short, fictional sketches of individuals, their life situations, and their feelings. None of the characters in the vignettes are real people. We made them up, inspired by people we read about and people we met.

Learning Through Comparison

Comparison and contrast are very important means of learning. The San spent all their lives in groups of 15 to 40 people, related by kinship. Imagine how hard it would be to teach them the concept of "bureaucracy." They have never waited in a line at the Department of Motor Vehicles or filled out forms for registration at college. When you study the San, you will learn how new and unusual bureaucracies are in the human experience.

Comparison has always been the essence of sociology. Sociologists know that when you are immersed in your own society, you take for granted and assume that its ways are part of human nature, universal and unchanging. We most easily discover what our own society is like when we learn about a different society. As sociologists say, "The fish is the last to discover water."

Comparison is a wonderful means by which to apply concepts and theories and deepen your understanding of their meanings. Comparison is also a challenge to intolerance. Studying world societies shows us that there is no one *right* way to live, and that the most fundamental characteristic of "human nature" is our tremendous flexibility in creating diverse cultures.

Active Learning

Suppose you wanted to learn to play basketball and someone told you to listen to another person talk about the game, and then watch other people play it. You would be disgusted with this advice because you know that in order to learn basketball, you must play the game yourself and then practice, practice, practice. If you have a coach or someone else to watch you and give you pointers, you will learn even faster.

Will you be surprised to hear that learning sociology (or any other college subject) works the same way? Just reading or hearing someone else present sociological ideas isn't enough. You must practice your own sociological reasoning, aloud and in writing, and have others coach you in your work in order to learn the subject.

Global Sociology is designed so that you can practice applying sociological concepts to a descriptive "database" of information about five different societies. As you read this book, ask yourself: "Can I talk about these societies using the language of sociology?" Try to describe the values of each society, or the roles they expect men and women to play. Think about how family life is organized in each society, or what social groups are most important in people's lives. Questions at the end of each chapter will help you put your knowledge of sociology to active use.

One of the best ways to practice sociological thinking is to make comparisons. We invite you to compare each of these societies to your own society: What similarities and what differences can you see? You can also compare the societies in this book with one another. In writing this book, we have been greatly tempted to make comparisons ourselves, but we have tried to discipline ourselves and stick to description. We want to leave the work and play of comparison to the students and instructors who use *Global Sociology*.

Preface: To the Instructor

We wrote this book to give students a broader context for understanding both sociology and their own societies. For several years both authors had assigned William Kephart's *Extraordinary Groups* when teaching introductory sociology. We liked Kephart's case-study approach. Reading his descriptions of a variety of American religious groups, students were exposed to diverse cultures and social structures. Despite these advantages, we were unhappy confining our comparisons to religious sects. Linda's student Mike Godino put it nicely when he told us, "You know, introductory sociology is great. I'm learning about ways of life I never imagined, and it makes me see my own society so much more clearly by contrast. But I'm not sure I want to know this much about these little religious groups. Isn't there a book that does the same thing for countries, important countries that we should understand?"

Mike's comment crystallized our desire to extend the range of comparisons, and we searched around, but there wasn't such a book. There were plenty of ethnographies, but these were anthropological rather than sociological. Then there were "global" textbooks. We liked these texts, but we were looking for a supplement with in-depth case studies.

Finally, we decided to write the book ourselves: *Global Sociology* is a soft-cover supplement to any standard sociology text, providing broad and comprehensive sociological description of five diverse contemporary societies. We aimed for wide geographic distribution: We chose one Asian society—Japan; one Latin American society—Mexico; one European society—Germany; and two African societies—Egypt and Namibia. Two of the societies are wealthy and industrial, and two are poor "developing" nations. For greater contrast we include a special focus on the hunting-and-gathering San of Namibia.

One of our concerns in writing *Global Sociology* has been to create a text that instructors can use without being specialists in the study of Japan, Mexico, Egypt, Germany, or Namibia. General knowledge and a sociologist's understanding of how societies work provide ample background for using *Global Sociology*. We are confident that you will see how easily *Global Sociology* can be introduced into your courses. Although it is interesting to read some of the more specialized studies we have recommended, it is by no means a requirement for the effective use of *Global Sociology*.

A Comparative Framework

The five societies described here vary in many ways: in their definitions of male and female roles, in their degree of inequality, in the salience of religious values and norms in their cultures, and in their population dynamics. *Global Sociology* includes two societies that once were socialist, the former East Germany and Egypt, and it discusses the impact of earlier socialist institutions and cultures on society today. The book also examines two different wealthy capitalist societies—Germany and Japan—whose styles of capitalism contrast with that of the United States.

Global Sociology is structured to parallel the major sections of a standard sociology text. Each chapter is organized around basic sociological topics: culture, social structure and group life, socialization, deviance, social institutions, social stratification, and social change. Earlier chapters place more emphasis on topics usually introduced first in introductory sociology. Chapters on Japan, Mexico, and the Bushmen of Namibia provide much discussion of culture, social structure, socialization, and deviance, although they include other topics as well. Later chapters on Egypt and Germany touch more briefly on beginning concepts and emphasize social stratification, social institutions, and social change.

Global Sociology will help bring to life abstract textbook presentations of concepts with a wealth of vivid illustrations. Reading about Japanese greeting norms, or Mexican patronage politics, or the effects of population growth in Egypt, or incompatibilities in German and Turkish marriage norms, or how the San avoid conflict, students will see the universal relevance of sociological ideas. Questions posed at the end of each chapter lead students to make sociological comparisons and to apply sociological concepts to descriptive knowledge.

Comparison is one of the great strengths of sociology. By comparing other societies with their own, students learn about the range of social variation, and they learn what makes their own society distinctive. Reading *Global Sociology,* students will spontaneously make comparisons with their own society, and they can be encouraged to compare the diverse societies described in the book. To aid in this effort, the text provides a variety of tables that summarize important comparative data for Japan, Mexico, Egypt, Germany, Namibia, and the United States.

Although most of our students were born and raised in the United States, an increasing number are from countries as diverse as El Salvador, Haiti, Nigeria, Iran, China, Pakistan, and the former Soviet Union. It is exciting to see that these students can use *Global Sociology* to make meaningful comparisons with the societies and cultures they have been born and raised in. *Global Sociology* doesn't require that students carry the assumptions, insights, and values of an American childhood and schooling.

Learning about other societies helps all students become aware of their ethnocentrism and reach beyond it. Students develop a sense of attachment to the societies they study, even when some of what they read disturbs them. To help students use their imaginations in picturing unfamiliar societies, we have included fictional vignettes of individuals in each society. Vignettes help students make human connections across cultural divides.

We have found that reading *Global Sociology* heightens student interest in other societies. News from abroad becomes absorbing when students have a framework in which to place it. *Global Sociology* presents societies that are often in the news, and our own students have become alert to news coverage about the societies they study. After 2003, with the United States fighting wars in Afghanistan and Iraq, our students became very interested in news coverage of Islamic societies. As they compared Egypt with Afghanistan, Iraq, and Pakistan, they learned that while Muslim societies are linked by a common religion and face similar problems of wrenching economic and political transformation, they respond very differently because of their diverse histories and cultures.

The Fifth Edition

World events move quickly. The fifth edition has been revised to keep students up to date. First of all, the statistical tables have been updated with the latest information available. We have searched out the best sources of world statistics on the Internet, and Web references are noted with the tables and in the bibliography. You and your students can continue to update data by using these sources. In many cases, Web sources will allow you to generate your own tables by selecting variables.

  Global Sociology has been carefully revised to reflect current events. The chapter on **Japan** traces changing work roles and changing norms in the culture of work, as these affect women and men, young and old, schooling, careers, and patterns of inequality. We have reorganized the chapter on **Egypt** to provide fuller discussion of deviance and social control, gender roles, and social groups in rural and urgan settings. The chapter on **Mexico** lays new emphasis on the ubiquity of conflict in Mexican society, the growing impact of crime, and especially drug trafficking, on Mexican life, and the importance of recent government action in moderating economic inequality. We now report on three different groups of San in **Namibia,** to better portray various ways San have adapted to social change as their hunting and gathering life disappears. In the fifth edition the chapter on **Germany** has been most radically changed. We have deemphasized comparison of the former East Germany and the former West Germany, as reunification recedes into the past. Instead, we have explored the issue most pressing now in Germany: immigration and ethnic diversity. We think that today, in our era of massive global migration, this topic will have broad resonance. And because of their nation's history, Germans are particularly sensitive to issues concerning minorities, national identity, and discrimination based on notions of race, ethnicity, or religion.

  As we follow events in *Global Sociology*'s five societies and the world, we see two overarching themes of change, which we have tried to illustrate and incorporate in the fifth edition. First of all, we see everywhere the effects of **globalization.** We have reorganized the chapters of *Global Sociology* so that each chapter now ends with a section discussing social change and globalization, utilizing some standard themes: globalization and economic change, globalization and migration, globalization and the environment, demographic change, and cultural change. Global media and the global economy touch every society, making their material cultures more similar, and widening the secularizing impact of capitalist economic institutions and democratic politics. We ask ourselves, Will *Global Sociology* become outdated as all the world's societies become alike? Our answer is, No, because the secularizing and homogenizing effects of globalization have been greeted in every society by efforts to assert particularistic identities, be they national, cultural, or religious. So the world's societies—including those in *Global Sociology*—are becoming both more similar and more different all the time. *Global Sociology* describes this two-way flow of social change.

The following material is new to the fifth edition:

- More emphasis on the global impact of migration, both on societies which receive immigrants (Japan, Germany, Mexico) and also on societies from which people emigrate (Mexico, Egypt, Germany).
- Expanded discussion of the effects of economic globalization: on Mexicans who migrate and Mexicans who adapt to changing job opportunities at home; on Japanese who increasingly look toward Asia, rather than the United States, for economic competition, markets, and culture; on Germans who see themselves as Europeans, free to work and live anywhere in the European Union.
- Updated analysis of Egypt's religious revival, in the context of global Islam, highlighting its reshaping of gender roles and daily life.
- Broadened coverage of deviance and social control in Japan, Mexico, Egypt, and Germany, to facilitate cross-cultural comparison and the application of sociological theories.
- More analysis of class inequality and income distribution in Japan, Mexico, Egypt, and Germany. New discussion makes possible comparison of the impact of government policy on inequality in several societies.
- Fuller discussion of the lives of Namibian San in three different social settings: on reservations, in government-owned resettlement areas, and on Bantu-owned land.

Events, no doubt, will continue their rapid pace. We have tried to give you access to current news about the societies in this book so that it will be easy for you to keep up. Please use the Web Guide in the Instructor's Manual that accompanies *Global Sociology*. It includes English-language newspaper Web sites for all five societies. We have carefully selected sites that are reputable and reliable, easy to access, and constantly updated. They should be a good source for news for you and your students.

We have enjoyed using *Global Sociology* with our own students. We appreciate their sense of wonder as they confront diverse societies, and we are continually impressed with how much they learn about their own society when they study other societies. We hope you and your students will enjoy the book, too.

Supplementary Material

Accompanying *Global Sociology* is a combined Instructor's Manual and Test Bank. It opens with an Introduction that provides hints on "Using Global Sociology." For each chapter, it includes a chapter overview highlighting the important themes; an annotated list of suggested readings; a film/video guide; an annotated list of Web sites; exercises and assignments; discussion/study questions; essay questions; and multiple-choice and true/false test questions.

Acknowledgments

Any book is the product of many hands and *Global Sociology* has had a wealth of help from its inception as an idea that emerged from our classes in the early 1990s. We would not have moved to create *Global Sociology* without the questions and curiosity of our students. Our students at Nassau Community College have continually shaped and reshaped our work by their responses to what we have written.

The first edition of *Global Sociology* had an active advocate in Teresa Salas Imhoff of McGraw-Hill, who brought our project to the attention of Phil Butcher also of McGraw-Hill. Phil was willing to endorse what was and remains today a somewhat unorthodox text. The first four editions benefited greatly from the insight and hard work of Kathy Blake, who supervised the endless details of production and tactfully helped the authors avoid folly. Gina Boedecker, McGraw-Hill's current sociology editor, has actively supported our project. Without her support there would have not been a fifth edition.

We are fortunate enough to work in an academic department that gives active support to our writing. Our colleagues Lyle Hallowell, Elizabeth Wood, and Yih-Jin Young graciously assumed the burden of departmental committee work as we turned our hands to writing. Our colleagues also endured the continual burden of queries in their area of expertise: criminology, gender, and demography, respectively. Our departmental secretary Mavis Loschin went out of her way to make our lives easier and our work possible.

We owe a continuing debt to the Kamei family for their hospitality in Japan. As in previous editions, Tsubasa Kamei made us aware of currents in contemporary Japanese culture that had not yet made it into the scholarly literature. Norman Tjombe and Romy Noeske, the director and librarian of Namibia's Legal Assistance Centre, took time out from the enormously valuable work of the Centre to respond to our requests and send us material on contemporary Namibia. We are also indebted to Thomas Krebs of the Statistisches Bundesamt, who helped us make our way through the detailed statistical resources of the German Federal Statistical Office.

We were able to obtain photographs with the active assistance of Kaori Kamei and Sada Aksartova in Japan, Jim Gibbons and Edeltraut Patterson in Germany, and Jerry Kugler in Egypt. Many of these photographers came to our assistance through the good offices of Daniel Schneider of Princeton University. We greatly appreciated the willingness of the Maruzen Company of Tokyo to let us use photographs of their offices, officers, and staff. *Domo Arigato Gazimasu.* John Day of Nassau Community College gave generously of his time in editing our photographs. As in the past, Brian Pecko of McGraw-Hill offered us useful technical support and advice in searching McGraw-Hill's photo archives.

Alicia Sanchez of Nassau Community College's Library was indispensable to our efforts to read and review the wide range of contemporary scholarship on our subject matter. The librarians of the Rochester, Vermont, Merrick, New York, and the New York Society Library went out of their way to find sources and provide a comfortable working environment during our sabbatical leaves.

Our reviewers' suggestions are always important to us as we prepare a new edition. Their response to our work is a most useful guide. For this edition the reviewers include: Joseph Healy, Christopher Newport University; Dale Howard, North West Arkansas Community College; Susan Cox, Bellevue Community College; and Gary Brock, Missouri State University. We thank them all.

Our spouses, Peter Schneider and Ruth Silverman, carefully read the entire manuscript and offered invaluable and detailed advice on revisions. Needless to say, they continued to offer their support in other ways as they have through four previous editions of *Global Sociology*.

Linda Schneider
Arnold Silverman

About the Authors

LINDA SCHNEIDER is Professor of Sociology at SUNY—Nassau Community College. She received her PhD in sociology from Columbia University. Professor Schneider has for many years enjoyed teaching introductory sociology and has long been involved in activities related to undergraduate instruction. She has published in the American Sociological Association's journal *Teaching Sociology,* contributed to panels about teaching at conferences of the Eastern Sociological Society, the Community College Humanities Association, the Community College General Education Association, and the American Association of Community Colleges. Professor Schneider has directed several grants from the National Endowment for the Humanities, the Fund for the Improvement of Postsecondary Education, and the National Science Foundation for multidisciplinary and global curriculum development.

ARNOLD SILVERMAN is Professor of Sociology at SUNY—Nassau Community College. He received his PhD in sociology from the University of Wisconsin, Madison. Professor Silverman has published widely, and his articles have appeared in the *American Sociological Review, Built Environment, Contemporary Sociology, Social Service Review,* and elsewhere. He is the coauthor of *Chosen Children,* a longitudinal study of American adopting families. Professor Silverman has also been active in efforts to improve the quality of undergraduate instruction. He codirected a faculty development effort financed by the Fund for the Improvement of Postsecondary Education to encourage active learning in undergraduate teaching. He has been chair of the Eastern Sociological Society's Committee on Community Colleges, and coordinator of Nassau Community College's Freshman Learning Communities program.

Global Sociology

Introducing Five Contemporary Societies

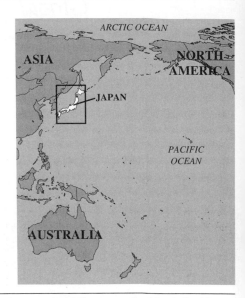

To reach Japan from the United States or Canada you would fly across the North Pacific almost to the mainland of Asia. Narita airport outside Tokyo is one of the busiest airports in the world. Rising from defeat in World War II, Japan has become the world's second largest economy.

LOCATION: Japan is located on the eastern edge of Asia, 200 miles from Korea and across the Sea of Japan from China and Russia. East of Japan lies the Pacific Ocean.

AREA: Japan consists of four large islands of Hokkaido, Honshu, Shikoku, and Kyushu (145,000 square miles). Together they are the size of California or Germany. Honshu is the largest island and the site of Tokyo, the capital, and other large cities.

LAND: Japan is mountainous and rugged. Mt. Fuji, a dormant volcano, is 12,000 feet high. Less than 1 acre in 6 is flat; most of this is along the coasts where cities compete with farms for space. Almost half the population lives in three major metropolitan areas.

CLIMATE: Similar to the east coast of the United States. It is colder on Hokkaido and nearly subtropical in southern Kyushu.

Japan receives 50 inches of rain a year, much of it falling as snow.

POPULATION: In 2007 there were 127 million people; by 2050 the population will likely fall to 101 million. Japan's population is aging; 20% were over age 65 in 2005.

INCOME: In equivalent U.S. purchasing power, $32,530 per capita GDP in 2005.

EDUCATION: Japan has one of the highest average educational levels and the highest literacy rate in the world.

RELIGION: Seventy-five percent combine Buddhism and Shinto, a unique Japanese religion; less than 2% are Christian.

MINORITIES: Korean Japanese, Ainu, *Burakumin,* immigrants.

CHAPTER ONE

Japan: The Importance of Belonging

INTRODUCTION

If you visit downtown Tokyo today, you might think you are in New York, or London, or Beirut for that matter. Young people sit in coffee bars and talk on their cell phones. The women carry Vuitton bags and wear Prada and Burberry clothes. You can eat lunch at McDonald's or KFC, shop at The Gap, and see the latest Hollywood action movie. In some ways, all our societies are becoming more similar, as a global consumer culture spreads around the world. Perhaps in your society, people eat both hamburgers and sushi, watch both *Survivor* and Japanese anime. Does it still make sense to read a book like this one, devoted to describing what makes five societies different from each other?

This is an old question in Japan, a really old question, going back at least 1,000 years. Japan's history has a very clear story line. It is the story of a society that repeatedly adopted elements of culture from other societies, but nevertheless remained distinctly "Japanese."

JAPAN'S HISTORY

Japanese history is interesting and contradictory. It shows us long conservative periods when the Japanese guarded and preserved their traditions and shut out foreign influences. It also displays repeated crises in which Japanese society transformed itself, rapidly adapting foreign cultures and creating new Japanese "traditions."

The Great Opening to China

A great turning point in Japan's history occurred 2,500 years ago. Immigrants from China and Korea introduced rice cultivation to Japan. This productive crop enabled the Japanese to support many more people on their limited farmland. These immigrants also introduced many aspects of China's culture: Buddhism, literacy, legal systems, city planning, and architecture. By the 7th century a unified Japanese state

3

had emerged based on Chinese models (Totman, 2005, pp. 20–67). Typically for Japan, planned change and the adoption of foreign ideas was orchestrated from the top, by the elite of Japanese society. For the next three centuries, Japan's rulers continued to study China and adopt Chinese institutions, arts, and technology, deliberately "improving" Japanese society. But it is important to understand that this was a self-transformation. Japan was not conquered or colonized by China. All of its borrowings were voluntary. In fact, after the 9th century, Japan retreated into isolation and slowly digested all its borrowed Chinese culture, blending it with native ways, and finally producing a new, distinctly Japanese culture (Bellah, 2003, pp. 9–15; Reischauer, 1977, pp. 41–51).

The Tokugawa Era: Contact with the West Refused

In the 16th century the door to Europe opened briefly, then slammed shut for nearly 300 years. The 16th century was a time of great disorder in Japan. Europeans arrived in the midst of conflict. Their guns fascinated Japanese warriors who soon copied them and put them to use. Christianity was very attractive to people whose lives were in chaos: More than 300,000 converted in less than a century. When order was forcibly restored, Japan's rulers found both guns and Christians threatening to their rule. Christians had to renounce their religion or face execution. By 1638 rulers had completely sealed off Japan from the outside world. Laws banned firearms and forbade the Japanese from building oceangoing ships or trading with foreigners. Only a few foreign traders—Koreans, Chinese, and Dutch—were allowed to enter Japan. During two centuries of isolation, from 1638 to 1853 (known as the Tokugawa Era, after the leading family of *shoguns,* or rulers, of the period) Japan was peaceful and stable. Important changes took place, though, including the development of a class of entrepreneurs, the rise of a centralized government, and the forging of a strong sense of national identity. A few Japanese scholars read Dutch books and kept up with news of the scientific and political revolutions taking place in the West (Bellah, 2003, p. 22; Christopher, 1983, pp. 47–48; Totman, 2005, 211–219).

The Meiji Restoration: The First Opening to the West

Japan's second contact with the West had a very different outcome. It resulted in another great self-transformation. By mid-19th century, Western powers had colonized Africa, India, and much of Southeast Asia, forcing trade concessions upon China as well. Finally, in 1853, the American navy forced Japan to open its ports to American ships and sign a series of trade treaties. Fear of subjection to foreign powers brought on a national crisis in Japan. In 1868, rebel provincial rulers, backed by reform-minded middle- and low-ranking *samurai* (members of Japan's hereditary warrior caste) seized power from the shoguns. Their rule was called the *Meiji Restoration,* because they claimed to restore power to the emperor, the heredity monarch. In fact, however, they ruled in his stead. Japan's new rulers decided to take radical defensive action against European colonization. They successfully argued that the only way Japan could enjoy equality with Western powers was to modernize and adopt Western technology. Under Meiji leadership Japan was able to deliberately bring about its own modernization and fend off European colonization.

The new government soon abolished feudal domains and began dismantling the caste system. It instituted universal primary education and universal conscription. Then, the top leaders of the new regime went off on a long voyage during which they visited the United States and many European countries. In effect, the Meiji government went shopping for new institutions, finding a model for its navy in Britain, its army in France, its universities in America, and its constitution in Germany (Bellah, 2003, pp. 30–31; Tasker, 1987, p. 21). Meiji rulers created a new government bureaucracy, based on European models and staffed by a new university-educated civil service. They adopted a modern court system and public school system. Meiji Japan promoted economic modernization, making peasants owners of the land they farmed, and encouraging modern agriculture, based on American models. The government created Western-style banks, railroads, and ports, and developed mining, steel and weapons production, and silk manufacture. They sent students abroad to learn Western skills and hired Western experts to come to Japan. And all of this was done by the end of the 19th century!

Japan also emulated the imperial ambitions of Western countries, both to demonstrate its military strength to the West, and also to build an empire of its own. In 1894–1895, Japan defeated China in a war for control of Korea, and in 1904–1905, it fought again for Korea, this time against Russia, gaining Korea and several other possessions in its victory. By World War I, Japan was a major colonial power, the equal of Western powers. Militarism intensified in Japan during the difficult years of the 1920s and 1930s. Imperial ambitions once again led Japan into war with China, a war that dragged on and finally escalated into the Pacific theater of World War II. Japan's defeat opened a new chapter in its Westernization and economic development.

The Occupation Reforms: The Second Opening to the West

Japan was utterly devastated by the war, and its people demoralized and disillusioned with militarism. They were open to change and new ideas. And the American occupying forces, in their self-confident, well-meaning American way, were eager to make over Japanese society. General Douglas MacArthur, acting as Supreme Commander for the Allied Powers, dismantled Japan's military, reformed its government and constitution, broke up its industrial monopolies, and redistributed land ownership. MacArthur's reforms were radical, giving individuals rights beyond what is guaranteed in the U.S. Constitution, including equal rights for women, the right of labor to bargain collectively, and the right of all individuals to an equal education. As we will see, in the years since the occupation, Japan has strengthened the reforms that were compatible with its culture and ignored the rest. A new combination of Western institutions and Japanese centralized government, created with Japanese-style drive, brought about Japan's postwar "economic miracle."

Japan rapidly rebuilt from wartime ruin and then went on to industrialize and develop cutting-edge export-oriented industries, producing cars, radios, televisions, computers, and other consumer electronics. Japan is a small country, essentially lacking in raw materials and energy resources. In 40 years, the nation grew to become the world's second largest economy. Japanese workers were content to dedicate themselves to the nation's goal of economic advance because they benefited. Wages doubled and redoubled. Companies promised job security and rising wages in exchange for worker loyalty, and once-radical unions were declawed. The Japanese "embraced the drama of business growth," making business their national identity (Chapman, 1991, pp. 120–121). People looked up to big companies and business life became glamorous. The company man going to work became a kind of warrior, headed into battle, with the nation cheering him on.

JAPANESE CULTURE

In its long history, Japan has repeatedly adopted foreign institutions and practices. And they haven't just nibbled a little around the edges. Japan has swallowed entire foreign institutional systems, technologies, and forms of government. Nevertheless, when they borrowed foreign ways, the Japanese didn't feel humiliated or dominated. Even in the case of the American Occupation, when the United States did indeed force changes on Japan, the Japanese remained confident that their society could digest all its foreign borrowings, while remaining true to itself in essential ways. In Japan, you can still hear an old slogan from the Meiji Era, "*wakon yosai*" (Japanese spirit and Western knowledge), and Japanese people will tell you that the foreign models they adopt are transformed by the addition of a "Japanese heart" (Feiler, 1991, pp. 36–37; Tasker, 1987, p. 21). What is this Japanese heart? It is the critical core of Japanese culture, consisting of elements of nonmaterial culture: values, beliefs, language, symbols, and norms and sanctions. **Values** are a central element in all cultures. They are ideals, abstract expressions of what people consider important. Even if people don't explicitly articulate their values, values infuse the decisions they make, the way they see the world, and how they relate to one another.

The Value of Belonging

In Japan, belonging is the most fundamental value. Let us take some time to thoroughly explore what belonging means in Japan. After all, in every society people want to belong. If you ever went to junior high school or high school, you have had intense, personal experience of the human need to belong. And belonging is the basic subject matter of sociology, which studies the groups people construct and how these groups shape their lives.

A Sense of "Peoplehood"

Belonging in Japan begins in a sense of national solidarity. People in Japan are told constantly that their society is special, like no other, because the Japanese people are, literally, one family. Tradition holds that Japan is a sacred land, created by the gods, and that all Japanese are biologically a single family, descended from a common ancestress, the sun goddess, Amaterasu. The emperor, said to be a direct descendant of Amaterasu, symbolizes the government, the people, and divinity, fused together (Bellah, 2003, pp. 35–38). The Japanese see themselves as a unique people, physically and racially different from all the rest of the world's peoples. Many Japanese people believe that their society's economic success, low crime rate, and high level of education are the result of its people's distinct racial stock.

But Japanese racial identity is in reality a social belief, not a physical fact. Anthropologists tell us that the Japanese people are part of the Mongoloid group of peoples, which includes the Koreans and the Han Chinese. There is some variety too in the appearance of the Japanese people—different shades of skin color, and hair and eyes ranging from black to brown reflect a heritage of Polynesian, Chinese, and East Asian ancestry. And while they believe that Koreans are physically distinctive, the Japanese are unable to identify Japanese-born Koreans by their appearance (Feiler, 1991, p. 135; Tasker, 1987, pp. 15–16, 34).

Although it is not a physical fact, the Japanese sense of "peoplehood" has a firm social foundation. Japan, like most other societies, is inhabited by people whose ancestors came from many places. Japan is a chain of islands, about 200 miles off the coast of Korea. The most ancient people to arrive in Japan were the Ainu, a distinctive race that dates back thousands of years into prehistory. After the Ainu, other peoples came to Japan from southern and northern Asia. But it is important to know that there has been no significant immigration into Japan for more than 1,000 years. For all that time, the peoples of Japan mingled, until they developed the world's most racially and culturally unified society. There are in fact some minority groups in Japan (which we will examine later), but they are few and small in size. The Japanese sense of distinctiveness is reinforced by language: Unlike the rest of the world's major languages, Japanese is spoken by only one ethnic group, and by relatively few foreigners (Tasker, 1987, p. 26).

Although the Japanese people are not the separate race they believe themselves to be, they are indeed an unusually homogeneous people, much more so than the people of other societies. Their sense of peoplehood has given them unique advantages that other societies don't have. They are able to merge the concepts of racial and national identity, and their acute sense of distinctiveness, carefully cultivated by Japan's leaders, helps foster an unusually strong feeling of group solidarity and national purpose in Japanese society.

"An Island Nation"

"Japan is an island nation," schoolchildren are repeatedly told, "surrounded by seas and enemies, so we must depend on each other." Though their country is perceived by others as a giant power in the global economy, the Japanese people share a sense of national vulnerability. Many Japanese think of their country as small, even weak, unprotected from assault by outside forces. They are acutely aware that Japan, though self-sufficient up to the 20th century, is now highly dependent on the world economy, more so than any other major power. Japan has no oil, almost no raw materials, and must import much of its meat and grain. Because the land is very mountainous, only a small portion is suitable for agriculture, and almost the entire population is squeezed into only one fifth of the total area. The Japanese play down their early-20th-century history as an aggressive imperial power, which invaded China and other Asian nations and provoked the United States to war (Feiler, 1991, pp. 88, 141; Tasker, 1987, pp. 8–10).

Group Membership

The importance of belonging in Japan starts on the level of the nation, or people, but this group membership is then expressed in all the social groups that make up Japanese society. Japanese groups are like little "family states, tightly cohesive and all-consuming in their demands," American sociologist Robert Bellah explains. Individuals owe their groups intense loyalty and devoted service (Bellah, 2003, pp. 39, 188). In Japanese society, the group comes first. Being alone, outside the web of group life, is unthinkable. In the Japanese view, it is only in groups that people develop as individuals, experience the pleasures of human feeling, and enjoy a sense of secure interdependence with others.

Do you remember the craze for Pokémon cartoon superheros? It is interesting that Pokémon was such an international success because it teaches quintessential Japanese values, including the value of group membership. Unlike American superheros, who generally work alone, the Pokémon characters work as a team, taking risks to save one another from danger. The older, more experienced Pokémon characters befriend the younger ones and guide them, and in return the younger ones give them loyalty (Strom, 1999b, p. WK4).

Of course there are individualists in Japan: brilliant entrepreneurs who start billion-dollar companies alone, and iconoclastic artists and writers. But they are not celebrated in Japanese society. They are not cultural idols and children don't look up to them and imitate them. Popular legends attach instead to the loyal company man, the "salaryman," who puts his company first, despite his personal wishes and problems.[1] A recent television series in Japan chronicled the lives of quality control engineers (Fackler, 2006b, pp. A1, C4).

Group Life and Adaptability

Now that you know something about the importance of belonging in Japan, you can begin to understand why Japan has so readily incorporated practices and institutions borrowed from other societies. Bellah explains that group life is the heart of Japanese culture. It is, in his words, like a "container," uncommitted to any particular set of beliefs or institutions, which persists even when the "contents"—all those foreign borrowings—change (Bellah, 2003, pp. 189–190). In fact, group life, or belonging, is the "Japanese heart," which can encapsulate and transform foreign culture by implanting it firmly within the structure of Japanese group life. So Japan was devoted to war and conquest in the 1930s and 1940s, and then when Japan was defeated and occupied by the Americans, the society turned around and devoted

---

[1]*Sarariman* translates in English to "salaryman." It is used to describe managers who are, almost without exception, men. Women work in business as "office ladies"—secretaries. There is no gender-neutral language in Japan (like "businessperson") to describe employees, because men and women play sharply different workplace roles.

itself to economic growth and peace. The transition was smooth because the whole culture of group life continued; only the "content" changed.

Values and Norms

In every society, values name shared ideals, shared goals. Values are usually stated abstractly: "belonging is important," "it's good to be part of a group." Also, in every society, people follow **norms** which are often linked to values. Norms are instructions; they tell people, in detail, how they are expected to behave, or think, or feel in specific situations. Some norms are enacted into laws, but others are interpersonal **social expectations,** no less powerful for being informal. Norms tell what is expected, or **normative,** but we can't assume that people always follow norms. Let's see how these two key terms—*values* and *norms*—help us describe and understand Japanese culture.

Group Harmony

Harmony is a major Japanese value. People in Japan will tell you that because their island is crowded it is important to maintain public harmony and avoid conflict. But, as sociologists, we can see that restricting conflict helps people keep up important relationships in groups. In a huge traffic jam, no one honks; no one drives on the shoulder. It would be very rare to see people arguing in public or come upon a fight outside a bar. Japanese norms require people to apologize sincerely when their actions threaten group harmony. So after a car accident, both drivers will jump out and apologize and bow to each other. They both apologize because in Japan an apology shows sincerity; it is not an admission of guilt. Japanese television mysteries don't end with the arrest of the criminal. In the final 10 minutes, the criminal tells the detective or someone else about his hardships or mental stress and he apologizes, often tearfully (Azuma, 2001, p. 36).

As you can imagine, lawsuits are uncommon in Japan; people are more likely to avoid confrontation and reach informal compromises. But lest you get the idea that the Japanese are inhumanly perfect, you should understand that people must work very hard to maintain public harmony and order. Japanese people get insulted or angry just like anyone else, but in their society values and norms forcefully promote self-control and the avoidance of direct personal confrontation. Even to express yourself too clearly violates Japanese norms. You might force others to disagree openly and the confrontation would disrupt group harmony. When Darius Mehri, an American engineer, started work at a car manufacturer in Japan, he suggested his coworkers all contribute to buy a coffee-maker for the office. His suggestion created a crisis: No one knew how to respond (Mehri, 2005, pp. 23–26). If he had followed Japanese norms, Mehri would have expressed his wish indirectly, without making a demand. He could have said, "it would be nice to be able to get some coffee without having to leave the office, don't you think?" Then others could have shown their sensitivity to his needs by spontaneously taking up a collection to buy a coffee-maker—or not—without the risk of open refusal. In business or personal life, people avoid committing themselves to hard-and-fast positions. They try not to acknowledge or clarify their disagreements. Instead, Japanese people proceed by cautiously feeling out one another, making ambiguous statements, and using nonverbal clues to figure out what others prefer, aiming for compromise without revelation of conflict.

The Importance of Relationships

Japanese people place great value on warm interpersonal relationships. People see their primary task in life as fitting into or adjusting to social relationships (Shimizu, 2001, p. 16). To foster relationships, people believe, it is more important to understand other people's feelings than it is to express your own. Norms tell people not to be egotistical or to call attention to themselves. This *enryo* or "reserve" restrains people from publicly giving opinions, expressing desires, or even making choices if they are offered. But how can a group function if no one can express their wishes? Because of enryo, it is of fundamental importance that people are highly sensitive to the unspoken wishes of others. The Japanese value *ninjo* means compassion and mercy, and *omoiyari,* empathy or rapport (Shimizu, 2001, p. 9). A good person should strive to empathize—to understand the feelings of others and the situational difficulties others may be experiencing.

In ordinary Japanese life a good host should know a guest well enough to anticipate what food will be pleasing and set it before the guest, so no choices are required. Good guests are expected to eat what they are given and not to cause embarrassment by implying that the host has misunderstood their desires. If you make your wishes known, it is an insult to others: It implies that you believe the other person is too insensitive to perceive them. Members of Japanese groups also expect other group members to anticipate their unexpressed desires (Smith, 1983, pp. 57–58). For example, when you go out drinking with friends or colleagues, you must watch carefully so you can pour them refills when their glasses are empty. You should never refill your own glass or say "pass me that pitcher please."

How do the Japanese manage to follow such demanding norms? For one thing, spending a lot of time together helps. People who are in constant contact, in informal as well as formal situations, come to understand each other intuitively. Also, the Japanese place great emphasis on nonverbal communication. Because of enryo, people's words are not a good guide to their feelings. From childhood, people practice observing others' behavior for tiny hints in body language, tone of voice, the timing of silences. Just as children in many cultures can read their parents' disapproval in a glance or body posture, so members of Japanese groups come to read one another. In fact, a person who insists on explicit rational explanation is called a "reason freak" and is considered immature (Smith, 1983, p. 58).

Conformity

Conformity helps people fit into groups. It is related to reserve, a Japanese reluctance to stand out, an unwillingness to separate oneself from the group. Conformity means following the norms. If you observe the way people dress in Japan you will see conformity in action. Businessmen dress very conservatively; the salaryman outfit of dark blue suit, white shirt, and unobtrusive tie is legendary. A gray suit or a blue shirt stands out. Salesclerks in department stores wear uniforms and so do all the workers and supervisors in factories. Adult women usually dress quite conservatively too; they wear skirts and avoid bright colors. When they shed their school uniforms, rebellious adolescents conform to the styles of their "tribes," like the subculture of young people who tint their skin dark and wear braids or Rastafarian hair.

People also conform to the norms of public life. Subway riders wait in two neat rows for the train doors to open. Householders carefully separate their trash into as many as 44 different categories for recycling (Onishi, 2005e, p. A4). If you visit Japan, you will see no litter at all in public places, and no one eating on the street. A person who finds a lost object in the subway or on the street turns it over to the police, who carefully catalog it and place it in the local lost and found center. In 2002, people brought $23 million in lost cash to the Tokyo center (of which 72% was returned to its owners) and 330,000 umbrellas, among many other items. Unclaimed money or objects are eventually offered to the finder (Onishi, 2004a, p. A1).

The Values of Loyalty, Duty, and Self-Sacrifice

Loyalty, duty, and self-sacrifice are traditional Japanese values that date back to the time of the *samurai,* Japanese knights of the feudal period. Samurai had a code that told them they should be proud to sacrifice themselves, in battle or suicide, to uphold their lord's honor. Before World War II, during the whole Meiji Era, the bonds of duty were very strong. Bellah (2003) says that at the time "any pursuit of purely private happiness was considered almost criminal" (p. 205). And social obligation was often set in hierarchical situations where someone in a position over you made demands that you demonstrate your loyalty and do your duty. A folk saying from this time, that everyone still knows, says "you can't be there when your father dies." It reminds people that public duty to nation, company, community, or school often takes priority over your private feelings. During World War II, the government leaned heavily on the values of loyalty and self-sacrifice. We remember the kamikaze pilots, but all Japanese were asked to make terrible sacrifices to show their loyalty to the emperor and Japan. Today, in a peaceful Japan, the bonds of loyalty and duty still tug on people.

During the economic recession of the 1990s, some small businessmen struggled to keep their enterprises from going under because they felt obliged, by ties of loyalty, to continue to employ their workers. Some ran up enormous debts borrowing money to pay wages. One man used his entire personal savings to pay his workers "sorry money" when the company finally went under (Belson, 2002, p. BU1). Now the meaning of group loyalty is shifting, from a context of threatened punishment, to a softer dependence on reward. People remain loyal because of the rewards of group membership, because they find acceptance in groups and feel dependent on other group members, or because bosses and teachers and others with authority demonstrate caring (Bellah, 2003, pp. 194–205).

Achievement

Japan is an achievement-oriented society. People believe that what you accomplish in life should be more important than who you are when you are born. They want Japan to be a society in which hardworking people of even the most modest background can rise to positions of prestige and power.

Today, more than ever, the kind of achievement that matters is educational achievement. By the time they reach junior high school, children must understand that excelling in school is the unavoidable gateway to good jobs and high status. Education is becoming more and more important all over the world, but in Japan, it has been the supreme arena of achievement for a long time because entrepreneurship garners little prestige. If you do well on the high school entrance exams, you can go to a prestigious academic high school. Do well on the college entrance exams and you can get a high-status job with a major corporation or the government bureaucracy. Flunk the exams, and you will find yourself restricted to part-time, temporary manual labor. This pattern of advancement through exams has been generalized throughout Japanese society. The arts are organized in "schools" of painting, flower arranging, acting, calligraphy, and so on. To advance in your art you take classes and exams.

The value of achievement is linked to several other Japanese values, including perseverance, discipline, dedication, endurance, and perfectionism. Children must endure after-school cram classes and long nights of study to pass their high school and college entrance exams. Principals tell their students that school is "life's first big battle," and they must put their all into it. Businessmen must endure after-hours parties with clients, even if they would rather be home sleeping or spending time with their families. Players on high school baseball teams are expected to arrive at school at dawn to practice before classes start and then practice again after school for another 4 or 5 hours. They practice in scorching heat and downpours of rain.

Perseverance is linked to another traditional Japanese value, dedication, or *seishin.* People judge others by how hard they try, how hard they work at whatever task or role is their lot. They are willing to make excuses for poor work, as long as great effort went into it, while good work produced without effort does not impress them. *Seishin* literally means "spirit"; it means the spiritual development that results from effort, discipline, and self-control. It doesn't matter what the task is: It can be studying for exams, paving a road, or learning the tea ceremony; if you persevere in working at it and try to do it perfectly, you will become a better person and people will respect you (Bayley, 1994, pp. 118–119).

Respect

An important part of being comfortable in a Japanese group is knowing where you stand in relation to others. The members of a group are assumed to be unequals and that inequality pervades even close-knit groups. Many important norms in Japanese life are connected to dealing with unequal personal status. People of unequal status expect different behavior from one another. Generally, lower-status people show deference, respect, and loyalty to higher-status people. Politeness is very important. In a group, older people walk first. In an office, or at formal meetings or parties, people are seated in order of status, and it is a common sight to find people jammed up at the door, deferring to one another and trying to sort out the correct seating. If people of higher status, or people you don't know well, come to your house, you will treat them with great deference, seating them in the best spot in the best room, and serving them special food and drink on the best dishes, and choosing topics of conversation they will enjoy (Bachnik, 1994, pp. 160–162).

But those in higher statuses also owe much to the people below them. They are expected to act their age, or live up to their positions. Acting like "one of the boys" or "like a kid" is felt to be extremely unbecoming and embarrassing. Higher-status people are expected to treat those below them with parental kindness. A common relationship in Japan, particularly in business, is that of a mentor and protégé in which an older, higher-status man helps his younger protégé, not only in business, but in his personal life, advising him and helping him find a wife, if he is single. The protégé relies upon, and positively enjoys, his dependence on his mentor. In the rare female-owned Japanese businesses, female executives play this mentor role in relation to their female employees.

In Japan, when you meet another person, you must be able to assess whether your status is higher or lower than his or hers. Then you will be able to follow the appropriate norms: bowing lower or higher, choosing the right forms of address. Gender helps establish status because women are assumed to be of lower status than men. For this reason, it is extremely rare to find a woman in a position in which she supervises or gives orders to men. In fact, the few women who are business owners tend to surround themselves with female employees.

In a group that is all men or all women, like a group of women at a flower-arranging class, people hasten to find out how old each member is, so that everyone will know where they are ranked by age. A group of businessmen will immediately ascertain one another's job titles, eagerly offering their business cards to each other. Business cards show a person's name, but in larger print they tell his title and what organization he works for. Once occupational statuses are clearly established, Japanese men feel more comfortable: They know how to treat one another as unequals.

When sociologists discuss Japan they try to do so from the standpoint of **cultural relativism.** Cultural relativism encourages us to see other cultures from the inside, to see how values and norms fit into the lives of people in other cultures. This is very different from **ethnocentrism,** judging another culture from the standpoint of your own culture. Ethnocentrism can often make it difficult to accept the way people in other cultures behave. Do you think you have responded ethnocentrically to Japanese culture?

Religion and Japanese Culture

In some societies (like Egypt) religion is of major importance and norms and values are closely linked to religious belief. Some people think that it is only when people are religious that values and norms are taken seriously. This is not the case in Japan. Though most people carefully conform to the society's norms, very few Japanese people consider themselves religious believers and few are observant of religious practices. You could say that in a general sense religion has influenced Japanese values, but the norms that people follow so carefully are not religious norms. See Table 1.1, p. 14.

These Japanese businessmen conform to their culture's norms of greeting. You bow higher or lower depending on whether your status has more or less prestige than the person you are greeting. Where you stand is not always clear. If you are the president of a small company greeting a Toyota executive, do you bow lower or does he? Japanese must be able to make these decisions rapidly. Does your culture have norms for greeting others? Do you greet superiors in the same way you greet equals?

TABLE 1.1 God, Morality, and Government

In Japan, relatively few people think one must believe in God in order to be moral. In contrast, in Egypt almost everyone thinks so. At the same time, nearly half of Egyptians want religion and government to be separate. The question seemed so irrelevant in Japan that it wasn't asked.

	Must Believe in God to Be Moral (%)	Completely Agree That Religion and Government Should Be Separate (%)
Japan	33	—
Germany	39	67
Mexico	53	38
United States	57	55
Egypt	99	47

Source: From the Pew Research Center for the People and the Press, *What the World Thinks in 2002,* 2002, http://people-press.org/report/165/what-the-world-thinks-in-2002.

Note: Dash indicates not applicable.

There are many religious traditions in Japan—Shinto, Buddhism, Confucianism, Taoism, and Christianity—as well as a number of more modern religious sects usually referred to as the New Religions. Except for a very small number of people (less than 2%) who are practicing Christians, most Japanese don't feel they must choose a single religious identity from this heritage. Instead, they practice a kind of folk religion, observing Shinto, Buddhist, and Christian holidays, having Buddhist funerals, and weddings that combine elements of Shinto and Christian rituals, and choosing lucky days by the Taoist calendar.

Shintoism is the most ancient Japanese religion; its tradition extends back to Japan's prehistoric past. Shinto reveres nature in the form of *kami*, deities that embody natural objects, like trees, mountains, the sun, and animals, and represent the life force. Perhaps we can see the influence of Shinto in the immaculate tiny gardens people maintain in their very small front yards. Kami are everywhere and they are worshipped at Shinto shrines where people ask for their blessings (Earhart, 1984, pp. 16–17). No one takes the Shinto kami literally today, but Shinto is a lively part of Japanese folklore, and shrines and shrine festivals figure in folk religion. In cities, ancient Shinto temples often own a great deal of land, which they lease, but don't sell, for apartment houses and office towers.

The Meiji rulers who militarized Japan in the 20th century revived Shinto and separated it from Buddhism, identifying the emperor as a living kami to heighten group identification and create nationalism (Bellah, 2003, pp. 35–39). Today, militarized state Shinto is rejected, but Shinto influence survives in a love of nature which is a deep current in Japanese culture, expressed in poetry, landscape painting, and traditions of pottery, landscaping, and architecture that stress subtle, natural materials. Buddhism, a religion that began in India, came to Japan via China in the 6th century AD. In Japan it is both a monastic tradition and a family religion that honors family ancestors and offers the possibility of salvation and an afterlife in a Buddhist paradise. For almost 1,000 years, Buddhism was a very important part of Japanese culture and society, until, in the 16th century Japan's Tokugawa revolution attacked Buddhism as the religion of the old political system and substituted a new emphasis on Confucianism (Reischauer, 1988, pp. 206–207). Today Buddhism permeates Japanese values in a very subtle way: The Japanese belief in perfectionism, the idea of improving one's spirituality through dedication to any task, no matter how humble, is deeply Buddhist. It is notable that in Buddhism (and Shinto), it is the family, not the individual, that is the basic unit of religious participation. Traditional religions helped shape Japan's dominant group consciousness, but today fewer people are choosing traditional Buddhist funerals and temple membership is down (Earhart, 1984, pp. 69–71).

Confucianism is not a religion in the same sense that Buddhism, Shinto, or Christianity are religions. It is a philosophical tradition, named for Confucius, its originator in China in the 5th century BC. Confucianism became prominent in China in the 12th century AD, as a rational, ethical system with strict norms, stressing loyalty to the ruler, obedience toward one's father, and proper behavior. Confucianism has no priests, no temples, no religious rituals. From the 16th century to the late 19th century, Confucianism was very important in Japan, shaping values in a lasting way. Its influence is felt today in the Japanese stress on loyalty and obedience, and in the importance of education, hard work, and doing one's duty to family, employers, and the nation (Reischauer, 1988, pp. 203–204).

Christianity came to Japan in the 16th century and it spread rapidly before being suppressed by the Tokugawa rulers. When Christianity was permitted again in the late 19th century, Protestant and Catholic missionaries entered Japan but found only small numbers of converts. Today, however, Christian culture has come to Japan as part of a larger Western influence. People who are not Christians celebrate Christmas, and Christian "white weddings" are all the rage. The bride wears white, and the wedding takes place in a fake chapel, with a Western actor dressed up like a priest officiating (Brooke, 2005b, p. A4).

Japanese people today who feel a strong need for religious faith generally turn to the New Religions, popular religious movements, the best-known of which are *Soka Gakkai* and *Tenrikyo,* which combine ideas and rituals from Shinto, Buddhism, Taoism, and sometimes Christianity. The New Religions offer their members help in solving personal problems through faith and religious observance, and perhaps even more important, they offer close-knit communities, with festivities, rallies, study groups, and leadership hierarchies (Inoue, 1994, pp. 220–228).

Shinto shrines like these are found everywhere in Japan, but almost all their visitors are elderly. The man at the fountain in this photo is carrying out a cleansing ritual. Knowledge of Shinto rituals has declined so much in Japan that many shrines put up signs to instruct the occasional worshipper. Often these signs depict children, so as not to embarrass adult visitors.

SOCIAL STRUCTURE AND GROUP LIFE

In Japan, group life comes first. People think of themselves primarily as members of groups, and only secondarily as individuals. Japanese sociologists consider this **group consciousness** or **group identification** a traditional part of Japanese culture.[2] Over the course of the 20th century, different groups have risen to preeminence in Japanese life, but group identification remains the basic pattern.

Up to the start of World War II, people in Japan lived out their lives "embedded" in **extended,** multigenerational families and in their village or neighborhood (Fukutake, 1981, p. 214). Villages were small, consisting of not more than 100 households, and they were closed, self-sufficient communities, within which most people spent their entire lives. Villages were self-governing units, responsible as a whole for collecting taxes imposed on the village, not its households. The households of a village worked together in the fields, or in maintaining the village irrigation system. They helped one another build and repair houses and hold weddings and funerals. Ties between superiors and subordinates were emphasized in the village as well as in the family because wealthier, landowning families and their tenants and laborers were in constant interaction (Fukutake, 1981, pp. 33–39).

Group Life in Modern Japan

The old-fashioned family and village community have all but disappeared in Japan today. Since World War II, the size of Japanese households has gotten smaller and smaller. Japan has one of the world's lowest birthrates, with Japanese women bearing an average of only 1.29 children each. As a result, the size of the average household numbers only about three people. Twenty-eight percent of households are single-person households. More young people are living alone away from home (although it is still only 6.8% who do so) and almost half of all elderly people live alone or with a spouse instead of with extended family (Jones, 2007, pp. 7, 20; Onishi, 2005f). See Table 1.2, p. 18.

The modern nuclear family is a much less dominating group than the traditional extended family. Typically, the husband has less authority than the old head of household and he almost always works outside the home, often quite far away. Long commutes and many hours of work result in fathers spending little time with their children. Salarymen, whose long hours are legendary, must return home after their children are asleep and leave home before the children awaken in the morning. Mothers and children are close, but children typically spend long hours at school and after-school activities. Husbands and wives usually have different friends and don't socialize as a couple. Their leisure activities and even their vacations are spent separately (Fukutake, 1981, pp. 123–126).

Postwar industrialization has also broken up the village community. After World War II, massive migration from the countryside to cities emptied the villages, as young Japanese searched for industrial jobs. Today, most Japanese, even those in

---

[2]See, for example, Nakane (1970), pp. 1–22; or for a recent discussion, Kuwayama (1994), pp. 121–151.

TABLE 1.2 Household Size (2005–2007)

People in Japan and Germany are far more likely to live in small households than people in Egypt, Mexico, or Namibia.

	Year	Population in One-Person Households (%)	Population in Households of Two to Four Persons (%)	Population in Households of Five or More Persons (%)	Population in Households of Eight or More Persons (%)
Japan	2007	11	68	22	1
Germany	2005	18	73	9	—
United States	2006	11	69	20	—
Mexico	2005	2	45	53	11
Namibia	2006	2	26	73	36
Egypt	2005	1	29	70	20

Sources: F. El-Zanaty, and A. Way, *Egypt Demographic and Health Survey 2005,* Ministry of Health and Population, National Population Council, 2006, http://www.measuredhs.com/pubs/pdf/FR176/FR176.pdf

Instituto Nacional de Estadística Geografía e Informática, *Conteo de Población y Vivienda,* 2005, http://www.inegi.gob.mx/inegi/default.aspx?s=inegi

Ministry of Health and Social Services (Namibia), *Namibia Demographic and Health Survey 2000,* 2003, http://www.measuredhs.com/pubs/pdf/FR141/00FrontMatter.pdf

Ministry of Internal Affairs and Communications Statistics Bureau, *Japan Statistical Yearbook 2007,* 2007, http://www.stat.go.jp/English/data/nenkan/index.htm

Statistisches Bundesamt Deutschland, *Haushalte nach Haushaltstypen,* http://www.destatis.de/jetspeed/portal/cms/Sites/destatis/Internet/DE/Content/Statistiken/Bevoelkerung/Haushalte/Tabellen/Content50/Haushaltstypen, templateId=renderPrint.psml

U.S. Bureau of the Census, *Current Population Survey 2006,* 2006, http://www.census.gov/population/www.socdemo/hh-fam/cps2006.html

rural areas, commute long distances to work, so few people both live and work in the same community. People are less involved in local community life, and less concerned about what their neighbors think of them, especially in big cities (Fukutake, 1981, pp. 134–36).

Many Western sociologists expected Japan to follow a pattern observed in Europe and North America: When societies industrialize, people spend less time in **primary groups** (small, personal, face-to-face groups), like families and villages, and more time in **secondary groups** (large, relatively impersonal, goal-oriented organizations), like cities and corporations. Then, group membership becomes less important in people's lives and they begin to think of themselves as individuals and to value their liberty to make individual choices. Away from the close supervision of family and neighbors, people feel freer to defy social norms. You can think of individualism and community as a kind of sliding scale. Western societies have gone very far in the direction of emphasizing individualism, for some societies, over into what Bill McKibben (2007) calls "hyperindividualism" (p. 96).

Japan is fascinating to sociologists because there the social consequences of industrialization have been different than in the West. When Japan became a modern, industrialized nation, the family and the community became much less important. But individualism didn't take their place. Instead, Japan has so far kept its group focus, making group life in school and at work the center of Japanese life.

Group Life in School

School dominates the lives of Japanese children. They have long school days and short summer vacations. Being on a sports team is a 7-day-a-week commitment, for both the children and their teacher-coaches. Children are often away from home from seven in the morning until seven in the evening (Fukuzawa & LeTendre, 2001, pp. 98–100).

In elementary and junior high school, Japanese children are taught to see themselves first and foremost as members of their homeroom class, or *kumi*. (The word *kumi* is old: Originally it meant a band of samurai warriors.) Starting in first grade, children spend 9 years together in the same kumi. In elementary school, the kumi stays with each teacher for 2 years. Each kumi of about 40–45 children is encouraged to think of its classroom as the children's own collective home. The children in the kumi arrange and rearrange furniture, bring in plants and flowers from home, and each day the kumi and teacher completely clean the room—scrubbing the desks and floors, washing windows, cleaning blackboards and erasers. Each kumi also takes a turn cleaning the school halls and toilets, the teachers' room, and the street outside the school. The kumi eats lunch in its own room, and even in junior high school, teachers for different subjects move from classroom to classroom, while the students stay in their own room. On the playground, members of a kumi play on the same team, competing with other kumi in their grade.

Teachers divide kumi into smaller groups called *han*, which are like study or work groups. Han stay together for several months before they are reshuffled. Each han elects a leader or *han-cho*, whose job it is to lead the group into harmonious decision making by patiently eliciting a consensus. Han members are expected to resolve conflicts and solve problems themselves, without appealing to adult authorities (Duke, 1986, pp. 25–29). Japanese schools do not practice ability grouping. The emphasis is on keeping the whole class moving through the work at the same pace, with the more able students helping their slower han-mates. Hans function as teams that compete against each other in the classroom.

Keiko's Story: The Han

Keiko is nervous as she arrives in her seventh-grade classroom. Today her han must present its report on the Tokugawa Era. The students have been working on it in school and for the past 2 days they have met after school at Yukichi's house to practice making the oral presentation. Keiko is afraid she will make a mistake and let down her han. She hardly hears the music over the loudspeaker that signals the official start of the school day, and she follows the kumi through the prescribed exercises without even noticing. But her teacher, walking up and down the rows, does notice. "Keiko seems distracted; not concentrating," she writes in her little notebook. After the presentation, Keiko is giddy with relief. They did well! The teacher gives Keiko's han gold stars for preparation and presentation. It is the only han with no demerits! Today Keiko's han has its turn to serve lunch and she gaily wraps herself in the white apron and puts on the surgical mask. She and her han-mates haul the heavy pots and bins of rice, stew, and salad up to the classroom from the school kitchen and dish them out. The whole kumi chants grace together, then breaks out in laughter and conversation while they eat. Keiko is particularly animated. She has done her part in supporting her han.

Working and playing so closely together, members of a kumi come to know each other intimately and think of themselves as a group. Children work hard, not to please the teacher, but to avoid letting down their han-mates. Habits of group loyalty, a preference for uniformity, and the learned skill of building group consensus through patient negotiation prepare children for the all-important work groups of Japanese adult life (Feiler, 1991, pp. 99–102; Leestma, 1987, p. 3).

But as much as group life in school illustrates the strength and importance of group life in Japan, it also illustrates its dark underside. It was American sociologist William Graham Sumner (1840–1910) who long ago articulated the principle that the more closely people identify as a group and the stronger their **in-group** feelings, the more hostility they direct toward **out-groups** or people outside the group. We see this in Japanese schools in the practice of *ijime,* or bullying, usually after school or during free play, or even through e-mail, when children single out one child who is different in some way (perhaps Korean, or foreign-born, or poorer or richer than the others) and subject him (it is usually a boy) to ceaseless torment. They tease him, make fun of him, kick and punch, sometimes extort money, or pressure him to commit petty theft. The Japanese are ashamed of ijime, but even though they are disturbed about it, they seem unable to prevent it. Sometimes teachers ignore bullying or even abet it. Every year there are several reports of suicides of 12- or 13-year-old children who are victims of ijime. Bullying shows us that as much as the Japanese value harmony, it is harmony within the group that matters; hostility toward outsiders, toward those who are different, is tolerated. Is it possible that bullying those who are different is essential to maintaining the tight cohesion of Japanese school groups (Sugimoto, 1997, pp. 127–128; Yoneyama, 1999, pp. 161–185)?

The Work Group

Following World War II, as Japanese industry expanded, and drew in an ever larger workforce from the farms and villages, Japanese companies encouraged their workers to see the company as their family. They invented a new focus for group identity in modern Japanese life: Large corporations hired their employees right out of high school or college. Promised lifetime employment and guaranteed promotion, employees spent their whole working lives in one company, advancing in step with all those hired in their year. Company housing, company sports teams and recreation complexes, cafeterias, health clinics, and company discount stores re-created the all-absorbing village within the company. Today, although no more than a third of Japan's labor force is employed by large corporations, their organization has set the tone for Japanese work life. Government employees, as well as employees in smaller companies, look to work for a sense of community. They find it in the work group, or "section," of the office or factory.

Hiroshi's Story: The "Section"

When the bullet train suddenly slowed, Hiroshi glanced out the window and saw beside the track the village where he had been born. Staring, Hiroshi thought about how different his life was now from his village childhood. He spotted his family's old house—a large wooden structure with its own courtyard and small garden, where he had lived with his parents, brother and sisters, and grandparents. Hiroshi looked down into the quiet streets of the town where he had spent his days at play, even as a 2-year-old, watched by his brother.

Now Hiroshi lives in an apartment house outside of Tokyo. He is home so little that he doesn't even know his neighbors and his children never play outside. They hurry from school to lessons to homework. Really, his office is now the focus of his life. Hiroshi knows his family wants him at home, but he feels he has to give his all to his job. He doesn't do it to get a raise, or even a promotion; he just wants to do a good job.

Every morning the nine men of his section assemble, greet each other, and drink their first cups of tea together. Takeshi has become a close friend: He really knows what is in Hiroshi's heart. But all the men are important to him. That year when Hiroshi's mother was dying so painfully, they knew how he felt without his having to explain. They took over most of his duties at work and took him out after work, making sure he ate and gently distracting him with stories and songs. Kenji-san had introduced Hiroshi's son to his niece, and they were soon to be married. Mr. Fuji, the department chief, looked after them all, and was now arranging a marriage for Masao, the only unmarried man in the section. After work, and before the long commute home, the section and its chief usually go out together to a local bar, to drink and chat more informally. Hiroshi enjoys the monthly evening parties paid for by the company, and the twice-yearly weekend retreats when the whole section goes away together to a country inn. His real home, he thinks, is at the office with his office "family."

SOCIALIZATION

Japan is a demanding society: It asks of individuals a high level of conformity with very detailed norms, and it demands self-discipline in subordinating individual needs to the requirements of the group. Most people conform. The Japanese pride themselves on how orderly their society is, and they find it threatening if order seems to break down. Most people embrace Japanese values, identify with their roles, and do what is expected of them. Foreigners often wonder how Japanese society achieve such a high level of conformity.

Conformity is carefully taught in Japan. Japanese people learn the beliefs and role expectations of their culture and learn to play their roles properly through the process sociologists call **socialization.** While all societies and social groups socialize their members, in some cases the process is haphazard and disorganized and people may be largely unaware that socialization is taking place. In Japan, socialization is highly consistent, explicit, and carefully planned. Studying Japan provides a wonderful opportunity to understand the process of socialization, how socialization actually takes place, because the Japanese carry out socialization so thoughtfully.

The Process of Socialization: Explicit Instruction

In school, at work, and in many other situations, Japanese people are used to receiving a great deal of **explicit instruction** about what is expected of them, followed by opportunities to **practice** proper behavior. Elementary schools in particular are designed to socialize children into Japanese values and norms. Teachers consider this "moral education" even more important than teaching reading and writing and math (Lewis, 1995, pp. 44–61).

In school, posters on classroom walls and in hallways exhort, "Let us not run in the corridors," "Let us keep our school toilets clean," "Let us greet people with a smile," and so on. Students actually make up these goals themselves, and then later hold self-criticism sessions in which they decide whether they have met the goal, and if not, what should be done next. So the exercise also teaches children to take responsibility, because no one in authority tells them, "You are still running in the corridors." They are expected to recognize this themselves and devise a remedy.

Schoolchildren through junior high school are drilled in proper bowing, formal greeting, sitting and standing (all together), answering their teachers (immediately and loudly), and arranging their desktops for study (in a set format). A teacher, preparing eighth graders for a class trip, arranges chairs on the floor of the gym in the shape of a bus, and for hours students practice getting in and out of the seats in orderly fashion (Feiler, 1991, p. 264; Hendry, 1981, p. 102; Leestma, 1987, p. 27).

Several Western analysts of Japanese society have called Japan a "nanny state" because of the active role the government takes in giving its citizens corrective advice. Loudspeakers tell bus and train passengers to be careful getting off and even warn bus riders to hold on because "the bus is turning a corner." A passenger running for a train and gratefully slipping in just before the doors close, can expect to be reprimanded by the loudspeaker: "never run for a train." Bruce Feiler reported that highway signs approaching his town proclaimed "patience and humility prevent accidents." On the ski lift too, messages blare out: "remember to lift your ski tips" (Feiler, 1991, p. 16; McGregor, 1996, pp. 113–114).

Role Models Aid Socialization

The Japanese believe in providing **role models** to help people learn expected behavior. Mothers and teachers consciously "model" correct behavior for children. Nursery school teachers wash their hands and brush their teeth alongside their charges, and elementary school teachers eat lunch with their students and work alongside the students during the regular daily cleaning period. At home and at school older children are urged to set a good example for younger ones, and take pride in their roles as "elder brother" or "elder sister" (Hendry, 1981, p. 149).

Ceremonies Support Socialization

Initiation ceremonies, marking the transition to new roles, are an effective part of Japanese socialization. Ceremonies help people learn to recognize that they are in a new stage of life, with new roles and norms. Carefully staged ceremonies are an important part of children's progress through school. Interestingly, the Japanese place more emphasis on ceremonies that mark the beginning of different stages of education than on graduation ceremonies. Children begin their elementary schooling with a special welcome ceremony. Their mothers attend, dressed in their best clothes, and the children dress up too. Usually there is a formal photo taken of the whole class and their mothers. It is customary in Japan for parents to give each child a special study desk at the beginning of elementary school. The desk is expensive. It has a special built-in

Sumo wrestlers stretch before a match in Tokyo's big sumo stadium. Sumo is an ancient Japanese martial art. Aspiring wrestlers must live for years in a strictly regimented, hierarchical, and competitive "training stable." They eat a special diet to bulk up their bodies and follow strict rules and rituals handed down for centuries. After years of training, a sumo match lasts just minutes. One wrestler forces the other out of the circle and that's it: no second chances. The Japanese are not sure how they feel about sharing sumo with the world: One third of sumo wrestlers now are foreigners and the reigning grand champion is from Mongolia.

light, shelves, and drawers. The message is clear: "You are embarking on a new stage in life that really matters. We're investing a lot of time and effort in you."

Defining the Situation

Sociologist Peter Berger used the term **"the definition of the situation"** to explain that the way people respond to situations is conditioned by how they "define" or interpret and evaluate those situations (Berger, 1993, p. 94). If you get together with your friends, it is up to you to define the situation as a party or a study session. Depending on which you choose, you will behave differently, in fact adopt different roles. But we find ourselves in many situations that others have defined. Think of a courtroom. When you enter the court, it is not up to you to define the situation and decide how to behave. Those who designed the court have already decided that your role is to be humble and respectful, to literally look up to the judge, seated on his platform. We find ourselves in many situations that have been defined, or socially structured, to induce us to view reality in particular ways and adopt certain roles and ways of relating to others. This is an indirect form of socialization. If you are Japanese, from infancy through adulthood you find yourself in situations defined in such ways to emphasize group consciousness and dependence on the group.

Socialization to dependence on the group begins at birth, according to Takeo Doi, a famous Japanese psychiatrist, because of the way mothers define the situation for their babies. Care of infants is based on the assumption that babies should experience as little anxiety as possible. Caregivers try to anticipate the baby's needs, and satisfy them before crying and fretfulness signal a problem. Cribs are placed beside adult beds, and children are never put in their cribs to fall asleep alone; they are sung to sleep before being laid down. The Japanese also avoid playpens, preferring instead that the child be protected by the constant close attention of an adult. They almost never employ babysitters. Doi argues that mothers' all-embracing, unconditional love and support fosters in children a taste for dependency that is later expressed in adult group life. Children learn implicitly that if you conform, and do what others expect of you, then people will be kind and considerate, and they will gratify your wishes without your having to ask (Christopher, 1983, pp. 68–70; Doi, 1977; Hendry, 1981, pp. 18–25, 97, 116).

Defining the Situation in School

Japanese preschools and kindergartens carry out the crucial job of first socializing children for *shudan seikatsu,* "life in a group." At home, they may be indulged only children; they have to learn to enjoy group life. At one kindergarten, children end the day with a game that is like musical chairs, but with a significant difference: When the music stops the object is to make physical contact with as many children as possible. For the next round, these linked-up groups race around together and repeat the game until everyone is joined up (Kelly, in Shimizu, 2001, p. 173). How does this game define the situation? In what way is it different from musical chairs?

Many preschools provide blocks for play, but these blocks are different from the ones you may be familiar with: They are very large, 3 to 5 feet long. Just think about how these blocks define the situation. The children must work together in order to carry them. In fact, they organize themselves to carry the blocks all over the school—from gym to classroom to yard—and build enormous structures with them, two-story buildings sometimes, in which they play, even eat their lunches (Lewis, 1995, pp. 20, 114, 115).

Elementary schools carry out a tremendous amount of **anticipatory socialization,** socialization that prepares children for adult roles by teaching them to be part of Japan's all-important groups. Schools stress the similarity of all children, and the importance of the group. As discussed earlier, in the typical elementary school, teachers put a lot of thought into forming *hans.* For example, the teacher will pair an immature, needy child with a child who enjoys taking care of others (Lewis, 1995, p. 82). The purpose is to bring children to enjoy belonging to the han, to find pleasure in their dependence on others. Teachers seldom address children individually, or overtly recognize differences in individual ability, and they minimize situations in which children compete individually with one another. Instead, each han is held responsible collectively for the progress of all its members.

Also, teachers try to deal with students as a class, rather than as individuals. If a class or an individual is unruly, the teacher will turn to that day's assigned monitor and request him or her to restore order. The classroom situation is structured to emphasize group participation, group loyalty, and the responsibility of the individual to the class. In this situation, students experience no conflict between loyalty to their friends and conformity with school norms (Feiler, 1991, pp. 30, 100–102; Leestma, 1987, pp. 3, 27).

Teachers are well aware of the importance of defining the situation for socialization. For example, Feiler (1991) describes a seventh-grade class trip to Tokyo's Disneyland defined in such a way as to encourage students' dependency on their han. Students were required to stay with their han during the visit. In each han one member was assigned to carry the money, one to wear the watch, one to take the photos, and one to take notes. "The management of this trip," Feiler explained, "revealed the skill with which Japanese schools transfer abstract goals into concrete educational practices" (p. 266).

A Japanese office is a large, open area filled with desks lined up side by side in islands. Office workers must be very conscious of one another in these close quarters. They need to consider others when they do their work; they must speak softly when others are on the phone. The arrangement of desks defines the situation in a way that reinforces the Japanese values of harmony and teamwork. Have you ever worked in an office? Was its arrangement different? What values did it convey to you and other office workers?

Socialization in the Workplace

Socialization doesn't end with childhood. We all continue to be socialized and **resocialized** throughout our lives. When people in Japan leave school and enter the world of work, they find familiar patterns of socialization. Companies use explicit instruction and drill. Large companies maintain an in-house staff of trainers, who create company slogans and chants, inspirational comic books and poems, and conduct training sessions. Corporations often provide elaborate welcome ceremonies for new recruits (described by one observer as "a cross between a coming-of-age ceremony and initiation into an American fraternity"). Starting in the 1950s, companies devised rituals in which cohorts of new employees, and in some cases their parents too, were first greeted and lectured by company officials in welcome ceremonies at the factory, then escorted on several days of touring and partying (Chapman, 1991, pp. 131–134).

Corporations also rely on role models to socialize employees. Building on the familiar pattern of the elder child as role model, companies appoint "elder brothers" to instruct new recruits in proper behavior. In business, government, and even organized crime, young men seek out "mentors" to guide their progress.

Companies take care to define the situation in the workplace to maximize group identification. The employees of offices and factories are organized in "sections," groups of eight or nine workers who share responsibility and are expected to make suggestions for improving efficiency and to monitor their own progress in implementation. The arrangement of the furniture actually helps define the situation. Offices are huge undivided areas, but each section's desks are arranged in two facing rows, all touching, to form one huge tabletop, with the section chief's desk perpendicular across the end. Among the eight or nine section members, every conversation is a group affair, every memo can be read by all. Even telephones are shared. The director's desk stands alone, but nearby, not in a separate room (Feiler, 1991, pp. 19–20, 28).

DEVIANCE IN A DEMANDING SOCIETY

There is **deviance** in every society. Despite socialization and group pressure, people violate norms, incurring disapproval and possible punishment. But in some societies there is a great deal more deviance than in others. If you look at Table 1.3 you will see that for every million people in Japan there are 6 murders a year. In the United States, there are 59 murders for every million people, and in Mexico, 101. Comparisons like these generate useful questions for sociologists. Is there something special about Japanese society that minimizes deviance?

There is a very influential school of thought in Japan that sees Japanese society as a **functionalist** sociologist would. In this view (called *nihonjinron*), which has influenced many scholars in both Japan and the United States, Japan is unique in its harmony. Everyone shares the same values; everyone conforms and subordinates their personal desires to the needs of the group (Yoder, 2004, pp. 41–42). In this view, it is not surprising that rates of deviance are low. But this theory can't explain why deviance is increasing.

TABLE 1.3 Murder and Suicide (2001–2005)

Japan and Germany have much lower murder rates than Mexico and the United States. Although Japan has a low murder rate, it has a high suicide rate. Mexico has a very low suicide rate.

	Year	Total Number of Murders	Number of Murders per Million People	Year	Total Number of Suicides	Number of Suicides per Million People
Japan	2006	1,309	11	2004	30,247	240
Germany	2005	1,206	15	2001	11,566	135
United States	2006	17,034	57	2005	31,647	108
Mexico	2002	13,144	130	2001	3,784	38

Sources for Homicide Data:

U.S. Federal Bureau of Investigation, *Uniform Crime Reports, Crime in the United States 2006,* 2006, http://www.fbi.gov/ucr/cius2006/data/table_01.html.

National Police Agency, *Crimes in Japan in 2006,* 2007a, http://www.npa.go.jp/english/seisaku5/20071019.pdf.

Statistisches Bundesamt Deutschland, *Criminal Prosecution Statistics; Persons Convicted 2005,* n.d., http://www.destatis.de/jetspeed/portal/cms/Sites/destatis/Internet/EN/Content/Statistics/Rechtspflege/Strafverfolgung/Tabellen/Content75/VerurteilteStrafart.psml.

United Nations Office on Drugs and Crime, *Eighth UN Survey on Crime Trends and the Operations of Criminal Justice Systems,* n.d., http://www.unodc.org/pdf/crime/eighthsurvey/8pc.pdf.

Sources for Suicide Data:

Ministry of Internal Affairs and Communications, *Japan Statistical Yearbook 2008,* 2008, http://www.stat.go.jp/English/data/nenkan/index.htm.

E. Niska and J. Xu, *Advance Data,* No. 386, June 29, 2007, http://www.cdc.gov/nchs/data/ad/ad386.pdf.

World Health Organization, *World Health Statistical Information System Mortality Database,* n.d., http://www.who.int/whosis/database/mort/table1.cfm.

Low but Rising Levels of Deviance

Crime rates are unusually low in Japan. With a population one half the size of the United States, Japan has fewer robberies in a year than take place in 2 days in the United States; fewer rapes than in 1 week. In 2005, there were 1,392 homicides in all of Japan, compared to 16,992 in the United States. Twenty-two of the homicides in Japan were committed with handguns, while nearly 9,000 killings were done with handguns in the United States. Japan controls firearms very tightly. In 2006 police reported only 53 incidents of gunplay and most of these involved members of organized crime. Ordinary Japanese citizens may possess rifles and shotguns, but they are strictly licensed and licenses must be renewed every 3 years. In 2005 there were only 388,856 licensed rifles and shotguns in Japan, about a tenth of those produced every year in the United States for domestic use. More minor kinds of deviance are also uncommon in Japan. There is little drug use, low rates of out-of-wedlock childbearing, and no graffiti on the streets (Nakamura, 2007; National Police Agency, 2005; U.S. Department of Justice, 2006a; U.S. Federal Bureau of Investigation, n.d.; See also Table 1.3 above.)

But despite their society's low crime rates, people in Japan are worried about deviance. While Japan's homicide rate is low, compared to other countries, nevertheless, there were more homicides in 2005 than in 1990 (when there were 1,238). The rate of robbery (though low) more than tripled between 1990 and 2005, and there were twice as many cases of extortion. Newpapers give enormous publicity to juvenile crime, particularly unusual and grisly murders committed by teens. At the same time, juvenile delinquency has become more conspicuous. People see kids, who are neither in school nor at work, hanging around convenience stores, smoking and drinking, even sniffing paint thinner. Arrests of girls for "paid dating" are up, as are bicycle thefts and vandalism. It turns out that although there is little deviance in Japan compared to other countries, nevertheless deviance is increasing, and the increase is what people notice (Ministry of Internal Affairs and Communications Statistics Bureau, 2004; National Police Agency, 2005).

So we have two interesting questions to answer: Why are rates of deviance in Japan relatively low, and why is deviance increasing? Luckily, sociology offers three powerful theories to help us answer these questions: **control theory, labeling theory,** and **strain theory.**

Effective Social Controls: Control Theory

Control theory, as developed by Walter Reckless (1973), explains that when social controls work effectively, people are more likely to conform to society's norms. One reason why rates of deviance are relatively low in Japan is that social controls are very powerful. Thorough socialization to strict standards is followed by constant supervision and effective **social sanctions.** In every society sanctions are the muscle behind social control. Social sanctions reward those who conform and play their roles well, and punish those who fail to shape up. In Japanese society there are a variety of **positive sanctions** that are real incentives, coupled with **negative sanctions** that people wish to avoid. You could say that in Japanese society people are managed very effectively. The Japanese themselves say, "The nail that sticks up, gets pounded down."

With great consistency and regularity, the reward for role conformity in Japanese society is inclusion in the warm and pleasant life of the group. Those who fail to play their roles correctly face exclusion: Misbehaving children are excluded from family activities or left standing alone outside the classroom or playground, ignored by teachers.

In Japanese corporations social sanctions back up all the slogans and chants and exhortations to work hard and be loyal to the company. Full-time jobs, especially those with big companies, with lifetime security are hard to find. They pay much more than part-time jobs. But a man who leaves such a job may find it hard to get another one, because most companies won't hire a man they label as disloyal for leaving his company. Salarymen who disappoint or annoy their bosses may be punished by bullying—looked through as if they don't exist, moved to a desk all alone in a distant office, transferred to a company branch in another city far from their families. In effect, they are pointedly expelled from the group, though not usually fired. Positive and negative sanctions ensure that it pays for a corporate employee to

TABLE 1.4 Prison Population (2002–2005)

Japan imprisons a far lower percentage of its citizens than Mexico does. Imprisonment rates are highest in the United States.

	Year	Number of Prisoners	Number of Prisoners per 100,000 Population
Japan	2004	64,047	50
Germany	2006	64,512	78
Egypt	2002	61,845	93
Mexico	2002	172,888	172
United States	2005	2,186,230	738

Sources: Ministry of Internal Affairs and Communications, *Japan Statistical Yearbook 2008,* 2008, http://www.stat.go.ip/English/data/nenkan/index.htm.

Statistisches Bundesamt Deutschland, *Mehr als 64 000 Strafgefangene in deutschen Gefängnissen,* n.d., http://www.destatis.de/jetspeed/portal/cms/Sites/destatis/Internet/EN/press/pr/2006/12/PE06_517_024.psml.

United Nations Office on Drugs and Crime, *Eighth UN Survey on Crime Trends and the Operations of Criminal Justice Systems,* n.d., http://www.unodc.org/pdf/crime/eighthsurvey/8pc.pdf.

U.S. Department of Justice, *Prison and Jail Inmates at Midyear 2005,* 2006b, http://www.ojp.usdoj.gov/bjs/abstract/pjim05.

act loyal, even if he doesn't feel loyal (Chapman, 1991, pp. 137–139; Mehri, 2005, pp. 84–91, 184–185).

Criminal sanctions in Japan are a serious matter. Japan's prison population has grown in the last decade, but it is still comparatively small—only 50 people out of every 100,000 people are in prison, compared to 738 per 100,000 in the United States and 78 per 100,000 in Germany. See Table 1.4. Jail sentences are relatively short, but harsh. Prisoners are often kept in isolation and not even allowed to talk to each other. There are no gangs in Japanese prisons, nor any prison rapes or assaults. White-collar offenders are treated the same as ordinary criminals. Also, Japanese people are ashamed to have relatives in jail. They seldom visit them and often refuse to accept them back home once they are released (Kristof, 1995a, pp. 1, 8; McGregor, 1996, p. 94).

"Friendly Authoritarianism"

Japanese society is unusual in the sureness with which negative sanctions follow deviance. You can be certain that if you violate norms in Japan, someone will notice and will definitely take action, and you will surely pay a price. Yoshio Sugimoto calls the Japanese system of sanctions "friendly authoritarianism," because authority figures in Japan are usually warm and caring. They help people and give them rewards and people come to trust them. But people also know that if they don't conform, these same authorities can be very harsh. Police, for example, are polite and helpful. They lend people umbrellas when it rains and they lend money to people who have lost their wallets or are short on trainfare (and people almost always return the umbrellas and pay back the money) (Kristof, 1995b; Sugimoto, 1997, pp. 245–258). Police often decide not to prosecute for minor offenses, but only if the suspect writes out a sincere apology. The same police, however, are given great leeway in searching and questioning people. If you attract attention and fall under police suspicion, you have few rights and protections. Police can hold suspects without a formal hearing for up to 21 days, and often subject them to long interrogations and pressure to confess. Evidence obtained illegally is admissible in court. The very high conviction rate in criminal cases (99.8%) is partly the result of coerced confessions (Kristof, 1995a, p. 8; Onishi, 2007b, pp. A1, A10).

Surveillance

In Japan, strict norms are enforced through constant surveillance. People come to feel that the eyes of others are always upon them. People have a word for this in Japan; it is called the *seiken* (the watchful community). A good example is the "garbage guardians," volunteers who examine their neighbors' garbage bags to ensure trash is sorted properly for recycling. Some towns require each household to put an identification number on every bag. In other towns, guardians look for mail with names and addresses in bags of improperly sorted trash. Being personally reprimanded is embarrassing. Worse, the guardian may complain to your landlord who might evict you (Onishi, 2005e, pp. A1, A4).

Feeling watched all the time is stressful. There are a couple of interesting aspects of popular culture in Japan that we can see as escapes from the eyes of others. In Tokyo "media immersion pods" are a popular retreat. You can rent a cubicle with unlimited access to video games, DVDs, magazines, television, and Internet. For about $10 you can stay all night. Holed up anonymously, one writer said, "your identity can be in flux. You go to these places not to present yourself, but to lose yourself" (Heffernan, 2006, pp. AR11–AR12). Robots are popular in Japan. People like interacting with them because you don't have to think about a robot's feelings or what the robot thinks of you. In experiments, Japanese people are more likely to look a robot in the eye than a real person (*The Economist,* 2005b, pp. 58–59). Finally, you can escape the eyes of others by leaving Japan. In the past decade a wave of young women especially have gone to New York where they feel free of other people's expectations and judgments (Adachi, 2006, pp. CY1, CY10; Prasso, 2006, pp. ST1, ST6).

Formal and Informal Social Controls

Now that you see how powerful social controls are in Japan, you can see why deviance rates are low compared to other countries. But we still have to explain why deviance rates are rising. **Informal social controls** have always been important in Japan. They are the social sanctions applied spontaneously, unofficially, informally by those around you: your neighbors, family members, friends, coworkers, and so on. But many of these controls are no longer as effective as they once were. We can see this clearly in the case of teen deviance. Fewer people live in villages now. More mothers are working; they aren't home to supervise their children every hour of the day. There are fewer people watching the street. Teachers and police officers find no one at home when they make their regular visits. In response, in the past decade, Japanese society has placed increased reliance on **formal social controls**—official, legal, formalized responses.

Policing and Juvenile Crime.   The police have recently become much more proactive. In 2006 nearly 1.5 million juveniles (about 1 in 10 of those aged 10 to 19) were under "police guidance." Children who are caught smoking or drinking, or engaging in "Internet dating," as well as those caught in actual criminal acts are investigated by a special police branch, then monitored by community volunteers, referred to counseling centers and, when appropriate, required to meet their victims in "restorative conferences." Police say their goals are "to correct [the child's] deficient character and improve his/her environment"; "to improve their sense of social norms" (Nawa, 2006, pp. 13–17). Although juvenile crime and deviance remain at record high rates, increased police activity may have had some impact. Between 2002 and 2005, street crimes like purse snatching were cut in half. In 1990, there were less than 6 robberies per 100,000 juveniles per year, and in 2003 there were 25. By 2005, the rate had dropped to 18 per 100,000, still three times the rate in 1990 (National Police Agency, 2007b).

The Importance of Inner Controls

What is your reaction to reading about social controls in Japan? Are you saying to yourself, "I would never go along with a system like that"? Studying social control lets you see just how demanding and exacting Japanese society is. Why do most Japanese go along? The answer is that for most people the rewards of being part of Japanese society are sufficiently satisfying to compensate for the difficulties. Sociologist Travis Hirschi (1969) explained that the **outer controls** of social sanctions are complemented by **inner controls.** The more strongly connected we are to our social groups, the more we want to conform. We want the approval of our fellow group members. We want the group to accept us. The more we care about belonging to the group, the more we **internalize** group values and norms and make them our own. We are moved by inner controls. In Japan, most people feel like they belong, like they are part of a team—a *han,* a section, the nation itself. Also, as part of the group, people find they share in the nation's prosperity and participate psychologically in its prestige. And in Japan it is important that people share equally in prosperity, so no one feels that he or she has sacrificed and someone else has benefited. You can also see that if order, belonging, and social equality were ever undermined, Japanese society might well be in trouble.

Defining Deviance: Labeling Theory

Sociologists have long understood that deviance is a matter of social definition. **Symbolic interactionists,** who use **labeling theory,** point out that actions are deviant only if people see them that way. Behavior labeled as deviant in one society might not be considered a problem at all in another society. One reason why there is so little deviance in Japan is that a lot of behavior condemned as deviant in other societies is acceptable in Japan, as long as it remains private.

The paired concepts of *omote* and *ura* are fundamental to Japanese life. They describe two kinds of situations: Omote is the official, public face of a person, event, or social institution. Ura is the back, the private side. Japanese society requires outward conformity in a person's omote or public life, but behind the scenes, on the ura side, Japan is very accepting. What matters is that you keep your behavior appropriate to the social situation. On the ura side, people can relax with close friends or family and be relaxed and spontaneous and express their emotions. It's okay to make demands or be egotistical. People will sit in the informal family room and loosen their clothing, drink from the old teapot and cups, and joke and gossip. Women friends or male coworkers spending the weekend together at an inn will put on *yukata,* the cotton robes the hotel supplies, and drink and eat in a private room, after relaxing together in the hotel's hot tub. In ura settings people can express individualism and rebellion and let off steam that builds up in the pressure cooker of Japan's conformist public life.

Drinking is one such release. Alcohol plays an important role in Japanese life. Most drinking takes place in groups, in bars or restaurants. Levels of habitual alcohol consumption that would be labeled alcoholism in other societies are not seen as deviant in Japan. Drinking together, business associates or coworkers are able to ease the tensions of formal, omote relations (Sugimoto, 1997, p. 227).

It is common for the whole staff of a work section, including the boss (and sometimes the female workers), to go out drinking together after work. Drunk, the boss may make a fool of himself, singing and crying, but the next day in the office, when he is once again his proper, formal self, no one's respect for him will be diminished in the least. Employees, under cover of "drunkenness," may complain to the boss openly about their treatment, but the next day no one will "remember" that it happened.

Japanese society is matter-of-fact about sex—in its proper ura place. Although a husband would never kiss his wife goodbye in public at the train station, nevertheless Japan is dotted with conspicuous "love hotels"—fantastically decorated as castles, or pirate ships, or chalets—which rent rooms by the hour. These hotels are much used by young people, adulterous couples, and even married pairs looking for privacy. Pornographic *manga* (comic books), often filled with violence, are sold in vending machines and porn videos are shown in bars. Popular animated films have many scenes of sex and violence (often cut from the exported versions of the films) (Tasker, 1987, pp. 111, 113–114). In the entertainment districts of big cities, bar hostesses offer men flirtation and flattery. Teenaged girls look cute and innocent in their school uniforms, going about in giggling groups, but behind the scenes two thirds of the girls engage in sex by age 15. Some teenaged girls go further, working on telephone sex lines or even as prostitutes (White, 1993, pp. 170–189).

Sexual Harassment

You can see how much deviance is a matter of social definition if you consider the topic of sexual harassment. Until very recently, sexual harassment didn't exist in Japan. Of course there was and is sexual molestation, quite a lot of it in fact. Men grope young women on trains, and in offices men take advantage of women's subordinate position to touch them, make unwanted sexual advances, and spread sexual rumors about them. Recently, 70% of female government workers told interviewers they had been sexually harassed. But all of this was just taken for granted. Police ignored sexual molestation, and women were warned not to complain, because complaining would bring them shameful attention and people would assume they had dressed or acted provocatively. It was not until 1999 that the government estab-lished regulations banning sexual harassment in the workplace. But the rules lack clear penalties and very few women have dared to sue. So even though the govern-ment is conducting a campaign against sexual harassment, with posters in the Tokyo subway, most people don't yet see harassment as deviant. It is complaining about sexual abuse that is labeled the deviant act (French, 2001b, pp. 1, 10).

Domestic Violence

In Japan, as in other societies, there are groups of people who try to redefine certain behaviors, or certain people, as deviant. Sociologists call such activists **moral entrepreneurs.** In the past few years, several organizations in Japan have worked to change the way the Japanese view domestic violence—specifically assaults by men on their wives. In a nationwide government survey in 2000, 27.5% of Japanese wives said their husbands had beaten them, but most Japanese don't see such vio-lence against women as a crime. Nevertheless, activists, lawyers, and some outspo-ken victims of wife battery actually succeeded in 2001 in getting the Japanese legislature to pass a law permitting courts to issue restraining orders against wife beaters. It is one step in relabeling spousal abuse as an act of deviance, rather than a domestic dispute that should be hushed up (Kambayashi, 2004, p. 11).

Labeling People

It's not just behavior that gets labeled as deviant or acceptable; sometimes people get labeled, too. Police and school authorities look at kids differently depending on what high school they go to. They assume that students at low-ranked schools in working-class neighborhoods are failures and troublemakers. The places where these students hang out are policed more actively and the rules at their schools are extra strict. Stu-dents end up more likely to have a police record, more likely to drop out of school, and more likely to live out the adult world's low expectations for them. Kids at pres-tigious schools have fewer restrictive rules to follow and are more likely to get away with everyday delinquency like smoking and drinking. They don't get labeled, or as we say **stigmatized,** as a result of their deviance (Yoder, 2004, pp. 51–56). Is this kind of social-class-based labeling something that happens in your society, too?

Deviance and Stigma

You may be surprised to learn that in Japan it is sometimes seen as more deviant to adopt a deviant identity than to engage in deviant behavior. **Primary deviance,** that is, deviant acts, is much more readily forgiven than is **secondary deviance,** or the adoption of deviant statuses. When Japanese people adopt a deviant identity—one that proclaims their difference from other Japanese—they are strongly stigmatized or publicly labeled as different and deviant. For example, homosexual sex acts are not seen as perverted or sinful in Japan, but people who announce that they are gay scandalize others and bring shame on their family members who will experience difficulty getting jobs and finding spouses. Having AIDS is a matter of the deepest shame, and many people living with AIDS move to Hawaii before their symptoms show to spare their families from ostracism. We can say that in a very real way being different is deviant in Japan.

How Strain Theory Accounts for Deviance

Why is it that in Japan (or in any other society for that matter) some people decide to risk negative social sanctions and stigmatization and commit acts of deviance? You might look at this as a matter of individual choice, but sociologists see patterns in who engages in deviance, and they locate the causes for deviance in society.

Robert Merton's (1956/1968) **strain theory of deviance** offers a powerful analysis of social patterns of deviance. Every society, Merton said, has both generally approved goals (its values) and widely approved means for achieving those goals (its norms). If people who follow the norms regularly achieve the values they treasure, then conformity pays off and people will generally conform. Deviance arises when some people find obstacles in their path to achieving the approved goals by following the approved means. The more obstacles people encounter, the more they will experience strain or frustration and the more likely they are to resort to deviant behavior (Henslin, 2004, pp. 148–149).

Merton saw four possible kinds of deviant responses to strain. **Innovators** continue to strive for the accepted goals of society, but resort to disapproved means for achieving them. **Ritualists** give up on the accepted goals, but continue to cling to following the norms. **Retreatists** give up entirely, rejecting both the accepted goals and the normative means for achieving them. And finally, **rebels** reject both the goals and the norms, but try to substitute new goals and new norms they consider superior.

Sources of Strain in Japanese Society

Merton's strain theory is enormously helpful in understanding Japanese society. It explains both why there has been so much conformity in Japan and why deviance has recently increased. In the 40 years that followed World War II, the Japanese created a remarkably successful society. People devoted themselves to work, sacrificing their personal time and family lives. Children studied intensively for exams, denying themselves time for hobbies and social life. But nevertheless, people found life good. They conformed by working hard, but they were rewarded. Children who excelled in school got good jobs and men who loyally worked for their companies enjoyed constantly rising pay, economic security, and eventual promotions. They were sought after as husbands and found fulfillment as valued members of their companies. They took pride in helping create Japan's economic miracle. Wives were told they made it all possible by taking over all the household responsibilities. Everyone belonged.

Today, however, the postwar social order is breaking down. Change is rapid; there are many signs of strain and rising levels of deviance. Much of the disruptive change in Japan today results from the long recession that lasted from 1991 until approximately 2004. Some changes are the product of efforts to adjust to economic and political globalization. Economic growth and prosperity were the basis of the late-20th-century Japanese social order. But with the recession came unemployment, job cutbacks, rising insecurity, and a serious blow to national pride. It threatened the team spirit that came with being part of an economic miracle. Now the economy is recovering, but it is not at all clear that Japan can make the old social order work again.

Japanese men who once assumed that their loyalty to their company would be rewarded with lifetime security now must worry about being cast out of the company. Salarymen don't seem so attractive anymore to young women; they have an odor of failure about them. The lasting strain of the recession is particularly clear when we look at young people and their lives in school.

Social Controls in School. Japan used to have a very powerful system of social controls in schools, because a student's school performance had serious effects that could last a lifetime. School systems haven't changed, but the effectiveness of the controls has. Junior high schools in Japan are neighborhood schools, but high schools are not. At the end of junior high school, students all take admissions tests to high schools, which are ranked, with the higher-status schools serving as feeders for the most prestigious universities. Only students with good school records are even allowed to take tests for the highest-ranked high schools. Then, at the end of high school there are once again competitive exams for college admission. People hired for upper-level government jobs and the best companies are chosen almost exclusively from a few select universities. Students who attend technical high schools are expected to seek jobs through their high school placement offices, which have close, semiformal relationships with companies. If you haven't worked hard in school and made a good impression on authorities, you have no chance of getting a good job. Keep in mind that if you don't get a good full-time job when you leave school, there is very little chance that you will ever get one.

This system kept Japanese students tightly controlled; there was no alternative to conformity if you wanted to have a good life. But during the recession, the jobs dried up. Companies tried to retain their loyal employees and didn't hire any new graduates. In 1992, Japanese companies offered 1.67 million permanent full-time jobs to high school graduates. In 2003, only 220,000 such jobs were offered. The number of college graduates recruited for full-time work dropped by a third in the same 10-year period (Honda, 2003; Kosugi, 2004, pp. 52–53). Also, because families have gotten smaller, there are now fewer students competing for university admissions. It has become easier to get into the less prestigious universities, at the same time that the rewards of attending have become less impressive. Could you predict the effect of these strains on rates of deviance in Japan? Let's see what evidence we can find of the four types of deviance Merton predicted would result from strain.

Innovative Deviance in Japan

There is certainly innovative deviance to be found in Japan, but in a way it is the most acceptable form of deviance. Deviant innovators still embrace the supreme Japanese value of belonging; they just find ways of belonging that are deviant.

The Yakuza. Japan's organized crime syndicates, called the *Yakuza,* are a form of innovative deviance with a long history. Approximately 90,000 Yakuza members are organized into three main syndicates and 3,000 groups, running prostitution, pornography, gambling, drugs, extortion, and labor rackets, and taking in billions of dollars a year. The Yakuza also engage in violence on behalf of legitimate authorities who wish to avoid the use of violence themselves. The members have broken strikes, silenced dissenters, and evicted tenants from valuable real estate. The Yakuza have worked for corporations, the ruling Liberal Democratic Party, the American CIA, and the police. The Yakuza also police the ranks of criminals, making sure that all who engage in crime belong to one of their organizations.

The Yakuza occupy a somewhat contradictory position in Japanese society. Obviously they are seen as engaging in deviant activity. But as an organization, the Yakuza enjoy a legitimacy and acceptance in Japanese society very different from their American counterparts. The Yakuza are accepted as a public presence in Japan; their offices publicly display gang insignia on the door, like an insurance office or loan company. Members wear gang badges, like the company pins Japanese salarymen wear. People who join the Yakuza become part of a social group like others in Japan—one that stresses group identity and conformity to group norms (Sterngold, 1992, pp. A1, A6; Tasker, 1987, p. 78; Wildeman, n.d.).

The Yakuza have long attracted Japanese who have the hardest time being accepted by Japan's mainstream groups: outsiders, mostly people of Korean and *Burakumin* ancestry. (Koreans in Japan are mostly descendants of people brought to Japan in the early 20th century when Korea was conquered by Japan. Burakumin are descendants of Japan's ancient hereditary **outcaste** group. See pages 52–55 for more on both these **minority** groups.) Today, Yakuza advertisements for new members are drawing responses from high school dropouts and disgraced former employees (*Mainichi Daily News,* 2003, p. 1).

Yakuza members are genuinely innovative. They constantly come up with new rackets to adapt to changing times. Since environmental activism has increased in Japan, the Yakuza have started creating fake environmentalist groups that make demands that are inconvenient for companies. Then, in exchange for bribes, they cease their campaigns. Another new Yakuza business is contract killing of suicidal unemployed men who want to die without depriving their families of their life insurance (Pearson, 2004, p. 44; Shih, 2004).

Cult Groups.   There are about 18,000 groups classed as New Religions in Japan, groups neither Shinto nor Buddhist (McGregor, 1996, p. 29). Japanese society is ordinarily very tolerant of religious cults. They, too, fit the pattern of innovative deviance: They offer a way to belong to people who feel alienated from mainstream society. Most cult groups follow the familiar pattern of a secretive group, led by a mystical guru, who demands members' loyalty and total involvement. For example, Pana Wave is a doomsday cult whose members dress all in white and do not bathe. They travel Japan in caravans searching for places to avoid electromagnetic waves (French, 2003b, p. A10).

Ritualist Deviance in Japan

There are a few examples of ritualist deviance in Japan, but these cases don't excite much outrage. They are seen rather as pathetic. One example is the sad ex-salarymen who have been forced by their companies to retire prematurely. Some of them continue to leave the house every morning in suit and tie and take the train into Tokyo. Then they while away the hours in the public library, public buildings, or movie theaters before returning home. They are ashamed of being fired and don't want their neighbors to know. Some have not even told their wives.

Retreatist Deviance in Japan

Many of the forms of deviance that upset the Japanese the most could be classified as retreatist. That's not surprising when you remember the importance of belonging, of group membership, in Japanese culture. Retreatists reject belonging in a way that is the ultimate threat to Japanese society.

Suicide.   Suicide is clearly the most radical possible retreat from society, and the Japanese are very concerned about their rising suicide rate. Japan began the 1990s with a relatively moderate rate of suicide, comparable to that of most European countries. But with the economic recession, the suicide rate shot up, rising 50% between 1990 and 1999. Since 2001, the rate has remained high and relatively stable. The suicide rate has been highest for men between the ages of 55 and 64, precisely the group that devoted their lives to the company and then abruptly faced new company demands, layoffs, and forced retirements. This is the same age cohort that is also experiencing an increased divorce rate. These men continued to follow the norms as usual, but nevertheless felt rejected both at work and at home (Ministry of Internal Affairs and Communications, 2008, Chapter 25, Table 15; Nathan, 2004, pp. 74–75; World Health Organization, 1999, Table 1). See also Table 1.3, p. 27.

Japanese newspapers carry many reports of suicides on the rail lines, particularly the express lines that lead from Tokyo to the surrounding suburbs. One company has installed mirrors across the tracks from passenger platforms in the hope that if jumpers see themselves, they may hesitate. All the rail lines now charge the families of suicide victims for the expenses caused by the suicides. It is widely rumored that the most suicides take place on the rail line that charges the least (French, 2000, p. A4). Recently there have been many news articles about young people using the Internet to enter into group suicide pacts with strangers. How ironic that people who feel so alienated from society that they would take their lives still want company as they do so (Brooke, 2004, p. A11)!

School Refusal.   Another form of deviant behavior that is of serious concern in Japan is the growing number of children, usually of junior high school age, who refuse to go to school. There are many news articles about school refusal. Teachers and parents worry about it, and the government conducted a special study in 1999. It found that by 1997 over 20,000 elementary school students and over 80,000 junior high school students were identified as school refusers (an eightfold increase over 1978). In 2005 the Ministry of Education reported that 2% of students enrolled in high school never attended (Zielenziger, 2006, p. 53). School refusal worries the Japanese way out of proportion to its rate of incidence, because it challenges their belief in school as a "family society," an all-inclusive group to which children should enjoy belonging (Fukuzawa & LeTendre, 2001, pp. 81–87; Nathan, 2004, p. 39).

Some school refusers become *hikikomori* (which translates as "one who withdraws from society"). Hikikomori are recluses who won't leave their houses. Sometimes they even barricade themselves in their bedrooms, dependent on worried parents to deliver food. Eighty percent of hikikomori are males, some schoolboys and some adult men in their 20s and 30s. They have completely abandoned the normal progression of life in Japan: from school to university to work. Some Ministry of Health studies estimate that more than 1% of Japanese families include a hikikomori, though they usually keep the problem secret (Zielenziger, 2006, pp. 16–19, 40–41).

Youth Violence.   School refusal is often associated in public discussion with youth violence, also a much publicized problem. There are constant stories in the media about students armed with knives, horrible murders committed by middle schoolers, and attacks on drunken salarymen by gangs of youths. Rates of juvenile crime have risen since 1990, but are actually much lower than they were back in the 1960s and 1970s (*The Economist,* 2003, pp. 39–40; Fukuzawa & LeTendre, 2001, p. 87; Nathan, 2004, pp. 31–37; Zaun, 2004, p. A12).

Japanese experts understand child violence and disobedience in terms that resemble Merton's. Parents' expectations for their children are rising; they have smaller families and demand that their one or two children excel in school, attend prestigious colleges, and get high-status jobs. But children see the means to achievement collapsing. They see young people with excellent records in school who still fail to get secure jobs with good companies. They lose their trust in society, their belief that following the approved norms will lead to achieving desired goals (French, 2002b, p. A6, quoting Noaki Ogi, an education expert).

Responses to Deviance

Characteristically, Japanese society responds to deviance by assuming there has been a failure of human relations in groups. The focus is less on the deviant individual and his or her problems and more on devising a way to reintegrate that individual into a close-knit group. When LeTendre interviewed teachers in Japan, they kept telling him that school refusal and school violence came about when teachers had been unsuccessful in creating emotional connections with students, in building a sense of community (*kazoku-teki shakai,* or "family-society") in the class. They saw violence in school resulting when teachers didn't work together, when divorce disrupted families, and when employment kept mothers from participating in the PTA, breaking connections between parents and school (Fukuzawa & LeTendre, 2001, pp. 86–87).

Some schools and communities have set up programs for students who avoid school and seem at risk of dropping out. Often school nurses set up a special room for these children, where they can be coaxed out of their shells. "They need to be closer to teachers. They need to feel the teacher's warmth," one nurse said. New alternative schools offer school-refusing children a chance to start over in a rural town, boarding with local families and forming an accepting group of their own in school. The few programs that exist for *hikikomori* all offer a protective environment where isolates can learn to interact with others (Fukuzawa & LeTendre, 2001, p. 85; Nathan, 2004, pp. 40–43; Onishi, 2004c, p. 3; Zielenziger, 2006, pp. 76–92).

Recently, the *Yomiuiri Shimbun,* Japan's major conservative newspaper, detailed the decade-long rise in crime rates and fall in arrest rates. The cause, the newspaper explained, was selfishness by police officers, who were neglecting routine police work in order to concentrate on cases that might help them win promotion. To control crime, the newspaper recommended that the focus of policing return to the *koban,* the local "police box," from which officers make themselves part of the community (Masui, 2003).

GENDER ROLES: A FOCUS FOR REBELLION

Most rebellious deviance in Japan today centers on rejection of traditional gender roles. Young men and women spurn the goals their society assigns them and the approved means for achieving those goals and instead adopt new, alternative goals and norms. To understand the rebellion of young people, you must first know what are the dominant role expectations and then recognize what forces have created stress around these expectations. So far, young Japanese women are far more rebellious than young men, but there are signs of rebellion among men too. Despite change, sex remains a **master status** in Japanese society, defining the gender roles that men and women play in school, work, and other areas.

Traditional Gender Roles for Women

The subordination of women is built into Japanese institutions, shaping family life, education, and the economy. Women are seen as fundamentally different from men and inferior to men. Almost everyone assumes that the purpose of a woman's life is to serve others: her children, her husband, perhaps her in-laws, the men at work. Women are expected to be patient and "endure" and put their own needs last. They are expected to defer to men—they giggle behind their hands, act shy, cute, and submissive, and lower their eyes. They are taught to listen and quietly observe men to interpret men's feelings and anticipate their needs. When women do speak, they are expected to have small, high voices and to use forms of speech that express hesitation.

Although women are certainly subordinate in the public realm of life, "off-stage" at home they exercise considerable power. Japanese wives are in charge of family budgets and with their husbands away at work so much, they are the emotional center of family life. In a way Japanese men are dependent on their wives, both physically and psychologically. Anthropologist Takie Sugiyama Lebra describes the traditional wife as offering her husband so much "around the body care" that he cannot even find his socks without her (Kato, 1994, pp. 184–185; Lebra, 1984, p. 133).

Shoko's Story: A Conformist Marriage

Shoko Sato was born in 1965 in a small city near Kyoto. She graduated high school and began working in the office of a local construction company. She enjoyed working very much. Her department chief was very kind to her and he allowed her an unusual amount of responsibility for organizing the paperwork on contracts. When she was 24 Shoko married Taichi. The match was semiarranged. She knew Taichi from high school and from neighborhood temple festivals. When Taichi's boss, who knew her father, suggested the marriage, they found themselves drawn to each other. Shoko wanted to continue working after she married, so she felt terribly flustered and confused when her boss immediately began to talk about a party for her "retirement" when he learned of the engagement. It was too embarrassing to try to explain that she had imagined she could keep working, and she didn't want to suggest that he hadn't understood her. So Shoko went along. Anyway, her first child was born just a year after the marriage, and Shoko firmly believed that she should fully devote herself to her children.

While Shoko plunged into the world of babies and mothers, she was still in some ways disappointed in her marriage. The companionship she and her husband Taichi had enjoyed in the beginning of their marriage seemed to vanish in the face of his obligation to work long hours and travel frequently for his company. Shoko made his breakfast every morning, and waited up for him at night until he returned at 10 or 11, because he didn't carry a key to the apartment. At any rate, she wanted to give him dinner and run his bath for him and lay out his clothes for the morning. Taichi turned his paycheck over to her and she arranged the family finances. They moved several times and each time Shoko searched for the new apartment and made the decision to buy it, because her husband was too busy at work to join her. Raising her children was a great joy to Shoko. At every milestone, like starting first grade, or graduating junior high school, she relived her own happy childhood and strove to make her children's as secure and loving as her own. Shoko became active in the PTA and kept up her friendships with several women she had known ever since junior high school. Now, helping her son and daughter with their homework and driving them to lessons take a lot of her time. She works on the yearly festival of their local shrine and studies flower arranging in the town cultural center. Last year she began working part-time for a nearby bank. Shoko feels her life is full, but she doesn't really know her husband very well anymore.

Gender Segregation

One thing is clear about Japanese adult men and women: Their roles are highly segregated. They lead separate lives. The word *wife* in Japanese literally means "inside person" (Condon, 1985, p. 1). It is the wife's role to be in charge of the home and children. The husband is the "outside man," who goes out into the world, relieved of all worries at home. In a real way, the primary ties in the family are those between mothers and children. Women are expected to live through their children, taking pride in their successes and blaming themselves for failures. Child care and housework are demanding jobs in Japan. Mothers are expected to teach their children to read at home before they enter kindergarten and to spend hours a day helping their children with homework. Apartments are very small and few women have cars, so they must shop for groceries every day. A significant obligation for women is care of elderly family members. They are expected to care for their husband's parents, and often their own as well.

Women and Work

In Japanese society, everyone is expected to marry, and almost everyone does, though people are marrying later and later these days. Between high school or university graduation and marriage, women are expected to work outside the home. But when their first child is born, usually within a year of marriage, three quarters of women leave work. They begin working again, on a part-time basis, once their last child has begun school. See Table 1.5, p. 41.

TABLE 1.5 Working Women (1970–2004)

Increasing numbers of women work, but in Japan, Egypt, and Mexico their income is less than half of men's income.

	Percentage of Adult Women Employed			Women's Income as Percentage of Men's Income
	1970	1990	2004	2004
Japan	39	49	51.2	46
Egypt	—	30	36	26
Mexico	19	34	40.6	36
Germany	39	48	48	54
Namibia	39	53	53.7	51
United States	37	56	59.6	62

Sources: United Nations, *Human Development Report 2005,* 2005 (1990, 2004 data), http://hdr.undp.org/en/reports/global/hdr2005/; United Nations, *Human Development Report 1997,* 1997 (1970 data), http:/hdr.undp.org/en/reports/global/hdr1997/.

Note: Dash indicates data not available.

Young Women and Work. Young women find they have few job alternatives. The jobs available to them keep them dependent, separated from and subordinated to men, usually without prospect of promotion. Unmarried women work in offices, in factories, and in retail stores. A job considered appropriate for young women is "office lady" (called OL), especially with a prestigious company. OLs are selected for looks, as their duties are minimal: They do photocopying and filing, make tea, and tidy up. They are really a corporate status symbol, employed to be decorative and act as hostesses for business guests. Newly hired OLs are trained in bowing, greeting phone callers correctly, and offering tea. See Table 1.5.

Within the last decade it has become possible for women to get "career-track" managerial or professional promotion track jobs, but, in fact, very few women do so. A woman in a career-track job must work overtime, be willing to transfer to distant offices, and work through her childbearing years, just like a man. Only university graduates are eligible and only 21% of female high school graduates go to a university.[3] Even women who make it onto the management track often drop out once they have children. Sometimes women can find promotion-track jobs with foreign companies or in the very few female-owned companies. But overall, few women in Japan hold high-ranking jobs. Although women make up almost half of Japan's workforce, only 10% of managers are women (Fackler, 2007d, pp. A1, A6).

Working Mothers. The typical Japanese woman today reenters the workforce once she is in her 40s and her children are school age or grown, both to occupy her time and to help pay rising family expenses. Since 1977, more employed women have been married than single, and 40% of the workforce is female (Condon, 1985, pp. 219, 263; Sugimoto, 1997, p. 142). But married women

[3]Of that 21%, only 1% take career-track jobs (Sugimoto, 1997, pp. 145–147).

work on terms even more disadvantageous than do single women. Accommodating the needs of their families, most married women find unskilled part-time work, near home, in supermarkets, fast-food shops, department stores, and small factories (Condon, 1985, p. 194; Tasker, p. 1987, p. 103). Under the pressure of economic competition, more and more Japanese companies now hire a small core of men for full-time, lifetime security jobs, and then adjust their workforce to the ups and downs of the business cycle with part-timers, often women.

Women and Men

Japanese women are still seen primarily as wives and mothers, and it is as wives and mothers that they are registering their strongest rebellion against their roles. Women are postponing marriage, prolonging that pleasurable time after leaving school and before marrying when they are relatively independent and have jobs and money of their own. Although 90% of all Japanese marry by the age of 40, young women are postponing marriage more and more. More than half of all Japanese women are still single at age 30, compared with 37% in the United States (Orenstein, 2001, p. 31). Japanese men complain about their difficulty in finding wives. Farmers and fishermen find it particularly hard to persuade women to live in rural areas and in the same house with their in-laws. Marriage bureaus do a big business in arranging marriages for Japanese men with Chinese, Taiwanese, and Filipino women (Jolivet, 1997, pp. 40, 146–147).

What do Japan's young women want? They are not demanding job equity. Most women say they don't envy men their long hours, grim devotion to work, and lack of time for any other activity. What women do want is even more subversive. Over and over again, unmarried women in their 20s in Tokyo told journalist Peggy Orenstein, "I just want to live for myself and enjoy my life" (Orenstein, 2001, p. 34). This statement might sound completely ordinary to you, but it is revolutionary in Japan where self-sacrificing devotion to family and duty has been the unquestioned norm for women. The popular name for unmarried women in Japan is now "parasite singles." They live with their parents, pay no rent, do no housework, and do as they please. Though their wages are not high, they have disposable income for cell phones, designer clothes, restaurant meals, and travel. These women are *wagamama*, people say, meaning selfish and willful. And the parasite singles have defiantly adopted *wagamama* as their own self-characterization, moving its meaning toward "self-determining" (Orenstein, 2001, pp. 32–33).

Makiko's Story: Parasite Single

Makiko Yokimura is 29 years old and still unmarried. She lives with her parents in Tokyo and works as an OL for a big pharmaceutical company. Her work, she says, isn't unpleasant, but it's unchallenging. Mostly she answers the telephone and acts as receptionist for visiting businessmen. She earns the equivalent of $28,000 per year. But her life, she says, is good. She wears Comme des Garçons clothes and carries Gucci handbags. She lightens her hair in the trendiest salon and spends a fortune on makeup. Her cell phone seems to ring constantly. After work at 5 o'clock she meets her friends in fashionable cafes. She takes lessons in conversational French and classical shoko playing. Last summer she and a friend took a trip to Paris.

"Sure I'll get married," Makiko says, "someday. But I don't want to think about it now. If I were married I'd be stuck at home all the time, worrying about what my husband wants. I'd have to do all the housework and be a servant to my in-laws. My mother tells me I should get married, but she also complains all the time about how her in-laws exploit her and how my father is a stranger to her." But doesn't she miss having a man in her life, we asked Makiko? "You have to understand," she replied, "Japan is not a 'couples culture.' Even if I were married, or had a regular boyfriend, I'd still be spending most of my time with my girlfriends. Men and women just aren't companions for each other."

Married Women Rebel

Apparently, many married women in Japan feel that they have empty marriages. Their husbands have been busy working, essentially "absent" from the marriage. In a recent survey, 35% of couples reported that they had sex less than once a month (*The New York Times,* 2007, p. A6). The divorce rate for middle-aged couples has shot up. The real crisis seems to come when husbands retire and, for the first time, they are around the house all day. Seventy-five percent of all divorces are initiated by women (Hogg, 2007). Middle-aged divorcees must be determined and brave because although the legal requirements for divorce are simple, there are tremendous social barriers for older, divorced women. They face the disapproval of family and neighbors, who expect a wife to deny herself for the sake of her family. Middle-aged divorced women find it hard to get jobs, loans, mortgages, or even credit cards (French, 2003a, p. A3).

Unhappy wives who are afraid to divorce have initiated an unusual new trend: They arrange to be buried separately from their husbands, leaving them in death, if not in life. Cemeteries that accommodate such women have appeared only since 1990, but there are now close to 400 of them (French, 2002a, p. A4).

Imagining New Ideals. Japanese women say they are seeking a new kind of man, one who is devoted and attentive. A popular new café for women in Tokyo offers service by male servers dressed as butlers, who treat customers like "princesses." Devotees of the café choose a favorite "butler" and visit often to get close to him (*The Economist,* 2006d, p. 40). "Host clubs," which employ as many as 20,000 men nationwide, offer young women the same kind of attention men get from bar hostesses. Customers visit several times a week and spend hundreds of dollars drinking and talking with their favorite "hosts" (Onishi, 2005c, p. A4).

Japanese Men: Trouble with Roles

You must pity the poor Japanese male! Even the most willingly conformist man is likely to have trouble with his roles, at work and at home. Japanese men know they are expected to devote themselves to their jobs, out of loyalty to their company, and to help Japan compete and advance. But the economic crisis in Japan has produced a collapse of careers. Men can no longer count on what used to be stable patterns of hiring, promotion, and compensation. Middle-aged salarymen who have been dedicated team players all their lives may suddenly experience harassment designed to drive them into retirement. And the executives who do the bullying also feel ashamed, because they can no longer reward their subordinates for loyal efforts. Those who keep their jobs may be overwhelmed by the increased workload (Strom, 1999a, p. A8).

At the same time, men experience a kind of loss of meaning. It wasn't so long ago that Japanese men saw themselves as players in a grand national drama. They were like a band of samurai warriors, fighting to bring Japan back from its defeat in World War II and make it a world economic power. That fight was won, but by the 1990s Japan was mired in recession and China was the ascendant economic power. Japan is no longer the envy of the world. Americans no longer fear that Japan will take over the U.S. economy, and Japanese men no longer understand what it is that they are to sacrifice for. John Nathan (2004) quotes a 48-year-old bank manager who told him:

> We had big dreams until the early nineties. . . . We wanted things and we worked desperately hard to bring our material life up to the American standard. The family cooperated; it was a team effort. No matter how late we had to stay at the office working, Saturdays and Sundays and no vacations, they understood and supported us. And we created unbelievable wealth. . . . But since the bubble burst it feels as though our hard work is unavailing. And people my age and older have to ask ourselves why are we working so hard. What's the point. . . . We've lost our dreams and now we must rethink our way of life. (p. 67; also see Roberson & Suzuki, 2003, pp. 6–7, 9)

Marriage and Family Life

Today, Japanese men's battered self-esteem has come under further assault by dissatisfied women. Being a salaryman is suddenly *dasai* (uncool). Younger women call the ubiquitous dark-suited company warriors *nakakenai* (clueless) and their wives call them the *nure-ochiba zuku* (the "wet leaf tribe," "clingy, musty, and emotionally spent" (French, 2002c, p. A4).

When it comes to marriage, men find themselves caught between contradictory demands. If they are lucky enough to find full-time, salaryman-style jobs, their employers demand that they marry. But young women don't want the lifestyle of the salaryman's wife. At the same time, young women are also reluctant to marry men without secure incomes. A recent large Japanese government survey of family relations found that 68% of Japanese wives believed that husbands should give first priority to their work. Remarkably, at the same time, 77% believed husbands should share equal responsibility for childrearing! Another 48.3% said they were unsatisfied with their husband's participation in household work and childrearing (National Institution of Population and Social Security Research 2000).

Men Respond: Ritualism, Retreatism, and Rebellion

As discussed earlier, we can see many examples of men engaging in retreatist deviance in Japan: from suicide to *hikikomori*, to dropping out. There is a small but growing number of homeless middle-aged men who have lost their jobs and left their families because of shame. You can see them in orderly squatter settlements in public parks and under bridges, or in spotless shelters put up by city authorities (French, 2001a, pp. A1, A8). Some men go on working and supporting their families, playing the expected male roles, but they find no meaning or fulfillment in any of it. It does not look like deviance, but Merton would call it ritualistic deviance.

The varied forms of rebellion among Japanese men deserve fuller description. Some men are rejecting the traditional role of company man and instead, like the "*wagamama* girls," are seeking a more personal self-fulfillment. Some men try to become more the kind of person women are demanding in a boyfriend or husband: more emotionally expressive and more devoted to family life. The Japan Aisaika Organization provides this statement of purpose: "Perhaps the world will become a little nicer and more peaceful if more of us start to show our appreciation and care for our wives. With this sweet concept, we are promoting the lifestyle of Aisaika, or Adoring Husbands." The group was founded by a businessman whose first wife divorced him because he was never home. When he remarried, he promised to change. The group started a "Beloved Wives Day," and published "five golden rules," including "call your wife by her name instead of grunting," and "look into her eyes when you talk" (*BBC News,* 2006; Japan Aisaika Organization, n.d.).

Some men have rebelled in their work lives too, rejecting conventional jobs, choosing to work only for the money they need to enjoy life. They are called *freitas* (from a combination of the English word *free* and the German word *arbeiter,* or worker). The government estimated in 2000 that there were 4.17 million freitas, aged between 15 and 34, up from 1.5 million in 1997 (*Japan Today,* 2004). Freitas take part-time jobs or temporary jobs; they are unmarried and live with their parents. They travel, pursue personal hobbies, and enjoy free time.

Not all men who rebel do so by dropping out in search of personal fulfillment. In some recent cases, highly publicized in the media, salarymen rejected Japan's values of loyalty and sacrifice for the company and insisted on personal recognition and gain. Shuji Nakamura sued his company for a share of royalties on patents for a device he invented: a blue-light emitting diode. The company had originally given Nakamura a bonus of less than $200 for his invention. A record court settlement now has awarded him $8.1 million. Other engineers and inventors followed Nakamura's example and sued their companies (Onishi, 2005d, p. 16; Zaun, 2005, p. C3). Japan may have limited tolerance, however, for this kind of individualism. In several recent public scandals, two self-made young billionaires, Takafumi Horie, who started an Internet company, and Yoshiaki Murakami, a self-styled "corporate raider," were first lauded and then prosecuted for business fraud (Onishi, 2007a, p. A4). Recently, some salarymen have become corporate whistle-blowers, exposing their company's deceptions and scams. Some whistle-blowers who, for example, exposed adulterated or mislabeled food products became folk heroes, even starred in comic strips, but most pay a heavy price for their "disloyalty," are fired by their companies, shunned by neighbors, relatives, and coworkers, and are unable to find other work (Fackler, 2008, p. BU4).

Interlocking Changes

The 1990s were a period of rapid change in Japan. Against a background of economic recession, crime rates rose, suicide rates spiked, and women and men began to challenge traditional roles. Now we need to examine patterns of inequality in Japan and how these too have been changing.

SOCIAL INEQUALITY IN JAPAN:
CLASS, STATUS, AND POWER

Inequality is universal; it can be found in every society, but that doesn't make all societies similar. Actually, societies differ quite a lot, both in how much inequality they contain and what forms these inequalities take. Max Weber's classic discussion of social stratification is useful for understanding the varieties of social inequality in Japan. Weber said that there are three basic aspects of inequality: class, status, and power. **Class** has to do with the wealth and income people enjoy as the result of their property or job. **Status** refers to prestige. It is the cultural dimension of inequality, because it results from the way a culture views different groups of people—men and women, ethnic or racial groups, people in different occupations, people from particular families. Weber defined **power** as the ability to make people do what you want, even against their will. In every society, some individuals and groups have more power than others.

In Japan, class inequalities make people uncomfortable. The Japanese don't want to have great inequalities of wealth or income or opportunity in their society, and they have made great efforts to minimize them. But the economic recession and the economic restructuring that resulted from it have strained class equality in Japan, creating new tensions in the society. There are interesting changes in status inequality as well. Women, as we have seen, are challenging their subservience to men. But other status inequalities are growing, as Japan's minority populations expand. Inequalities of power in Japan have seen little change. Power is still closely held in the hands of a small elite of government bureaucrats, politicians, and business leaders. Significant challengers have appeared on the scene, but it is not yet clear how successful they will be in dislodging the elites. You should be aware, however, that changes in the structure of inequality are not without precedent in Japan. Japan's history is full of such transformations.

A History of Change

For most of its history (up until the Meiji Restoration) Japan was a society of hereditary status rankings: it was a **caste society.** Everyone was born into their parents' **caste,** as warrior-rulers (samurai), peasants, artisans, or merchants. Those who didn't fit any of these categories, like landless laborers, servants, entertainers, and pariahs who did dirty work like animal slaughter, were outside the caste system and at the very bottom. Caste was destiny: Everyone had to live and marry within the caste, no matter what his or her talents might be, and there were rules regulating what members of different castes and subcastes were permitted to do and wear (Neary, 2003, p. 269; Reischauer, 1977, p. 158).

Meiji Inequality

Then, in one of Japan's most remarkable self-transformations, the Meiji government declared that "the four orders are equal" and legal distinctions between the castes were officially discarded (Fukutake, 1981, pp. 27–28). Remarkably, most caste distinctions faded from people's awareness after they were legally abolished. But inequality by no means disappeared from Meiji Japan; rather, it changed its character. In the early 20th century, class inequalities grew as Japan industrialized. Rural land was concentrated in the hands of a wealthy landlord class, while the growing industrial economy quickly came to be dominated by a small number of vastly powerful, family-owned business conglomerates with close ties to government and the military (Chapman, 1991, p. 198).

Postwar Equality

But the story is far from over, for remarkably, World War II ushered in yet another era of Japanese social stratification. Defeat destroyed Japan's industry and left nearly everyone poor. Many inequalities were leveled by the American Occupation reforms, which broke up the landlords' estates and distributed the land to the peasants, dismantled the great industrial empires, and purged their executives as war collaborators. Occupation authorities instituted progressive income taxes and (briefly) supported labor unions. Building on occupation reforms, Japan's leaders reconstructed the society on egalitarian foundations. Contracts between labor and management followed the principle of equal pay for equal work, regardless of the education, skill, or status of the employees. Unions aimed for a "livelihood wage" for all, and there was little difference in the pay received by blue- and white-collar employees. For employees of the same age, those in the highest-paid positions made no more than about 25% more than those in the lowest-paid positions. Salarymen all started their careers with the same low wages and advanced as a cohort with others hired at the same time. Wages increased year by year, growing quickly after the age of 50 until retirement, when the worker received a bonus of about 3 years' salary before starting on his pension (Chapman, 1991, p. 198; *The Economist,* 2008, pp. 68–70).

New schools, shaped by the Occupation authorities and by teachers' socialist unions, tried to create equal opportunity through education. Teachers told their students that everyone had equal ability; hard work and perseverance were what counted for success. Schools did no IQ testing or ability grouping, so each class was a cross-section of the community. Individuals in high positions took their cue from the government and tended to disguise their wealth. Executives avoided conspicuous luxury in dress or housing and took buses and trains like their employees (Chapman, 1991, p. 199). In the postwar years the Japanese came to believe that class inequalities of wealth, income, and opportunity were unfair and should be minimized, and this belief persists today.

Class Inequality in Japan Today

People in Japan don't like to acknowledge the existence of class inequalities in their society. People value equality, and they try to maintain an *omote* depiction of Japan as an egalitarian society. Traveling in Japan, you will not see run-down, crime-ridden ghettos, and because Japan is ethnically homogeneous, people can't visually identify any particular group with the poor. There are no class accents or styles of dress; even the newspapers and magazines people read vary little along class lines. It's pretty easy to pretend that everyone is equal. Official government statistics make it hard to learn about class inequality in Japan. For example, official government statistics on income distribution include the earnings of full-time workers, but omit part-time workers. Let's try to figure out how much class inequality there really is in Japan.

Slums and mansions are hard to find in Japan. Even though as a society Japan is rich, most Japanese live modestly in the middle class. This residential neighborhood in Roppongi, Tokyo, is typical of Japan's crowded cities. The houses are small and close together on a narrow street, with a tangle of electric poles and wires overhead. There is no room for front lawns or gardens, but the carefully pruned pine tree is a reminder of traditional Japanese esthetics. In the background you can see the tip of the Tokyo Tower, a glitzy downtown landmark.

Continued Equality

To some degree, postwar equality has survived into the present, with class disparities weaker in Japan than, for example, in the United States. According to Yoshio Sugimoto, about 10% of Japanese are part of an upper middle class of university-educated managers and professionals. They have income more than twice the national average and they have some wealth—fancy cars, stocks and bonds, costly memberships in sports clubs. They can afford expensive sports like golf and sailing, and attend theater and concerts. At the other end of the income spectrum is a much larger working class—as much as 30% of Japanese who have completed only junior high or high school. They are manual workers and farmers and their incomes are only about half the national average.

Most Japanese fall somewhere between the richest 10% and the poorest 30%, and for this large population, class differences are blurred. If you go to college and become a manager or professional you can expect to enjoy higher prestige and more power but not much higher income than those without college education. Men with university degrees earn, on average, only about 20% more than those with only high school degrees. Big companies still pay on the seniority system: All employees at the same rank earn about the same amount and pay increases for everyone the longer they work at the company. Many self-employed workers—owners of small businesses and skilled tradesmen like plumbers and electricians—earn more on average than the salarymen, though they enjoy less prestige (Jones, 2007, pp. 8–9; Sugimoto, 1997, pp. 37–39; Tachibanaki, 2005, pp. 52, 109, 111).

The best-paid Japanese earn less than the best-paid Americans—and they accumulate less wealth, too. According to a 2001 survey by an American management consulting firm, the average income of chief executive officers of U.S. manufacturers with annual sales of at least $500 million was $1.93 million. Equivalent Japanese CEOs averaged only $500,000. Without high incomes, Japanese executives are unable to accumulate great wealth. For years, high inheritance taxes and heavy taxes on high incomes made it difficult to pass on any wealth amassed. As a result, while the U.S. economy is twice the size of Japan's, America's billionaires outnumber Japan's 10 to 1: 277 to 22 (*The Asahi Shimbun,* 2003; Chapman, 1991, p. 200; *Forbes,* 2004).

Table 1.6 displays differences in income distribution in five societies. In the United States, those in the poorest 20% of the population receive 3.4% of the total income earned by all individuals. In Japan, the poorest 20% receives almost twice as much—6.6% of all the income earned. The richest 20% in the United States gets 49.9% of total national income, but in Japan the corresponding figure is only 41%. You can see that inequalities between the richest fifth of the population and the poorest fifth are greater in the United States than in Japan, more than twice as big.

TABLE 1.6   Distribution of Income

Income is shared more equally in Japan and Germany than in the United States, Mexico, or Egypt. In Japan, the income share of the richest fifth of the population is about 6 times the share of the poorest fifth. In Mexico and the United States, the share of the richest fifth is about 14 times the share of the poorest fifth. Income is distributed more unequally in the United States than in any other developed society.

	Year	Income Received by Poorest 20% of (Percent of Total) Population	Income Received by Richest 20% of (Percent of Total) Population	Ratio of Income Share of Richest 20% to Income Share of Poorest 20%
Germany	2004	7.7	39.1	5.1
Japan	2006	6.6	41.0	6.2
Egypt	1997	6.7	46.6	6.9
Mexico	2004	3.9	55.0	14.0
United States	2006	3.4	49.9	14.7

Source: United Nations University, World Institute for Development Economics Research, *World Income Inequality Database,* Version 2.0b, 2007, http://www.wider.unu.edu/research/Database/en_GB/database/.

Growing Inequality

Remember that the degree of class inequality in Japan has changed over time. That's true of other countries, too. Everywhere, economic cycles of boom and recession, the dynamics of globalization, demographic change, economic restructuring, and government action influence how equal or unequal people are in their income and wealth. In Japan, an economic boom in the 80s made the rich richer. And then the crash of the 90s made some people poorer. Some people saw their wages and benefits cut, others were unemployed, and the number of people who have no savings or receive welfare or are homeless increased (Tachibanaki, 2005, p. 67).

Polarization

To recover from the recession, Japanese businesses began to restructure. Manufacturing companies moved some factories to China and Vietnam, where wages were a fraction of Japanese wages. Within Japan, the biggest change is that companies now hire fewer career workers with lifetime security, and more part-time and contract workers, who don't receive benefits or bonuses and earn only about 40% of what full-time workers earn. They don't belong to unions either (*The Economist*, 2006c, p. 47; Jones, 2007, pp. 9–10). The growth of part-time work in Japan has created what sociologists call a **polarized** economy. A minority (less than a quarter of full-time workers) are still in the old lifetime security system. They tend to be middle-aged men. Wage inequality for them has actually declined (Jones, 2007, p. 8). But then there is the growing number of part-time workers, who earn much less. Strikingly, this group is mostly women—85% of them are female, and the rest are mostly elderly or teenagers. It is remarkable that most of the new income inequality in Japan turns out to be **gender inequality.** Income has also increased for a small elite of Japanese, including highly skilled technology specialists, celebrities in sports and the arts, financial managers, and successful new entrepreneurs. At the same time, the government has lowered taxes on the rich and decreased health and pension benefits. People think that receiving welfare is shameful, but as inequality grows, the percentage of people on welfare has inched up: from 0.84% of the population in 2000 to 1.18% in 2006. Local governments make it very difficult for people to get welfare benefits. In the last couple of years a number of cases of older men starving to death after being denied government help have made news across the country (Onishi, 2007c, pp. A1, A12). Though Japan still values equality, and retains some elements of postwar equality, the society has set out on a path toward more inequality. The population has become more polarized between rich and poor (Jones, 2007, p. 8; Onishi, 2006a, pp. 1, 6; Tachibanaki, 2005, p. 75).

Inequality and Opportunity

Japanese society prizes equality in two different ways. First, people think it's right that incomes and wealth should be relatively equal throughout the population. (We call this **equality of reward.**) Then, they also think everyone should have an equal chance to compete for the more prestigious, somewhat better-paying jobs. (This latter kind of equality is called **equality of opportunity.**) A system that provides equal opportunity is often called a **meritocracy.** Advancement in a meritocracy is based on "merit," not on inherited privilege or disadvantage. Japan's meritocracy makes education the route to advancement. This kind of system, founded on ancient Chinese models, already existed in Japan at the beginning of the 20th century and was expanded and became even more central to Japanese society after World War II. Japan's meritocracy is overwhelmingly focused on school achievement, which makes some sense in a modern, technological economy. In Japan, academic excellence and high scores on achievement tests are the ticket to high-status jobs. Other good qualities like creativity, or entrepreneurial flair, which aren't measured by tests, are not rewarded.

Public elementary and junior high schools include everyone. At the end of junior high school, students going to high school are admitted by exam to selective academic high schools that prepare children for university. Those who fail or don't choose the academic route go to vocational high school. Schooling is thus set up to be competitive and children have to work very hard studying. People believe that where you end up depends on your ability, how hard you work, and some element of luck. The emphasis is all on effort. School sorts people, and with lifetime employment, how well you do in school has permanent consequences (Kariya & Dore, 2006, pp. 137–138).

To make effort the basis of the competition, the Japanese government has gone to great lengths to give everyone an equal chance to get a good education and eliminate inherited advantage or disadvantage. Public schools are all controlled by the Ministry of Education, which designed all elementary and junior high schools to be of uniform quality, with identical facilities and budgets. Teachers receive high salaries in all schools. (Teaching is a prestigious career in Japan and a very competitive field to enter.) Teachers are even rotated from school to school around a district to make sure all children have the same quality of instruction.

An Era of Equality

For 30 years or so after World War II, Japanese people felt good about the system they had created. With rapid economic growth, many new jobs were created in manufacturing and service industries. Young people left poverty-stricken rural villages and found better jobs in the cities. As productivity increased, pay rose for everyone, making income more equal. More families could afford to send their children to high school and university. Aspirations were equalized too: More young people aspired to go to university. In a society with rather equal incomes, values, and home cultures became more similar too (Kariya & Dore, 2006, p. 139; Tachibanaki, 2005, p. 113). Children who worked hard and finished high school could count on getting jobs, full-time jobs, with benefits and job security. In a labor-short economy, high school graduates were so prized by employers that they were known as "golden eggs" and were well rewarded. Some companies, like Toyota, even set up their own high schools that they paid young men to attend, training them for assembly-line and white-collar work. Young men who finished college could expect prestigious jobs in large companies or with the government. Through all the years of economic growth Japan's meritocracy worked to provide greater upward mobility for poor children than exists in most other industrialized nations.

Threats to Meritocracy

Today in Japan, social mobility is slowing down and opportunity is becoming less equal. During the long recession of the 1990s, there was less hiring, more intense competition for education and jobs, a greater number of losers in the competition, and more anxiety all around. For middle-class children, the pressure to compete and excel has increased. Parents feel desperate to ensure their children prosperous futures. Especially in urban areas parents who afford it send their children to private schools that combine junior high and high school, schools with special relationships with the most prestigious colleges. Their students don't have to take the difficult high school entrance exams. But the private schools are selective, so at age 12 children who apply have to take entrance exams. They are tutored at *juku* (cram schools) from age 8 to 10, attending cram school many afternoons and evenings a week after school and sometimes on weekends too. Overall, the 30% of Japanese children who go to private schools are four times as likely to be admitted by Tokyo University, the top university, as the 70% who go to public school. In 1992 a Japanese television special revealed that at Tokyo University, the top university, half of the students were graduates of the 20 top high schools in Japan and 18 of those high schools were private schools. The elite of the private schools are the experimental schools attached to schools of education at the elite universities. The 3,000 or so children who attend those schools are 1,000 times as likely to get into Tokyo University as are public school graduates. Education has become more expensive, too. Jukus are expensive and tuition at private schools equals 1 to 2 months' income for an average family (Kariya & Dore, 2006, pp. 143–144).

Some wealthy parents are able to pass on their advantages to their children in other ways. Doctors pass on their practices to their doctor offspring and the children of politicians take over their fathers' seats in parliament and their carefully nurtured political support groups (Chapman, 1991, p. 203).

Working-class children are losing faith in Japan's meritocracy. Vocational school no longer reliably leads to secure, well-paid jobs. While academic standards have been maintained at elite high schools, they have slid down at ordinary schools. Students at those schools have become anxious and disillusioned and angry. They resent the relentless emphasis on tests that no longer guarantee success in adult life. More and more working-class children feel "thrown away." If they don't plan to go to college, they don't see how working hard in high school will benefit them.

Is this story of polarization and competition familiar to you? In many ways, the changes in social stratification we have been describing have become a worldwide pattern, experienced in all the rich nations. Do you notice polarization in the job market, and increasing competition for good jobs, in your society? Are students whose families are not wealthy finding it harder to pay for education? We lack studies to show whether there is less or more social mobility in Japan than other industrialized societies. People see a decline in mobility in Japan, but they don't see how much mobility remains. In one study done in prefectures that have no private schools 45% of children from the lowest socioeconomic group were achieving at the highest levels in public high school, along with 77% of the highest socioeconomic group. That's a pretty remarkable achievement for children from low-income families. Is it equaled in your society (Kariya & Dore, 2006, p. 154)?

Status Inequality in Japan: Minority Groups

Japan is a rather homogeneous society; it has few groups that differ racially or ethnically or socially from the rest of the population, and those it does have are very small. At most, 4–5 million people out of the total population of 120 million could be classified as members of **minority groups,** groups which are seen as inferior and are treated unequally by the **majority** population. About 1,800,000 of these are foreigners—about 1% of the total population. Japan's minority population is growing, but rather slowly, as low birthrates and a changing economy have created a niche for immigrant workers. Most Japanese minorities look little different from other Japanese. Though they can't be recognized by their physical appearance, minorities are nonetheless treated with distaste and face considerable discrimination (Reischauer, 1977, pp. 32–33; Tasker, 1987, pp. 23–24).

Sociologists note that there is a variety of ways that societies treat their minority groups, ranging from pluralism to genocide. A **pluralistic** society takes a positive view of group diversity and minorities are permitted, or even encouraged, to keep their separate identities, languages, and customs. Pluralistic societies believe that people can be different without being unequal. Many societies reject pluralism and aim for **assimilation** of minorities, requiring that they adopt the values, language, and customs of the majority. If assimilation works, minorities join majority culture and they are accepted and become equal. Although Japanese society officially promotes assimilation of minorities, minorities, who may not be very different from majority Japanese, are often excluded from mainstream society. They face **discrimination** in employment and marriage, and **segregation** in their place of residence. But in modern times Japan has never gone to the extreme of **genocide,** the physical extermination of minorities, which has happened in many other societies.

Korean Japanese: The Zainichi

About 600,000 people in Japan are ethnic Koreans. They face many identity conflicts because neither Japan nor Korea really accepts them. Most are the descendants of people who came to Japan for economic opportunity after Japan annexed Korea in 1910. Other Koreans came to Japan against their wills as forced laborers during World War II. In 1952 Japan revoked the Japanese nationality of all ethnic Koreans, even if they had been born in Japan. They were barred from voting and from civil service jobs, and faced widespread rejection and discrimination. A civil rights movement in the 1980s got many discriminatory laws repealed. Eventually *Zainichi* were allowed to apply for Japanese citizenship and about 10,000 people a year do so now (*The Economist,* 2006b, p. 40; Ministry of Justice, 2003).

Ethnic Japanese

A new minority in Japan is the growing community of approximately 300,000 people of Japanese descent who were born in Brazil and Peru. Faced with a shortage of unskilled workers, and fearful of illegal immigration from other Asian countries, the Japanese government decided to welcome Japanese of foreign descent whose ancestors had left Japan in the past. These new immigrants are racially identical to the Japanese, but culturally they are different. They speak and laugh loudly and embrace in public, and hold street festivals with salsa and samba music. The Latin Americans face discrimination in Japan: They are treated fearfully in restaurants and stores and often exploited by labor contractors. "The Japanese treat us like some kind of inferior race," said one Brazilian immigrant (Ministry of Justice, 2003; Sellek, 1997, pp. 187–192: Weisman, 1991, p. 1).

Immigrants

Japan's population of recent Asian immigrants, mostly from China, the Philippines, and Vietnam, is growing but still small. Demographers say that Japan needs immigrants. If the nation wants to keep Japan's population of 120 million from falling to 60 million by the end of the 21st century, immigration will be necessary. Businesses and farmers are openly calling for Japan to allow in more immigrants. But foreigners, even other Asians and immigrants who have adopted Japanese names and speak fluent Japanese, are not well accepted in Japan. "Living in Japan," said one student from China, "is like staying in a hotel forever, never in a home. I'm always waiting to go home." Though the government has agreed to encourage migration of immigrants with specialized skills or knowledge, in fact most immigrants fill the most undesirable jobs, providing cheap labor to a polarizing economy. They work in what the Japanese call 3-K jobs, translated in English as dirty, dangerous, and difficult. Many Thai and Filipino immigrants work in construction, and farmers employ Chinese students and so-called foreign trainees as seasonal workers. Many immigrant women, especially those from Thailand, Colombia, and the Philippines, work in the sex trades, and some have been illegally trafficked to Japan.

There are more than 100,000 foreign students in Japan, 65% of them Chinese. Many foreign students overstay their visas or work illegally to support themselves in expensive Japan. It is widely believed that foreign students are responsible for rising crime rates in Japan and criminal acts by foreigners get headlines in the press. Recently, in reaction, the government tightened visa requirements for foreign students (French, 2003c, p. A1; Onishi, 2004b, p. 3; 2005a, p. A3).

The Burakumin

Not all Japanese minority groups are racial or ethnic minorities. The *Burakumin* are Japanese, but they are rejected nonetheless. They are the descendants of Japan's former outcaste groups. In Tokugawa times the Burakumin were required to live in separate villages and were forbidden to enter temples, shrines, and festivals. Though the Burakumin became legally equal to other Japanese during the Meiji period, discrimination continued. The Burakumin today are physically and culturally indistinguishable from other Japanese. Only their family names and sometimes the neighborhoods where they live mark them for discrimination and distaste. Estimates of the number of Burakumin today range from 1.2 to 3 million, no more than 2% of the population (Pharr, 1990, pp. 76–77).

Burakumin have faced discrimination in employment and marriage. It is common practice in Japan for families to hire a "marriage detective" to research the background of a prospective spouse whose family is not known to them. Marriages are canceled when the family is traced to a Burakumin village. The same thing happens when employers research the family background of new hires. As a result of this discrimination, Burakumin have lower incomes and less education than majority Japanese; they follow more insecure occupations, and have higher crime rates than other Japanese, and this feeds the contempt in which they are held, perpetuating their disadvantage (Pharr, 1990, pp. 77–79). Pushed by the Burakumin Liberation League, starting in the 1960s the government provided extra help to Burakumin—for example, financing special programs in schools in Burakumin neighborhoods, health clinics, and rent subsidies—even though it never made discrimination against Burakumin illegal. To some degree, these programs worked: The Burakumin population is now less segregated than it once was. As Burakumin have blended into the majority population, the Burakumin liberation movement has weakened. In 2002 the government ended all national programs to help Burakumin, declaring the problem solved. Today debate swirls around questions of whether discrimination continues, and whether identifying and helping Burakumin communities stigmatizes them more than it helps them. Some people say that if everyone ignored Burakumin background the problem would be solved, but others say that would just allow discrimination to continue (Gordon, 2005, pp. 183–184; Neary, 2003, pp. 269–294).

Inequalities of Power in Japan Today

Everyone in Japan knows that political and economic power is unequally distributed. Power is concentrated in the hands of a small elite—a three-way partnership among government bureaucrats, legislators, and industrialists. But the truth is that as long as Japan enjoyed its long post–World War II prosperity, no one cared. People were willing to entrust their nation's rule to an elite that was wisely managing the society for the good of the entire nation. But once Japan's economy got stuck in recession, people became cynical about the power elite of their society. Politicians had never been much respected in Japan. Now people began to question the honesty of bureaucrats too, and their respect for business leaders faltered as the economy failed. So far, discontent has not led to any real change, but the nature of inequalities of power in Japan has become clearer.

Government and Business: Western Structures, Japanese Spirit

Formally and officially, Japan is a Western-style parliamentary democracy. After Japan's defeat in World War II, democracy was imposed by the American occupying forces. Occupation authorities created a legislature (the Diet) with an upper and a lower house, political parties, a prime minister, and a liberal constitution guaranteeing free speech, universal suffrage, labor's right to organize, and the rule of law. In theory, the people govern by electing representatives who make laws implemented by the bureaucracy. Japan's economy was also remade to resemble Western ideals. The Occupation destroyed Japan's powerful family-owned conglomerates hoping to encourage a free-enterprise economy in which economic power also would be widely and equally distributed among a great many small companies.

Japanese society did not turn out the way Occupation forces intended. After the Occupation, the Japanese retained the American preference for a weak executive who cannot make decisions alone and a weak military excluded from political power. To the American formula they added a very Japanese preference for centralized power, for cooperative over confrontation, and for behind-the-scenes compromise over public debate. Though Japan today has a legislature, political parties, corporations, labor unions, and stockholders, these Western institutions function in a distinctly Japanese fashion. As they say, it is a case of *wakon yosai,* Western structures transformed by

Japanese spirit. Most power-holders are not elected, and power is exercised almost entirely behind the scenes.

The Iron Triangle

In Japan's tripartite power structure, commonly called the "iron triangle," the central government bureaucracy in Tokyo stands at the top, coordinating its power with that of business leaders and elected officials. Bureaucrats today, who work in the various government ministries, actually draft the legislation that is brought to the floor of the Diet. According to Atsushi Ueda, "we might go so far as to say that a Diet session is a kind of ceremonial performance, to give people inside and outside Japan the impression that decisions are being made democratically" (Ueda, 1994, p. 129). Then after passage, the bureaucracy implements laws and policies it has developed and sent to the legislature. But bureaucratic power extends further, because the bureaucracy doesn't simply mechanically apply the law; it exercises what is known as "administrative guidance," flexibility in enforcing regulations. Businesses cultivate their relationships with bureaucrats. In a way it is difficult to decide whether bureaucrats are the masters or the servants of business, because all their efforts are aimed at maximizing the long-run expansion of industry.

However, when the recession of 1990s set in there was a crisis of public confidence in the bureaucracy. Faced with the stubborn economic recession, the ministries stumbled. They couldn't seem to get the Japanese economy moving again; they couldn't deliver on the goals people had trusted them to accomplish. As a result, distrust in the bureaucracy grew. Japanese bureaucrats had never been viewed as corrupt or incompetent, but now scandals involving bureaucrats began to surface. The Japanese public also became much more cynical about relationships between businessmen and bureaucrats, and business entertainment spending, formerly accepted as a normal part of business, came to be seen as a form of bribery.

Japanese Business

Today industry in Japan is far different from the thousands of competing small firms Occupation authorities envisioned. Japan's business structure is capitalist, and despite the recent recession, it has been highly successful, raising Japan from ruins after World War II and constructing the second largest economy in the world, on a small island lacking in natural resources. But Japan's capitalism is different from capitalism in the United States or Europe, and it is distinctly Japanese in nature. Japan's economy has been dominated by big businesses, world-renowned companies like Toyota and Sony and Hitachi, that are organized into even larger conglomerates and associations. Big companies have both dominated and protected their smaller subsidiaries, suppliers, distributors, and contractors, as they protected their employees. Businesses and banks have been closely linked, too. Company managers, with lifetime job security, could afford to take the long view, aiming for company growth and market domination, rather than this quarter's profits. Selling one's company has been seen as a humiliating failure (van Wolferen, 1989, pp. 34, 46–47).

Some of this has changed, as Japan struggles to emerge from recession. Corporate mergers are up, though companies prefer to define them as "mergers of equals," rather than takeovers, to avoid embarrassing the company being bought.

Some companies, such as Nissan and Mitsubishi, have brought in foreign CEOs to shake things up Western style, and some companies have been bought by foreign investors. In the past, most shares of stock in companies were held by other companies and by banks, who shared management's perspectives, but today there are individual investors and foreign institutions holding stock and they pressure management to raise profits.

The business world and the public are ambivalent about these changes, one day making heroes of home-grown "corporate raiders" and the next day characterizing American-style businessmen as "vultures." The general sentiment seems to be a sense of inevitability, rather than welcome. "Japan must learn to live with these vultures," as one salaryman said, or risk losing out in the global economy (Belson & Zaun, 2005, p. BU5; Fackler, 2007a, p. C1).

The Elected Government

The official institutions of Japanese power—that is, the legislature, the political parties, the prime minister, the cabinet, and the electorate—are probably the weakest partner in Japan's ruling triumvirate. Since the 1950s the Liberal Democratic Party (the LDP) has held power and dominated Japanese politics, running what is essentially a single-party system. The LDP is a vote-getting machine: Politicians treat politics as the business of getting elected. The legislature seldom legislates. The prime minister is often a relative unknown installed by behind-the-scenes kingmakers and has very limited power; and the cabinet serves a merely ceremonial function, automatically approving policies developed by the bureaucrats (van Wolferen, 1989, pp. 45, 110).

So what do Japanese politicians really do? What power do they have? Politicians are mostly engaged in what Americans call "pork barrel politics"—securing government funding for their constituents in exchange for political support (Kristof, 1998, p. A4; Ogawa, 1998, p. 4). Politicians play the role of go-between linking citizens with business and bureaucrats and helping all three groups informally trade favors and influence one another. The politics of the construction industry illustrates this relationship. The Ministry of Construction controls licenses for the entire industry, and it spends trillions of dollars building bridges, railroads, airports, museums, dams, and roads. Politicians, especially those from rural areas, use their contacts in the ministry to get construction projects approved for their home districts. The communities that elected them benefit from jobs and local spending and vote for the LDP. Local construction companies are big contributors to political campaign funds, and they are rewarded with contracts. Then politicians reward retired construction ministry bureaucrats by helping them gain election to the Diet (the legislature), reinforcing the connections between politicians and the ministry (Strom, 2001, p. 16; van Wolferen, 1989, pp. 114–120).

SOCIAL CHANGE

A recent earthquake can perhaps serve as a metaphor for the condition of Japanese society. On July 24, 2007, a powerful earthquake struck northwestern Japan, killing 11 people and damaging a nuclear power plant, which leaked radiation. The plant had unknowingly been built directly above an active seismic fault. Japan is both prone to earthquakes and very dependent on nuclear power. Its nuclear technology is advanced and the plants are supposed to be highly earthquake-proof, so the quake and the discovered fault came as a distressing surprise. Japanese society devotes great effort to maintaining a smooth surface, but underneath lurk dangerous social faults, which are now creating change and disorder and threatening Japan's omote harmony (Fackler, 2007c, p. A3). What are these faultlines in Japanese society?

Demographic Change

People in Japan are acutely aware that their society has a population crisis. We have heard so much in the past few decades about the problems of rapid population growth that you may be surprised to hear that Japan has the opposite problem: Its population is shrinking! How can a country's population grow smaller? It is easy to understand. Demographers tell us that for population size to remain stable in Japan, the number of births per woman (the **total fertility rate**) would have to average 2.1 children. At this rate, taking childhood mortality into account, each couple would just about replace themselves with their children. If each woman has more than 2.1 children, total population grows, and if each woman has fewer than 2.1 children, population falls. By 2000, Japanese women were averaging only 1.4 children each. According to sociologist Merry Isaacs White, we can see the problem more clearly if we look separately at married and unmarried women. Birthrate data for all women aged 15–49 show 1.3 children born per woman. But married women in that age bracket have an average of just over two children each. So postponement of marriage is the real culprit in Japan's birthrate problem (White, 2002, pp. 209–210). Do you think that a shrinking population would be a good thing for a society? It would definitely reduce crowding, but there is a downside too. Not only are there fewer children in Japan, there are fewer people in their prime working years. And, there are more and more older people.

Fewer Children

In Japan there has been a great deal of discussion about the problem of falling birthrates. It is clear that there are several ways to halt population shrinkage. One strategy is to follow the example of the United States and open Japan to immigration. People in poor countries all over Asia—China, Thailand, the Philippines, Indonesia, and others—would like to immigrate to Japan. But the number of immigrants would have to be quite large. The United Nations (UN) estimates that Japan would need to admit about 380,000 immigrants a year to stabilize its population at the 2005 projected level. This is a solution that is profoundly distasteful to Japanese policymakers. They attribute Japan's economic success and social harmony to its racial "purity." Sentiments like those of Tokyo mayor Ishihara, who said that foreigners in Japan commit "atrocious" crimes, are widespread in Japan (Sims, 2000, p. A6; United Nations Population Division, 2000, p. 49).

What else could Japan do about its falling birthrate and shrinking working-age population? Another possible solution is to allow women a more active role in the labor force. If more women worked and worked full-time in real careers, this would add to the labor force and help support the old. Recent studies comparing birthrates in many countries show a surprising result. In societies that make it easier for women to get good jobs, birthrates are higher. For Japan, that would mean full-time career jobs for women, combined with better support services like child care facilities. It would also mean shorter work hours for men, so they could be involved in family life. This is commonly called "a better work–life balance," a term that has no equivalent in Japanese (*The Economist*, 2007a, pp. 24–26).

More Older People

At the current low birthrate, not only will Japan's population shrink in the 21st century, it will age. More of the population will be elderly, especially because older people are living longer and longer. In 2000, the number of Japanese over 65 topped the number of those below age 15 (Sims, 2001, p. 4). Rural areas in Japan are aging faster than cities. Many young people leave the countryside, leaving the elderly behind. Who will support these people? Twenty years ago, there were four working-age people for every retired elderly person in Japan. Taxes on the working people provide retirement benefits for the older people. But in 20 years there will be only 2.2 people of working age for every elderly person (*The Economist*, 2000, p. 28). People in Japan know that today's unemployment problems will soon disappear: There will be a shortage of workers.

Japan will have to become a pioneer in figuring out how to run a society top heavy with older people. Natural disasters are particularly difficult for the elderly. An earthquake in July 2007 struck a rural area with a large percentage of retirees. Many of the elderly people were ill, or had special needs. Some had no one to take them to a shelter and many lived in rickety old houses toppled by the quake. Earthquakes and snowstorms disproportionately kill older people (Fackler, 2007b, p. A3).

You might not anticipate it, but Japan's prison population is aging along with its general population. Now 12.3% of prison inmates are over the age of 60. (Compare that to the 4.6% of inmates in the United States who are over age 55.) Through trial and error prison administrators are learning that they must stock adult diapers; that elderly inmates tend to forget their identification numbers; and that they must provide low-sodium diets and handrails along the prison corridors. Many elderly prisoners will have nowhere to go when they leave prison. Welfare benefits are hard to get and there are few nursing homes. Prison officials fear that prisons will become a sort of de facto nursing facility for elderly prisoners (Onishi, 2007d, pp. A1, A11).

Cultural Change

Later marriage and a declining birthrate are part of a larger pattern of cultural changes, many of which we have already discussed in this chapter. Young people lead the way in cultural change. *Wagamama* girls put personal goals before their duty to marry and serve others. *Furita* boys reject a lifetime of devotion to company and nation. As early as 1993, 40% of Japanese told survey-takers they would prefer to spend their lives doing "what you find interesting, regardless of money or honor." Only 4% said they would like best "to live a life devoted entirely to society without thought of self." In 1940, 30% had chosen that option (Sugimoto, 1997, p. 70). More homegrown "vulture capitalists," more lawsuits, more defiance and delinquency by schoolchildren, more divorces initiated by wives, and more local activists challenging government projects all spell out an increase in individualism and a corresponding lessened willingness to sacrifice oneself to duty, to the group, to the preservation of harmony.

Westerners, particularly Americans, tend to assume that Japan has embarked on a sort of inevitable process of becoming more and more like the United States. They expect its economy to become more of a free-enterprise system, its government more voter oriented, its men and women more individualistic. If you are familiar with the American context, Japan today will remind you of the 1960s in the United States, with its rapid social change, disillusionment with government and business, challenges to gender roles, rebellious youth, dropouts, and hippies. But let the comparison be your guide: In the United States, the revolutionary days of the 1960s were followed by decades of reaction, in which the society became more religious, more conservative and business oriented, and in which traditional gender roles and "family values" were reinvigorated. Which way will Japan go—toward continued liberalization, or toward a conservative reaction?

Globalization and Social Change

Japan has been dealing with globalization for a long time. You could say that the nation spent the whole second half of the 20th century working out its response to the dominating economic and military power of the United States—first as an occupied nation, then as a host for U.S. bases, junior ally and economic competitor. The United States was Japan's best market and its cultural ideal. Every Japanese schoolchild learned English, and hundreds of English "loan-words" worked their way into Japanese, along with McDonald's, Kentucky Fried Chicken, Hollywood movies, and country and western bands. But now the Japanese are losing interest in the United States. Politically, militarily, and economically, Asia is now the focus of Japan's response to globalization. China and India are the rising giants in the global economy. North Korea and China are possible military threats. Japan's anxiety is clear in a book by Kenichi Omae, *China Impact,* which argues that "for most of its history Japan has been a peripheral country to China. . . . In the future, Japan will be to China what Canada is to the United States, what Austria is to Germany, what Ireland is to Britain" (Brooke, 2002, pp. BU1, BU11).

Economic Globalization

Now that China is growing in importance in the global economy, it is no surprise that China's economic importance to Japan is also growing. Some people say that China is the engine of Japan's present economic recovery. China (and to a lesser extent Russia and Southeast Asia) plays a dual role for Japan, both as a location for cheap manufacture of Japanese products and as a market for Japanese goods.

Wages in Japan are 20 to 30 times higher than wages in China, where a very good factory job pays $95 a month. So Japanese companies have swallowed their scruples about lifetime security for Japanese workers and moved manufacturing, particularly low-cost mass production of simple products, overseas to China. More than 16,000 Japanese companies do business in China and China has overtaken the United States as Japan's biggest trading partner, a huge market for Japanese goods. Imagine 2 billion people buying their first refrigerators, cell phones, cars, and computers! Lately Japanese manufacturers have been moving on from China to India and Vietnam, where costs are now lower (Brooke, 2005a, p. C5; *The Economist,* 2005a, pp. 23–25; 2007b, pp. 68–69: French & Onishi, 2005, pp. A1, A10).

World Politics

At the same time that economic globalization is drawing Japan and China closer together, political tensions between Japan and its Asian neighbors—China, South Korea, and North Korea—are rising. Provocations large and small have sparked conflict between Japan and its Asian neighbors, but underlying it all is a national identity crisis in Japan, about its role in Asia and the world. First among the provocations is North Korea's nuclear weapons program and its test of an armed missile that could potentially reach Japan. Japan and China have worked together to try to persuade North Korea to stop its nuclear program, but that has led to sparks between Japan and South Korea, which feels more sympathy for its northern brother than for Japan, its former invader. China has increased its own military spending and has tested Japan's detection systems with a submarine incursion. Then there are the territorial disputes, with China over an island chain near undersea oil and gas deposits, and with South Korea and Russia over other islands (Choe, 2006, p. A8; *The Economist,* 2006a, pp. 25–27; Onishi, 2006c, p. A6).

Political Disputes.   The fundamental dynamic behind all these disputes is this: Some Japanese see China's rise as an economic and military threat. They want Japan to reassert itself militarily and politically. But to China and South Korea, Japanese military might evokes the nightmares of World War II and Japanese occupation of their nations. They react with anti-Japanese demonstrations and demands for apologies for war atrocities. Japan reacts with anti-Korean and anti-Chinese outbursts.

The Rise of Neonationalism

In Japan these squabbles have fueled the reinvigoration of nationalism: a social movement demanding greater military strength and a return to the old-fashioned virtues of patriotism, self-sacrifice, and tradition.

After World War II, the United States supplied Japan with a "pacifist constitution" that forbids the use of military force except in self-defense and forbids the development of nuclear weapons. The neonationalists want to change that clause of the constitution, and about 60% of the population supports the idea. Japan already spends about $40 billion a year on its military, one of the largest in the world, but it is alone in the world in constitutionally forbidding offensive action (Orr & Sims, 2008).

For nationalists, like the popular mayor of Tokyo, Shintaro Ishihara, the problem with Japan is that the nation has become weak and the people have lost their confidence. Ishihara traces Japan's problems to the nation's humiliating subservience to the United States. Japan is still apologizing, he says, for its supposed misdeeds in World War II, while no one mentions the cruelty of the United States' firebombing of Tokyo and the atomic bombing of Hiroshima and Nagasaki. The nationalists have succeeded in changing school textbooks to whitewash Japan's wartime activities, with some texts even claiming that Japan did not invade other Asian countries, but rather liberated them from Western domination (Sims & Orr, 2008).

The claim has infuriated South Koreans and Chinese who are still demanding official apologies for the famous "Rape of Nanking" in China during World War II and the use in that period of forced labor and sex slaves by the Japanese military. Japanese schools used to feature extensive "peace education." That curriculum has been replaced by a new "patriotism bill" that will require teachers to inculcate "a love of one's country" (Onishi, 2006b, p. 26).

The neonationalists see their program as a solution to all of Japan's ills: individualistic, unmanageable children, women who won't marry and have children, immigrants who are slowly filtering into Japan and threatening the nation's "racial purity." For many Japanese, especially older people, this kind of talk evokes the militarism of the World War II era. They find it frightening and repellent; pacifism has been engrained in Japan since the Occupation. But many people are sympathetic to the neonationalist nostalgia for a time of greater national confidence and glory. They are tired of being ashamed of their past. The neonationalists seem to suggest that if a more assertive Japan could rally its people behind some grand national enterprise, devotion to duty and a sense of belonging would return.

Thinking Sociologically

1. When you read Chapter 1, were you ethnocentric in your reaction to the Japanese?
2. Using a highlighter pen, go through pages 6–16 of Chapter 1. Highlight descriptions of Japanese values in blue and descriptions of norms in yellow. Are you confident you understand the difference between values and norms?
3. When some large American luxury cars were recently put on display in Tokyo, many Japanese shoppers said they wouldn't want to purchase them. "I would get a lot of attention if I drove that car," one woman said. Using what you now know about Japanese society, decide what kinds of cars you would choose to export to Japan if you were making this decision for an American auto company.
4. What are some Japanese values that contrast sharply with values in your own society?
5. What social groups are most important in the lives of the Japanese? What groups are most important in your life, in your society?
6. How are offices in your society physically arranged? (Are the desks separated, or all touching, as in Japan? Are there cubicles? Separate offices with doors?) Are offices in your society similar to Japanese offices or different? What kinds of interaction and attitudes does office arrangement in your society encourage?
7. Review Table 1.3 (p. 27) and compare homicide rates in Japan to those in the United States. Thinking sociologically, can you explain what causes the tremendous difference in these rates?
8. Are there any similarities in the roles of women in Japanese society and in your society? What differences are there?
9. Use Robert Merton's strain theory of deviance to explain the growth of *hikikomori* in Japan. Is there any deviance in your society that you would describe as retreatist deviance?

For Further Reading

Bellah, R. (2003). *Imagining Japan.* Berkeley: University of California Press.
Bumiller, E. (1995). *The secrets of Mariko: A year in the life of a Japanese woman and her family.* New York: Times Books, Random House.
Dower, J. W. (1999). *Embracing defeat: Japan in the wake of World War II.* New York: Norton.

Feiler, B. S. (1991). *Learning to bow: An American teacher in a Japanese school.* New York: Ticknor & Fields.

Fukuzawa, R. E., LeTendre, G. K. (2001). *Intense years: How Japanese adolescents balance school, family and friends.* New York and London: Routledge Falmer.

Lewis, C. C. (1995). *Educating hearts and minds: Reflections on Japanese preschool and elementary education.* Cambridge, England: Cambridge University Press.

Mehri, D. (2005). *Notes from Toyota-Land: An American engineer in Japan.* Ithaca, New York: Cornell University Press.

Osasawara, Y., (1998). *Office ladies and salaried men: Power, gender and work in Japanese companies.* Berkeley: University of California Press.

Roberson, J. E., & Suzuki, N. (Eds.). (2003). *Men and masculinities in contemporary Japan.* London and New York: RoutledgeCurzon.

Sugimoto, Y. (1997). *An introduction to Japanese society.* Cambridge, England: Cambridge University Press.

White, M. I. (2002). *Perfectly Japanese: Making families in an era of upheaval.* Berkeley: University of California Press.

Yoder, R. S. (2004). *Youth deviance in Japan: Class reproduction of non-conformity.* Melbourne: Trans Pacific Press.

Yoneyama, S. (1999). *The Japanese high school: Silence and resistance.* London and New York: Routledge.

Bibliography

Adachi, J. (2006, January 30). How Q found her groove. *The New York Times,* pp. CY1, CY10.

The Asahi Shimbum. (2003, July 19). More firms put directors' retirement bonus out to pasture.

Azuma, H. (2001). Moral scripts: a U.S.-Japanese comparison. In H. Shimizu & R. LeVine (Eds.), *Japanese frames of mind* (pp. 29–50). Cambridge, England: Cambridge University Press.

Bachnik, J. (1994). Kejime, defining a shifting self in multiple organizational modes. In N. R. Rosenberger (Ed.), *Japanese sense of self.* Cambridge, England: Cambridge University Press.

Bayley, D. (1994). The forces of order in Japan and the United States. In G. Carter, (Ed.), *Empirical approaches to sociology* (pp. 101–119). New York: Macmillan.

BBC News. (January 31, 2006). *Japan marks "Beloved Wives Day.* Retrieved from http://news.bbc.co.uk/go/pr/fr/-/-2/hi/asia-pacific/4664734.stm

Bellah, R. (2003). *Imagining Japan.* Berkeley: University of California Press.

Belson, K. (2002, December 28). Struggling in debt, sacrificing pride. *The New York Times,* p. C1.

Belson, K., & Zaun, T. (2005, March 27). Land of the rising gaijin chief executive. *The New York Times,* p. BU5.

Berger, P. L. (1993). *Invitation to sociology: A humanistic perspective.* New York: Anchor Doubleday.

Brooke J. (2002, November 21). Japan braces for a "designed in China" world. *The New York Times,* pp. BU1, BU11.

Brooke, J. (2004, October 18). Strangers in life join hands in death as the Web becomes a tool for suicide in Japan. *The New York Times,* p. A11.

Brooke, J. (2005a, April 14). For Japan and China, strains from a line in the sea. *The New York Times,* p. C5.

Brooke, J. (2005b, July 8). Here comes the bride, looking very Western. *The New York Times,* p. A4.

Chapman, W. (1991). *Inventing Japan: The making of a postwar civilization.* Englewood Cliffs, NJ: Prentice Hall.

Choe, S.-H. (2006, July 12). Japan and Korea wrangle over response to north's missiles. *The New York Times*, p. A8.

Christopher, R. C. (1983). *The Japanese mind: The Goliath explained.* New York: Simon & Schuster.

Condon, J. (1985). *A half step behind: Japanese women of the eighties.* New York: Dodd Mead.

Demographic and health surveys. (2000). Retrieved from the STAT compiler database, http://www.statcompiler.com

Demographic and heath surveys. (2005). Retrieved from the STAT compiler database, http://www.statcompiler.com

Demographic and Health Surveys. (n.d). *STAT compiler, 2000, 2005.* Retrieved from http://www.statcompiler.com

Doi, T. (1977). *The anatomy of dependence.* Tokyo: Kodansha.

Duke, B., (1986). *The Japanese school.* New York: Praeger.

Earhart, H. (1984). *Religions of Japan.* San Francisco: Harper & Row.

The Economist. (2000, July 1). After Japan's election: Sunset for the men in suits, pp. 26–28.

The Economist. (2003, October 25). Crime in Japan, insecure, pp. 39–40.

The Economist. (2005a, March 26). China and Japan: So hard to be friends, pp. 23–25.

The Economist. (2005b, December 24). Better than people, pp. 58–60.

The Economist. (2006a, May 13). Japan and its neighbors: A giant stirs, a region bridles, pp. 25–27.

The Economist. (2006b, June 3). Koreans in Japan: What a little sunshine can do, p. 40.

The Economist. (2006c, June 17). Inequality in Japan: The rising sun leaves some Japanese in the shade, pp. 47–48.

The Economist. (2006d, September 2). Japanese comics: Kick-ass maidens, p. 40.

The Economist. (2007a, July 28). Briefing Japan's changing demography: Cloud or silver linings? pp. 24–26.

The Economist. (2007b, July 28). Japanese companies in China: Questioning the middle kingdom, pp. 68–69.

The Economist. (2008, January 5). Sayonara, salaryman, pp. 68–70.

El-Zanaty, F., & Way, A. (2006). *Egypt demographic and health survey 2005.* Ministry of Health and Population, National Population Council. Retrieved from http://www.measuredhs.com/pubs/pdf/FR176.pdf

Fackler, M. (2005b, July 8). Here comes the Japanese bride, looking very western. *The New York Times*, p. A4.

Fackler, M. (2006b, September 21). Japanese fret that quality is in decline. *The New York Times*, p. A1.

Fackler, M. (2007a, March 29). Merger and acquisitions no longer shock Japanese. *The New York Times*, p. C1.

Fackler, M. (2007b, July 20). Japan's elderly suffer hardest shock from earthquake. *The New York Times*, p. A3.

Fackler, M. (2007c, July 25). Japan's quake-prone atomic plant prompts wider worry. *The New York Times*, p. A3.

Fackler, M. (2007d, August 6). Career women in Japan find a blocked path. *The New York Times*, pp. A1, A6.

Fackler, M. (2008, June 7). The salaryman accuses. *The New York Times*, pp. BU1, BU4.

Feiler, B. S. (1991). *Learning to bow: An American teacher in a Japanese school.* New York: Ticknor & Fields.

Forbes. (2004). The world's richest people. Retrieved November 2, 2004, from http://www.forbes.com/billionaires.

French, H. W. (2000, June 6). Japanese trains try to shed a gruesome appeal. *The New York Times,* p. A4.

French, H. W. (2001a, February 2). Brooding over its homeless, Japan sees a broken system. *The New York Times,* pp. A1, A8.

French, H. W. (2001b, July 15). Fighting sex harassment, and stigma, in Japan. *The New York Times,* pp. 1, 10.

French, H. W. (2002a, May 9). Death does them part (wives make sure of that). *The New York Times,* p. A4.

French, H. W. (2002b, September 23). Educators try to tame Japan's blackboard jungles. *The New York Times,* p. A6.

French, H. W. (2002c, November 27). Teaching Japan's salarymen to be their own men. *The New York Times,* p. A4.

French, H. W. (2003a, March 25). As Japan's women move up, many are moving out. *The New York Times,* p. A3.

French, H. W. (2003b, May 14). Japanese cult vows to save a seal and the world. *The New York Times,* p. A10.

French, H. (2003c, July 24). Insular Japan needs, but resists immigration. *The New York Times,* pp. A1, A7.

French, H. W., & Onishi, N. (2005, October 31). Economic ties binding Japan to rival China. *The New York Times,* pp. A1, A10.

Fukutake, T. (1981). *Japanese society today* (2nd ed.). Tokyo: University of Tokyo Press.

Fukuzawa, R. E., & LeTendre, G. K. (2001). *Intense years: How Japanese adolescents balance school, family and friends.* New York and London: Routledge Falmer.

Gordon, J. A. (2005, March). Inequities in Japanese urban schools. *The Urban Review, 37*(1), 49–62.

Heffernan, V. (2006, May 14). Climb in, log on, drop out. *The New York Times,* pp. AR1, AR12.

Hendry, J. (1981). *Marriage in a changing Japan: Community and society.* New York: St. Martin's Press.

Henslin, J. (2004). *Essentials of sociology* (5th ed.). Boston: Pearson.

Hirschi, T. (1969). *Causes of delinquency.* Berkeley: University of California Press.

Hogg, C. (2007, March 26). Divorce fears for Japan baby boomers. *BBC News.* Retrieved from http://news.bbc.co.uk/go/pr/fr/-/-2/hi/asai-pacific/6495009.stm

Honda, Y. (2003, February). The reality of the Japanese school-to-work transition system at the turn of the century: Necessary disillusionment. *Social Science Japan, 25,* 8–12.

Inoue, S. Religions old and new. In A. Ueda (Ed.), *The electric geisha: Exploring Japan's popular culture* (pp. 220–228). Tokyo: Kodansha.

Instituto Nacional de Estadística Geografía e Informáca. (2005). *Conteo de población y vivienda.* Retrieved from http://www.incgi/gob.mx/inegi/default.aspx?s=inegi

Japan Aisaika Organization. (n.d.). *Aisaika Organization prospectus, 2005–2007.* Retrieved from http://www.aisaika.org/en/prospectus.html

Japan Today. (2004, February 6). *Living in an era of "Freeters."* Retrieved from http://www.japantoday.com/e/?content=kuchikomi&id=284

Jolivet, M. (1997). *Japan: The childless society? The crisis of motherhood.* London and New York: Routledge.

Jones, R. S. *Income inequality, poverty and social spending in Japan.* Organisation for Economic Co-operation and Development, Economics Department Working Papers No. 556.

Kambayashi, T. (2004, February 4). A defender for Japan's battered women. *Christian Science Monitor,* p. 11.

Kariya, T., & Dore, R. (2006). Japan at the meritocracy frontier: From here, where? *Political Quarterly.*

Kato, R. (1994). Japanese women: Subordination or domination. In J. Curtis & L. Tepperman (Eds.), *Haves and have-nots: An international reader on social inequality.* Englewood Cliffs, NJ: Prentice Hall.

Kosugi, R. (2004, Winter). The transition from school to work: Understanding the increase in freeter and jobless youth. *Japan Labor Review, 1*(1), 52–67.

Kristof, N. D. (1995a, May 14). Japanese say no to crime: Tough methods, at a price. *The New York Times,* pp. 1, 8.

Kristof, N. D. (1995b, June 4). A neighborly style of police state. *The New York Times,* p. E5.

Kristof, N. D. (1998, July 5). Japan voters send message: No change. *The New York Times,* p. A4.

Kuwayama, T. (1994). The reference other orientation. In N. L. Rosenberger (Ed.), *Japanese sense of self* (pp. 121–151). Cambridge, England: Cambridge University Press.

Lebra, T. S. (1984). *Japanese women: Constraint and fulfillment.* Honolulu: University of Hawaii Press.

Leestma, R. (1987). *Japanese education today.* Washington, DC: U.S. Government Printing Office.

Lewis, C. C. (1995). *Educating hearts and minds: Reflections on Japanese preschool and elementary education.* Cambridge, England: Cambridge University Press.

Mainichi Daily News. (2003, November 16). Yakuza place want ads to find new blood. Retrieved from http://mdn.mainichi.co.jp/

Masui, S. (2003, January 18). Back to basics to beat crime. *Daily Yomiuri.* Retrieved from http://www.yomiuri.co.jp/index-e.htm.

McGregor, R. (1996). *Japan swings: Politics, culture and sex in the new Japan.* Tokyo: Yenbooks.

McKibben, B. (2007). *Deep economy: The wealth of communities and the durable future.* New York: Henry Holt.

Mehri, D. (2005). *Notes from Toyota-Land: An American engineer in Japan.* Ithaca, New York: Cornell University Press.

Merton, R. K. (1968). *Social theory and social structure* (Enlarged ed.). New York: Free Press. (Original work published 1956)

Ministry of Health and Social Services (Namibia). (2003). *Namibia demographic and health survey 2000.* Retrieved from http://www.measuredhs.com/pubs/pdf/FR141/00Front Matter.pdf

Ministry of Internal Affairs and Communications Statistics Bureau (Japan). (2004). *Japan statistical yearbook 2004.* Retrieved from http://www.stat.go.jp/English/data/nenkan/1431-25.htm

Ministry of Internal Affairs and Communications Statistics Bureau (Japan). (2007). *Japan statistical yearbook 2007.* Retrieved from http://www.stat.go.jp/English/data/nenkan/1431-25.htm

Ministry of Internal Affairs and Communications Statistics Bureau (Japan). (2008). *Japan statistical yearbook 2008.* Retrieved from http://www.stat.go.jp/English/data/nenkan/index.htm

Ministry of Justice (Japan). (2003). *Statistics on foreign residents.* Retrieved from http://www.moj.go.jp/ENGLISH/

Nakamura, A. (2007, June 5). Headline-grabbing gun crimes mar safe image. *Japan Times.* Retrieved from http://search.japantimes.co.jp/cgi-bin/nn20070605i!.html

Nakane, C. (1970). *Japanese society.* Berkeley: University of California Press.

Nathan, J. (2004). *Japan unbound: A volatile nation's quest for pride and purpose.* Boston: Houghton Mifflin.

National Institute of Population and Social Security Research (Japan). (2000). *The second survey of Japanese households report.* Retrieved from http://www.ipss.go.jp/ps-katei/e/nsf_2nd/jinko4.pdf.

National Police Agency, prepared by the National Police Academy (Japan). (2005). *Crimes in Japan in 2004.* Retrieved from http://www.npa.go.jp/english/index.htm

National Police Agency, prepared by the National Police Academy (Japan). (2007a). *Crimes in Japan in 2006.* Retrieved from http://www.npa.go.jp/english/seisaku5/20071019.pdf

National Police Agency, prepared by the National Police Academy (Japan). (2007b, March). *Situation of juvenile delinquency in Japan in 2006.* Retrieved from http://www.npa.go.jp/english/syonen1/20070312.pdf

Nawa, S. (2006, March). Postwar fourth wave of juvenile delinquency and tasks of juvenile police. *Journal of Police Science, 58*(1), 1–19.

Neary, I. (2003, Spring). Burakumin at the end of history. *Social Research, 70*(1), 269–294.

The New York Times. (2007, March 15). Japan: Not tonight, Dear. Or tomorrow, p. A6.

Niska, E. W., & Xu, J. (2007, June 29). National hospital ambulatory medical care survey: 2005 emergency department summary. *Advance Data,* No. 386. Retrieved from http://www.cdc.gov/nchs/data/ad/ad386.pdf

Ogawa, A. (1998, July 19). Public works opposed, but system hard to break. *Asahi Evening News.*

Onishi, N. (2004a, January 8). Never lost, but found daily: Japanese honesty. *The New York Times,* pp. A1, A4.

Onishi, N. (2004b, March 28). Mood sours for Japan's other Asian students. *The New York Times,* p. 3.

Onishi, N. (2004c, June 6). An aging island embraces Japan's young dropouts. *The New York Times,* p. 3.

Onishi, N. (2005a, February 16). Japan, easygoing till now, plans sex traffic crackdown. *The New York Times,* p. A3.

Onishi, N. (2005b, February 19). A samurai and Japan get samba night fever. *The New York Times,* pp. 12, 17.

Onishi, N. (2005c, April 5). It's 3:30 a.m. The off-duty hostesses relax. With hosts. *The New York Times,* p. A4.

Onishi, N. (2005d, May 1). A jolt to team Japan: Bonus demands. *The New York Times,* p. 16.

Onishi, N. (2005e, May 12). How do Japanese dump trash? Let us count the myriad ways. *The New York Times,* pp. A1, A4.

Onishi, N. (2005f, December 24). Japan's population fell this year, sooner than expected. *The New York Times,* p. A8.

Onishi, N. (2006a, April 16). Revival in Japan brings widening of economic gap. *The New York Times,* pp. 1, 6.

Onishi, N. (2006b, June 11). Japan's conservatives push prewar "virtues" in schools. *The New York Times,* p. 26.

Onishi, N. (2006c, July 11). Missile tests divide Seoul from Tokyo. *The New York Times,* p. A6.

Onishi, N. (2007a, January 6). A renegade's tale of his scorn for Japan's "club of old men." *The New York Times,* p. A4.

Onishi, N. (2007b, May 11). Pressed by police, even innocent confess in Japan. *The New York Times,* pp. A1, A10.

Onishi, N. (2007c, October 12). Starving man's diary suggests harshness of welfare in Japan. *The New York Times,* pp. A1, A12.

Onishi, N. (2007d, November 3). As Japan ages, prisons adapt to going gray. *The New York Times,* pp. A1, A11.

Orenstein, P. (2001, July 1). Parasites in pret-a-porter. *The New York Times Magazine,* pp. 31–35.

Orr, M., & Sims, C. (2008, June 27). *Rearming Japan: A film. The New York Times.* Retrieved from http://video.on.nytimes.com/?fr_story=96c8dc2685bfd9f9f373fc110a8453e87cfOae42

Pearson, B. (2004, January 23). Japan despairs of dying trends. *Australian Financial Review,* p. 44.

Pew Foundation. (2007). *47-nation Pew global attitudes survey, 2007.* Retrieved from http://pewglobal.org/reports/pdf/258.pdf

The Pew Research Center for the People and the Press. (2002). *What the world thinks in 2002.* Retrieved from http://people-press.org/report/165/what-the-world-thinks-in-2002

Pharr, S. J. (1990). *Losing face: Status politics in Japan.* Berkeley: University of California Press.

Prasso, S. (2006, October 15). Escape from Japan. *The New York Times,* pp. ST1, ST6.

Reckless, W. (1973). *The crime problem* (5th ed.). New York: Appleton.

Reischauer, E. O. (1977). *The Japanese.* Cambridge, MA: Harvard University Press.

Reischauer, E. O. (1988). *The Japanese today: Change and continuity.* Cambridge, MA: Harvard University Press.

Roberson, J. E., & Suzuki, N. (Eds.). (2003). *Men and masculinities in contemporary Japan.* London and New York: RoutledgeCurzon.

Sellek, Y. (1997). Nikkeiin: The phenomenon of return migration. In M. Weiner (Ed.), *Japan's minorities: The illusion of homogeneity.* London and New York: Routledge.

Shih, B. (2004, May 15). Yakuza, the Japanese mob. *National Public Radio* (weekend edition).

Shimizu, H. (2001). Japanese cultural psychology and empathetic understanding. In H. Shimizu & R. LeVine (Eds.), *Japanese frames of mind* (pp. 1–28). Cambridge, England: Cambridge University Press.

Sims, C. (2000, April 11). Tokyo chief starts new furor, on immigrants. *The New York Times,* p. A6.

Sims, C. (2001, June 30). Japan: Census shows gray. *The New York Times,* p. 4.

Smith, R. J. (1983). *Japanese society: Tradition, self and the social order.* Cambridge, England: Cambridge University Press.

Statistisches Bundesamt Deutschland. (n.d.). *Haushalte nach Haushaltstypen.* Retrieved from http://www.destatis.de/jetspeed/portal/cms/Sites/destatis/Internet/DE/Content/Statistisken?Bevoelkerung/Haushalte/Tabellen/Content50/Haushaltstypen,templateId=renderPrint.psml

Statistisches Bundesamt Deutschland. (n.d.). *Mehr als 64 000 Strafgefangene in deutschen Gefängnissen.* Retrieved from http://www.destatis.de/jetspeed/portal/cms/Sites/destatis/Internet/EN/press/pr/2006/12/PE06__517__024.psml

Statistisches Bundesamt Deutschland. (n.d.). *Criminal prosecution statistics; persons convicted 2005.* Retrieved from http://www.destatis.de/jetspeed/portal/cms/Sites/destatis/Internet/EN/Content/Statistics?Rechtspflege/Strafverfolgung/Tabellen/Content75/Verurteilte Strafart.psml

Sterngold, J. (1992, October 21). Mob and politics intersect, fueling cynicism in Japan. *The New York Times,* pp. A1, A6.

Strom, S. (1999a, July 15). In Japan, mired in recession, suicides soar. *The New York Times,* pp. A1, A8.

Strom, S. (1999b, November 7). Japanese family values: I choose you, Pikachu! *The New York Times,* p. WK4.

Strom, S. (2001, July 27). The twist of Koizumi's reforms: Supporters could suffer. *The New York Times,* p. 16.

Sugimoto, Y. (1997). *An introduction to Japanese society.* Cambridge, England: Cambridge University Press.

Tachibanaki, T. (2005). *Confronting income inequality in Japan: A comparative analysis of causes, consequences, and reform.* Cambridge, MA: MIT Press.

Tasker, P. (1987). *The Japanese: Portrait of a nation.* New York: Penguin Books, New American Library.

Totman, C. (2000). *A history of Japan.* Oxford, England: Blackwell.

Totman, C. (2005). *A history of Japan.* Oxford, England: Blackwell.

Ueda, A. (1994). How bureaucrats manage society. In *The electric geisha: Exploring Japan's popular culture* (pp. 127–138). Tokyo: Kodansha.

United Nations. (1997). *Human development report 1997.* Retrieved from http://hdr.undp .org/en/reports/global/hdr1997/

United Nations. (2005). *Human development report 2005.* Retrieved from http://hdr.undp .org/en/reports/GLOBAL/HDR2005/

United Nations Office on Drugs and Crime. (n.d.). *Eighth UN survey on crime trends and the operations of criminal justice systems.* Retrieved from http://www.unodc.org/ pdf/crime/eighthsurvey/8pc/pdf

United Nations Population Division, Department of Economic and Social Affairs. (2000, March 21). *Replacement migration: Is it a solution to declining and ageing populations?* New York: Author.

United Nations University, World Institute for Development Economics Research. (2007, May). *World income inequality database,* Version 2.0b. Retrieved from http://www .wider.unu.edu/research/Database/en_GB/database/

U.S. Bureau of the Census. (2006). *Current population survey, 2006.* Retrieved from http:// www.census.gov/population/www/socdemo/hh-fam/cps2006.html

U.S. Department of Justice, Bureau of Alcohol, Tobacco, Firearms and Explosives. (2006a, January 18). *Annual firearms and manufacturing report, 2004.*

U.S. Department of Justice. (2006b, May). *Prison and jail inmates at midyear 2005.* Retrieved from http://www.ojp.usdoj.gov/bjs/abstract/pjim05

U.S. Federal Bureau of Investigation (n.d.) *Supplementary homicide reports, 1976–2005.*

U.S. Federal Bureau of Investigation. (2006). *Uniform crime reports, crime in the United States 2006.* Retrieved from http://www.fbi.gov/ucr/cius2006/data/table_01.html

Van Wolferen, K. (1989). *The enigma of Japanese power: People and politics in a stateless nation.* New York: Knopf.

Weisman, S. R. (1991, November 13). "In Japan, bias is an obstacle even for the ethnic Japanese. *The New York Times,* pp. A1, A10.

White, M. (1993). *The material child: Coming of age in Japan and America.* New York: Free Press.

White, M. I. (2002). *Perfectly Japanese: Making families in an era of upheaval.* Berkeley: University of California Press.

Wildeman, J. (n.d.). *Crime and crime control in modern Japan.* Unpublished manuscript.

World Bank. (2006). *World development indicators 2006.* Retrieved from http://web.worldbank .org/WEBSITE/EXTERNAL/DATASTATISTICS/0,,contentMDK:20899413~pagePK: 64133150~piPK:64133175~theSitePK:239419,00.html

World Health Organization. (1999). *Statistical information system mortality database.* Retrieved from http://www.who.int/whosis/database/mort/table1.cfm

Yoder, R. S. (2004). *Youth deviance in Japan: Class reproduction of non-conformity.* Melbourne: Torans Pacific Press.

Yoneyama, S. (1999). *The Japanese high school: Silence and resistance.* London and New York: Routledge.

Zaun, T. (2004, June 2). World business briefing: Asia: Japan: wages rise, p. A12.

Zaun, T. (2005, January 12). Japanese company to pay ex-employee $8.1 million for invention. *The New York Times,* p. C3.

Zielenziger, M. (2006). *Shutting out the sun: How Japan created its own lost generation.* New York: Nan A. Talese.

MEXICO

You can fly to Mexico from New York in 5 hours, from London in 10, or you can walk across a border bridge from Texas in 5 minutes. You will find yourself in a society created from two clashing cultures: the Native American culture of Mexico and the Spanish culture of the European conquerors.

LOCATION: Mexico is a North American country just south of the American states of Texas, New Mexico, Arizona, and California. Mexico is bordered on the east by the Gulf of Mexico and on the west by the Pacific. To the south Mexico borders Guatemala and Belize.

AREA: One fifth the size of the United States or Canada, Mexico (756,000 square miles) is four times the size of Germany.

LAND: A rugged, mountainous country. Mexico City, the country's capital, is several thousand feet above sea level.

CLIMATE: Hot, humid, and tropical in the south; arid and desertlike in the north. Temperatures cool as one climbs higher. The year alternates between rainy and dry seasons.

POPULATION: In 2007, 108,700 million people. As many as 28.5 million people live in the capital. The population is relatively young. One third of the population is under the age of 15.

INCOME: In equivalent U.S. purchasing power, $11,369 GDP per person per year in 2005. Between 15 and 20% live in absolute poverty.

EDUCATION: Ninety percent of adult women and 92% of adult men are literate.

RELIGION: Ninety-three percent are Roman Catholic; 3% are Protestant.

MINORITIES: Seven million people (8% of the population) belong to indigenous Indian groups, including the Nahua, the Zapotec, the Maya, the Totonac, the Mixtec, and many smaller populations.

CHAPTER TWO

Mexico: Conflict and Cooperation

INTRODUCTION

Visitors to Teotihuacan, the ancient Indo-American ruins 25 miles northeast of Mexico City, come upon richly carved walls, crammed with intricate patterns, picked out in sharp relief by the bright sunlight of the mountains. These stone carvings might well symbolize Mexico itself, a diverse society marked by strong social and cultural contrasts. There are many Mexicos: urban and rural, rich and poor, European and Indo-American.

Mexico City is a 21st-century megacity. It points the way to the problems of urbanization increasingly visible all over the world. Twenty million people live crowded into Mexico City's high, mountain-ringed valley: in apartment towers, leafy middle-class suburbs, and squatter shantytowns. They jam its highways, buses, subways, and markets, their cars spewing out a toxic haze of air pollution, their accumulating sewage and garbage a constant hazard. But when city people go home to visit their relatives in the countryside, they find a very different way of life. Most villages now have electricity and roads; some have Internet service and regular bus transportation. But people still grow some of the food they eat, often without machinery, and build their own houses; some wear traditional Indian dress. In the most remote villages, paths, not streets, link the houses; there are seldom any newspapers, and perhaps not even a telephone.

Even in Mexico City, the rich and the poor live so differently they might inhabit different societies. A rich teenager may drive an imported car, live in his family's air-conditioned house, wear European designer clothes, and dance at a club built to look as much as possible like one in New York or Los Angeles. The family's maid will probably travel 4 hours a day on packed buses and trains, returning at night to a one-room shanty with a bare light bulb (wired illegally to a city streetlight), a single mattress, and no refrigerator or running water.

Understanding Mexico: The Conflict Perspective

Mexican society seems to call for analysis with the **conflict perspective.** When we examine Mexico, we see all sorts of divisions and disagreements within the society. Diverse groups struggle for control of scarce resources and justify their claims with conflicting worldviews. Those who hold power use it to dominate others and to protect their own privileges. Disagreement about values is common. A conflict theorist, looking at Mexico's long history, would contend that conflict and value **dissensus** (disagreement, the opposite of consensus) are the normal condition of society, and any period of order is really a period of domination by one or another ruling group.

A HISTORY OF CONFLICT

To better understand both the conflict perspective and Mexican society, you must first know something about Mexico's dramatic history. Mexicans themselves believe that their history holds the key to their character, and they relish its romance and extravagance. In every period in Mexican history, different groups struggled to control society to benefit themselves. Mexico's history is divided by dramatic events into three clearly marked periods: the pre-Columbian, the colonial, and the modern.

The Pre-Columbian Period (c. 300 BC–AD 1519)

The earliest period of Mexican history was the longest: This was the pre-Columbian period (c. 300 BC–AD 1519) when the great Maya and Aztec and other Indo-American empires ruled Central America. By the 1st century BC, there were great civilizations in Mexico, the equal of anything in Europe. The Indo-Americans built large cities, developed sophisticated systems of writing and mathematics, kept astronomy records, and built monumental works of architecture. These empires also fought frequent wars to subjugate neighboring peoples and made them pay **tribute** (goods that conquered people had to pay to their conquerors) and also to take captives who were made into slaves or sacrificed to the gods (Rudolph, 1985, pp. 5–8; Ruiz, 1992, pp. 18–20).

The Aztecs

The last Indo-American empire was that of the Aztecs, who rose to power in the 14th century. Dedicated to conquest, the Aztecs glorified fighting and bravery. Nobles ruled and merchants enjoyed a relatively high status, but commoners, conquered people, and slaves labored hard to build the gleaming pyramids, roads, and aqueducts of their capital, Tenochtitlán (site of today's Mexico City). The Aztecs exacted more and more tribute from subject peoples to make their gorgeous feathered cloaks and jewelry, and the resentment and hatred of the conquered peoples grew (Kandell, 1988, pp. 49–54; Rudolph, 1985, p. 14; Ruiz, 1992, p. 24).

The Conquest

The pre-Columbian period in Mexico ended in a new episode of struggle and domination in 1519, the year of the Spanish Conquest, led by Hernán Cortés. At the time of the Conquest, Spanish society had much in common with Aztec society: Both were shaped by war and religion. The most important force in Spain was the *Reconquista,* the politico-military "crusade" to recapture all of Spain from the Muslims or "Moors" who had ruled it for seven centuries. Under the leadership of Ferdinand and Isabella, Granada, the last bastion of the Moors, was reconquered in 1492. The crusader mentality glorified war and looked down on agriculture and manufacture, which it associated with the Moors, and also looked down on finance, associated with the despised Jews (expelled from Spain in 1492). Spanish warriors found it proper to live off the labor of those they conquered, the crown rewarding them with land grants and "infidel" serfs.

Cortés and Moctezuma.   Hernán Cortés was the very model of a *conquistador,* thirsting for adventure, greedy for gold, aggressive, brave, and ruthless. He was a brilliant strategist, able to switch gears instantly and turn misfortune to advantage. In 1519, at the age of 33, Cortés assembled 11 ships, 500 soldiers, 100 sailors, 200 Cuban Indians, weapons, and 16 horses and sailed from Cuba for the Yucatán (the southeastern coast of Mexico).

Cortés's invading force was tiny compared to the military might of the Aztecs. Two special weaknesses made the Conquest possible. First, the Aztecs had made many, many enemies among neighboring peoples, who gladly joined Cortés, swelling his army from 500 to 10,000. It was not really Cortés who conquered the Aztecs, but the Aztecs' Indian enemies. Also, if any European force really mattered, it was an army of European germs: smallpox—absent in the Americas—which arrived with the Spanish and ravaged Tenochtitlan.

The Colonial Period (1519–1810)

The Conquest ushered in 300 years of colonial rule in Mexico, now christened New Spain. Mexico's native peoples were inclined at first to see the Spanish as just the next in a long series of conquerors, but in many ways the Spanish empire was harsher and more destructive than any previous Indo-American rule.

The Spaniards wanted wealth from Mexico, gold or silver, ideally, but also sugar, indigo (a valuable dye), cattle, or wheat for export. They were not much interested in settling Mexico. The Spaniards in Mexico wanted to become rich and they wanted to do so by using Indian labor to extract the wealth of the land. The Spanish monarchy had similar ambitions: The king and queen hoped to tax Mexico's exports. The colonizers in Mexico had another goal too: They wanted to save souls and to convert the Indians to Catholicism and stamp out the worship of pagan gods.

A Genocidal Beginning

Spanish rule turned out to be much more disastrous for the native Mexicans than Cortés's Indian allies could ever have imagined. First of all, Spanish rule began with a tragedy—a "biological catastrophe"—a terrible plague of Old World diseases to which the Indo-Americans had no immunities. Measles and influenza, minor diseases in Europe, became killers in Mexico (as everywhere in the New World). Smallpox became epidemic. Demographers estimate a population of 25 million in central

Mexico at the time of the Conquest; by 1650, only 1 million native Mexicans survived there (Kandell, 1988, p. 149; Wolf, 1959, p. 195). Disease wiped out families, villages, ruling classes, and whole cultures.

The Hacienda System

Without an abundant Indian labor force, Spanish colonizers' plans for wealth were frustrated. It took them until the 17th century to work out a sustainable system for colonizing Mexico: the *hacienda system*. The hacienda was an estate or plantation on which Indians were forced into a kind of slavery. Spanish colonizers helped themselves to the best land, and then offered to employ the now-landless Indians. They tricked the Indians into debt by giving them advances on their wages until they owed so much money they could never finish working off the debt. Haciendas were land-hungry: the more Indian land they could take, the more Indians they could force into dependence. They also imported some Black slaves (Rudolph, 1985, p. 23; Ruiz, 1992, pp. 81, 102–103; Wolf, 1959, pp. 203–208).

The society the Spanish created in Mexico was highly race conscious and racially stratified. Every person had an official racial classification: White, followed by *casta* (mixed White and Indian), with Indian and Black at the bottom. People had different rights based on their race.

The Modern Period (1810–Present)

The modern period in Mexico began with the War of Independence, which freed Mexico from Spanish rule. Much of the modern period has been characterized by a high level of conflict among different groups. From 1810 until the early 20th century, Mexico was in an almost constant state of upheaval as the different strata of Mexican society fought for justice, recognition, equality, or power. Every group had grievances: The wealthy colonists wanted more political independence, the middle class wanted greater economic opportunities, and the poor and the Indians wanted land, food, jobs, and an end to slavery and to tribute payments.

After declaring independence from Spain in 1824, rural guerrilla bands, royalists, and republicans fell to fighting each other. The next 50 years were marked by government instability and corruption and a succession of coups by generals. There were 42 different governments between 1821 and 1855 (Kandell, 1988, p. 319). During this period of disintegration, Mexico lost Texas to the United States, lost the Mexican-American War, and suffered a French invasion and occupation. Finally, a new middle class emerged as the ruling elite. They looked toward Europe and sought to remake Mexico according to the ideals of the French and American Revolutions, as a capitalist republic. Mexico abolished slavery, established constitutional government on the American model, and guaranteed freedom of religion, but these paper reforms had little practical effect.

Order and Revolution

Order was finally imposed by a brilliant politician, Porfirio Díaz, whose eight terms of office as president between 1876 and 1911 are known as the Porfiriate. Díaz advocated order and progress and threw all his tremendous power into modernizing the economy, securing international recognition, and attracting foreign investment. He built railroads and ports, extended electric and telephone service, modernized Mexico City, strengthened mining and agriculture, began oil exploration, and balanced the national budget. Díaz was ruthless in his exercise of power. He executed rival generals, massacred rebellious Indians, held fraudulent elections, and censored the press. The wealthy enjoyed a golden age during the Porfiriate, but the misery of the poor intensified, paving the way for Mexico's next great upheaval.

Mexico's revolution, begun in 1910, was one of the great early-20th-century revolutions, like the Russian Revolution. The Mexican Revolution spoke for workers and peasants whose living and working conditions had steadily worsened in the late 19th century. The revolution rejected Europe as a model, asserted an Indian identity for Mexico, and committed the government to providing security for peasants and workers by redistributing land and income.

Middle-class liberals who wanted democracy started the revolution, but it blazed into violent struggle as it attracted those who had suffered most under the Porfiriate. Peasants and Indians, led by the famous Emiliano Zapata and by Pancho Villa, waged guerrilla struggles to take back land from the *haciendas*. Fighting continued for almost two decades, with every region convulsed by conflict between rival armies. A radical constitution promulgated in 1917 stipulated restoration of all Indian lands and national ownership of all natural resources, guaranteed free public education, an 8-hour workday, equal pay for equal work, and the right to organize and strike. Amid the prevailing disorder, most of these provisions were not put into practice for years, if ever (Fuentes, 1992a, pp. 299–306).

Revolutionary Change

It was not until the 1930s, and the presidency of Lázaro Cárdenas, that the government finally made good on its promises to retrieve for the Indians lands stolen by the *haciendas*. Cárdenas redistributed 46 million acres of land. Two thirds of Mexican farmers received land, mostly through the creation of *ejidos*—landholdings given to villages to be held in common and assigned by the village for individual use—on the traditional Indian model. Cárdenas also nationalized the whole oil industry (mostly foreign owned), another enormously popular action.

Finally, poor rural Mexicans saw some improvements in their lives. Schools, roads, electricity, and hospitals began to reach the countryside. The number of people dependent on haciendas decreased. Now it became possible for the government to move from revolutionary change to the consolidation of power. Those who had benefited from reform were readily rallied as supporters of the government: Ejidos, trade unions, and government workers were all organized into subsidiary units of the Institutional Revolutionary Party, the PRI. The party dominated Mexico for the next seven decades, making politics orderly, channeling benefits to organized peasants and workers, but also substituting one-party rule for democracy.

Mexico Today

Mexico today remains riven by conflict. Poverty, especially rural poverty, remains a major problem and source of tension in the society. In some rural areas left-wing insurgent groups have challenged local governments and attempted land takeovers.

Even in more conventional politics, contention continues between the PAN, a modernizing party in the Porfirio Díaz tradition, which advocates neoliberal free-trade policies, and the PRD, a party of the left focused on issues of inequality in income and land ownership. Also, throughout Mexico, drug cartels battle each other and resist all government efforts at control.

Ordinary Mexicans do their best to survive and support their families in an insecure environment. They rely on family networks to till the land, find paid work, establish small businesses, and care for children. In many cases, family networks extend to both sides of the border with the United States, helping migrants cross over, get jobs and housing in the cities of the north, and aid relatives in Mexico with money sent home.

MEXICAN CULTURE

Every era of Mexican history has left its own ambiguous cultural legacy. A distinctive society developed, in which Indo-American, Spanish, western European, American, socialist, and Catholic influences were adapted and combined. Mexicans debate the effects of Spanish colonialism on their society. In one view, Spanish and Indo-American cultures blended in Mexico. The Spanish colonizers tried their best to destroy Aztec civilization—its religion, cities, government, army, and system of social stratification—and to substitute their own church, Spanish law, and the *hacienda* system. They succeeded in eliminating Aztec institutions, but were less successful in destroying Indo-American culture. Instead, similarities between the two cultures facilitated blending: Both cultures were warlike, hierarchical, and religious. Their family structures and norms were similar. Celia Falicov (1982) argues that "today the Spanish and Indian heritages are so fused that it is difficult to separate them" (p. 135).

Some analysts (like Mexican writer Octavio Paz) have seen the colonial legacy as much more destructive. Paz argued that the experience of conquest and colonial domination caused lasting damage to the Mexican psyche. Mexicans, he contended, saw their origins in a historical act of violation and wished to deny both their Spanish and their Indian origins. Some contemporary socialists argue that today Mexico continues to be enmeshed in economic colonialism, distorting its development to serve the needs of multinational corporations, while unemployment, poverty, and undernourishment increase. In this view, relations of economic dependency are deeply embedded in Mexican society, shaping its political system as well as its economy (Barkin, 1990, pp. 11–22, 93–95; Paz, 1961, pp. 86–87).

Other Mexicans identify with their country's revolutionary tradition. Mexicans still see the revolutionary murals of Diego Rivera, and they faithfully remember President Lázaro Cárdenas. Insurgent leaders align themselves with Mexico's historic revolutionaries. They stress Mexico's heritage of resistance rather than dependence— resistance to Spanish colonialism, to the hacienda system, to undemocratic government. The legacies of cultural blending, colonial domination, and resistance can all be seen in Mexico's religious heritage.

Catholicism in Mexican Culture

The most enduring legacy of the Conquest was Catholicism. Mexico became, and remains, a Catholic country. Colonial churches and images of Catholic saints are seen everywhere. Catholicism is so much a part of Mexico that it is as multisided and contradictory as Mexican culture itself.

Catholicism arrived with the Conquest. Spanish friars immediately set about converting the conquered Indians. In Mexico City, one friar, Pedro de Gante, baptized Indians at the rate of 14,000 per day. Many writers have wondered why the work of conversion was so successful. In some measure, force was responsible: The Catholic Church drove out the old priests, destroyed the idols and temples, ended human sacrifice, and burned sacred books. Indians who refused to accept the new religion were sometimes tortured or whipped. But the Catholic clergy also offered genuine concern and care for the Indians and sometimes defended them against abusive colonial practices. Probably most important, the Church declared Indians to have immortal souls, to be human. In a dehumanizing colonialism, the Church offered Indians hope for justice.

In some ways too, Catholicism offered the Indians a way to continue their religious traditions after their own gods had failed. Colonial Mexico, like Aztec Mexico, was a society permeated by religious faith and ritual. There were similarities between Catholicism and Indo-American religions, so it was not difficult to join them. The Indians looked on the Catholic saints as an array of gods, similar to their own. They were familiar with rituals of baptism, confession, and communion, enacted in their own religion too. The cross was even familiar to the Maya, though their cross emerged from a base of carved snakes and represented the god of fertility.

In fact, the Indians adapted Catholicism to meet their own needs for religious grace and human respect. Nowhere is this clearer than in the legend of the Virgin of Guadalupe, still today the patron saint of Mexicans. The story tells that in 1531, the Virgin Mary appeared before a humble Indian man at Tepeyac, just north of Mexico City, at the site of a temple to Tonantzin, the Aztec mother of gods. Miraculously her image appeared on his cloak, and lo! she was a dark-skinned Mary. Worship of the Virgin of Guadalupe spread rapidly in Mexico, and after initial opposition the friars accepted her, implicitly conceding the full humanity of the Indians (Ruiz, 1992, pp. 66–70; Wolf, 1959, pp. 165–175).

Catholicism in Mexico (as elsewhere in Latin America) absorbed and became joined to deep Indo-American religious feeling. Shrines and altars, incense and flowers, religious ceremonies and processions make Catholicism in Mexico "a sensuous, tactile religion" (Fuentes, 1992b, p. 410).

Popular Religion

Everywhere that it has gone in the world, the Catholic Church has adapted to local practices of folk religion, and Mexico is no exception. Mexican Catholicism has absorbed local *fiestas* (festivals) and local Indo-American saints. All over Mexico, villages celebrate the saint's days of their patron saints with brass bands and processions, bright costumes, special masses, colorful decorations of the church and town, fireworks, bullfights, sports contests, food, drink, and dancing, and street sales of fruits, candy, and toys. Some fiestas, like Holy Week, Christmas, and the Festival of Our Lady of Guadalupe, are national holidays.

El Día de Los Muertos.   Probably the most famous of Mexico's *fiestas* is El Día de Los Muertos (The Day of the Dead). By an odd coincidence, both the Spanish and the Aztecs commemorated the dead on November 2, and this holiday fuses the two celebrations (as well as the Christian All Saints' Day, November 1).

Weeks before November 2, candy vendors begin selling skulls of white sugar, decorated with sequins, ribbons, and foil, with first names on their foreheads. People buy skulls with the names of their dead relatives and set them on homemade altars, along with statues of saints, ears of corn, fruit, candy, foods the dead especially liked, soda, liquor and cigarettes, incense, and candles. People give each other gifts of cookies shaped like skeletons, or chocolate skulls, or sugar coffins (Braganti & Devine, 1989, p. 156; Nolen, 1973, pp. 48–49).

Before midnight on November 1, Mexicans spread a path of flower petals from their doors to the altar, and settle down to await a visit from the dead. The next day, they jam the roads to the cemeteries, to bring flowers and candles and perhaps a toy for a dead child, and to clean up gravesites. There is a party atmosphere, as people picnic and chat with graveside neighbors. Afterward, at home, they feast on the food that the dead have enjoyed in spirit (Reavis, 1990, pp. 194–198).

The Saints.   Every village in Mexico adopts a patron saint who watches over villagers. If you visit a village church, you will see a statue or doll representing the saint at a special altar. People pray to their patron saint and ask for miracles, often cures for illness, or good harvests. The saint of San Juan Jaltepac, for example, is a 3-foot-tall plaster statue of the Virgin of Candelaria. In Zapopan, the tiny doll-like Our Lady of Zapopan, covered in jewels, is said to protect against floods (Oster, 1989, p. 200; Reavis, 1990, pp. 200–203). People often devote part of the main room of their house, or a special separate room to a home altar where they light candles, hang religious pictures, and spend time in prayer.

Doña Ana's Story: The Believer

Doña Ana is a woman in her 50s who works as a maid for a middle-class family. Every night she takes the subway and two buses and returns to her family in Colonia Caultepac at the northern edge of Mexico City, where she lives with her husband, daughter, and granddaughter. When her granddaughter fell ill with hepatitis, the doctors at the clinic said they weren't sure they could save her. Doña Ana prayed to the Virgin of Candelaria. A special room in her house contains an altar: a shelf covered with a lace tablecloth, decorated with marigolds and a picture of the saint. Doña Ana burned candles to the Virgin and prayed every night. When her granddaughter recovered, Doña Ana cried with joy. She felt bad that she couldn't go to the Virgin's own church in San Juan Jaltepac to thank the saint. So Doña Ana saved her money and the next year, on the Virgin's own

On Good Friday in Oaxaca local residents of Zapotec background participate in a colorful parade. You can see a traditional figure of Christ on the cross, flanked by paraders on stilts covered in bright drapes, a vivid example of the blending of Spanish Christianity and indigenous Indian religious rites in Mexican Catholicism. This festival is changing today, as it becomes more and more of a tourist attraction.

saint's day, she made the long trip to her village, bringing the saint flowers and candles. Doña Ana's foolish son José laughed at her, but she felt she did the right thing and that there could be no better use for her precious savings.

Some saints are of more recent origin. In Sinaloa, pilgrims come to the shrine of Jesús Malverde, "the Angel of the Poor," in Culiacan. Malverde was a legendary late-19th-century bandit said to have stolen from the rich to give to the poor. He is also known as "the Narcosaint," the patron saint of Sinaloa drug smugglers. The shrine is hung with thank-you letters, plaques from grateful pilgrims ("thank you for saving me from drugs") and pleas from other visitors ("please let them leave my family alone") as well as plastic flowers, faded baby pictures, and the odd artificial limb (Quinones, 2001, pp. 225–232).

In Jalisco, Toribio Romo, sainted by Pope John Paul II in 2000, is known as "The Patron of Immigrants." He is known to appear to desperate immigrants as a miraculous *coyote,* bringing them safe passage across the border. Thousands come for special masses, or to kiss the saint's coffin or buy medallions of his portrait. Vendors sell a small "Migrants' Prayer Book" which includes "the Prayer for Crossing Without Documents: I feel I am a citizen of the world and of a church without borders" (Thompson, 2002d, p. A4).

Popular Religion and the Church

Religion permeates Mexican culture, but there is always a tension between folk religion, religion created by ordinary people, often poor Indian farmers or slum dwellers, and religion as laid down by the Catholic Church. Mexicans have long felt suspicious of the political role of the church in their society. In the beginning, the Church worked hand in hand with the conquistadors, although some clerics, like Fray Bartolomé de las Casas, criticized the treatment of the Indians and spoke movingly on their behalf. Many leaders of the fight for independence were clerics like Miguel Hidalgo, but the Church, itself a huge and wealthy landowner, was seen as part of Spanish colonialism by the independence fighters. The revolution was anti-Church, and the Constitution of 1917 institutionalized a strict separation of church and state, making the Catholic Church subject to civil authority and forbidding clerics from teaching in primary schools or even from wearing their religious robes in public.

Catholic Deacons.   In rural Mexico, especially in the State of Chiapas, the poorest, most Indian state, local bishops have appointed several hundred deacons, or lay preachers. They are married men who perform baptisms and weddings and conduct services. However, they don't serve communion or hear confessions. Almost all the deacons are Indians, who preach in their native languages. In many places, deacons' wives are considered deacons too and help with services, baptisms, and teaching. The Vatican has now ordered Mexican bishops to stop appointing deacons. This controversy is linked to an ideological dispute within the Catholic Church (Thompson, 2002b, p. A8).

Evangelical Protestants.   In Chiapas, it has been clear that the appointment of deacons was a defensive measure taken by the Church to try to counter the growth of evangelical Protestantism in Mexico during the past 20 years. Evangelical missions first came to Mexico from the United States and Europe, but Mexico and Guatemala now have organizations of their own. The evangelical movement has been particularly successful in Chiapas, where almost 14% of the population is now Protestant (overall for Mexico, 7.3% of the population is Protestant, mostly evangelical).

Two explanations stand out in accounting for the recent success of evangelicals in Mexico, particularly among the indigenous population. First of all, these groups are less hierarchical than the Catholic Church. Worshippers are able to take a more active role in evangelical churches, preaching and using native language, songs, and symbols. Second, evangelical opposition to the use of alcohol has proved very popular. In poor Mexican communities, male alcoholism is a scourge of family life. Wives are attracted to the evangelical church, and then coax their husbands to join. It gives them a church-based social life that is alcohol free, in contrast to the culture of Catholic folk religion, in which many traditional festivals involve heavy consumption of alcohol (Brandes, 2002, p. 33; *The Economist,* 2002, pp. 34–35; Thompson, 2002b, p. A8).

A Culture of Opposites

Mexicans tend to see the world divided into two opposite realms: the "City of God" (the world of the sacred, of religion, home, and loyal friends) and its opposite, the "City of Man" (the public world of power struggle, appearances, and dishonesty). It could certainly be argued that Mexicans' colonial experience contributed to their dualistic view of the world. In colonial times, the public world was indeed a hostile, exploitative place for Indo-Americans. Developing a strong, protective family life was a healthy response.

Family and home represent loyalty, trust, and warmth to Mexicans. The family is "a fortress against the misery of the outside world" (Goodwin, 1991, pp. 3, 6). It is "the hearth, the sustaining warmth" (Fuentes, 1992b, p. 410). Today, Mexicans who can afford it build high, solid walls around their homes, sometimes topped with broken glass. The mother is seen as the caring heart of the family, taking pleasure in serving her children and treasuring the loyalty they return. Respect for the father may keep him a somewhat remote figure, but siblings are often very close, even in adulthood. For men, a small group of old friends may form another inner world of trust in which they freely let down their defenses and express their feelings, especially in the forgiving setting of a drinking party. In the popular mystery novels of Paco Taibo, for example, the hero is always rescued in a crisis by his drinking buddies or his sister and brother.

Idealization of the Mother

In Mexican culture, women and men are often depicted as deeply and tragically different from each other. Women, as mothers, belong to the City of God, set apart in the protected and protecting home. Motherhood is a sacred value in Mexico, and through motherhood, women become spiritual creatures, long-suffering, and patient, offering unconditional love and care to their families. The treasured national symbol of the mother is the Virgin of Guadalupe, the miraculous Mexican Virgin Mary, the virtuous, humble mother who looks after her suffering Mexican children.

The Macho

Corresponding to the sacred ideal of the mother in Mexican culture is an equally stereotyped image of the *macho* (more or less, "the real man"). Men are depicted as belonging to the City of Man. They live in the dangerous public world where they must guard their honor, protect their families, and battle for respect. Every man's life is an adventure story, a quest for recognition in a corrupt society. The macho is courageous and capable of violence, and it is understood that he is sexually active. Mexico's famous essayist, Octavio Paz, described these gender dualities so forcefully in his 1950 book *The Labyrinth of Solitude* that his work helped confirm the ideals, even though he wrote about them critically (Paz, 1961, pp. 29–31, 38–39).

We must investigate what connection there may be between the cultural ideals of the mother and the macho and the roles people actually play in real life. You will find that discussion on pages 89–92. But for now, let's look further into the cultural implications of Mexican's dualistic view of the world. Important traditional norms help Mexicans, especially men, negotiate the dangers of the City of Man.

Negotiating the Public Realm.   In contrast to the inner world of family and friends, the outer world is perceived as a dangerous, treacherous, corrupt place. Business, government, the police, unions, schools, towns, and neighbors are not to be trusted. Social relations in the public world require watchfulness. Outside the family, Mexicans hide their feelings and fears behind "masks of formality" (Riding, 1985, p. 10). Like actors, they practice what symbolic interactionist Erving Goffman called **role distance,** self-consciously playing a role fit for a situation, but not identifying with the role. Formal language, empty phrases, false promises, and even lies allow Mexicans to meet role expectations without risking their real selves. Goffman would say that for Mexicans the world outside the family is a **frontstage** where people play their roles carefully and engage in **impression management** to try to control how others see them, while at home in the **backstage** they relax their guard.

Respect and Dignity.   In the public world Mexicans try to attain and keep respect and dignity. *Respeto* in Spanish has a different meaning than does the corresponding word *respect* in English. In English, when one person respects another, it has a connotation of individuals acknowledging their essential equality. In Mexico, respeto is more like deference: It means that one person acknowledges the high status of another. Mexicans agree that people ought to be respected by others of lower status, by younger people and children, and that men ought to be respected by women. Respect allows people to preserve their *dignidad.* Mexicans attach greater importance to honesty and the preservation of their dignity than they do to individual achievement. People will proudly depict themselves and their families as "poor but honest" (Falicov, 1982, p. 138).

Individualism and Familism

The cultural ideal of the Mexican man bravely and aggressively making his way in a hostile world can certainly be described as "individualistic." In part, individualism in Mexico derives from a frontier mentality, what Sam Quinones calls "ranchero culture." *Ranchos* are the tiny settlements made by landless people who moved out to the arid frontier in central and northern Mexico, away from the *haciendas* and cities. Quinones (2001) quotes Esteban Barragán, a leading rural historian, who says, "people who live on the frontier have to take care of problems on their own. There's no police to solve conflicts, no judges to resolve problems with others, no ambulances. It's him alone against everything else. And an attitude develops around this. People who grew up in this don't feel tamed." "Ranchero culture values daring and individual initiative," says Quinones, as typified in the figure of the *valiente,* celebrated in Mexican *corridos* (ballads) and classic films. You could call the valiente a bandit, or a lone avenger (pp. 252–253).

The romantic individualism of ranchero culture is reflected in the way Mexicans admire the matador or the boxer more than the team player in soccer or basketball. Mexicans personalize their history, telling it as a story about heroes and villains like Cortés, Zapata, Porfirio Díaz, and Lázaro Cárdenas. Successful politicians are never simply party functionaries; they build their own faction or following within the party, and the most successful, like Cárdenas, attract supporters through charismatic appeal (Riding, 1985, p. 5; Wolf, 1959, pp. 238–239).

Although their culture idealizes the valiente, in real life Mexicans are **familistic:** They are intensely loyal to their families and pride themselves on their willingness to put their families first. It is not uncommon for Mexicans to sacrifice opportunities for individual advancement or enrichment in order to remain near their parents, or support their widowed sisters or other relatives. Individuals who work in the United States send a lot of what they earn home to their families. Mexicans see their status in society as an attribute of their families, not an individual quality.

Cynicism and Fatalism

Another aspect of the culture of the City of Man, of the *macho* individualist, is cynicism. Mexicans don't trust the government to make rational decisions and they are skeptical of government promises to solve social problems through legislation and government action. Mexicans believe it would be foolish to make business decisions or career plans based on government forecasts and foolish to plan too far ahead. If you save now for retirement, the banks could fail, inflation could skyrocket; it makes more sense to spend your money now on a house that will last or a business that will generate income.

Also, Mexicans are cynical about the idea of "progress," about the value of modern science and technology. When things go wrong—when corrupt governments disregard the Constitution; when modern technology pollutes the countryside—Mexicans are cynically unsurprised. If the bus fails to arrive, if the store is out of what you need, people shrug and cynically say *"ni modo"* (literally "no way," but with the connotation, "that's life"). They are likely to tell you that people always make mistakes; that something inevitably goes wrong, even with the best intentions. They cite the old proverb "There is no evil that does not come from good."

Anticipating your cynicism, Mexicans minimize their own accomplishments. A Mexican who is ambitious says, *"tengo ilusiónes"* ("I have illusions"). He calls his ambition a weakness, and if you call him ambitious, it is a criticism. It is more acceptable to praise a person for their good qualities—their strength, bravery, intelligence, or skill, than their accomplishments. People usually attribute a person's success to luck (Reavis, 1990, pp. 289–293).

SOCIAL STRUCTURE AND GROUP LIFE

Sociologists often find it useful to distinguish between **culture** and **social structure.** So far, we have been discussing Mexican culture: Mexicans' distinctive norms and customs, their particular beliefs, attitudes, and values. When we are introduced to an unfamiliar society, we notice culture first. Sometimes it seems exotic: Other peoples' religion, their holidays, food, art, and music may be noticeably different from our own. It takes longer to notice social structure, but it is equally important. Unlike culture, which always involves meaning, social structure describes how people organize their social lives. In Mexico, people may idealize the brave loner, but in fact they create a rich fabric of social groups: the family, the village, the political party, the evangelical church, the union, and others, to help them deal with life's difficulties. All of these groups are built out of **status positions,** like "student," "woman," or "employee," linked together in a **status system,** together with **roles** and **norms.** Don't confuse status positions with status in the sense of prestige. Sometimes status positions are ranked in a hierarchy, with different levels of prestige. But now we want to focus on status in its meaning of position, or social location. The social structures built out of status positions may be small—like a nuclear family built of three statuses: mother, father, child—or they may be large and complex, like a corporation or university. Three distinctive types of social structures are found in all societies: **social networks, groups,** and **social institutions.**

Social Networks in Mexican Society

People in every society are members of networks. Networks are webs of relationships that connect each person to other people, and through them to yet others. People have family networks, and networks of friends, neighbors, coworkers, and so forth, and sometimes these networks interlock. You may find a job, or an apartment, or meet your spouse-to-be through your networks.

Networks are of enormous importance in Mexican society. One 2005 study of Mexican mothers found that they averaged 21 face-to-face visits a week with members of their networks (not including their spouses and children). Children whose mothers have bigger extended kin networks are healthier, especially in poor families. People look to their networks for help getting medical care or medicine, for child care, transportation, or small loans (Kana 'Iaupuni, Donato, Thompson-Colon, & Stainback, 2005, pp. 1141, 1150–1151). One way people maintain their family and community networks, especially in rural areas, is by giving very large parties. A birthday, a baptism, or a wedding calls for a party at one's home in which a fancy traditional meal is served to hundreds of people (Rothstein, 2007, p. 121). Mexicans place great value on family loyalty, and as we have seen, they are distrustful of public institutions and nonrelatives. There is nothing in Mexican life equivalent, for example, to the importance of the company and the school in the lives of the Japanese. This leaves Mexicans with a problem: Everyone needs relationships beyond the family, particularly in modern cities where one cannot count on being surrounded by relatives.

Compadrazgo and Personal Networks

Mexicans create relations of trust beyond the family by developing personal networks. One way they do this is by adapting the traditional Latin American practice of *compadrazgo,* or godparenthood. It is customary for important occasions in a child's life—like baptism, confirmation, marriage, or even nonreligious events like graduation, or a first haircut—to be marked by the appointment of godparents, or "sponsors." A child then has many sets of godparents and the relationship between parents and their children's godparents is a special one. *Compadres,* as they are called, might be equals like neighbors, friends, or coworkers. Often people seek as compadres and *commadres* (the feminine of *compadres*) those of greater wealth or power, like bosses or local politicians. Compadres can turn to each other for favors, like a loan of money. Compadrazgo creates personal networks, but not necessarily social groups because each person's compadres are different, and one individual's compadres may not all know each other (Falicov, 1982, pp. 142–143; Goodwin, 1991, pp. 8–9).

Patronage

Mexicans also may construct networks by seeking out **patron-client relationships. Patronage** is a special kind of relationship between unequals—between a **patron,** a person with power of some kind, and a **client,** a person who gives the patron loyalty and perhaps something else of value in exchange for the patron's protection and help. Traditionally, in rural villages, people sought out the local elite as *compadres,* to establish a kind of protected relationship with them. Nowadays, ordinary people are likely to become clients (or dependents) of patrons (or bosses) in other ways: by joining a political party, or community organization, or by becoming a follower of a local boss who controls access to stalls in a market or unionized jobs. Clients owe patrons loyalty, sometimes votes, and often payments of one kind or another. Patrons will often lend money in time of need, attend the client's saints' day celebrations, or even find ways to register a favored client in the national social security system (Cross, 1998, pp. 123–127, 151–153; Selby, Murphy, & Lorenzen, 1990, p. 121).

Reciprocity Networks

Through kinship, friendship, *compadrazgo,* and patronage, ordinary Mexicans create what they call *redes de seguridad* (literally, "security networks"), or, as anthropologist Larissa Lomnitz terms them, **reciprocity networks.** Members of such networks are linked by exchange: They help one another find work; they lend food, money, pots, and pans, even clothing. They visit back and forth and watch one another's children. They care for one another when ill, and in a crisis they take in one another's children for a day, or even for years. Economists used to talk of reciprocity as a mode of exchange found only in traditional societies (like the San) and absent in modern industrial societies, except for minor practices like Christmas gift giving. Lomnitz (1977) argues that reciprocity remains an important pattern in complex, modern societies, existing alongside exchange of goods for money: "The enduring importance of social connections and influence peddling in societies as different as Mexico, the United States, and the Soviet Union attests to the fact that reciprocity as an economic force is today very much alive" (p. 4).

A good example of a Mexican reciprocity network is a *tanda,* an informal, rotating credit arrangement. The members of a tanda are usually close relatives, neighbors, or coworkers who join together to help one another save and who must trust one another to continue contributing (Lomnitz, 1977, pp. 88–89).

Rosa's Story: The Tanda

Rosa, Carmen's daughter, is desperate to get married and leave home, but there is no money. She has only a slim hope. Next month is Rosa's turn for the tanda. *She and Carmen and their two neighbors and two cousins each contribute 10 pesos weekly to the* tanda, *and then every month a different person gets to take the whole 240 pesos. When they began the* tanda *they drew lots to establish the order and now it is Rosa's turn. Her great plan is to use the money as a down payment on a sewing machine. With the machine, she figures that she and Héctor, her fiancé, will be able to afford to marry. They can live with Héctor's family, and she can sew piecework at home.*

Networks and Migration

Sociologists call it **chain migration**—the way people all over the world use their networks to emigrate to another country. Family networks often help Mexicans migrate to the United States. Your older brother in the United States lends you money and recommends a good *coyote* for the crossing. Your cousin picks you up at the border and sends you on to his wife's brother in Atlanta. Then you join your brother in North Carolina where there is a job for you in the slaughterhouse where he works. Three or 4 years later, you do the same for your younger brother, or your cousin. Studies have found that individuals with larger networks are more likely to find jobs, and to find higher-paying jobs, when they arrive in the United States. Similarly, poor people with large networks are more likely to be able to migrate than those lacking good networks. There are other positive results of good networks too. Communities with rich cross-border networks have lower levels of inequality (McKenzie & Rapoport, 2006, pp. 1–4).

Social Groups in Mexican Society: The Household

Groups are more highly structured than networks. Group members occupy statuses and play roles that are special to the group, and have some kind of group culture: shared values and norms, perhaps group folkways, and even some special way of talking. Finally, group members interact regularly and they see themselves as a group, drawing a boundary between those who are members and those who are outsiders. Most people belong to many social groups: families, friendship groups, work groups, teams, clubs, and other organizations.

The social group of greatest importance to most Mexicans is the household, the group of people with whom they live. For poor urban Mexicans, it is household sharing and reciprocity that enables them to get along, to feed and clothe their families. In the majority of cases, the members of a household form one **nuclear family** (a family composed of two parents and their children), but it is considered desirable for several nuclear units linked by kinship to join together in an **extended family** household. In fact, extended family households tend to be better off economically. Households may also include more distant relatives, godchildren, or even friends or neighbors.

Most urban Mexicans live in a detached house on a small plot of land (a *solar*). Ideally, they want a brick house with a wall to close the household off from the street. In this small domain, the household sets about *defendiendose,* or "looking after themselves" (Selby et al., 1990, pp. 70, 89). Many households are productive units, a functioning part of the economy. Households often raise animals for their own consumption or for sale; they sometimes open tiny workshops that produce textiles, carpentry, upholstery, or custom ironwork; or sidewalk businesses that do auto and truck repair or customize trucks. Sometimes household members take in washing or run sidewalk stands or rudimentary stores, selling fruit or milk, beer, crackers, and candy (Selby et al., 1990, p. 71).

Rothstein (2007) describes rural households that run tiny home workshops manufacturing clothing and employing unpaid family labor as well as occasional paid labor. The workshops occupy a bedroom, or sometimes the living room. Piles of garments take over the house and even small children help, picking off threads or hanging garments. Grandmothers care for small children while their daughters work. Teenaged daughters cook meals (pp. 63–91).

The Gómezes' Story: The Household

The Gómez household, consisting of 14 people, lives in Ciudad Nezahuacoyotl, the huge working-class neighborhood east of Mexico City. Their solar contains a series of rooms grouped in a U-shape around a central patio. Here live three related nuclear families and two individuals, linked to the household by kinship. There is Don Ramón, the head of the household, his wife Consuela, their two teenage children, and a 5-year-old godchild, who all share the main room. Don Ramón's older son and his family live in another room, and a younger son and his family live in a third room. Both daughters-in-law have orphaned younger siblings living with them too. When each son married, the whole family worked together to build a new room. The children of all three families are raised by everybody in the household, and the women go out together to shop and visit church. They borrow food, money, and other items from each other.

Many facilities in the solar are shared by the whole household. There is a small pen for pigs, rabbits, and chickens, and a privy. Also, there is a woodstove, a barrel for water, which all share in refilling, and laundry tubs used by all. Consuela and her two daughters-in-law help support the household by taking in laundry. The two teenagers carry the laundry for Consuela when she collects and delivers it, and the two young mothers wash the clothes at home. The married sons work in the same factory and the older helped the younger get a job. Sometimes, when the factory is busy, they are able to get Don Ramón hired too. Each nuclear family keeps its separate finances, but the two married sons give their father a weekly allowance in exchange for the use of his solar. Don Ramón says that they all "stick up for themselves and keep going." (See Selby et al., 1990, p. 70, and Lomnitz, 1977, pp. 112–114, for descriptions of similar households)

SOCIAL INSTITUTIONS

The Gómez household is a social group, but it also illustrates a third aspect of social structure. It shows us some of the characteristics of the Mexican family, a major Mexican **social institution.** Although social groups are concrete units of real people, social institutions are patterns of behavior. Sociologists use the term *social institution* when they need to discuss how clusters of social groups and organizations, statuses and roles, and associated norms and values operate to serve some important need in social life. In modern societies there are five major social institutions: the family, political institutions, the economy, educational institutions, and religious institutions, each performing functions that are vital to the continued existence of the society (we will discuss the first two in this chapter). Each of these institutions can be organized in a variety of ways, as you have seen in this book; but in each society, social institutions are long-lasting and widely accepted. Often, people don't even imagine different ways of organizing their society's institutions, and when institutions do change, they find it difficult to adjust.

Mexican Social Institutions: The Family

Families in all societies perform basic functions for society, though they do so in different ways. Families regulate sexual activity, supervising their members to be sure they conform to sexual norms. Families are in charge of reproduction to keep the society going, and they socialize the children they produce. Also families provide physical care and protection for their members. They provide emotional support and caring as well. When sociologists discuss "the family," they are talking about a cultural ideal: how families are supposed to work in a given society. The ideal may or may not coincide with what things are actually like in any given family group.

The Mexican family fulfills these universal functions in a distinctive way. The structures and the values, norms, beliefs, and attitudes that permeate family life are characteristically Mexican or Latin American. According to Selby and colleagues (1990), "it is difficult to overemphasize the importance of the nuclear family in Mexico, for it truly is the emotional center of the psychological and social life of all Mexicans" (p. 98). People in Mexico rely on families for order in a conflict-ridden, dangerous society. Ordinary Mexicans don't go downtown to shop, or eat out in restaurants, or go to clubs or concerts or sports events. Their lives revolve around home and work; family TV watching, family celebrations, visits among relatives and neighbors, and for men, going out drinking with close friends. Although Mexican families are typically large, only the well-to-do in Mexico live in houses with many bedrooms. Ordinary Mexicans will even rebuild the interiors of houses to make fewer bedrooms and more shared common space for family work and socializing (Selby et al., 1990, pp. 22, 26, 98).

Practically everyone in Mexico lives in a family-based household, and most of these are headed by a man who is the principal wage earner. In 2000, 20.6% of households were female headed (compared to 36% in the United States). Mexicans tend to marry young (only 37% of Mexican women aged 20 to 29 have not been married) and stay married. In Mexico there are only 6.2 divorces per year per 100 marriages.[1] Almost no one lives alone (only 6% of Mexicans lived in one-person households in 2000), and indeed it is almost unthinkable to do so, and very inconvenient too, because Mexican society assumes the presence of children or servants

---

[1]Mexico's extremely low divorce rate is puzzling. It results in part from the 17% of couples who live together in common-law marriages without a legal marriage. If they part, there is no divorce to register. Also, because Mexico is a Catholic country, people are reluctant to divorce. They are more likely to separate but remain legally wed. There is tremendous social pressure on wives to stay with their husbands, even in the face of physical or psychological abuse (Frank & Wildsmith, 2005, p. 927).

TABLE 2.1 Divorces per 100,000 Persons

Mexico's divorce rate rose between 1971 and 2005, but remains quite low. In the same period, the divorce rate in Egypt fell. The divorce rate in the United States remained essentially stable, but at a high level.

	1971	2003–2005
Mexico	41	62
Japan	99	212
Germany	131	259
Egypt	209	98
United States	372	380

Sources: United Nations, *Demographic Yearbook,* 1990 and 2004a, http://unstats.un.org; U.S. Department of Health and Human Services, *National Vital Statistics Reports,* 56, No. 2, 2007.

in every household to run errands, stand in line to pay bills (the mails are unreliable), or to carry messages (so many people lack telephones). The average household size in Mexico is still rather large: 4.3 persons (compared to 2.6 in the United States), because most adults have children living in the house with them, and often grandchildren as well. Forty-one percent of Mexicans live in households of five or more (Mexican National Institute of Statistics, Geography and Informatics, n.d.; U.S. Bureau of the Census, 2002a). See Table 2.1, and Table 1.2 on p. 18.

Family Structure

In Mexico the ideal nuclear family is part of an extended family network, and the household willingly expands to include grandparents, uncles, aunts or cousins, related children who are orphans or children of divorced parents, or relatives who are single, widowed, or divorced. People feel close to their third and fourth cousins. Extended family members rely on one another to take care of children, help with or provide friendship and support. People live in families at every stage of their lives and families demand loyalty. "What you have to do," an informant told Selby, "is care for your family, so your family will care for you" (Falicov 1982, p. 138; Selby et al., 1990, p. 5).

Families are also hierarchical: Older members have authority over younger members, and men have authority over women at every stage of the life cycle. People are expected to remain loyal to their family of origin throughout their lives. Married sons and daughters will try to live nearby and visit often, and sons will contribute money to their parents' household.

Roles in the Mexican Family

Earlier in this chapter we described a pair of gender stereotypes deeply ingrained in Mexican culture: the self-sacrificing mother and the *macho.* At the beginning of the 21st century, do these stereotypes still have power in Mexican culture? Do people accept these role ideals and try to portray them in their own lives? Did they ever? Mexico's gender dualities are contested terrain: Everyone knows them but not everyone accepts them, and not everyone who accepts them actually plays them in real life. Mexican women fought alongside men in the revolution, worked in factories, and participated in Mexican public life. Though they did not gain the right to vote in national elections until 1953, women have since become deputies and senators, have occupied seats on the Supreme Court, and have held high positions in political parties. In 2003, 116 out of 500 members of the federal congress were women. In the assembly of Mexico City, 33% of the seats are held by women (*The Economist*, 2003, p. 36).

On the other hand, most women do not work outside their homes (40% were in the labor force in 2004), and women are paid less than men. On average, working women earn only 36% of what working men earn (see Table 1.5, p. 41). In the government, women find themselves appointed to "soft-issue" ministries like tourism and culture, not the powerful departments of economy and justice. School hours run from 9 a.m. until 1 or 2 p.m., so children have to be picked up in the middle of the day, and there is very little formal day care available (*The Economist*, 2003, p. 36). Probably for most families, traditional role ideals still hold sway.

Role expectations for husbands and wives stress complementarity. Ideally, the husband is hardworking and continuously employed. He disciplines and controls the family. The husband hands over his wages to his wife, who manages the household. It is her task to maintain the home, physically and emotionally. She creates an emotional shelter, a refuge for her family, where they can recover from the stresses of life in the public world outside. Taking care of everyone is the mother's task: She sustains and nurtures and serves her family.

Traditionally, the roles parents play in relation to their children are considered much more important than the roles they play toward each other as spouses. They don't expect much romantic intimacy or friendly companionship, but rather respect, consideration and control of anger. As Falicov explains (1982), "it is thought that *el amor de madre* (motherly love) is a much greater force than wifely love" and "a Mexican woman feels more challenged to perform as a mother than as a wife, companion, or sexual partner" (pp. 140, 149). If adult children live nearby, husbands and wives are able to transfer their early involvement in raising their children to a lasting relationship with their grandchildren.

Children are expected to respect and obey their parents, but they wouldn't think of being friends with them. Ideally, children put the family's needs before their own. When they see their parents working so hard to maintain the family, they feel tremendous gratitude and a sense of protectiveness toward their mother. They are eager to help by working with their parents, or if they obtain paid work, by contributing their wages.

Siblings are expected to have very close ties throughout their lives. Brothers and sisters and cousins are encouraged to play together, and it is not unusual for Mexican children to have few friends who are not relatives. Older siblings are usually given some authority over younger ones and these age hierarchies may continue into adult life. Adult brothers and sisters may quarrel and carry grudges, but they seldom break off relations with each other, because family celebrations or crises reunite them.

Stability and Change in Family Life

To survive, Mexican families adapt to rapid change in a globalizing economy. However, some of their adaptive strategies transform, as well as preserve, family life. In other words, some of the things people do to help their families have **unanticipated**

consequences. We see this especially in the effects of migration, and we also see it in the family changes that result from women taking paid employment.

The Transnational Family.   The relationship between family life and migration to the United States is a complex one. People migrate to earn money to help their families and, as we have seen, the help of transnational family networks often makes migration possible. But migration also changes families, sometimes in positive ways, but sometimes in ways no one desired. In many communities, migration is the basis of a new pattern of family life, that of divided households, with fathers, and sometimes teenaged children, circulating back and forth between Mexico and the United States and sending money home while they are away. The family's access to capital improves, but its unity is fractured. Wives worry greatly about desertion by their husbands in the United States, and in fact divorce rates, though low, are twice as high for migrant families as for those in which husbands remain in Mexico. Husbands temporarily in the United States, free of surveillance by relatives and neighbors, are more likely to stray, and to think of themselves as "married here, single there" (Frank & Wildsmith, 2005, pp. 920, 923, 937). HIV/AIDs rates are rising rapidly in the rural Mexican states with the highest migration rates, as infected migrant husbands pass the disease on to their wives (Lacey, 2007, pp. A1, A12).

Fractured families are hard on children. More children are being left in Mexico with relatives, while both parents migrate to the United States. They are more likely to become depressed, or to rebel, than are children from undivided families, and more likely to join gangs, to drop out of school, and to head for the United States at a young age (Garcia-Navarro, 2006a).

A more ambiguous change is the altered norms that migrants bring back from the United States, a form of **social remittances** that accompanies migrants home. It appears that women who live in Mexican communities with higher rates of female migration have fewer children, even if they themselves never visit the United States. Migrants also learn American norms of family life: patterns of cooperation between husbands and wives in decision making, more sharing of domestic chores by men, and an expectation that sexual desire will join obligation as a basis for marriage (Frank & Wildsmith, 2005, p. 924).

Women's Work and Changing Gender Roles.   Migration and economic growth in Mexico are changing the roles women play. When men migrate alone, the women left behind assume new responsibilities and freedoms. They must make decisions for their families, and usually they must work. Many put on jeans and farm the family plot or even work as farmhands. They get used to more independence. If and when husbands return, it may mean a wrenching return to old roles for their wives. "Women have to slip quietly back into their traditional role," explains sociologist Monica Gendreau Maurer of the Latin American University in Puebla, Mexico (Tayler, 2001, p. A12). In some cases young women are the ones who migrate, leaving their families behind. When the first factories were built in the border region, people expected that they would employ men, but in fact, almost the only people hired were women, especially young women between the ages of 16 and 24. Young women come to Juárez, or other border cities, and suddenly find themselves freed from family control. *Maquila* cities have huge numbers of bars and dance halls, filled on weekend nights with groups of girls who arrive together and pay their own way. The clubs even feature male strippers. There are also many more female-headed families in the border cities, and more women who must fend for themselves without family or the other networks of village life to watch over them and back them up (Quinones, 2001, pp. 139–149).

Today in Mexico, more women are working for wages outside their homes. In 2004, 40% of Mexican women were in the labor force, double the percentage in 1970. See Table 1.5, p. 41. Women are also having fewer children. Obviously these two big changes are related in complex ways. Both changes may be a response to Mexico's economic problems, as families try to make ends meet. But it is also true that when women have fewer children they are freer to work, and conversely, when women work, they are likely to have fewer children. In 1967, Mexican women bore an average of 6.8 children in their lifetimes. By 1980, it had fallen to 4.6, and by 2004, this **total fertility rate** was down to 2.5. Falling fertility rates are reflected in smaller household sizes (United Nations, 2004b; U.S. Bureau of the Census, 2000b). See also Table 1.2, p. 18.

Changing Roles for Men.   If women can work, support themselves, or leave their husbands, then men's roles must also change. Matthew Gutmann documents the positive side of this change and Sam Quinones, the negative side. In his 1996 book *The Meaning of Macho: Being a Man in Mexico City,* Gutmann found Mexican men playing more companionate roles in their marriages, spending more time at home with their wives, and even discussing child care. He could find no case among ordinary working Mexicans of the legendary philandering *macho,* supporting a mistress on the side. Robert Fox and Pedro Solis-Camara found Mexican men as involved in child care as their American counterparts (Fox & Camara, 1997, pp. 489–495).

Though it is becoming more acceptable for the husbands of working women to "help out" at home, both men and women speak of it as helping out. The belief that the home is primarily the woman's responsibility is unchanged in Mexico. But when men help, especially with child care, they learn how much work it is, and it makes them think differently about how many children they want and whether use of contraceptives is acceptable to them.

Quinones (2001) describes husbands in Juárez who have become newly dependent on their wives and are angry and resentful about it: "*Maquiladoras* . . . created a new Mexican woman," Quinones says, "but this same process did not create a new man." Community activists in Juárez talk about men from rural areas who are used to controlling women. But when their wives get work in the maquiladoras, those women become more independent, talk back to their husbands, and socialize with coworkers, including men. Some men respond with violence, beating or even killing their wives (pp. 144–145; see also Shorris, 2004, pp. 535–536).

Mexican Political Institutions: Order and Conflict

Every society develops some means to maintain order, protect the members of the society from outside threats, control crime, and resolve conflicts among different groups. All modern societies have separate political institutions that exist to serve these functions: governments, political parties, the military, and legal institutions.

Mexico's political institutions are in transition. For years, Mexico was ruled by the PRI in a one-party patronage system, which imposed order on Mexican society, but at a cost. The PRI has been losing power since the start of the 21st century. As a result, Mexico's political institutions have become more democratic, but also more conflict-ridden and disorderly.

How the PRI Imposed Order

Until very recently, Mexico was really a **single-party system.** The PRI was a "big tent" party that worked to include everyone: Farmers, factory workers, small business-men, white-collar workers, and so on all found their place within the PRI. The PRI organized them all in confederations under its wings. These groups made the PRI a powerful machine for getting votes and channeling benefits (Riding, 1985, pp. 53–55). The party became the **patron** of all its subsidiary groups, and in exchange, all the **clients** acknowledged the supremacy of the party and accepted its choice of president. The PRI's success was based on its ability to deliver real benefits to Mexicans in exchange for their political loyalties.

One reason why the PRI was so successful is that it was firmly based in Mexican culture and social structure. The party was a hierarchical network of patron–client relationships, based on personal favors, gratitude, and personal loyalty. Sociologists and political scientists call this way of running a government **patronage politics.** Patronage politics is highly developed in Mexico, but it is found in many other societies too.

The system took shape under President Lázaro Cárdenas, who is remembered with gratitude to this day. Cárdenas began by organizing Mexican peasants into their own federations under the PRI. Between 1934 and 1940 Cárdenas redistrib-uted 46 million acres of land, formerly held in large estates, creating more than 180,000 ejidos (tracts of land held communally by villages, which could be inher-ited but not sold), farmed by 750,000 families. Peasants received land and vital loans from state banks to buy seeds and equipment. The government invested in rural development—road construction, power lines, wells, health clinics, and schools—that benefited peasants and also created jobs for construction workers, teachers, health care workers, and government bureaucrats. The PRI organized these workers into party-affiliated unions and professional organizations. Then these groups received wage increases, benefits, and also access to jobs in industries newly taken over by the state, like the railroads, the oil industry, and as time went by, thousands of smaller state companies as well. But people who didn't join and support the PRI were cut off from benefits.

Don Miguel's Story: The Patron

Don Miguel is a PRI jefe (or boss). He is the president of the Citizens Action Committee of Colonia "Lázaro Cárdenas," a newly settled colonia populare (or squatter neighborhood) on the outskirts of Oaxaca. Five years ago, Don Miguel got involved with his neighbors in order to build a much-needed school. To his own astonishment, he found he had a talent for organizing and leading people. With Don Miguel as president, the Citizens Action Committee collected signatures on petitions, visited the mayor's office, and searched for every possible personal connection to officials of the city government. Demonstrations in front of city hall finally culminated in a memorable visit by the mayor to the colonia, when he promised to provide sewer service. By the time the bulldozers arrived, Don Miguel found he had a new profession. Residents of the colonia came to him with all sorts of problems: This one's brother needed a job; that one's son was brilliant, but needed a scholarship; that one's mother was senile and kept wandering off and getting lost. As he got to know the officials at city hall better, Don Miguel found he could get help for some of his neighbors. They looked up to him as a kind of protector, a patron, and they willingly gave 5 pesos a month per family to finance the Citizens Action Committee. In turn, Don Miguel felt grateful and loyal to the mayor and the other PRI officials for their help. When they asked him to bring his people to a campaign rally in Oaxaca to cheer the mayor and the PRI, he was glad to do it, and his neighbors were happy to come to show their gratitude and loyalty to him. The PRI even served them all a free lunch when they arrived.

Although the citizens of Lázaro Cárdenas know, in an abstract way, that the city is obliged to provide sewer service, they haven't demanded it with a feeling of entitlement. Rather, they believe that it is their personal relationship with a patron, Don Miguel, and his relationship with his patron, the mayor, which made the sewers possible.

Social Mobility and the PRI.   Ambitious Mexicans often thanked the PRI for providing them with opportunities for **upward social mobility** (movement to a higher social rank or position). Like a good patron, the PRI "sponsored" the rise of politically talented individuals up the ladder of power. It was possible to become active in your local union or *ejido* or student group and then, supported by the power of the organization you controlled, to be tapped by the party for higher positions. Sociologists call this pattern of improving your social position **sponsored mobility.** In this way, some people who came from quite poor origins ended up in congress or in high government positions (Riding, 1985, p. 75). At the same time, the PRI created networks that linked together potentially opposed groups, granting benefits to each and absorbing into itself the natural leadership of each group.

What Price Stability?

If you are thinking that this political system sounds too good to be true, you are right. There is a substantial downside to a one-party patronage machine. Because for so long the PRI was in effect identical with the Mexican government, certain kinds of abuses of power readily occurred.

Co-optation and Repression.   Faced with any new organization, like a newly settled community, or a new union, the PRI/Mexican government followed a consistent policy. When local authorities judged the new group and its leaders willing to play the game, the organization was **co-opted**—that is, it was given some benefits, allowed to achieve some of its goals in return for becoming a loyal part of the PRI. Leaders could be co-opted personally with recognition and paid positions. But organizations with interests and goals that conflicted with those of the PRI, or organizations bent on achieving power independent of the PRI, were ruthlessly repressed. Because the PRI and the government were identical, it was an easy matter for the party to call out soldiers to bulldoze the too-independent shantytown, or police to crush the too-radical union.

Fixed Elections. In theory, the PRI gave representation to all groups through its subsidiary organizations. But in fact, this system was a far cry from representative democracy. Power was held by a hierarchy of bosses: union chiefs, or local leaders who were appointed by those above. Election was a mere formality. Even the president was essentially appointed (by his outgoing predecessor); the election just legitimated his selection. Basically, Mexican elected officials were accountable to the patrons who appointed them, not the people they represented (Cornelius & Craig, 1991, p. 25).

The PRI, as the governing party, organized all the elections held between 1929 and 2000. In national as well as in local elections, the PRI won through fraud, stuffing ballot boxes, destroying ballots, buying votes, and intimidating voters. Also, the PRI siphoned money from the public treasury to finance its party operations. It used government resources for party business, for example assigning public officials to run party election campaigns and using government cars and trucks to carry supporters to rallies. The PRI's subsidiary organizations also misused funds. In 2002 allegations surfaced that officials of the state-owned oil company, PEMEX, and the leaders of the oil-workers union had jointly siphoned $100 million out of union funds. The money was given to the PRI and used in the 2000 presidential campaign (Thompson, 2002a, p. A6).

Corruption. The practice of patronage, combined with the *sexenio,* the single 6-year presidential term of office for the president and legislators, fostered corruption in Mexico. Every high-level PRI politician had his following of loyal clients, who helped him rise. When a politician was elected, his patronage network struck it rich. Every client could expect a government job, or perhaps a government contract, an import license, sewers and streetlights for the community, or other government funds, a portion of which found their way into the private wealth of the client. But the largesse lasted only 6 years, after which another politician and other clients took over. The temptation to line one's pockets as fast as possible usually proved irresistible. Corruption filtered down to lower civil servants, police, judges, businesspeople, and the media.

Today's Political Parties: Conflict and Competition

Social institutions are crucially important building blocks of every society. It is not easy to change institutions, and when they do change, disruption and reorganization spread widely through the society. The PRI's hold on Mexican political institutions was so firm and lasted so long that no one believed the party could be dislodged. But the PRI lost its domination in 2000. It lost the presidency, a major blow, and it lost its majority in congress. Today, Mexico is much more democratic than in the past because there is competition among the three major political parties. The press is freer than it was during PRI rule and elections are cleaner. Nevertheless, it is not entirely clear whether a system of competition between parties will be institutionalized in Mexico or whether competition will deteriorate into open conflict.

The PAN and the PRD represent clearly opposed political philosophies. The PAN is a socially conservative party that speaks for business, and it is popular in the north. It favors limited government, free trade, and foreign investment, and it opposes unionization, increased environmental regulation, and abortion. The PRD is a Latin American–style party of the left. It speaks for peasants and poor city residents, primarily in the south. The PRD supports tariff protection to help small farmers and calls for redistribution of more land to peasants. It is in favor of increased government help for the poor and higher taxes on the rich. It opposes private investment in Mexico's government-owned oil and gas industry.

The PRI has the potential to become a centrist party, between the extremes of right and left, of the PAN and the PRD, but its policies are a contradictory mix. It favors free trade, but also advocates government spending to help the poor, largely through the sort of patronage programs that have supported its power in the past. The PRI is divided between two factions. The "technocrats" are the younger, mostly U.S.-educated leaders. They are opposed by the "dinosaurs," the old-style operators of the political machine.

By the 2000 presidential election many Mexicans had lost faith in the PRI as a governing party. They were cynical about the honesty of elections and the effectiveness of the government. Then-president Ernesto Zedillo, a PRI "technocrat," opened the way to free election with the appointment of an autonomous agency, the Federal Elections Institute, with a budget of $918 million to prevent fraud and ensure an honest vote count. There were new voting booths, with curtains to ensure privacy, citizens selected at random to be pollwatchers, and a computerized vote-reporting system to ensure that results were posted on the Internet before tampering could occur. The government issued costly new photo-ID voter registration cards and compiled more accurate voting lists. Foreign observers monitored the vote (Dillon, 2000, p. A3; Dillon & Preston, 2000, pp. A1, A4).

The PAN candidate, Vicente Fox was elected president. He was the first non-PRI head of government in 70 years. The old system of "presidentialism," in which the president had almost unlimited personal power and was immune to justice, came to an end. The president now no longer dominates his party or congress. He no longer can use government funds as personal assets, nor can he order electoral fraud (Dominguez & McCann, 1996, pp. 14–15; Krause, 1987, 2004, p. A23).

The Fragility of Democracy

The 2000 election accomplished wonderful changes, but it didn't create effective government. By law, it takes the votes of two thirds of the members of congress to pass a bill. None of the three parties controls that many representatives, and as a result, President Fox was unsuccessful in enacting his legislative agenda. In 2006, the three major parties were once again positioned in a major struggle for power. Could the new system of multiparty competition survive? Would the PAN be willing to give up the presidency if it lost the election? Would the PRI be able to reestablish its old dominance?

The 2006 Election.   One of the most important features of democracy is a peaceful alternation of parties in power. Individuals and parties defeated in elections are willing to accept the election results and acknowledge the **legitimacy** of the winner. Many countries that have elections don't have democracy because elections are rigged, or because the military steps in to install its own choice of rulers. Does this happen in your society?

In Mexico, the 2006 election was a long-running drama of accusations and counteraccusations in which the PRD and the PAN, the main contenders for the presidency, challenged the legitimacy of each others' candidates. As early as 2004, when the PRD candidate Andres Manuel López Obrador, the mayor of Mexico City, seemed to be the front-running candidate, a series of highly publicized charges against him threatened to remove him from the race. The PAN and PRI joined in congress to try to impeach him as mayor and bar him from running. Luckily, this setback to orderly elections was unsuccessful. In the election, Obrador began in the lead, Felipe Calderón, the PAN candidate, gained on him, and Roberto Madrazo, the PRI candidate, trailed behind. It was an exceptionally dirty and polarizing campaign.

In the end Calderón won by the slimmest of margins—barely 240,000 votes (0.6%) and Obrador refused to accept the legitimacy of the election. He rallied his supporters to months of mass demonstrations. They blockaded the capital's main roads and accused the PAN of electoral fraud, even after the federal electoral court declared Calderón the winner. Before Calderón was sworn in as president on December 1, 2006, PAN and PRD representatives scuffled to control the dias and fistfights and catcalls broke out. Calderón had to be led in by bodyguards and inaugurated in a hurried 4-minute ceremony.

A Year Later. When the dust settled, President Calderón set himself to establishing legitimacy by patiently negotiating his agenda through congress. The PAN controlled a plurality of legislative seats, but not enough to do without coalitions. The PRD had the next largest block of seats. The PRI, although a minority in congress, still controlled 17 of 32 state governorships, many more than any other party, and many local governments too. By July 2007, Calderón's approval rating in polls was up to 65%. Democracy in Mexico had proved fragile, but not hopeless.

The Threat of Insurgency

Insurgent groups are social movements that reject participation in the political institutions of their society as a means to achieve their goals. Several more or less violent insurgencies have been active in Mexico in recent years. None of them has been powerful enough to be a real threat to Mexico's institutions of democracy, but all receive a lot of publicity and exert a kind of romantic attraction for Mexicans recalling their daring revolutionary history.

The Zapatista Rebels. The Zapatista National Liberation Army, a peasant revolutionary movement in the state of Chiapas, took the nation by surprise in 1994. It seized the major city of Chiapas, San Cristóbal de las Casas, and several other villages and towns, installing its own government, courts, and jails. In at least a dozen other towns, peasants took over their town halls and demanded the removal of local (PRI-selected) authorities. The Zapatistas demanded honest elections, redistribution of land, better treatment of Indians, and government development aid.

The Indian Zapatistas reminded Mexicans of the revolutionary heritage and their national hero, Emiliano Zapata, peasant leader of the 1910 revolution. Their masked leader "Subcommandante Marcos" (said to be actually a former college professor) captured Mexicans' affections with his clever manifestos and good humor. He was treated as a celebrity and public concern kept the government from using the military to wipe out the rebels. The Zapatistas keep much of the territory they took over, while the military stands at the ready without attacking. The government has invested in local schools and antipoverty programs, but resists giving Indian communities more official autonomy. Marcos remains a public figure, appearing in his mask on television and attracting large crowds when he speaks around the country, trying to organize what he says will be a nonviolent movement free of the corruption of other Mexican political parties (McKinley, 2006a, p. A4).

Insurrection in Oaxaca.   Studying Mexico's insurgencies sociologically we can see that these movements have several characteristic features. Insurgencies generally develop in states with large, poor, Indian populations, especially those with old-fashioned, corrupt, PRI governments, and they often have some middle-class leadership. A recent, violent protest movement in the city of Oaxaca illustrates these patterns.

The conflict in Oaxaca in 2006 grew out of a routine teachers' strike, into a "low-intensity urban war," with thousands of protesters occupying the main square, several radio stations, and public offices. The protesters belonged to a new organization, the Popular Assembly of the People of Oaxaca, a combination of more than 100 community and political groups, some from the far left, but others pushed into action when police, sent by the state governor, Ulises Ruiz, attacked and beat strikers. The protesters demanded the resignation of Governor Ruiz, who is an old-style PRI authoritarian and whose election in 2004 was widely believed to be fraudulent (*The Economist,* 2006c, p. 48). The occupation of the town was finally ended by heavily armed federal soldiers, with water cannons and helicopters, who cleared the main square and arrested protesters. At least 13 people had been killed by the end of the conflict. The governor remained in office.

The Popular Revolutionary Army.   This Marxist group, which formed in Guerrero state, emerged from obscurity in 2007 when it blew up natural gas pipelines belonging to Pemex, Mexico's state oil company, three times in 3 months. The group has a history of financing its operations by kidnapping people for ransom, raising millions of dollars in 88 kidnappings since 1999. They have kidnapped businessmen, police, even relatives of big drug dealers. Mexicans speculate that the bombing were a response to the federal crackdown on the protests in Oaxaca and to the defeat of PRD candidate Lopez Obradór in the presidential elections. The revolutionary group is small, perhaps no more than 100 people, based in the slums of Mexico City (McKinley & Betancourt, 2007, p. A3).

CONFLICT AND DEVIANCE

Every society experiences deviance, though the amount of deviance, the forms it takes, and its causes vary greatly. In Mexico there is a great deal of deviance that is criminal in nature, and deviance is very much a political issue. Deviance not only reflects conflicts and divisions within Mexican society, it adds to them by undermining faith in the government's ability to fulfill its primary purpose: to protect the people.

Drug Trafficking and Ineffective Social Controls

Have you ever lived in a neighborhood or town where there was a lot of illegal drug dealing? If so, you will understand how much drug trafficking increases crime. Dealers fight over turf and commit assaults and murders. Drug addicts feed their habits with holdups and thefts. And the gangs that transport the drugs corrupt police and courts and border agents with bribes. All this and more has taken place in Mexico, starting in the 1990s, as Mexico became a major route for the transport of cocaine from Colombia to the United States, and more recently a center for the manufacture of heroin and methamphetamines.

About 90% of the cocaine used in the United States now goes by ship to Mexico and from there is smuggled across the border. That's between 500 and 700 tons of cocaine a year. In October 2007, law enforcement agents made their largest seizure ever of cocaine: 23 tons, with a street value $2.7 billion, found on a ship that arrived from Colombia. This may be a sign of progress in Mexico's war against drug traffickers, but it also shows how far authorities still have to go. Also in 2007, Mexico took steps to extradite the former governor of Quintana Roo state to the United States, where he was wanted on drug chargers. He was accused of taking millions of dollars in payoffs from the Juarez drug cartel, $500,000 for each shipment of the 200 tons of cocaine that he stored and sent on its way. A decade ago, drug addiction was rare in Mexico, but today the drug cartels have begun local sales of cheap, highly addictive drugs like crack cocaine and methamphetamine (McKinley, 2007c, p. A6; 2007e, p. A1; 2007h, p. A10).

Mexicans believe that when it comes to crime and punishment, the whole system is a mess. Crime rates are rising, but many police seem to be implicated in the crime, not controlling it. In 2005, Mexico's government was forced to send troops to take over control of three major high-security prisons from wealthy drug dealer inmates who had bribed wardens and guards to let them bring guns into the prisons and run their gangs from jail. One drug lord had an enemy assassinated in the visiting room of the prison.

A remarkable symbol of the ties between police and drug gangs is Sandra Avila Beltrán, the niece of two major drug smugglers who was married to the commander of the federal police in Sinaloa (before he was assassinated) and later to the commander of the National Institute for the Combat Against Drugs (before his murder). Her last partner before her arrest was the infamous Colombian trafficker Juan Diego Espinosa (McKinley, 2007g, p. A3).

Even aside from police corruption, the criminal justice system is almost ludicrously disorganized and ineffective. The central part of Mexico City has about 8 million people, about the same number as metropolitan New York City, but it has only one third as many police, divided into three poorly coordinated forces. The SSP (the Ministry for Public Security) can only patrol to prevent crime; it cannot investigate or prosecute it. That function belongs to the PGR (the Prosecutor-General's Office).

Then there is the federal police force and several special police forces devoted to the drug trade. Police are poorly paid and poorly trained. Mexican experts estimate that only 20 in 100 crimes are reported to the police. In Oaxaca only 4 or 5 of those 20 are actually investigated and of those, more than three quarters are never solved. Prosecutors usually follow up minor crimes and crimes in which the perpetrator was caught in the act. The poor go to jail, while well-connected professional criminals go free (*The Economist,* 2005b, p. 45).

Felipe Calderón began his presidency in 2006 with a major assault on drug trafficking. Calderón's government had some success in extraditing major leaders of drug cartels to the United States for prosecution, and the price of cocaine rose in the United States. But with the kingpins removed, a bloody turf war broke out between rival splinter gangs. There were 2,200 drug-related murders in 2006, up from 1,600 in 2005, and more than 1,200 in the first half of 2007, including 60 police commanders, 22 soldiers, and 160 police officers. The brutality of attacks was unprecedented, with two dozen beheadings, a raid on a local police station with grenades and machine guns, and kidnappings and murders of top law officers. By early 2008 Calderón had ordered a major intervention of federal troops into the cities where drugs cross the border. Thousands of army troops are involved (6,000 in the state of Tamaulipas alone), with jeeps and machine guns, and navy fight jets flying reconnaissance missions. The troops are battling drug cartel members armed with rocket-propelled-grenade launchers. They search out cartel leaders, the cartel guards called *Zetas* (who were originally army commandos trained by the United States), and the local police, who protect the cartels in exchange for bribes. This is the biggest effort yet by the government to bring the drug cartels under control and restore law and order, but it is by no means clear the campaign will succeed. Some people find the violence worse than the drug trade and others are upset that gun battles have frightened away the American tourists they depend on economically (*The Economist,* 2007a, p. 33; 2007b, p. 45; McKinley, 2006e, p. A1; 2007f, p. A20; 2008a, pp. A1, A9).

In a bizarre and puzzling accompaniment to drug gang violence, in the past year and a half there has been a series of murders of Mexico's country music stars. Thirteen have been murdered, many in shocking, grisly ways. Sergio Gómez was kidnapped, tortured, and strangled in December 2007. Some musicians seem to have had ties to drug gangs. Others composed popular ballads known as *narcocorridos,* which idealized the world of drug dealing. In still other cases no one has been able to establish how the singer angered his gang killers (McKinley, 2007i, pp. A1, A20). All this unchecked crime and violence has undercut what little confidence Mexicans have left in their criminal justice system. Also, it has become clear to criminals that if you commit a crime you have a very good chance of getting away with it. Ineffective sanctions result in increased deviance.

Murder and the Breakdown of Social Organization

As many as 400 women have been murdered in the industrial border city of Juarez since 1993, many of them raped, some mutilated, their bodies dumped in ditches or in the desert. Most of the victims have been young, between 15 and 25 years old. They were poor and relatively dark skinned: students, store clerks, and many, many *maquiladora* workers. Officials say that at least 100 of them were victims of serial killers, but that more than one killer is involved. Very few of the killings have been solved. The police have arrested several suspects, each time declaring the crime wave at an end, only to see the murders resume while the suspect was in jail. Several suspects made false confessions under torture. In fact, only half the bodies have been identified, and there are no missing persons reports or descriptions to match up with the unidentified women.

What is going on? We probably need to investigate many factors to understand the unsolved murders, including police incompetence and male rage over the displacement of male workers by women. But one factor that stands out is the changes in the city of Juarez. Women have come to Juarez from all over Mexico, many without their families. The population of the city has grown rapidly, from 407,000 inhabitants in 1970, to probably 1.5 million today. Thousands of people arrive and depart every day, on their way to the United States, on their way back home to their villages. But the social organization of the city has failed to keep up with its rapid growth. The business district of the city is safe and modern, filled with industrial parks, shopping malls, and gated housing developments for managers. The rest of the city is shantytowns spread out into the desert, without water or sewers, lighting, or paved streets. There are no street addresses. Five different gangs battle for control of the streets (*The Economist*, 2005a, p. 37).

The poor parts of Juarez have the kind of anonymity that goes with a new city. Not only is there a lack of formal government, family networks have not yet developed and neighborhood organization is just beginning. Many of the murdered women were unknown to their neighbors, and their families back home had lost touch with them or assumed they were in the United States. Lack of social organization means there are fewer informal controls on crime (Guillermoprieto, 2003; Navarro, 2002, p. B3; Quinones, 2001, pp. 139–148; Thompson, 2002e, p. A20).

Kidnapping and Social Strain

There were 732 kidnappings for ransom officially reported in Mexico in 2001— 197 in Mexico City alone in 2004; but because so many others went unreported, the real total was probably five times as large. In 2005 the famous soccer coach Rubén Omar Romaro was abducted. Most kidnapping victims are wealthy businessmen or their relatives, targeted for multimillion-dollar ransoms. Recently, more middle-class people have been kidnapped for ransoms of "only" around $100,000. And then there are the "express kidnappings" in which people are grabbed and forced, over a period of hours or days, to use their ATM cards to empty their bank accounts. The number of kidnappings rose rapidly after the serious economic recession of 1995. In 2005 there was an outbreak of kidnapping of Mexicans and visiting Americans in the cities along the border with Texas. Often the kidnappings are done by city police officers who are working for local drug gangs that have gone into the business of kidnapping for ransom.

It makes sense to look at a great deal of the crime and corruption in Mexico in the context of Merton's social strain theory of deviance (see p. 34). When Mexicans cannot achieve a widely accepted goal like making money in a legal, conformist way, some people (but by no means all) engage in **innovative deviance.** They find deviant means of achieving conformist ends. Police officers, who make as little as $250 a month, find ways to supplement their salaries. These range from the familiar small bribes to major and disruptive acts of deviance. Some police rent out their uniforms and badges to con men, called godmothers. Other Mexicans turn to car theft, picking pockets, and petty theft: such crimes all abound. In 2006 there was a wave of thefts of colonial era religious art from churches. Recently, many kidnappings have turned more violent, with female victims raped and male victims beaten and mutilated, ears cut off and sent to relatives. Some speculate that this reveals an edge of class hatred, born of economic hard times (*The Economist,* 2004; Malkin, 2006, p. E3).

Issues concerning inequality come up repeatedly in discussing deviance in Mexico: Some poor Mexicans resort to crime as a means to escape poverty. Relatives of the young women murdered in Juárez charge that the police are uninterested in solving crimes against poor people. Drug trafficking ends up enriching corrupt, high-level officials, while street dealers are jailed, killed, or sometimes addicted. It is clear that in order to really understand Mexican society and analyze why it is so conflict-ridden, we need to know more about social inequality.

SOCIAL INEQUALITY AND CONFLICT

Sociologists who take the **conflict perspective** on deviance see inequalities of wealth and power as the most important characteristics of societies. Their perspective derives from Karl Marx, who studied European societies in the 19th century, at a time when there were very deep inequalities between the rich and the poor, between those who owned the means of production and those who were obliged to sell their labor in order to survive. Marx predicted that this **class conflict** would dominate capitalist societies. He predicted it would be manifested in the criminal system being used as a means of oppression against the poor, in workers organizing and striking against business owners, in labor parties contesting elections against parties of the wealthy, and even in revolutionary movements leading insurrections against the government. How much of the conflict that we see in Mexican society today is the product of social inequality? How deep are the inequalities in Mexican society?

To begin, we need to ask, what do sociologists mean when they say that a given society has deep inequalities, or that another is relatively egalitarian? How do we judge the extent of inequality in a society or compare the amount of inequality in different societies? In every society there are scarce resources that are distributed unequally: Some people receive more and others less. Sociologists usually point to three categories of scarce goods: **power, prestige,** and **wealth.** Then, in examining any society, they ask who, which groups or categories of people, has more or less power, prestige, or wealth.

In every society there is some degree of inequality between men and women. (We call this **gender inequality.**) We have seen how in Mexican society women are often economically dependent on men and defer to their husbands and fathers. In Mexican society (and in many other societies) there are also **racial inequalities** in which some races (or ethnic groups) enjoy higher status than others, more wealth, and more power over other races. Finally, in Mexico, as in many other societies, we can distinguish distinct groups or **strata** (layers) of the population whose access to power, prestige, and wealth differs because they start out with different economic resources. We call these groups **social classes** and this kind of inequality **class inequality.**

Two Mexicos

Mexican society has long been deeply divided by social class, and other divisions in Mexican society tend to be associated with class divisions. First of all, there is an increasing gap between the northern and southern regions of the country. In the industrialized north, average incomes are higher, the economy is growing faster, and voters lean toward the PAN, the conservative, business-oriented party. The southern states are mostly agricultural and poor. Growth is slow there, and many voters support the PRD, the left-leaning party. Many insurgent movements have their roots in the south. Agriculture is different in the two regions. In the north modern commercial farms produce for export, while in the south most farms are small or part of *ejidos* or cooperatives and farmers produce food mostly for their own consumption (McKinley, 2006d, p. WK3).

Significantly, southern states have much bigger Indian populations than northern states. Although Mexico collects no statistics about race, data are available about people who speak Indian languages. There are at least 7 million people (or 8% of the population) who speak 55 different Indian languages and dialects. Indians are much more likely than non-Indians to live in rural areas, and they are more likely than other Mexicans to be self-employed peasant farmers. They are also much poorer than other Mexicans. Of Indians living in Indian counties 77% earn less than the minimum wage (compared to 27% of all Mexicans). Half live in houses without electricity, 90% have no indoor plumbing, and 45% are illiterate (Ethnologue, n.d., Russell, 1994, pp. 125–128).

Class Inequality in Mexican Society

Our picture of a divided Mexico is broadly accurate, but how can we make it more exact? We can start with two relatively simple comparisons. First, we can ask, do most people in this society make pretty much the same amount of money? Are there just a handful of rich people and a sprinkling of poor people, with everyone else clustered in the middle? Or are people spread out over the whole range of incomes? Second, we can ask, how big is that range from the richest to the poorest? Do the richest people receive double the share of total income that the poorest receive? Ten times as much? One hundred times as much? These are questions about **income distribution.**

When we measure income distribution we divide a society's population into five equal-sized groups, called **income fifths,** or **quintiles;** the 20% who are the top income earners, the 20% who are the bottom income earners, and each of the three

Members of an Indian family at an outdoor market in Chiapas State
all wear the same serapes, woven at home. Each Indian village has
its own traditional woven pattern. For this family, the local market is
their point of contact with the market economy. They have no cell
phone, computer, or television, no access to big box stores, and little
cash income. They raise food mostly for their own consumption and
sell some extra produce at the market.

fifths in the middle. Then we ask, what percentage of the total income earned by
everyone goes to the richest fifth? The poorest fifth, and soon?

In Mexico in 2004, the richest fifth received 55% of the total income earned by
everyone and the poorest fifth received only 3.9%. That means the richest fifth
received 14 times as much income as the poorest fifth. Compare this to Germany,
where the richest fifth received only about 5 times as much income as the poorest
fifth. Mexico's income distribution is similar to that of the United States, where the
richest fifth received 49.9% of the income and had earnings 14.7 times as big as the
poorest fifth. See Table 1.6, p. 49.

Comparing the richest fifth with the poorest fifth tells us a lot about class
inequality, but it may also leave you with many questions. How poor are the poor in
Mexico? How rich are the rich? Are all the poor people in Mexico in the poorest fifth
of the population, or is the next poorest fifth almost as poor as the bottom fifth?
These are important questions that we can better answer by examining social classes.

Social Classes in Mexico

When we study **social classes** we are looking at unequal-sized groups with very different amounts of income, wealth, prestige, and power. In some societies the lowest class is very small and most people are in the middle class. Is your society like this? Mexico is not: The lower class is the largest class in Mexico. A huge percentage of Mexico's population is poor; in fact, about half the people live on less than the equivalent of $4 a day. The upper class is tiny. Sociologist James W. Russell (1994) estimates it at less than 1% of the population (p. 69). Some writers call the rest of the population "the middle class," but it isn't really. This half includes a wide range of people, from blue-collar workers, farmers, and self-employed people to small business owners, privileged bureaucrats, managers, and well-paid professionals. We might realistically say that about 30% of the population is **working class** and perhaps 20% is **middle class.**

One other thing you must know about class inequality in Mexican society is that the distribution of income is changing and becoming more equal. In 2000, the richest 20% of Mexicans received 19 times the income of the poorest 20%. In 2004 that figure was "only" 14 times. In contrast, in the United States the comparable figures for 2000 and 2006 are 8.48 times and 14.7 times. You may be asking yourself how that can be, how income distribution can change. Let's examine each of Mexico's social classes in turn and see how they are faring.

Two men at a café in the city of Oaxaca are at home in affluent modern surroundings. If you didn't know this photo was taken in Oaxaca you might think it was Barcelona or Rome or Paris. Although some Mexicans are as wealthy as Europeans, with sophisticated, cosmopolitan lives to match their assets, others live in a rural poverty that has changed little since the 19th century.

The Upper Class

Don't feel sorry for upper-class Mexicans! Their share of total income has declined from 59% in 2000 to 55% in 2004, but that is still a very large share. And the incomes and wealth of the very richest Mexicans are rising.

Carlos Slim Helú is not only the richest man in Mexico, he is the richest man in the world! In 2007 he pulled ahead of Bill Gates, with a fortune of $59 billion. There are nine other Mexicans who also number among the world's 946 billionaires. Carlos Slim may be the most powerful man in Mexico, too. His family controls Telmex, Mexico's phone monopoly, as well as the largest cell phone company in Latin America. His family also owns the Mexican Sears, as well as other retail and industrial companies, including shopping centers, railroads, mines, cigarette companies, and construction firms, together earning $8.5 billion in 2007. His cell phone and telephone companies earned $37 billion that year (Porter, 2007, p. A20).

Slim's rise to wealth and power began during the late 1980s privatization of government-owned businesses. Then-president Carlos Salinas de Gortari sold Mexico's national phone company to his friend Slim and for years kept Telmex's monopoly in place. Salinas also awarded Telmex the only national cell phone license. The 96 government-owned companies that were privatized between 1982 and 1991 were sold to only 17 individuals and businesses, many of them friends of government leaders, and the prices they paid were rather low (Rothstein, 2007, p. 35).

Most upper-class Mexicans are not as wealthy as Slim, but they have sufficient money to live like the wealthy of rich Western societies, with cars, vacations abroad, designer clothes, and investments in foreign real estate. They think of themselves as an elite group and many of them share a common social life, living in the same neighborhoods, socializing at the same private clubs, sending their children to the same private schools, and marrying within their class. Many upper-middle-class Mexicans—lawyers, architects, real estate brokers, car dealers, owners of expensive boutiques—make their living entirely by serving upper-class Mexicans. See Table 2.2, p. 107 .

Ana María Dominguez Castañeda's Story

Ana María lives in Dallas, Texas, with her son Jorge, who attends a local private school. Her husband lives mostly at the family home in Mexico City, where he works, but he visits his family often in Dallas. Ana says she'd rather not live in Mexico City because it is so dangerous. She has to take her son to school there in an armor-plated car with an armed driver for fear he will be kidnapped for ransom. She can't even wear her jewelry or go to a good restaurant because she might be robbed. In Dallas she lives in a $1.6 million luxury home in a gated golf community with high walls, a staffed entrance, and patrol cars. Many other wealthy Mexican families live in the same community.

Ana María lives in Dallas legally, of course. She has a special business visa issued to Mexicans who are making a sizeable investment in a business in the United States, or whose Mexican companies do business in the United States. About 70,000 such visas are issued a year. Ana María owns an art gallery in Dallas, and her husband, who works for Pemex, makes frequent business trips to Texas. (Some information for this vignette came from Meyer, 2007, p. BU 19)

TABLE 2.2 Inequalities in Pay and Income (2002–2006)

Average annual income in Mexico is much lower than in Japan, but executive pay is similar.

	Average Income ($)	Average Pay and Benefits for CEOs of Top Companies ($)	For Every $100 the Average Person Takes Home, Top CEOs Take Home ($)
Mexico	7,870	369,890	4,700
Germany	36,620	439,440	1,200
Japan	38,410	422,510	1,100
United States	44,970	21,360,750	47,500

Sources: Public Broadcasting System, *NOW with David Brancaccio*, Executive Excess, April 12, 2002, http://www.pbs.org/now/politics/executive.html; World Bank, *World Development Indicators 2006*, 2006, http://web.worldbank.org.

The Middle Class

Middle class in Mexico is an elusive term. Some people, like teachers, have professions usually considered middle class, but in Mexico they are paid so little that in terms of their income they are poor. Other Mexicans own businesses, but their businesses are so small that they have no employees and their earnings don't keep them out of poverty. Nevertheless, about 40% of Mexican households have incomes between $7,200 and $50,000 a year. It might make more sense to call those at the lower end of this income range working class. But working class or middle class, this large group of Mexicans see themselves as much better off than the poor. Those who started in poverty justifiably feel proud of their achievements. In fact, Mexicans think of being middle class less in terms of income or occupation and more in terms of **assets** (what they own). Owning a home is a key marker of middle-class status. So is owning a car and other durable consumer goods like a big television or a computer. Finally, middle-class and aspiring parents are willing to spend a large portion of their income to send their children to college. They see a university degree as essential to ensure their children will be middle class, too (Smith, 2006, pp. 51–52).

The big news is that after years of stagnation Mexico's middle class is growing. One recent estimate is that about 1% of the population (about 100,000 people) has moved out of poverty each year since 2001 (Thompson, 2006b, p 8). That doesn't sound like much, but it adds up. And it stands in sharp contrast to the 1990s when a series of economic crises, with high inflation and high interest rates, made the middle class shrink. What has made current expansion of the middle class possible?

Part of the answer is economic growth. The economy is growing at a rate of 4–5% a year. In 2006, it created 900,000 new jobs and that, in combination with lower birthrates, meant that job growth kept up with the growth of the labor force. Some of the new jobs are in new industries or service businesses and with a stable economy some owners of tiny, informal enterprises have seen their business grow enough to support a middle-class life. Also, as more women go to work for wages outside their homes, that also helps family income grow.

A Larger Middle Class.   Some of the growth of the middle class results from financial innovation. It used to be very hard to get a mortgage in Mexico. People had to save up cash to buy a home. Now Mexican and foreign banks are competing to give mortgage loans. Storefront outlets offer mortgages, credit cards, auto loans, insurance policies: all the modern financial instruments that weren't available to ordinary people in the past. The government helped too, providing 3.5 million low-interest mortgages to public employees and others since 2000. Mexico is in the midst of a housing boom, with millions of people moving out of squatter settlements and into tracts of modest one- or two-family rowhouses. Education is expanding, too. University enrollment has doubled since 1990, with private universities, and especially foreign-based, for-profit technical colleges growing fastest (*The Economist,* 2007c, pp. 22–23; Smith, 2006, pp. 51–52; Thompson, 2006b, pp. 1, 8).

If Mexico can keep up this rate of growth, despite rising oil prices and threats of recession in the United States, it is likely the middle class will continue to grow. Right now, though, while poor people have more hope of escaping poverty, Mexico remains a deeply divided society, with half of its people in poverty.

Enrique and Elena Hernandez's Story

Enrique, 27, and Elena, 25, are jubilant. Today they are moving into their own home, a two-story concrete row house with two bedrooms in a newly built subdivision outside Mexico City. They have been living with Enrique's parents in their house in an informal settlement. Now the government's low-interest home loan program has helped them buy their own house. They will have clear title to the house and regular water, sewer, and electric service. It's only possible because Enrique "permits" Elena to work, as an aide in a public hospital. Her government job qualifies them for the loan, and her income, added to what Enrique makes as a billing clerk in an appliance store, let's them make their mortgage payments. Enrique's parents never had a mortgage. They squatted on the land and built their house themselves, concrete block by block over several decades. They used their income instead to pay tuition and school fees for Enrique so he could finish high school and study business and accounting at a private university.

Elena and Enrique were big supporters of President Fox and his PAN party, whose government created the home loan program, and they voted for Felipe Calderón in 2006. They are proud of themselves and of the government that made their upward mobility possible. The only problem, as Elena sees it, is how she will ever be able to stop working to have children.

The Lower Class

Mexico's **lower class** is enormous. In fact, a majority of Mexicans are lower class. In the past decade, their average incomes have improved a bit, but they are still poor. Mexico's government sets a **"poverty line"** to measure how many of its people are poor. The line is set at the equivalent of $4 a day per family member. By that standard about half of Mexican families (that's 50 million people out of 107 million Mexicans) fall below the poverty line. Between 15 and 20% of the poor live in "extreme poverty," lacking sufficient income to meet basic food needs. They cannot afford meat or milk and survive mostly on tortillas and beans. In early 2007, when the price of corn soared on the world market, there was a crisis in Mexico. The price of tortillas doubled (to 8 pesos or 75 cents a kilo) and thousands of Mexicans turned out to demonstrate in Mexico City's central square, women banging pots and pans on the iron fences in what was dubbed the "tortilla riots." Newly inaugurated President Calderón was booed and heckled as he traveled the country. He finally agreed to fix prices for tortillas and cornmeal, despite his devotion to free-market economics (*The Economist,* 2006d, p. 7; 2007c, p. 22; McKinley, 2006c, p. A8; 2007a, p. A12).

Absolute Poverty.   The bottom line for Mexican families is that, if they cannot somehow earn enough for necessities, they will simply have to do without. If they cannot afford rent, they will live in a shack in a squatter settlement, without electricity, running water, or sewage pipes. In 2004, a quarter of Mexicans had no toilet, not even a latrine. It is usual for the families of an apartment building or a squatter neighborhood to share a single water tap that runs continually. Often there is a rotating schedule for filling each family's containers at the tap: today your turn may come at 3 a.m. When you learn about the poorest Mexicans, the term **life chances** really becomes vivid. Lack of food results in malnutrition for children and mothers, weakening their health. The poorest Mexicans also lack access to good medical care, which results in high infant mortality rates. See Table 2.3.

How the Poor Make a Living

You have to admire the resourcefulness, tenacity, and hard work with which lower-class families struggle to put together sufficient income to survive. For most families, making ends meet requires several sources of income.

TABLE 2.3 Death and Disease (2000–2005)
The relative poverty of Mexico, Egypt, and Namibia is reflected in shorter lives and the deaths of mothers in childbirth.

	Number of Adults 15 and Over with HIV/ AIDS	Number of Mothers Dying in Childbirth for Each 100,000 Births	Women Not Expected to Survive to Age 65 (%)	Men Not Expected to Survive to Age 65 (%)	Number of Tuberculosis Cases per 100,000 Persons
Mexico	180,000	83	16	25	43
Egypt	5,000	84	21	31	35
Namibia	210,000	300	63	68	586
Germany	49,000	8	10	18	6
Japan	17,000	10	7	14	39
United States	1,200,000	17	13	21	4

Sources: United Nations Statistics Division, *Statistics and Indicators on Women and Men,* n.d., http://unstats.un.org/unsd/demographic/products/indwm/default.htm; United Nations, *Human Development Report 2006,* 2006, http://hdr.undp.org/hdr2006/statistics/indicators/.

If a family has more than one adult wage earner, a favored strategy is for one person to find a job for wages—in a factory, as a bus driver, or even as a teacher. Such jobs often pay no more than minimum wage, but they are desirable if they carry health benefits, pension, and access to other government subsidies. Other family members look for work in the **informal sector,** where there is a chance of earning more, but no benefits.

The Informal Sector.   One important difference between Mexico (and other "developing" nations) and the "developed" industrial nations is that most Mexicans lack "formal" paying jobs in business or government. Mexican economists estimate that only a little more than one fifth of the workforce of 50 million people has a job in the formal sector. Many of the rest are informally self-employed in tiny businesses that usually have no employees, or employ other family members working without wages. These businesses have no official licenses and pay no fees or taxes. Often people work for wages when they can, but if they are laid off they hustle work until they can find employment again (*The Economist,* 2005c, p 39).

There are few chain stores or chain restaurants in Mexico, but lots of "Mom and Pop" groceries and cafés. Outdoor markets are crowded with stalls selling fruit and candy, cooked food, appliances, new and used clothing, and anything else you might want. In sidewalk workshops people make and sell shoes; they print stationery and business cards; they sew dresses. On a busy street or square you can buy a song from a mariachi band, have your shoes shined, hire a child to watch your car, or watch a sword swallower or fire-eater who hopes for your tip. In Mexico City, 2,500 people work as garbage pickers, sorting through the city's huge garbage dump for recyclable materials to sell. (Incidentally, most of these informal sector occupations can't be adopted casually. The market or the street corner or the dump has its boss, and you must pay him or her for your spot. You will become his client and he will try to provide you some protection from shakedowns by police and competition from other peddlers.) Struggling for a livelihood, poor Mexicans find every possible niche in the economy.

Work in the Formal Sector.   About 11 million Mexicans work in "formal sector" jobs; for the government, or in businesses that are legally registered and pay taxes. After NAFTA—the free trade agreement between the United States, Canada, and Mexico—was signed in 1994, American companies flocked across the border setting up factories to manufacture clothing, appliances, television sets, and cars. Many of those manufacturers were later lured away by lower wages in China, so the number of manufacturing jobs in Mexico rose and then fell. Wages fell too, to an average of $2.50 an hour in 2004 (Uchitelle, 2007, p. WK4). But many Mexicans, especially women, make higher wages in these factories than they could in Mexican-owned firms or in the informal economy. Men who work in coal mines, steel mills, and the oil industry can earn more, but conditions are often dangerous and unhealthy. Recently, the retail sector has been expanding. Big American companies like Wal-Mart and Costco are now in Mexico and new shopping malls are opening alongside the new suburban housing tracts. So there are more retail jobs, too.

Work in Agriculture.   More than half of Mexico's poor families live in the countryside, especially in the depressed rural villages of the southern states of Chiapas, Oaxaca, Campeche, Yucatán, and Quintana Roo. A third of the people living in poverty in rural areas work their own farms or *ejido* plots. They produce most of the food they consume: corn tortillas and beans and possibly eggs, chicken, and pork. Any surplus they sell for cash. A small percentage of households (3.2%) are living outside the modern money economy: The value of what they grow for their own use exceeds their money income. Two thirds of the rural poor have no land. They work for the large landowners, increasingly as seasonally employed migrants, moving around the country from harvest to harvest, living in shacks in the fields, and often paid less than the minimum wage (Rudolph, 1985, pp. 125–126; Russell, 1994, pp. 71, 79).

Historically, rural Mexicans have tried to improve their lives through political action, supporting the Mexican Revolution and then petitioning the government to create or expand ejidos. Though the government was obligated under Article 27 of the Constitution to redistribute land to any Mexican who would work it, after Lázaro Cárdenas, government enthusiasm for this commitment weakened greatly. Ejidos were created on the poorest land: steep, rocky, and dry. Although it was forbidden to sell ejido land, many peasants found their only alternative was to enter into arrangements with landowners in which they lost control of their land and had to work it as employees. Many found that as the fertility of their land decreased, and their families grew, they could no longer make a living off the land. See Table 2.4.

TABLE 2.4 Men and Women Working in Agriculture and Their Families

In Mexico and Egypt the number of people working the land has not changed substantially in 25 years, but at the same time farmers and their families are a smaller percentage of the total population.

	Number of Men and Women Working in Agriculture and Their Families 1979/1981	Agricultural Families as a Percentage of the Total Population 1979/1981	Number of Men and Women Working in Agriculture and Their Families 2004	Agricultural Families as a Percentage of the Total Population 2004
Mexico	26,411,000	39	22,164,000	21
Egypt	26,541,000	60	24,954,000	34
Germany	5,405,000	7	1,724,000	2
Japan	12,452,000	11	3,895,000	3
Namibia	652,000	64	921,000	46
United States	8,556,000	4	5,828,000	2

Source. Food and Agriculture Organization, *Statistical Yearbook, 2005 2006*, 2006, http://www.fao.org/statistics/yearbook.

Bernardo and Francesca's Story

Bernardo and Francesca live in the village of San Bartolomeo del Valle in Oaxaca in a house Bernardo built on Francesca's grandmother's land. Francesca's parents live nearby and so do her two sisters and their families. Bernardo and Francesca and their relatives have pieced together a livelihood, seizing any opportunities that come their way, never prospering, but surviving. Francesca's younger brother has been working in the United States and he manages to send $50 a month to Francesca, in addition to the money he sends his parents. Francesca has been able to save some of the money and with it she and Bernardo bought three industrial sewing machines from a foreign company that moved to China. Francesca and her older daughter and one of her sisters work the machines, sewing skirts and aprons that Bernardo sells to market stalls and small shops in nearby towns. Bernardo and his father-in-law also work the family's small field, growing enough corn to make tortillas for everyone, come what may in the economy. In harvest season Bernardo temporarily leaves the business and the fields to work the coffee harvest. He earns very little, but every bit of cash helps. Bernardo and Francesca's son, Ernesto, is in seventh grade. They are trying to save up money for him to attend high school. There is no high school in San Bartoloméo, but he can stay with his grandmother, Bernardo's mother, in the nearest large town and go to school there. Ernesto is resisting; he wants to drop out of school and follow his uncle to the United States.

Social Mobility

Social mobility means moving up or down in class position, for example from poverty into the middle class (or vice versa), either within your own adult career or in comparison to your parents' class position. You may see social mobility as a personal matter, one that depends on an individual's talents, or determination, or hard work. Sociologists, however, look at social mobility differently. They are interested in **rates** of social mobility. They ask, why is it that the rate of upward mobility in Mexico has been higher since 2000 than it was between 1990 and 2000? They ask, why are rates of mobility higher in some societies than in other societies? When they study social mobility, sociologists ask what kinds of **opportunities** are available in a society at a given time. They ask, what kinds of **resources** do people have: Do they have access to financial capital, to education, to useful social networks?

In Mexico the rate of social mobility has recently increased after many years of stagnation. More people are moving out of extreme poverty into ordinary poverty and more people are moving up from the working class to the middle class, or from the upper class to the very very wealthy. We see two reasons why social mobility has increased. It doesn't have to do with changing attitudes or motivations. Rather, Mexicans are getting more help from their government, and economic changes associated with globalization are helping make mobility possible.

Government Policies and Social Mobility.   Back in 2000 when Vicente Fox was elected president he started off by using the government to help the rich. But then he developed excellent government programs that helped the lower middle class and the poor. We've said already that privatization of Mexico's government-owned monopolies like the telephone company helped the rich. Now we want to emphasize the importance of two programs that helped the poor. The first was the government low-interest mortgage program we have already described. That assistance not only helped families buy their own homes, it also sparked a construction boom that created jobs and boosted the economy (Thompson & McKinley, 2006, p. 8).

The government program most important for the poor is an antipoverty program called *Oportunidades*. It gives poor people money, but with strings attached. Depending on how many children they have and what grades their children are in, poor women can get cash grants of between $36 and $370 a month, but only if the children stay in school and if the women and children keep all their medical appointments. Mothers are also required to attend classes on health, nutrition, and family planning. The program is available only to those in extreme poverty, living on less than $2 a day per person, but that is as much as a quarter of the population. In some southern towns three quarters of the population receives Oportunidades help. The cash grants have had the biggest impact for poor families. The extra money has helped shrink the number of families in extreme poverty from 37% to 14% of all families. The government hopes that more knowledge about health, better health care, and more education will also help. So far, the effects of more education are not impressive. Only 1% of the students in higher education are from the poorest 20% of the population (*The Economist,* 2006d, p. 9; Rivera, 2007, pp. B1, B6).

Globalization and Social Mobility. Globalization has opened up some opportunities for poor Mexicans and it has helped some families improve their resources. Much of the least-skilled work in foreign assembly plants has moved to China, but the factories that stayed have moved up the skill ladder. There are fewer garment factories and more auto plants. Some industrial workers have learned new skills and moved up to better jobs. But the most important impact of globalization is probably migration. Every year about half a million Mexicans cross over into the United States to work. The money they send home (called remittances) amounted to $24 billion in 2006, which was one third more than the value of foreign investments in Mexico. Remittances have boosted the incomes of the poor, and for some families made it possible for them to invest in businesses, homes, or education. Because globalization has had such a big impact on Mexicans, it's time we examined it in greater detail (*The Economist,* 2006d, p. 7). See Table 2.5.

TABLE 2.5 Money Sent Home by Those Working Abroad

In only 5 years the amount of money sent home by Mexicans has tripled and the amounts sent home by Egyptians and Namibians have nearly doubled. Households in all these countries are increasingly dependent on money sent home by family members working abroad. Most Mexicans working abroad find jobs in the United States. The largest number of Egyptian migrants work in Saudi Arabia.

	Value of Money Sent Home by Those Working Abroad ($)	
	2000	2005
Mexico	7,525,000,000	21,917,000,000
Egypt	2,852,000,000	5,017,000,000
Namibia	9,000,000	16,000,000

Source: World Bank, *World Development Indicators 2006,* 2006, http://devdata.worldbank.org/data-query/.

GLOBALIZATION AND SOCIAL CHANGE

Mexico today is in the midst of major economic change. Increasingly it is part of a global economy, with especially tight links to the United States. We hear about globalization all the time these days, but you may not be quite sure just what globalization means. Often, when we think of globalization we think of products. We think that all over the world people are wearing Nike sneakers or eating McDonald's hamburgers or buying Hello Kitty accessories. But it is important to realize that it is not just consumption that has been globalized; social institutions have been globalized too. In Mexico, globalization has had profound effects on where people live, what work they do, and how their families and communities are organized.

Anthropologist Frances Abrahamer Rothstein has studied the small community of San Cosme Mazatechochco in Tlaxcala, Mexico, for more than 30 years. When she first went there San Cosme was an isolated place, on a dirt road, with only a few stores selling basic goods like canned sardines and cigarettes. Most people raised their own food on small family farms. Now a new paved highway runs through the community. There are cars and buses, taxis, and minivans. Residents can, if they wish, travel to work in the foreign-owned assembly plants in a nearby town, or to shop in the Wal-Mart there. Access to the Internet is available (Rothstein, 2007, pp. 1–3). In what ways have the people of San Cosme, and other Mexicans, gained— and lost—from this globalization?

Global Free-Market Capitalism

Mexico's people, like people all over the world, have been drawn into a system of global, free-market capitalism. The United States has been the world's strongest advocate for this kind of modern capitalism. Basically, it means that countries agree to remove barriers (like tariffs) to foreign trade and investment, so companies can invest their money and build their factories and stores wherever in the world they can make the most money. Governments are also supposed to agree to let market forces run the economy, avoiding government intervention. The idea is that Mexico, and other poor countries, will benefit from jobs and foreign investment, and American corporations will benefit from a cheaper workforce. It is a new international division of labor. Mexico signed up for globalization as the result of an economic crisis in the 1980s, getting rid of subsidies and tariffs, deregulating much of the economy, and privatizing many government-owned companies like the telephone company. Some people call this global free-trade philosophy "the Washington Censensus."

Rothstein calls global capitalism a system of "flexible production," a useful term (Rothstein, 2007, pp. 71–72). Companies are free to move around the world seeking to maximize their profits. They have few or no obligations to their workforce, and they can readily escape from environmental and other government regulations by operating in countries without any. In many ways Mexico and Mexican people have benefited from participation in the system of flexible production, but they have also had to adapt themselves to a very rapid pace of social change.

In the 1970s, many of the men of San Cosme were small farmers. In the 1980s they started commuting to the growing number of factories in nearby Puebla and in Mexico City, 60 miles away. In the 1990s, with globalization, those factories were driven out of business by competition from the new *maquiladoras,* foreign assembly plants, and by cheaper goods imported from China. Those new maquilas employed women, not men. Men found themselves pushed out of farming too, by competition from larger farms and by food imported from the United States. But a new opportunity opened up: Some men migrated to the United States for low-wage work in farming, construction, and food processing. The money they sent home allowed relatives to start informal businesses, mostly garment workshops producing for local sale. Now that work is threatened by Chinese imports and big box stores like Wal-Mart. And the migration route to the United States is shutting down because of growing American opposition to immigration.

What will the people of San Cosme do next? They have become experts in adaptation. Life is speeding up and people know much more about the wider world. They are linked to relatives elsewhere in Mexico and in the United States. They have computers and television. It is much easier to travel to other towns and cities. They have gained the know-how to get schools built in San Cosme and there are more professionals in town, working as teachers, or doctors, or dentists.

These are all significant benefits from globalization. But the people of San Cosme, like other Mexicans, also feel more vulnerable to outside forces. They feel their lives are precarious. A change of opinion in the United States, a change in markets in China, a change in the price of corn or oil on world markets, and their painstakingly constructed livelihoods are blown away. And it happens again and again (Rothstein, 2007, pp. 1–41). Let's look at some of the components of global change as it has affected Mexico: maquiladoras, free-market agriculture, and migration.

Maquiladoras

Most foreign assembly plants in Mexico are owned by United States–based multinational firms that send partly finished materials to Mexico for assembly into finished goods. When the *maquiladora* boom started in the 1980s, the plants were clustered along the border, where transportation of materials to Mexico and finished goods back to the United States was easy. The factories offered unskilled assembly-line work, making apparel, textiles, toys, small appliances. By the end of the 1990s Mexico had 3,700 maquiladoras employing 1.3 million people. For the corporations, wages in Mexico were an incredible bargain—$4 to $5 a day for entry-level unskilled workers, and an average for all employees of about $65 a week.

The assembly plants employed mostly young women, and for them, these were good wages, much more than they could earn in Mexican-owned factories (Villarreal & Yu, 2007, p. 386). For women this was an unprecedented opportunity to earn money, to learn industrial work, perhaps to acquire skills for better jobs later. Young women moved to the border towns, some alone and some with their husbands and children. But there wasn't much work for men.

The Ortegas's Story: Maquiladora Workers

Pedro and María Ortega count themselves lucky. Because they both have maquiladora jobs, they are able to earn as much as $120 a week. Back home in their village there was no work for María, and Pedro managed to find work only during the planting and harvest seasons. Now that they both work and earn equal wages, María says their marriage feels more like a partnership. But it isn't completely equal, she says. The way Pedro budgets their money, his wages pay for food and rent and water, the essentials, and her wages pay for "extras"— school uniforms, money sent home, and so on. María is still "in charge" of the cooking and housekeeping, even though she works full-time, just like Pedro.

They live in San Isidro, a settlement on the east side of Juarez, a huge border city with 1.3 million inhabitants and almost 300 maquiladoras. Although San Isidro is 15 years old, it still doesn't have running water or a sewage system, so Pedro and María spend $12 per week for bottled water, delivered by truck. The Ortegas and their son Juan take showers twice a week, by standing on their back step and pouring water over themselves with a dipper. María gives Juan as much drinking water as he wants, but she restricts herself to one glass a day.

Pedro has dug a pit for an outhouse out in back of the one-room tin-roofed shack they rent for $15 a week. San Isidro smells of human waste and of the garbage that piles up, because there is no city garbage collection. The Ortegas are saving up money to buy concrete blocks to build their own house, and they also send money home to their elderly parents in the village. When Juan started school this year, he needed sneakers, a book bag, the school uniform, notebooks, and pencils. María figured out that it took her 44 hours of work to pay for it all. (Dillon, 2001, p. A6; Thompson, 2001a; Young, 1992, p. 66).

The year 2000 proved to be the peak of the maquiladora boom. When the U.S. economy went into recession, the border region went with it. In 2001, more than 500 maquiladoras closed and 280,000 jobs were lost. By 2004, the industry was reviving, but it had changed profoundly. Much of the light manufacturing of textiles and small electronics moved to China. These products were easy to ship, and total costs for unskilled labor are much lower in China: 25¢ an hour, as compared to $1.50 to $2.00 in Mexico. Nowadays it is heavy industry that is moving to Mexico: cars, auto parts, televisions, and refrigerators that are expensive to ship from Asia. Factories employ more machinery and fewer, but more skilled, higher-paid workers, most of them men. It is a great opportunity for Mexican engineers and technicians. Many women left the region to join male relatives in the United States. What will happen when there is another recession in the United States and demand for cars and heavy appliances falls? In global production people have to adapt to international business cycles (Barclay, 2006; Thomson, 2007, p. 3).

Free-Market Agriculture

During the 1980s Mexico's president applied the principles of free-market economics to agriculture. The goal was to replace the inefficient subsistence farmer with modern "agribusiness"—big farm companies, often multinationals, growing food for export to the world market. Small farmers lost most of the help the government had given them in the past and found it harder and harder to remain in farming. Today there are still 2.6 million small farms in Mexico, but four fifths of them produce food only for their peasant owners and not for sale (McKinley, 2008b, p. A10).

After 2000, when the provisions of NAFTA were applied to agriculture, remaining small farmers experienced another shock. Cheap corn subsidized by the U.S. government flooded into Mexico. The price of corn dropped 45% in 3 years, to levels below the costs of production for Mexican farmers. The same thing happened to other staples like rice, sugar, and coffee. Small farmers protested, and got some help from the government, but economists estimate that as many as 1.4 million were forced off the land (Andreas, in Wise, 1998, p. 212). Where did they go? Some got industrial jobs; some left for the United States; and many found marginal, temporary jobs working on big export farms in Mexico. Vegetable growers in Sinaloa send buses south every year to recruit 200,000 poor Mexicans to pick fruits and vegetables, mostly for export to the United States. Whole families come north, to live in workcamp shantytowns, one room per family, and bathe in pesticide-soaked irrigation canals (Thompson, 2001b, p. 10).

Today, Mexican agriculture produces more food for export and more grain to feed animals, but production of food for domestic consumption has fallen. Mexico is in the seemingly contradictory situation of no longer being self-sufficient in food, even while foodstuffs are a major export. Rural Mexicans especially (like many people in other third-world countries that export food) are eating less and eating worse amid growing agricultural abundance (Barkin, 1990, pp. 11, 16–22, 28–32; Klein-Robbenhaar, 1995, pp. 395–409).

The Story of San Jeronimo

San Jeronimo Progreso is a remote mountain village in Oaxaca. It is so remote that there wasn't even any road linking the village to the nearest large town, until the villagers built one themselves 15 years ago. There are about 2,000 inhabitants in 250 households. All land is owned communally and all the land that could possibly be cultivated has already been cleared. There is no more land for growing families to farm. Nowadays, the people of this apparently isolated "traditional" Mixtec Indian village survive through their connections with the global economy.

Luis Ortiz, his wife Ana, and their three children can raise only enough corn and beans to feed themselves for 2½ months of the year. They must find some source of cash to buy food the rest of the year. Twenty years ago, when Luis was a boy, his whole family wove palm hats in the wintertime. They got 10¢ a hat from the merchant who bought them and each of the six family members could weave two hats a day. Last winter, Luis and his oldest son spent 4 months in El Campo de Las Pulgas (Flea Camp), a labor camp in Baja California, where they picked tomatoes for export to the United States. The money they earned bought food for the family, fertilizer for their plot of corn and beans, and last winter, bags of cement to pour a floor for their house.

Luis and Ana are considering moving the whole family to Tijuana next winter. San Jeronimo has a "daughter enclave" in a squatter settlement there, where they can live near relatives and neighbors from their town who will help them get jobs and find a place to live. Luis may even decide to risk a trip to the United States to live in another daughter enclave in Oregon and work the apple harvest there. Luis says that if he is to go, it must be soon. By age 35 he will be too old and worn out for migrating. He will "retire" to San Jeronimo and work the family land, with the help of cash that his migrating sons and daughters will send. (This vignette is derived from research presented by Nagengast & Kearney, 1998, pp. 453–469).

We must add the latest twist in this story. In 2008, the situation of poor rural and urban Mexicans worsened in the midst of a global food crisis. Having left the land because they could not compete with cheap corn from the United States, Mexico's former farmers saw the price of corn spike 70% in 1 year. Prices for corn and for tortillas, the staple foods of Mexico's poor, rose sharply. There were food riots in 2008 in 30 countries where poor people could no longer afford their basic foods. Bad weather, probably resulting from global warming, rapidly rising oil and fertilizer prices, and a huge increase in the use of corn for ethanol in the United States drove up food prices. The World Bank reported that almost the entire growth in global corn production between 2004 and 2008 went into American ethanol. Also, growing prosperity in China and India has driven up food prices. That is because the growing Asian middle classes eat more meat, so more grain is devoted to cattle feed, leaving less for people who cannot afford meat and rely on grain for protein. Meat-eating magnifies grain shortages because the same amount of grain that could feed seven vegetarians, when fed to cattle produces enough meat for only one person (Bradsher & Martin, 2008, pp. A1, A8; *The New York Times,* 2008). Has the food crisis created opportunities for Mexico's former small corn farmers? So far, it appears that few of them are in a position to seize the new opportunity. They have lost or sold their land, moved away to the north or to the United States, or lack the capital and connections to markets to get back into farming commercially.

Globalization and Migration

Today, the Mexican government estimates that there are 10–12 million Mexicans living in the United States, as much as 12% of Mexico's population of 100 million. An estimated 400,000 more arrive every year. As many as 6 million of the migrants are "undocumented," that is, they have no immigration documents and would be arrested and deported if found by the Immigration and Naturalization Service (INS). Three quarters of all Mexicans in the United States live in seven states: the border states of California, Texas, and Arizona, nearby Colorado, and also Illinois, Georgia, and New York. Mexican population, though smaller there, is growing rapidly now in Arkansas, North Carolina, Missouri, and Minnesota (Archibold, 2007a, pp. A1, A20; Dowd, 2005, p. A17; Garcia-Navarro, 2006b).

At least half a million people from the dry, impoverished state of Zacatecas work in the United States. The isolated town of El Porvenir ("The Future"), population 1,200, is silent and empty; half the working-age men are in the United States. Population is shrinking in 35 of Zacatecas's 57 counties. There are 80 people living in the ghostly village of Jomolquillo, but 300 others live in Los Angeles. It is surprising that many of these empty towns look fairly prosperous. Their unoccupied houses are built of concrete with American-style facades. The streets are paved, and there is a new bridge or a school yard playground. These improvements have been paid for by remittances, money sent home by migrants working in the United States. One bank study found that one Mexican in five regularly receives money from relatives north of the border. The money goes, first of all, to pay for food and clothing and housing, but an increasing percentage is invested in small businesses or higher

The border between Mexico and the United States is
unmistakable, not only because of the fence, but also because the
two sides look so different. On the Mexican side, at Juárez, a
dusty shantytown stretches to the horizon, filled with tiny houses
local maquiladora workers have constructed themselves out of
scrap materials. They can look across the border
to the wide-open spaces of the United States.

education. Mexicans are also organizing home town clubs that put together money to
finance village development. The Mexican government now matches these funds
with state and federal money on a two-for-one basis, to build roads, schools, and
health clinics (Lizarzaburu, 2004; O'Murchu, 2001; Thompson, 2002c, p. A3).

Migration and Social Mobility

Mexicans in the United States work as farmworkers, as laborers on lawn-care
crews, in restaurants, on construction sites, in factories, increasingly in slaughter-
houses and in meat-packing plants. They are willing to struggle across the border,
leaving their families behind, to do difficult and unpleasant jobs for minimum
wages because they can make roughly as much in 1 hour in the United States as in
1 day in Mexico. The wage differential across the United States–Mexico border is
the largest in the world. Do Mexicans get stuck in these unskilled, low-paid jobs?

The evidence so far is that many Mexican immigrants who remain in the United States move up economically.

The earnings of first-generation male Mexican immigrants are only half of those of White American men. But those immigrants' children earn more than Black American men and earn three quarters as much as White men. Many Mexican immigrants start businesses. They are three times as likely to do so as other Americans. Alberto Queiroz, for example, crossed the border illegally 12 years ago. He picked blueberries by the box, then worked for years in a slaughterhouse. Savings from his earnings of $10 an hour paid for a home back in Mexico. Then he started a taco stand with his brother, expanding it eventually into a restaurant (*The Economist,* 2006a, pp. 31–32).

Global Migration.   Migration is clearly part of today's pattern of economic globalization. Just as capital now moves more freely across borders all over the world, so does labor. Immigration brings U.S. employers a cheap, willing workforce and relieves Mexico of poor, unemployed, or underemployed people who might be a source of opposition to the government. It is worth noting that even as Mexicans migrate to the United States, Guatamalans illegally cross Mexico's southern border, seeking the jobs Mexicans have left behind, which pay more than they can earn in Guatamala. Average annual per capita income is $2,640 in Guatamala and $7,870 in Mexico. For the same reason, Haitians migrate to the Dominican Republic; Nicaraguans migrate to El Salvador or Costa Rica, and Colombians migrate to Panama and Venezuela. Worldwide, according to World Bank estimates, 74 million people leave one poor country to migrate to another poor country every year (DeParle, 2007, pp. A1, A16; Thompson, 2006a, p. 12).

Opposition to Migration.   But in the United States (as in many other countries) opposition to immigration is growing. You could say that anger about immigration is the way Americans express their fear of globalization. They feel their jobs are vulnerable, that they could be replaced by someone in India or someone who just crossed the border from Mexico. They see strangers moving into their local community. In response to anti-immigration sentiment, the U.S. government has beefed up the border patrol, hiring many more agents and jailing immigrants caught crossing illegally in some areas. One effect has been to push immigrants into crossing in more and more remote and rugged desert areas. The number of people who die attempting the crossing doubled between 1995 and 2005, with reported annual deaths up to 472 (Archibold, 2007b, p. A12; *The Economist,* 2006a, p. 32; McKinley, 2007b, p. A10).

Within the United States, the government has conducted raids on factories and farms, fining employers and imprisoning and deporting illegal immigrant workers. In 2006, Immigration and Customs Enforcement agents deported 183,000 people. Some American towns have passed anti-immigrant ordinances, forbidding people to share apartments or solicit work on the streets (McKinley, 2007d, p. A4).

The campaign has had impressive effects, not all of which were intended. Judging by the number of migrants caught by border agents, attempted crossings are down. So are remittances (Garcia-Navarro 2006b; McKinley, 2007b, p. A10).

Immigrants say it has gotten harder to find work in the United States because employers are afraid to hire them. Many immigrants now feel unwelcome and frightened in towns where Mexicans in the past had established enclaves. Men who routinely traveled back and forth across the border, for example, working construction in Florida in the winter and farming in Mexico in the summer, now remain in the United States year round. Some who would formerly have left their wives and children in Mexico now bring them along to cross the border, so they can all remain in the United States (*The Economist*, 2006b, p. 31).

Migration and Population. What will Mexicans do if they can no longer migrate to the United States? It would be wonderful if the remittance money already sent back to Mexico turned out to be sufficient capital to power an expansion of local business that would absorb Mexico's labor force. If not, Mexicans will have to find yet another strategy to cope with the rapidity of change in a global economy. Perhaps rising fuel costs for shipping will bring more factories back to Mexico from China.

However, in the long run, say in the next 20 years, it looks like the need for migration will decrease because of demographic change in Mexico. Population growth dropped by half in the last 50 years, with fertility rates falling from 6.9 children per woman in 1955 to 2.5 today. If this trend continues, Mexico's population will age and there will be more jobs for the young. A shortage of labor will raise wages and people will be less motivated to migrate (Dowd, 2005, p. A17). Mexico may even have a problem with too many older people. When Mexicans currently working in the United States grow old, where will they live? Mexico has almost no system of social security or health insurance for its elderly citizens. In the United States many illegal immigrants have paid into the Social Security system for years, but under false numbers, so they cannot claim benefits. If they retire to Mexico it will be a bonus for the United States, but a burden for Mexico (Porter & Malkin, 2005, pp. C1, C6).

Globalization and the Environment

Just as it has brought a contradictory mix of benefits and costs to Mexico's people, when it comes to Mexico's environment, globalization has been a two-edged sword. The economic development of the border zone has brought uncontrolled pollution to a fragile desert environment. Border cities like Tijuana, Nogales, Agua Prieta, and Ciudad Juárez have seen their populations increase by more than 50% in the last 10 years. In Ciudad Acuna, where Alcoa and GE and Allied Signal, among other companies, run *maquiladoras,* population has doubled. All along the border, the air and water are polluted with industrial and human waste. On average, cities can treat properly less than 35% of the sewage generated (*The Economist*, 2001). Resort development along the coast of Guerrero has polluted the beautiful bay the tourists come to enjoy. In Chiapas, timber companies and peasants have cut down most of Mexico's last rainforest. And in Mexicali, two new power plants will generate power for California, a very small number of jobs for Mexico, and abundant pollution for both sides of the border. The plants are built in Mexico because costs and environmental regulations are less there (Weiner, 2002a, p. A3; 2002b, p. 16; 2003, p. A4).

At the same time, globalization has brought Mexico's small environmentalist movement powerful international allies. Efforts to save Mexico's splendid natural landscapes—its deserts, rainforests, coasts, and offshore waters—and its stunning biological diversity have been embraced by powerful nongovernmental organizations (NGOs). The Mexican government has learned that if it seeks international investment, then it must also take into account international public opinion. For example, in 2000 the government canceled a joint project with the Mitsubishi Corporation of Japan to build an enormous salt plant on the shore of a lagoon in Baja California where gray whales give birth. The Natural Resources Defense Council, an American group, led the campaign against the plant, with ads throughout Mexico and the rest of North America, an international Internet and press campaign, and a planned campaign to boycott Mitsubishi stock and products.

But now another battle is looming with a salt-mining company and there are plans to drill for oil near the bay. In Baja and other states, a land boom, fed by speculators who plan to build resorts or second homes for Americans, threatens pristine landscapes. Several environmental organizations have arranged to protect land in Baja from development in exchange for a trust fund for the peasant ejido that owns the land. Some peasants fight hard to protect their land and trees from predatory logging companies, but others would rather sell and get much-needed cash (McKinley, 2005a, p. A10; 2006b, p. 3; Thompson, 2004, p. A11). There are no easy answers for the environment or the people exposed to powerful global economic change.

Thinking Sociologically

1. Describe some norms that are important in Mexican culture.
2. Are there any similarities in the roles men are expected to play in Mexican society and in Japanese society? What differences are there?
3. Explain what is meant by the term *reciprocity network,* using examples from Chapter 2. Do people in your society form reciprocity networks? Can you give an example of a reciprocity network from your own experience?
4. Compare the Gómez family household in Mexico (pp. 87) with the Sato family household in Japan (pp. 39–40). Which of these does your own household resemble more?
5. Can you explain what political patronage is and how it works? Can you find an example of political patronage in your own society?
6. Look up the most recent data you can find on income distribution by quintiles in your society. Is your society more like Mexico or more like Japan in its degree of inequality?
7. Refer to Table 2.1 (p. 89) and compare the rates of divorce in Mexico and in the United States. Use Chapter 2 and your introductory sociology textbook to help you explain why the divorce rate is so much higher in the United States than in Mexico.
8. Use Merton's strain theory to explain why crime rates are so high in Mexico. Can you compare crime rates in your own society with crime rates in Mexico? Explain sociologically why crime rates are higher or lower in your society than in Mexico.
9. Explain how Mexicans are helped and how they are harmed by economic globalization. How about in your society? What are the impacts of economic globalization there?

For Further Reading

Krause, E. (1997). *Mexico: Biography of power.* New York: HarperCollins.
Marnham, P. (1998). *Dreaming with his eyes open: A life of Diego Rivera.* New York: Knopf.
Martínez, R. (2001). *Crossing over: A Mexican family on the migrant trail.* Metropolitan Books.
Preston, J., & Dillon, S. (2004). *Opening Mexico: The making of a democracy.* New York: Farrar, Straus and Giroux.
Quinones, S. (2001). *True tales from another Mexico.* Albuquerque: University of New Mexico Press.
Rothstein, F. A. (2007). *Globalization in rural Mexico.* Austin: University of Texas Press.
Selby, H. A., Murphy, A. D., & Lorenzen, S. A. (1990). *The Mexican urban household: Organized for self-defense.* Austin: University of Texas Press.
Shorris, E. (2004). *The life and times of Mexico.* New York: Norton.
Stephen, L. (2002). *Zapata lives! Histories and cultural politics in southern Mexico.* Berkeley: University of California Press.

Bibliography

Archibold, R. C. (2007a, May 23). Mexico adds to consulates amid debate. *The New York Times,* pp. A1, A20.
Archibold, R. (2007b, September 15). At the border, desert takes a rising toll. *The New York Times,* pp. A1, A12.
Barclay, E. (2006, July 23). An unraveling industry: Apparel manufacturing jobs are in a steep decline. *Houston Chronicle.*
Barkin, D. (1990). *Distorted development: Mexico and the world economy.* Boulder, CO: Westview Press.
Bradsher, K., & Martin, A. (2008, April 30). Costs and shortages threaten farmers' crucial tool: Fertilizer. *The New York Times,* pp. A1, A8.
Bragante, N., & Devine, E. (1989). *The travelers' guide to Latin American customs and manners.* New York: St. Martin's Press.
Brandes, S. (2002). *Staying sober in Mexico City.* Austin: University of Texas Press.
Cornelius, W. A., & Craig, A. L. (1991). *The Mexican political system in transition.* La Jolla: Center for U.S.–Mexican Studies, University of California, San Diego.
Cross, J. (1998). *Informal politics: Street vendors and the state in Mexico City.* Stanford, CA: Stanford University Press.
Demographic and health surveys. (n.d.). Retrieved from the STATcompiler database, http://www.statcompiler.com
Deparle, J. (2007, December 27). A global trek to poor nations, from poorer ones. *The New York Times,* pp. A1, A16.
Dillon, S. (2000, June 28). Clean vote vowed in Mexico, but fraud dies hard. *The New York Times,* p. A3.
Dillon, S. (2001, February 15). Profits raise pressures on U.S.-owned factories in Mexican border zone. *The New York Times,* p. A16.
Dillon, S., & Preston, J. (2000, May 9). Old ways die hard in Mexican election despite the pledges. *The New York Times,* pp. A1, A4.
Dominguez, J. L., & McCann, J. A. (1996). *Democratizing Mexico: Public opinion and electoral choices.* Baltimore: Johns Hopkins University Press.
Dowd, M. (2005, August 1). The Mexican evolution. *The New York Times,* p. A17.
The Economist. (2001, July 17). Special report: The U.S.–Mexican border, pp. 28–30.
The Economist. (2002, July 27). Religion in Mexico staying alive, p. 34.

The Economist. (2003, September, 20). The Americas: A few shots at power; Mexico's women, p. 66.

The Economist. (2004, June 19). Crime in Mexico: Fear of captivity, p. 37.

The Economist. (2005a, June 4). Crime in Mexico: Lessons from Juarez, p. 37.

The Economist. (2005b, October 8). Mexico: Righting the scales, p. 45.

The Economist. (2005c, November 12). Mexico's trade unions: Unreformed, unrepresentative, p. 39.

The Economist. (2006a, June 17). Of meat, Mexicans and social mobility, pp. 31–32.

The Economist. (2006b, August 12). Migrants in Mexico: Waiting to cross, p. 31.

The Economist. (2006c, September 30). Mexico: Under the volcano, p. 48.

The Economist. (2006d, November 18). A survey of Mexico, pp. 3–16.

The Economist. (2007b, June 16). Mexico: State of siege, pp. 45–46.

The Economist. (2007c, August 18). Adios to poverty, hola to consumption, pp. 21–23.

Ethnologue. (n.d.). Retrieved from http://www.ethnologue.com/show_country.asp?name=mexico

Falicov, C. J. (1982). Mexican families. In M. McGoldrick, J. K. Pearce, & J. Giordano (Eds.), *Ethnicity and family therapy* (pp. 134–163). New York: Guildford Press.

Food and Agriculture Organization. (2006). *Statistical yearbook, 2005–2006.* Retrieved from http://www.fao.org/statistics/yearbook

Fox, R. A., & Solis-Camara, P. (1997, August). Parenting of young children by fathers in Mexico and the United States. *Journal of Social Psychology, 137*(4), 489–495.

Frank, R., & Wildsmith, E. (2005, March). The grass widows of Mexico: Migration and union dissolution in a binational context. *Social Forces, 83*(3), 919–948.

Fuentes, C. (1992a). *The buried mirror.* Boston: Houghton Mifflin.

Fuentes, C. (1992b, March 30). The mirror of the other. *The Nation,* pp. 408–411.

Garcia-Navarro, L. (2006a, May 9). Mexican migrants leave kids, problems back home. *National Public Radio, Morning Edition.*

Garcia-Navarro, L. (2006b, June 25). Mexican towns pinched by deportations, slowdown. *National Public Radio, Morning Edition.*

Goodwin, P. (Ed.). (1991). *Global studies: Latin America.* Guilford, CT: Dushkin.

Guillermoprieto, A. (2003, September 29). A hundred women. *The New Yorker,* pp. 82–93.

Gutmann, M. C., (1996). *The meaning of macho: Being a man in Mexico City.* Berkeley: University of California Press.

Kana'Iaupuni, S. M. Donato, K. M., Thompson-Colon, T., & Stainback, M. (2005, March). Counting on kin: Social networks, social support, and child health status. *Social Forces, 83*(3), 1137–1164.

Kandell, J. (1988). *La capital: The biography of Mexico City.* New York: Random House.

Klein-Robbenhaar, J. F. (1995, Summer). Agro-industry and the environment: The case of Mexico in the 1990s. *Agricultural History, 69*(3), 395–419.

Krause, E. (1997). *Mexico: Biography of power.* New York: HarperCollins.

Lacey, M. (2007, July 17). Mexican migrants carry H.I.V. home to unready rural areas. *The New York Times,* pp. A1, A12.

Lizarzaburu, J. (2004, May 18). *Mexican migrants growing influence. BBC News.* Retrieved from http://news.bbc.co.uk/go/pr/fr/-/1/hi/world/americas/3582881.stm

Lomnitz, L. (1977). *Networks and marginality: Life in a Mexican shantytown.* New York: Academic Press.

Malkin, E. (2006, October 4). Nothing is sacred, as looters rob Mexican churches of colonial treasures. *The New York Times,* p. E3.

McKenzie, D., & Rapoport, H. (2006). *Network effects and the dynamics of migration and inequality: Theory and evidence from Mexico.* Washington, DC: The World Bank.

McKinley, J. C., Jr. (2005a, July 13). In a logging war in Mexico, forests' peasant defenders are besieged. *The New York Times,* p. A10.

McKinley, J. C., Jr. (2005b, July 21). Coach abducted, adding focus to common Mexican dread. *The New York Times,* p. A6.

McKinley, J. C., Jr. (2006a, January 6). The Zapatista's return: A masked Marxist on the stump. *The New York Times,* p. A4.

McKinley, J. C., Jr. (2006b, March 12). Mexican land boom creates commotion in whale nursery. *The New York Times,* p. 3.

McKinley, J. C., Jr. (2006c, June 17). In race for Mexico's presidency, populist tilts at a privileged elite. *The New York Times,* pp. A1, A8.

McKinley, J. C., Jr. (2006d, July 9). Mexico faces its own red-blue standoff. *The New York Times,* p. WK3.

McKinley, J. C., Jr. (2006e, October 26). With beheadings and attacks, drug gangs terrorize Mexico. *The New York Times,* pp. A1, A12.

McKinley, J. C., Jr. (2007a, January 19). Cost of corn soars, forcing Mexico to set price limits. *The New York Times,* p. A12.

McKinley, J. C., Jr. (2007b, February 21). Tougher tactics deter migrants at U.S. border. *The New York Times,* pp. A1, A10.

McKinley, J. C., Jr. (2007c, June 22). Mexico moves to send ex-governor to U.S. on drug charges. *The New York Times,* p. A6.

McKinley, J. C., Jr. (2007d, September 3). Mexican president assails U.S. measures on migrants. *The New York Times,* p. A4.

McKinley, J. C., Jr. (2007f, October 3). Citing price rise, U.S. and Mexico see antidrug progress. *The New York Times,* p. A20.

McKinley, J. C., Jr. (2007e, October 3). Drug trade, once passing by, takes root, and toll, in Mexico. *The New York Times,* pp. A1, A10.

McKinley, J. C., Jr. (2007g, October 12). In Mexico, a fugitive's arrest captivates the cameras. *The New York Times,* p. A3.

McKinley, J. C., Jr. (2007h, November 29). Mexico tries to show resolve with big drug seizure. *The New York Times,* p. A10.

McKinley, J. C., Jr. (2007i, December 18). Songs of love and murder, silenced by killings. *The New York Times,* pp. A1, A20.

McKinley, J. C., Jr. (2008a, January 22). Mexico hits drug gangs with full fury of war. *The New York Times,* pp. A1, A9.

McKinley, J. C., Jr. (2008b, February 1). Mexican farmers protest end of corn-import taxes. *The New York Times,* p. A10.

McKinley, J. C., Jr., & Betancourt, A. (2007, September 26). With bombings, Mexican rebels escalate their fight. *The New York Times,* p. A3.

Mexican National Institute of Statistics, Geography and Informatics. (n.d.). Retrieved from http://www.inegi.gob.mx/incgi/dcfault.asp

Meyer, E. L. (2007, September 16). For rich Mexicans, parallel lives in U.S. *The New York Times,* p. BU 19.

Nagengast, C., & Kearney, M. (1998). Mixtec ethnicity: Social identity, political consciousness and political activism. In M. B. Whiteford & S. Whiteford (Eds.), *Crossing currents, continuity and change in Latin America.* Upper Saddle River, NJ: Prentice Hall.

Navarro, M., (2002, August 19). Who is killing the young women of Juárez? A filmmaker seeks answers. *The New York Times,* p. B3.

The New York Times. (2008, July 6). Man-made hunger, p. WK9.

Nolen, B. (Ed.). (1973). *Mexico is people: Land of three cultures.* New York: Scribner's.

O'Murchu, S., (2001, February 15). In Zacatecas, America's the future. *MSNBC News.* Retrieved from http://msnbc.msn.com/id/3071713/

Oster, P. (1989). *The Mexicans: A personal portrait of a people.* New York: Morrow.

Paz, O. (1961). *The labyrinth of solitude: Life and thought in Mexico.* New York: Grove Press.

Porter, E. (2007, August 27). Mexico's plutocracy thrives on robber-baron concessions. *The New York Times,* p. A20.

Porter, E., Malkin, E. (2005, August 4). Mexicans at home abroad. *The New York Times,* p. C1.

Public Broadcasting System. (2002, April 12). NOW with David Brancaccio, Executive Excess. Retrieved from http://www.pbs.org/now/politics/executive.html

Quinones, S. (2001). *True tales from another Mexico.* Albuquerque: University of New Mexico Press.

Reavis, D. J. (1990). *Conversations with Moctezuma: The soul of modern Mexico.* New York: Quill, Morrow.

Riding, A. (1985). *Distant neighbors: A portrait of the Mexicans.* New York: Knopf.

Rivera, R. (2007, April 25). In Mexican town, maybe a way to reduce poverty in New York. *The New York Times,* pp. B1, B6.

Rothstein, F. A. (2007). *Globalization in rural Mexico.* Austin, University of Texas Press.

Rudolph, J. A. (Ed.). (1985). *Mexico: A country study* (Area Handbook Series). Washington, DC: U.S. Government Printing Office.

Ruiz, R. E. (1992). *Triumphs and tragedy: A history of the Mexican people.* New York: Norton.

Russell, J. W. (1994). *After the fifth sun: Class and race in North America.* Englewood Cliffs, NJ: Prentice Hall.

Selby, H. A., Murphy, A. D., & Lorenzen, S. A. (1990). *The Mexican urban household: Organized for self-defense.* Austin: University of Texas Press.

Shorris, E. (2004). *The life and times of Mexico.* New York: Norton.

Smith, G. (2006, March 13). Piggybanks full of pesos. *BusinessWeek,* pp. 51–52.

Tayler, L. (2001, October 21). Changes in Mexican families. *Newsday,* p. A12.

Thompson, G. (2001a, February 11). Chasing Mexico's dream into squalor. *The New York Times,* pp. 1, 6.

Thompson, G. (2001b, May 6). At home, Mexico mistreats its migrant farmhands. *The New York Times,* pp. 1, 10.

Thompson, G. (2002a, January 21). Congress shifts Mexico's balance of power. *The New York Times,* p. A6.

Thompson, G. (2002b, March 12). Vatican curbing deacons in Mexico. *The New York Times,* p. A8.

Thompson, G. (2002c, March 25). Big Mexican breadwinner: The migrant worker. *The New York Times,* p. A3.

Thompson, G. (2002d, August 14). A saint who guides migrants to a promised land. *The New York Times,* p. A4.

Thompson, G. (2002e, December 10). Wave of women's killings confounds Juárez. *The New York Times,* pp. A1, A20.

Thompson, G. (2004, June 2). Where butterflies rest, damage runs rampant. *The New York Times,* p. A11

Thompson, G. (2006a, June 18). Mexico worries about its own southern border. *The New York Times,* pp. 1, 12.

Thompson, G. (2006b, July 2). Mexican vote hinges on conflicted middle class. *The New York Times,* pp. 1, 8.

Thompson, G., & McKinley, J., Jr. (2006, July 6). Suspense grows as vote count in Mexico race wraps up, p. 8.

Thomson, A. (2007, May 9). Skills and technology add value to product Maquiladora. *Financial Times (London),* p. 3.

Uchitelle, L. (2007, February 18). NAFTA should have stopped illegal immigration, right? *The New York Times,* p. WK4.

United Nations. (1990). *Demographic yearbook.* Retrieved from http://unstats.un.org/unsd/demographic/products/dyb/dyb2.htm

United Nations. (2001). *Human development report 2001.* Retrieved from http://hdr.undp.org/reports/global/ 2001/en/

United Nations. (2004a). *Demographic yearbook.* Retrieved from http://unstats.un.org/unsd/demographic/products/dyb/dyb2.htm

United Nations. (2004b). *Human development report 2004.* Retrieved from http://hdr.undp.org/statistics/data/index_indicators.cfm

United Nations. (2006). *Human development report 2006.* Retrieved from http://hdr.undp.org/hdr2006/statistics/indicators

United Nations. (2006/2007). *Human development indicators.* Retrieved from http://hdr.undp.org/en/statistics/

United Nations. (2007). *Human development report 2007.* Retrieved from http://hdr.undp.org/en/reports

United Nations. (n.d.). *Statistics and indicators on the world's women.* Retrieved from http://www.un.org/Depts/ unsd/gender/1-3dev.htm

United Nations Statistics Division. (n.d.). *Demographic and social statistics, statistics and indicators on women and men.* Retrieved from http://unstats.un.org/unsd/demographic/products/indwm/default.htm

U.S. Bureau of the Census. (2000a). *United States Census, American Fact Finder, Households and Families 2000.* Retrieved from http://census.gov

U.S. Bureau of the Census. (2000b). *International database 2000.* Retrieved from http://www.census.gov/ipc/www/idbsprd.html

U.S. Department of Health and Human Services. (2007, October 9). *National Vital Statistics Reports, 56,* (2).

Villarreal, A., Yu, W.-H. (2007, June). Economic globalization and women's employment: The case of manufacturing in Mexico. *American Sociological Review, 72,* 365–389.

Weiner, T. (2002a, September 17). U.S. will get power, and pollution, from Mexico. *The New York Times,* p. A3.

Weiner, T. (2002b, December 8). Growing poverty is shrinking Mexico's rain forest. *The New York Times,* p. 16.

Weiner, T. (2003, February 13). For all to read: A Mexican resort's dirty secret. *The New York Times,* p. A4.

Wise, C. (Ed.). (1998). *The post-NAFTA political economy: Mexico and the Western Hemisphere.* University Park: Pennsylvania State University Press.

Wolf, E. (1959). *Sons of the shaking earth.* Chicago: University of Chicago Press.

World Bank. (2006). *World development indicators 2006.* Retrieved from http://web.worldbank.org/WEBSITE/EXTERNAL/DATASTATISTICS/0,,contentMDK:20899413~pagePK:6413_3150~piPK:64133175~theSitePK:239419,00.html

Young, G. (1992). *Women, work and households in Ciudad Juárez.* Washington, DC: Institute for Women's Policy Research.

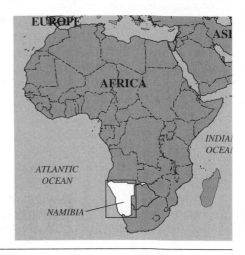

To get to Namibia you will have to fly to the southern tip of Africa. You may get a direct flight to Windhoek, the capital of Namibia, or you may have to fly to Johannesburg, South Africa, and change planes there. It will be a very long day's flight from Toronto or Los Angeles. In Windhoek you will need to hire a jeep and a guide if you want to visit the Bushmen described in this chapter.

LOCATION: Namibia is on the west coast of southern Africa. South Africa is to its south, Botswana to the east, and Angola to the north.

AREA: Namibia covers 318,261 square miles. It is about twice the size of California or Japan.

LAND: The Namib Desert extends along the entire Atlantic coastline. The rest of the country is a high, grassy plain, dryer toward the south and east and wetter in the north. In the Kalahari Desert along the eastern edge of Namibia there is dry grassland that gets less than 10 inches of rainfall yearly.

CLIMATE: In the desert areas, temperatures reach seasonal extremes—as high as 120 °F in the summer and as low as 10 °F in the winter.

POPULATION: Total population was just over 2 million in 2006. Namibia is a young country, with 43% of its people under age 15.

INCOME: Namibia is a developing nation. In equivalent U.S. purchasing power, its per capita income (GDP) was $5,200 in 2007.

EDUCATION: Eighty-five percent of Namibians are literate. Nearly all adult Namibians have at least some high school education.

MINORITIES: Namibia has many ethnic groups. The Ovambo number over 600,000 and are the largest ethnic group. There are 80,000 Whites and 36,000 San. The Kavango, Damara, and Herero groups number about 100,000 each. There are also many other, smaller groups.

CHAPTER THREE

The San Peoples of Namibia: Ancient Culture in a New Nation

INTRODUCTION

Of all the societies described in this book, Namibia may be the most unfamiliar to you. Perhaps you know little about any of the countries of sub-Saharan Africa. Many Westerners avoid thinking about Africa altogether. It seems to them to be a continent of disasters, plagued by drought, famine, war, and disease. You may know that most of the poorest nations of the world are in Africa. But we think you will find many surprises in this chapter. First of all, you will learn about African diversity. Do you think of Africa as a "Black continent"? Did you know that there are people of several different races in Africa and that there are many ethnic groups and many languages?

If you were born in the last decades of the 20th century, you may think it has been a long time since African countries were European colonies, and you may know little about the wars Africans fought for independence. We think you will be surprised to learn that Africa's colonial past is actually very recent and that it casts a long shadow over Africa today.

Namibia was the last colony in Africa to become an independent Black nation—in 1990! Today it is a stable democracy with a free press and the most democratic constitution of any African nation. Namibia is rich in resources: It mines diamonds, uranium, lead, and zinc and has a thriving fishing industry. Cattle and sheep ranching predominate on the dry central plain and Namibia exports beef and sheepskins. In the north, bordering Angola, where there is more rainfall, family farmers herd cattle and goats and raise crops for their own subsistence. Namibia is a "middle income" African country. Yearly per capita gross national product (GNP) is about $1,990 in dollar equivalents and the economy is growing by about 25% per year (World Bank, n.d.). But Namibia's income is very unequally distributed. Two minority racial groups stand out: In a country with a total population of about 2 million, there are 80,000 Whites whose incomes are way above average. They own most of the good land and live in modern European-style houses, with cars and servants, TVs, computers, and cell phones. Their children attend private schools and universities (Saunders, 1999, p. 764).[1]

---

[1]This pattern of a small White minority dominating land ownership is typical of southern African countries like Namibia, South Africa, Zimbabwe, and Mozambique.

At the other end of the economic spectrum are the 32,000 San who are the focus of this chapter. Looked down upon by Blacks and Whites alike, most San live in the Kalahari Desert, the driest, most undesirable part of Namibia. Most own no land and no cattle, and they are dependent on White commercial farmers and Black subsistence farmers for work, or on the government for life-saving food supplies. Yet the San are the original people of Namibia; they were here long before Whites or Blacks arrived. Their story is interwoven with the whole history of Namibia. When you understand the San you will know a lot about the importance of Africa in human history, about the tragedy of colonialism, and about the challenges facing African nations today.

Who Are the San?

The San of southern Africa are a people sharply different from all the other groups in this book. For centuries, and probably for thousands of years, they were a **hunting and gathering** (or **foraging**) people who lived in small bands of 10 to 50 individuals and gathered wild plant foods and hunted game. Systematically moving among food and water sources, the San were **nomadic:** They made no permanent homes and carried with them their few possessions. They had no rulers, no schools, no money, no written language, no police, no hospitals, and no inequalities of wealth or privilege. San lived in southwestern Africa long before Black people from southeastern Africa or Whites from Europe arrived. Archaeologists have found evidence of people like the San living in this region as long as 11,000 years ago and occupying the area without interruption ever since (Tobias, 1978, pp. 4, 30–31).

First Encounter

Bumping along sand tracks in the Kalahari Desert in dry season, you do not see the San camp until your jeep is almost upon it: a circle of shelters roughly built of sticks and grasses, facing inward toward a cleared area, and almost invisible in the surrounding landscape of dry brush. The full band of perhaps 20 individuals gathers around their campfires. You see small people with yellowish brown skins, partially clothed in animal hides, blending readily into their environment.

It is dusk and they are blowing their fires into flames to cook the evening meal. Women are sorting through their day's collection of wild foods: mangetti nuts, tsama melons, water-bearing roots, perhaps birds' eggs or a snake, or in a wetter season, wild onions, leafy greens, tsin beans, or baobab fruit. The men have killed a small antelope and they are distributing the meat among their relatives. You hear many voices: Men tell the story of their hunt; women report on the tracks they have seen while out gathering; people gossip, tease, and joke. You hear the children's games, played to a rhythm of clapping and singing. The San come forward to meet you, carefully leaving their weapons—their small bows with the lethal poison-coated arrows—behind. They will doubtless invite you to share their food and water, but they will expect you to return their hospitality.

The year is 1957.

When anthropologists and others talk about San "Bushmen," they are generally referring to people with three important traits. First of all, traditionally, San are hunters and gatherers; they feed themselves by foraging. They don't herd animals or farm.

Second, San are associated with a distinctive physical appearance. They are quite small in stature (the men under 5 feet 3 inches; the women considerably under 5 feet), and they have light brown or "yellow" skin, small heart-shaped faces with wide-apart eyes, eyefolds, and flat-bridged noses. Physically they are very different from the Black Bantu-speaking people of Africa, who are tall and dark.

Also, San are known for speaking "click languages," which will probably sound quite unusual to you. There are three related click languages that include a dozen or so click sounds, made by clicking the tongue against the teeth, the roof of the mouth, the cheek, and so on, as if you were going "tsk tsk" or signaling to a horse. The clicks usually function as consonants in forming words. San themselves have made no written language, so only anthropologists have attempted to write down these click sounds and they have developed a system of denoting the different clicks with symbols like these: !, /, //.

As you might expect, all San peoples are not exactly alike. The Ju/'hoansi or !Kung San, described in this chapter, fit the previous description best. Elsewhere in southern Africa, some San peoples (like the !Xu) live near rivers or in more fertile country, and do some fishing, herding, and gardening in addition to foraging. Other San peoples, like the Hai//om, speak languages related to those of the Nama and Damara, dark-skinned herding people. These San are also often taller and darker than the Ju/'hoansi (Barnard, 1992, pp. 6–13, 16–28).

Problems with Names

People who study the San have had a lot of trouble deciding what to call them. The San were called "Bushmen" by European settlers, a name derived from the Dutch *bossiesman* or "bandit." Recently the term San has been adopted in Namibia as a respectful name. In Botswana the Bushmen are now called *Basarwa*. Educated Bushmen adopt the name San, but many still call themselves Bushmen. Anthropologists use both terms. Because the San are so looked down upon in Southern Africa, all the names for them take on derogatory meaning. San is used to mean "tramps" or "rascals." Basarwa has picked up the insulting connotation of "those without cattle."(Barnard, 1992, pp. 8–9; Gordon, 1992, pp. 4–8; Kelso, 1993, p. 51).

Where Do the San Live?

Once Bushmen lived all over southern Africa, but today they are concentrated in the nations of Namibia and Botswana, mostly in the huge dry expanse of the Kalahari Desert. The Kalahari Desert is a vast basin of sand, occupying almost a third of the African subcontinent. Much of the Kalahari is too dry to sustain human habitation, but in the more northerly parts, around places like Nyae Nyae in Namibia and Dobe in Botswana, where the Ju/'hoansi live, and in the central Kalahari in Botswana, where the G/wi and the G/ana live, there is enough rain to support drought-resistant plants, grasses, scattered trees, and the animals that feed upon them. There are many kinds of antelope, like eland, kudu, and gemsbok; there are warthogs, hares, and tortoises, and also giraffe. There are predators too, like lions and hyena, and there are increasing numbers of elephants.

The rainy season leaves temporary pools of surface water, and greens up the landscape, so plants bear fruit, nuts, berries, and seeds. But rains are localized and unpredictable; at the same time that some areas receive abundant rainfall, others nearby may suffer drought. The whole region experiences drought approximately 2 years out of every 5, with severe drought 1 year in 4. There are dry riverbeds in the Kalahari, but they are rarely filled by runoff, perhaps only once in a decade. At a small number of permanent waterholes underground water comes to the surface.

The Kalahari is "big sky country," flat and monotonous, with endless vistas of brush out to the horizon. Outsiders easily lose their way in the markerless landscape. To this austere landscape is joined a harsh climate. During the hot, dry season of September and October, temperatures reach 115 °F in the shade, 126 °F in the sun, and the temperature of the sand reaches 140 °F. The Kalahari winter of May to August is cold and dry, with nighttime temperatures often below freezing (Lee, 1979, pp. 87–88; Marshall, 1976, pp. 62–71).

A few San peoples live outside the Kalahari: the Ovokango River San and the Hai//om of Namibia, the !Xu of Angola, and the /Xam and the "Mountain San of Lesotho" in South Africa.

The San and Prehistory

Using research by anthropologists, archaeologists, and historians, sociologists have concluded that in all of human history there have been just four basic kinds of societies. The first human societies were hunter-gatherer bands, like the San. Humans, and their prehuman ancestors before them, lived like this for hundreds of thousands and perhaps millions of years. They lived in small nomadic bands, following game and harvesting wild foods. It was only about 10,000 years ago that humans learned to raise their own food. They settled down, often along rivers, and made gardens and raised tame animals. These people lived in horticultural villages. At about this same time, other peoples began to live as pastoralists, herding animals and often moving about with their herds. Approximately 6,000 years ago what we think of as "civilization" began, with the invention of agriculture. Agriculture applied new technologies (the plow) and new methods (fertilizing and rotating crops) so people could farm the same fields generation after generation. Farming raised more food and made it possible for some people to live on food others grew. They became craftspeople, priests, monks and nuns, kings and queens, professional soldiers, sailors, cathedral builders, artists, scientists and inventors, and all the other inhabitants of cities in agricultural states. Finally, the most recent type of society to develop (in the last 250 years) is industrial nations, in which farming has become so productive that most people can devote their lives to other work, producing goods in factories, building large cities, inventing new technologies, waging war, and so forth. All four types of societies still exist today, but there are fewer and fewer hunter-gatherer and horticultural societies.[2]

[2]Sociologists owe this commonly used classification scheme to Gerhard and Jean Lenski (Lenski, Nolan, & Lenski, 1991).

The Importance of Hunter-Gatherers

Because the first humans were foragers, sociologists and anthropologists have long regarded hunter-gatherer bands as the cradles of human nature and culture. The first families must have been formed in hunter-gatherer bands, the first specialized roles and the first religions. It is easy to speculate (but difficult to prove) that early conditions of foraging bands fundamentally shaped human nature. Those who study hunter-gatherer societies have often asked whether widespread human characteristics—like competitiveness or aggression—are a heritage from those first societies.

It is hard to learn much about societies that existed 50,000 or 100,000 years ago when all the world's peoples were hunter-gatherers. Archaeologists dig up fossilized human and animal bones and the remains of hearths and sometimes huts, weapons, garbage heaps, and fossilized pollen, but these remains can tell us little about how people interacted in prehistoric times. To learn about humanity's ancient past, anthropologists and sociologists have turned to hunter-gatherer societies that still exist today. They have hoped that study of the San will open a window on the common ancestors of all humans—the ancient hunter-gatherer peoples.

Hunter-Gatherers and Human Nature

When you study the San, you must put away stereotyped images of "cavemen" fighting each other in a brutal competition for survival. The Bushmen are generally peaceful people which is quite typical of hunter-gatherers. They avoid conflict and competition and share what they have so that everyone can survive. They have no formal leaders, no privileged class or deprived lower class. They don't hate or fight their neighbors. Though they live in a harsh environment, their lives are not brutal or debased. They value generosity and graciousness, joking and kidding around, and they find plenty of time for relaxing, playing music and singing, dressing up, and holding ceremonial dances, like parties that go on all night. If this is what our earliest ancestors were like, then we cannot blame our own greed and violence on our evolutionary heritage.

Living with Nature

The San have exemplified a kind of society we may well call the most successful human way of life of all times. The hunter-gatherer life sustained humanity for millions of years. Variations of foraging cultures allowed people to live in many different environments, gentle or harsh: by the shore, in forests, open grasslands, deserts, rainforests, and arctic tundra. Wherever they live, hunter-gatherers live close to nature: Their food comes directly from nature, and everything they use—houses, tools, clothing, containers, jewelry, and weapons—is made by hand from natural materials. Hunter-gatherers use nature, but they don't use it up. They don't kill off the animals they depend on; they don't use up the water or pollute the land. They can go on living on the same land for thousands and thousands of years without harming it. Sociologists call this **sustainability.** In the last 10,000 years, since people learned to cultivate seeds and plants and to domesticate animals, human impact on the environment has constantly increased. Industrial society now pollutes the air and water and land. It pumps carbon dioxide into the atmosphere, creating a "greenhouse effect," and it alters ecosystems, so many animal species become endangered or extinct. Many people are now asking: Is our industrial way of life sustainable? Perhaps we can learn from the San about creating an environmentally sustainable society.

Anthropologists and the San

Eager to learn about hunters and gatherers, anthropologists have studied the San, especially the Ju/'hoansi in Namibia and Botswana, with exceptional thoroughness. Dutch and English scholars in South Africa began publishing studies of the San as early as the 19th century. From the early 1950s through the present, anthropologists, linguists, archaeologists, musicologists, and ecologists have almost continuously lived with and observed one or another group of San. These social scientists made a very detailed record of San life, in books and films, which we will draw on in this account.

The first major studies of the Ju/'hoansi and the G/wi were done by Lorna and Laurence Marshall in the 1950s. The Marshalls made many trips to the Kalahari, accompanied by their daughter, Elizabeth Marshall Thomas, who wrote a famous book about the San, *The Harmless People,* and their son, John Marshall, who filmed San daily life. In the 1970s, anthropologist Richard B. Lee and his team studied several groups of !Kung, as reported in his books, *The !Kung San* and *The Dobe Ju/'hoansi.* Today, a new generation of anthropologists, from South Africa, the United States, Norway, Japan, and other countries, has come to Namibia and Botswana to observe the San.[3] Their primary focus has been on how Bushman culture is now changing as former foragers settle in villages and adopt cattle herding.

Some present-day anthropologists such as Robert Gordon and Edwin Wilmsen (Gordon, 1992; Wilmsen, 1989) have questioned the portrait of the San painted by earlier anthropologists. These scholars, they suggest, were too eager to discover in the San an isolated living survival of Stone Age times. Anthropologists portrayed the San living in a timeless present and often failed even to mention what country they inhabited. Gordon and Wilmsen caution that for a long time—perhaps as long as 2,000 years—Bantu and Khoi herders lived near San, and well-used routes for trade in iron, glass beads, and shells passed through San territory. San, they contend, have long herded animals and traded goods when they could.

HISTORY OF THE SAN

We know very little about the history of the San for all the thousands of years before their contact with Europeans in the 17th century. The modern history of the San, recorded first by White settlers, then by colonial governments, and now by African governments, began in the 17th century. It is a tragic story of genocide and displacement.

---

[3]They include John Yellen, Susan Kent, James Denbow, Edwin Wilmsen, Robert Hitchcock, Robert Gordon, Thomas Widlok, Megan Biesele, James Suzman, Polly Weissner, and Claire Ritchie.

Settlers and the San

In the 17th century, an estimated 200,000 San lived all over southern Africa—in the desert, the mountains, on grasslands, and along the coasts. When the Dutch settled the Cape of Good Hope region at the southern tip of Africa in the 1650s, an indigenous (native) group of San, called the Khoi, were living there, fishing, hunting, gathering, and herding cattle and goats. Seizing their good land, the Dutch slaughtered the Khoi and drove them northward.

Other groups of San lived in more remote areas, in small bands, and without domesticated animals. The Dutch were especially contemptuous of them and considered them "wild" people, little better than animals. In the 18th century, White settlers moved north and almost completely exterminated the San, killing the men and enslaving the women and children. Some San fought back, raiding settlers' farms and stealing cattle, and in remote areas they were able to hold off the Whites for years. By the end of the 19th century, the San had been virtually wiped out in all of the country of South Africa. White South Africans then began to settle further north, in Namibia, joined by German traders and missionaries. However, few ventured into the harsh lands of the Kalahari Desert.

In the 19th century, the Kalahari Desert San came into contact with another group of settlers: Bantu-speaking Blacks from southeastern Africa. Relationships between the San and the Bantu peoples were not always harmonious. Both sides tell stories of armed conflict, cattle theft, and disputes over women, and the Bantu have considered the San an inferior people. However, these forms of conflict have never become as extreme as the European genocide against the San, and in the 20th century, trade and intermarriage between San and Bantu have peacefully developed. As a result of intermarriage, some San who live along the eastern edge of the Kalahari have come to resemble their Bantu neighbors physically. Two different Bantu cattle-herding peoples, the Tswana and the Herero, settled the margins of the Kalahari. The men worked for the Tswana as trackers and porters, and later as cattle herders, receiving tobacco and cow's milk in exchange for seasonal or temporary work. Many San, especially in Botswana, became attached to Herero farms as unpaid dependents (Lee, 1978, pp. 94–96; 1979, pp. 32–33, 77–84; 1984, pp. 17–18; Silberbauer, 1978, p. 181).

The Colonial Era in Namibia

Namibia became a German colony in 1884; it was known as German Southwest Africa. At that time Germany was a powerful industrialized society with advanced weaponry, and Namibia was sparsely populated and vulnerable. The Herero and Nama peoples were the largest ethnic groups in the country and they lived in the central plateau, grasslands well suited to animal raising. The German colonial powers gradually took over this land, between 1893 and 1903, pushing the Herero and the Nama onto the edges of the plateau, where there was less rainfall and the land quickly became overcrowded and the soil exhausted. When the Herero and the Nama tried to resist this policy of "highland clearance," the Germans responded with purposeful genocide. In two military campaigns, in 1904 and 1908, the German armed forces in Southwest Africa slaughtered three quarters of the Herero and half the Nama. The Herero and Nama population in Namibia today is still smaller than it was in 1904. As Leys and Saul (1995) point out, this first genocide in a century of carnage prefigured Nazism. It even began with an "extermination order" issued by the German chief of staff, Von Trotha (pp. 8–9; Slotten, 1995, p. 277).

Having killed off the native inhabitants, German settlers found there were not enough people available to work on their ranches and in the mines. So they set up a system of *apartheid* (separation of races), dividing Southwest Africa into two sections. The south was for Whites only, except for Blacks who had passes showing they worked for Whites. North of the official "red line" or "police line" the Germans created reserves for the Ovambo, Kavango, and Makololo peoples who were allowed to live under the authority of their own chiefs, as long as they responded to German recruiting and sent migrant laborers south to the German ranches and mines. There they worked as "contract laborers" for wages amounting to about 5% of White wages (Leys & Saul, 1995, pp. 9–10; Slotten, 1995, p. 1). In this period the first German settlers began to appear at the edges of the Kalahari Desert, taking over San waterholes and pushing them onto drier land. It wasn't unusual for settlers to kill San or kidnap ("blackbird") them and force them to work on White farms (Gordon, 1992, pp. 201–205).

South Africa Takes Over

Germany was defeated in World War I and as a result it lost its African colonies. The League of Nations awarded Southwest Africa to Great Britain, which turned it over to South Africa (a White-run former British colony, by then a member of the British dominion). For the people of Southwest Africa this was no improvement at all. They went from the hands of one brutal master into those of another. South Africa kept the German system of apartheid, as it did in its own territory. It gave the White minority in Southwest Africa some limited self-government and kept the Black majority suppressed and exploited. Afrikaner settlers (people of Dutch descent from South Africa) gradually replaced German settlers and kept pushing out the remaining Blacks on the plateau. By 1963, 48.7% of the land was controlled by White farms. Black migrant laborers from the north were not allowed to bring their families south with them. They were forced to live in miserable "compounds" and allowed to return home only once every 2 years. South Africa was as willing as Germany had been to use violence to maintain this system. The police, the army, and a counterinsurgency unit all made expeditions to punish resistance by northern peoples, and political activists were beaten, tortured, and killed (Gordon, 1992, p. 201; Leys & Saul, 1995, pp. 9–10; Saunders, 1999, p. 755; Slotten, 1995, p. 278).

Formalizing Apartheid

In 1964 South Africa formalized its system by creating "self-governing homelands" for Namibia's 11 ethnic peoples. In a kind of mockery of "separate but equal," Whites ruled Namibia, but Blacks were permitted their own local governments on reservations to which they were confined. Of course all the wealth, businesses, mines, diamonds, and minerals were in the south, so the northern reserves or *bantustans* had no tax revenues to work with (Leys & Saul, 1995, pp. 9–10; Slotten, 1995, p. 278).

Bushmanland

For the San apartheid meant the loss of most of their last refuge: the Kalahari Desert. South Africa established two "homelands" for the Bushmen, Bushmanland in the Kalahari and West Caprivi in the far north. But Bushmanland comprised only 10% of the land around Nyae Nyae, so the Ju/'hoansi lost 90% of their land and all but one of their permanent water holes. Most of the land they were left is deep sand, without water holes, with little plant or animal life. The government made southern Nyae Nyae into Hereroland East, a homeland for the surviving Herero, and joined northern Nyae Nyae to the Kavango homeland.

The San suffered further losses. The Southwest African government set up game and nature reserves on their land. In the 1950s the Hai//'om were driven off their lands that were turned into the Etosha Game Reserve. The Kxoe were expelled from their land on the Kavango River for another nature reserve. Finally, in 1968, about 6,000 Ju/'hoan people were evicted from the West Caprivi (Weinberg, 1997, p. 8).

The Fate of Hunter-Gatherers

As recently as 100 years ago, there were dozens of foraging peoples still living in isolation in the most remote corners of the globe—in the deserts of Africa and Australia, the rainforests of the Amazon, Africa, and New Guinea, and the arctic wastes of Canada. But modern societies have not been kind to indigenous foraging peoples. Industrial societies have penetrated every corner of the earth, exploring, searching for precious metals, or oil, for trees to log or land to clear for farming and ranching. Everywhere, they have dismissed indigenous hunter-gatherer peoples as subhuman savages. Settlers and explorers have not hesitated to kill indigenous people or take away their land, their means of survival. Western diseases spread through indigenous populations in devastating epidemics, and the bewildered survivors were converted by missionaries and enticed or forced into working for the outsiders. Under the assault of modern societies, indigenous cultures all over the world have disappeared. Surviving hunter-gatherers have been forced into the least desirable environments on earth.

Today, Namibia's San have lost almost all their land to encroaching White and Black farmers. How do they survive? Have they abandoned their culture to adapt to modern Namibia? This chapter is written in two parts. In the first part we will begin by describing San life as it was lived up until they lost most of their land in the late 1960s. Then, in the second part of the chapter we will continue our history of the San in Namibia and examine what happened to the San during Namibia's war for independence and after 1990 in independent Namibia.

Let's return, for now, to the 1950s, a time when the hunting and gathering life was relatively undisturbed. You must keep in mind that even in the 1950s, when there were many more people living by foraging, the San were not fossils of the past. Prehistoric hunters and gatherers lived in a world of hunters and gatherers.

Then, the whole world was wilderness; there were no towns, no governments, no roads, no lands cleared for farming. Small bands of people traveled about following game and harvesting wild plants, and meeting another band was a rare and important event. We can use our knowledge of 20th-century hunter-gatherers to help us picture the past, but we must remember that even in the 1950s, the Bushman world was shaped by governments, settlers, and world events.

PART I: SAN CULTURE—
A DESIGN FOR LIVING

You can do a brief "thought experiment" to help you understand San culture. Imagine that like characters in a movie, you and your friends are suddenly dropped into the Kalahari Desert, circa 1957. Will you survive? Unlike the animals of the Kalahari, you will not know instinctively how to find water or food or shelter, or how to organize your group life. You will lack special physical adaptations to desert life. Your evolved human capacity to create culture will have to see you through.

San groups, like all human societies, learned how to secure the necessities of life. They divided up their tasks efficiently. They learned to keep order, resolve conflicts, and protect the group from outside threats. Their beliefs about the meaning of life sustained them. Even reproduction was not left to nature; the San made sure they had enough children, but not too many, and they taught their children how to live in their society and their difficult environment.

Sociology textbooks often adopt anthropologist Clyde Kluckholm's definition of **culture** as **"a design for living."** Every human group must solve the basic problems of adapting to their environment: Groups do so through culture and **social structure,** and if they are successful, the group survives. But there are many possible designs for living (Kluckholm, 1949).

All the various Bushman peoples were similar in the fundamentals of their life, but they differed somewhat in their customs. For example, Ju/'hoansi San gathered in large groups in the dry season and dispersed into smaller bands in the wet season, but G/wi Bushmen in Botswana did the opposite. To avoid confusion in this part of the chapter, we will focus mostly on one group, the Ju/'hoansi San who live around Nyae Nyae in northeastern Namibia and directly across the border at Dobe in Botswana. The Ju/'hoansi are the most intensively studied Bushman group, so there is a lot of anthropological information to draw on.

Nyae Nyae: 1957

Let's describe traditional Ju/'hoan society in the present tense, so you can imagine yourself there, in the Kalahari, in 1957 or before. Even in their harsh environment the Ju/'hoansi San have found a way to live that is environmentally sustainable, psychologically rewarding, and physically healthy. Four elements of San culture make possible a more than adequate living in the Kalahari Desert. These are the Bushmen's comprehensive **knowledge** of their environment and its food sources; the custom of **nomadism,** or movement from one temporary encampment to another; customs of childbearing and childrearing that result in **population limitation;** and **values** that stress sharing, equality, modesty, and cooperation.

Knowledge

Foremost in importance is the San detailed knowledge of their environment, itself a form of control over nature. Knowledge of plants, water sources, and animal habits enables the San to use the desert as a larder, neither cultivating nor storing food, but rather turning systematically from one resource to another, each in its season. To some degree, knowledge is gender based because women gather plants and men hunt animals, but both women and men have some basic store of knowledge about animal tracks and plant properties.

San hunters are superb trackers. Not only can they identify animals from their tracks in the sand and their droppings, they are able to deduce detailed information from tracks. They can single out the tracks of a single animal (perhaps the one injured by an arrow) from those of a herd, tell if it is male or female, old or young, whether it is injured and how badly. Examining the freshness of tracks, hunters can deduce how long ago an animal passed, whether it was feeding, how fast it was going, whether it passed during the morning or afternoon (did it seek the shade to the east or west of bushes and trees?) or at night. Both men and women can read human footprints in the sand, identifying the tracks of every individual.

Intimate knowledge of resources makes the foraging life possible. The San know and name hundreds of plants, insects, animals, and birds. Tiny arrows derive their lethal power from a poison coating made from the larvae and parasites of three different kinds of beetles.[4] In the dry season, when plants wither to near invisibility, women unerringly locate underground water-storing roots from the evidence of a few tiny leaves hidden in the dry grass. They know exactly when each plant resource will be ready to harvest, under various weather conditions. And they know how much water each permanent and temporary waterhole can be expected to provide, so they are never caught short.

Nomadism

The San adapt themselves to the desert by living in small **nomadic bands.** The Ju/'hoansi have no permanent place of residence, but they cannot be said to wander either. They move about the desert in a planned, rational fashion, making temporary camps to exploit local resources of water and food, then move on when these become scarce. In the dry season, they retreat to permanent water holes. In this way, the San neither wear out nor pollute the desert; they distribute their impact over a wide area.

But nomadism means traveling light. When the Ju/'hoansi move, they carry on their backs all their possessions, plus their young children. In fact, all of a person's belongings can fit into a leather bag the size of an overnight carrier, and weigh no more than 12–15 pounds. Possessions include a woman's *kaross* (her leather all-purpose garment and blanket), her digging stick, items of personal adornment like beads and

---

[4]The poison acts on the central nervous system, through the bloodstream, so animals killed by the poison can be safely eaten.

headbands, ostrich eggshell water holders, and, perhaps, an iron pot. A man carries his hunting kit—arrows, bow, and quiver—and his fire-making kit; other possessions include musical instruments, toys, pipes, ceremonial rattles, tortoise shell bowls, nets, and leather bags. All possessions (except the pot) are handmade and can readily be made anew. Houses are built at each camp out of branches and grasses, and abandoned when the camp is moved. The San possess little, but until they become involved in the modern cash economy, they desire no more and feel no deprivation.

Population Control

Ultimately, the desert can support the San because they keep their population proportionate to its resources. In the 1970s, in the central Kalahari, population density was no more than one person per 4 to 6 square miles (Silberbauer, 1978, p. 184)! Significantly, it is a low birthrate, rather than an usually high death rate, that keeps the Ju/'hoan population small. Women generally don't have their first child until their late teens. Thereafter, children are widely spaced, without modern means of birth control, with an interval of approximately 4 years between babies. How this spacing is achieved has fascinated anthropologists. Elizabeth Marshall Thomas explains it clearly. Women work hard gathering and carrying food and so they are lean, with little body fat. As a result, they reach puberty late. Once they have had a child constant nursing inhibits ovulation. When the child is weaned, at around age 4, the mother resumes ovulation and probably immediately becomes pregnant again. Thomas observes that Ju/'hoan women rarely experience menstruation. Nowadays, we see that Ju/'hoan women who settle on cattle ranches or farms walk less and nurse their babies less frequently and also have more children more closely spaced together (Thomas, 2006, pp. 192–193).

The Ju/'hoansi understand the importance of spacing their children: It is very difficult for a mother to carry two children at once, and also, because young children live so entirely on their mother's milk, if a mother had two nursing babies, her milk would be insufficient and both would probably die. **Infanticide** (the killing of newborn infants) is infrequently practiced, but seen as a possible tragic necessity should a new sibling come too soon after the birth of a baby or in the rare case of twins. Infant and child mortality is high by modern Western standards, but not compared to most poor agricultural societies. Close to 20% of Ju/'hoan children die before their first birthday, and only half of those born live long enough to marry (Shostak, 1981, p. 182).

The Value of Sharing

Critical to San survival is the emphasis they place on sharing. The worst one can say of a person is that he or she is "far-hearted" or stingy. Generosity, graciousness, and modesty are highly valued. Indeed, it would be fair to say that sharing is a subject of constant discussion among the Ju/'hoansi, with the question "who will give me food?" always on people's minds. As the San see it, sharing is important because it is the way to create and maintain relationships.

A **functionalist** sociologist would explain sharing differently, as a practice that helps the society survive. A functionalist might say that sharing is the San "social security system." They cannot store food for future use and they cannot buy food with money or any other goods, so when food is scarce, life is threatened. A man could be the best hunter, but if he is injured or falls ill, there is no unemployment insurance or welfare, no savings account or pension plan. He must rely on the people in his family and band to feed him. Everyone needs to help others, so that they can be helped in turn. A person who shares gets something else of value in return also: prestige or social advantage. A hunter who shares shows he is fit to be a husband or qualified to be a hunting partner (Roue, 1998, p. 24).

Sharing is not only a prime value in San culture, it is a constant practice integral to their way of life. Sharing takes place on many levels. The plant foods women gather are cooked and shared with their immediate families. Big game is shared on a wider basis. The hunter to whom the meat belongs cuts it into large chunks and distributes these among his immediate relatives: his wife, in-laws, parents, and siblings. These recipients give some of their share to those who eat at their fire, but they also cut much of the meat into smaller pieces and make presents of these to their relatives, who pass it on in turn to theirs. In the end, everyone in a camp shares the meat, not in a wholesale distribution, but as a personal gift from some connection, and the meat is quickly consumed. The idea of a person hoarding meat is horrifying to the San: It seems savage and uncivilized. "Lions might do that; people could not," they explain. Lorna Marshall noted that in one large dry-season encampment, the meat of a single eland (a large antelope) was ultimately distributed to 63 individuals (Marshall, 1976, p. 302).

But the San struggle with sharing; it doesn't always come easily and sometimes hunger or possessiveness win out over generosity. People grumble if someone keeps a particularly desirable ornament or tool, instead of passing it on as a gift. Disputes often arise over the sharing of food. Among the Ju/'hoansi, custom facilitates sharing by blurring the ownership of meat. Meat belongs not to the man who brings it down, but to the owner of the arrow that first penetrates the quarry. A hunter will usually carry arrows from many individuals—his own, and also those borrowed or received as gifts from others. Even a poor hunter may thus come to be the owner of meat, and people will not be put in the position of constantly receiving gifts of meat from the same superior hunter.

Sharing takes place on a wider basis too: between bands as well as within them. Kalahari resources are unevenly distributed because localized drought may temporarily render one area barren while another is productive. At times like these, whole bands or individual families visit relatives in more fertile or better-watered areas. At another time, when conditions are different, they will reciprocate as hosts. Sharing evens out inequalities—between youthful and aging families, between talented and inept hunters, women and men, and people in different areas. Sharing constantly reinstates equality, ensuring that differences in individual ability or luck will not accumulate into institutionalized economic or status stratification.

A Flexible Culture

Knowledge, nomadism, low population growth, and sharing are critical elements of San culture. Together they make possible the distinctive flexibility of forager societies. People shift readily from one food source to another. Tsin beans, mangetti nuts, meat, government-supplied cornmeal—San turn readily from one to another. Without jobs or permanent houses, they are available to pull up stakes and go where food and water can be found. Small families are flexible, too. There aren't too many babies to carry, and as we will see, families easily break away from one band to join another, allowing band size to adapt to resources. Wherever they go, San can rely on their friends and relatives to share with them. There is no bureaucracy to slow down decision making, nor do possessions tie them down. It is customary to think of hunting and gathering societies as fragile, because we have seen so many destroyed by loss of their land; but actually, the fluidity and flexibility of San society is a great strength when they are forced to adapt to other peoples and societies. As Mathais Guenther points out, the San are as willing to forage for ideas and for new social connections as for food, making their culture relatively resilient in the face of outside influence (Guenther, 1996, pp. 73–74; Kent, 1996a, pp. 6–7, 12–14).

How Hard Is the Foraging Life?

Until recently, life in hunter-gatherer societies was believed to be harsh and difficult, with constant labor the only shield against starvation, and population kept from outrunning resources only by famine, disease, and infanticide. Late-20th-century studies of the Ju/'hoansi San and other foraging societies have advanced a much rosier view of foraging societies and, by implication, of early human history. One of the most significant new insights is that foragers don't work very hard. In fact, they spend fewer hours working and enjoy more hours of leisure than people in agricultural and modern industrial societies. In a typical band observed by Lee, women went out gathering on an average of 9 out of 28 days. Counting all foraging, tool-making and fixing, and housework, women put in an average workweek of 40 hours. Ju/'hoan men spent more days hunting, an average of 12 out of every 28 days, and counting all hunting, gathering, tool-making and fixing, and housework, their average work week was 44.5 hours. Even at this low level of work, the Ju/'hoansi are generally adequately nourished, and they have infant mortality rates and adult life expectancies somewhat better than those of most agricultural societies.[5]

Work and Affluence

The San work little, but from our modern Western point of view, they are poor and deprived. It is important to understand that San living traditionally don't feel deprived. They don't crave permanent houses, running water, refrigerators, Jeeps, or diapers. They accept occasional hunger, secure in the knowledge that there will be food soon enough. In effect, they have made a tradeoff—living at a low level of material affluence, they needn't work much, and can enjoy a great deal of leisure. And, in reality, because they live in a sparse environment, greater work would not necessarily produce greater abundance over the long run; it might instead disturb the ecological balance. For example, more intensive hunting might temporarily provide abundant meat, but it might also threaten the welfare of the wild herds, and therefore ultimately, the survival of the San.

---

[5]Richard B. Lee collected this data in 1964. See Lee, 1979, pp. 254–280. Lee notes that work in child care was not included in the calculations, but if it had been, the work totals for women would have been considerably higher, because they do 60 to 80% of all care of young children.

Leisure

The San devote their leisure to nurturing group life, cultivating relationships between individuals, and elaborating their culture. Perhaps it was the abundant leisure of foragers that allowed our ancestors to create human culture, incrementally freeing humanity from the bonds of instinct and biological necessity.

Those who study the San all note that they are great talkers. They spend an enormous amount of time sitting around their campfires talking, joking, arguing, exchanging news, telling stories, repeating the events of a hunt, planning tomorrow's hunting or gathering. There is a constant buzz of conversation in a camp, and uproarious laughter breaks out often. Group conversation takes the form of "call and response": a speaker's words are accompanied by cries of "eh, eh" and listeners repeat phrases as they are spoken (Guenther, 1999, p. 48). Women and girls sit close together at the campfire, their shoulders and knees touching, as do the men and boys. Members of a band truly seem to enjoy one another's company.

Playing Games.   Unlike the children of farming and herding societies, Ju/'hoan children do not have to work. This is, in its way, a sign of affluence: You could say that the Ju/'hoansi enjoy such abundance that they don't need the labor of their children (or of older people) to support the band. Because children don't go to school either, they are free to play all day long, until, in their teen years, girls and boys begin to accompany their elders in gathering and hunting. Adults also like to play games when they are at leisure in camp or in the evenings.

Surrounded by miles of open land, this band of Ju/'hoansi adults and children, men and women, cluster close together, talking, telling stories, joking, and arguing in typical San fashion.

The games the Ju/'hoansi play reveal much about their culture. There are no games in which people keep score or care greatly about winning or losing. Games are all played in groups, and in many, the players are bound together in rhythmic chorus and close physical contact. Typical is the ball game played by girls who stand in a line, singing and clapping. Each girl takes the ball in turn, at the right point in the music, dances with it, then tosses it to the next in line (Marshall, 1976, pp. 313, 322, 332–336).

A Musical Culture.   Music is not only a part of San games, but a constant accompaniment to camp life. The Ju/'hoansi have a rich musical culture in which everyone participates in some way. Their homemade instruments make subtle, vibrant sounds, and their compositions are always complex. For example, the traditional *guashi* is a stringed instrument made from a hollowed-out log strung with animal sinew or hair. People carry instruments with them on trips, and, traveling or in camp, they often sit listening to a musician, sometimes softly improvising a sung harmony interwoven with the intricate rhythm (Biesele, 1978, pp. 165–166; Marshall, 1976, pp. 363–375; Shostak, 1981, pp. 14, 310; Thomas, 1959, pp. 223–225).

Music is a means of individual self-expression for the San. People who are troubled or sad or bothered by some trying incident may sit alone and compose "mood music"—songs with titles, but without words, that touchingly express emotions, often wistful or ironic. Some songs are mocking and sung under cover of darkness, with words that reproach an individual for misbehavior.

Religion

Religion plays a part in San culture, but you may be surprised at how different San religious beliefs and practices are compared to those of your religion. The San believe in gods, spiritual beings who created the world and can intervene, if they wish, in life today. The San have creation stories and religious rituals, but no churches, no clergy, and, of course, no sacred books. Their religion features no laws or commandments, but rather reflects the uncertainly and unreliability of the world.

There are two main deities: a rather remote creator god, thought to inhabit the sky, and a lesser god, a trickster god, who has many disguises. Sometimes the trickster is a force for good, but he can also be capricious or destructive. He associated with the jackal, a devious animal. San also believe in the existence of the spirits of the dead, who live in a spiritual realm but may also do mischief among the living.

The San tell stories about a primal time when the earth was created. Many of these stories involve animal figures who have human traits. Both animals and the spirits of the dead feature in trance dances, the major religious ceremonies (Guenther, 1999, pp. 62–67, 88).

Sacred Dances.   *Trance dances* are a regular feature of San life, held on an average every 10 days, with dances more frequent during dry season, when the nearness of several bands at a water hole makes social life more intense and exciting. Dances involve everyone in the band or bands, and last entire nights, with the women seated in a line or circle, shoulder to shoulder, singing the sacred songs like the Gemsbok Song, the Giraffe Song, and the Sun Song and clapping complex rhythmic accompaniments. The men dance the animals, their steps emphasized by the shaking of cocoon rattles tied around their legs, Those who know how are able to use the dance to enter a trance in which they can converse with the spirits and heal the sick. Children excitedly dance and clap along, then, as the night wears on, fall asleep in their mothers' laps

Trance dances may begin spontaneously, as fun, often initiated by children, or they may be arranged in response to serious illness or misfortune. Trance medicine, *n/um,* is a kind of power, "owned" by the people who have learned how to achieve a trance state and use it to cure others. About half the adult men and a third of the women have achieved trance at some time. Smaller numbers are accomplished healers, the greatest of whom may travel from camp to camp when needed.

In trance, the healer is able to draw illness out of the bodies of the sick and throw it away. The Ju/'hoansi believe sickness (and misfortune and death) is caused by tiny invisible arrows shot into the sick person by the spirits of the dead. These spirits are not malevolent, but lonely, and wish the living to be with them. The spirits are especially likely to take away a person who is ill-treated by others. In trance, healers lay their hands on the afflicted persons and draw the arrows into their own bodies. Then, at a moment of crisis, healers violently shudder and shriek, hurling the arrows away again. It is believed that in deep trance healers' spirits can leave their bodies to meet and talk with the spirits of the dead, to find out why they want to take the sick person, and try to persuade them to reconsider (Biesele, 1978, pp. 167–168; Lee, 1984, pp. 109–113; Shostak, 1981, pp. 291–299). Megan Biesele emphasizes that the dancer's n/um cannot be activated without the support of singers (or drummers for the women's drum dance). Singing actually protects the dancers as their spirits leave their bodies. According to Biesele, the trance dance is thus "a concerted effort by the entire community to banish misfortune" and a central unifying force in San life. As **Emile Durkheim** (1965) pointed out a century ago (in *The Elementary Forms of the Religious Life*), dances like these are important shared experiences. Joining together in a sacred and risky ceremony intensifies group feeling, strengthening the bonds of group solidarity. Trance dances have both manifest and latent functions. **Manifest functions** are the consequences of behavior that people intend and recognize. **Latent functions** are the unintended and unrecognized consequences of behavior. Often latent functions are as important or even more important than manifest functions. Although the San may think of their dances as serving a practical-spiritual purpose (a manifest function), such as curing the sick, dances also fulfill a latent function of reinforcing solidarity. The San are unaware of this secondary purpose of drawing the group more closely together (Durkheim, 1965, p. 432).

Gift-Giving and Visiting. A great deal of the Sans abundant leisure is devoted to cultivating relationships—in talk and games, music-making and ceremony—that reinforce group solidarity. Leisure activities also link individuals with individuals in ties of friendship and reciprocal obligation. Ju/'hoansi all over northern Namibia are connected as *xaro*—gift-giving partners who maintain relationships by exchange and gifts and visits. In rainy season, individuals, couples, and small family groups break off from their bands to visit relatives and partners, especially people they like (Lee, 1979, p. 72; Marshall, 1976, pp. 180–181).

Gifts are also bestowed within the band and exchanged by spouses. Gift-giving is a constant preoccupation and a subject of talk second in prominence only to food. Interaction about gifts expresses feelings and carries weight in relationships. People talk about whom they plan to give gifts to; sometimes they complain about gifts they have received, or about people who take too long to reciprocate gifts. A person may ask someone for the gift of a particular object, as a way of inviting a closer relationship, or to cause discomfort because of jealousy or anger. It would be rude to refuse a gift, and one must reciprocate, but not too soon, for owing a return gift links people together in friendship and is the whole point of the exercise.

The objects given as gifts are really of secondary importance to the relationships created and sustained. Think of gift-giving, and sharing itself for that matter, as a way of creating **social capital,** relationships that help people survive and thrive and enjoy acceptance within their social groups. Anyone can make any of the objects in daily use, or readily borrow them, and people tend to keep the gifts they receive for just a short while, before passing them on as gifts to someone else. People give objects in common use: ostrich shell bead headbands and necklaces, musical instruments, wooden bowls, arrows, pipes, dance rattles, or valued materials like eland fat (Marshall, 1976, pp. 303–305, 309–310).

SOCIAL STRUCTURE AND GROUP LIFE

One important lesson you can learn from studying the San is that people create social structure themselves, through interaction. When you live in a large, complex society, statuses and roles and institutions often seem like "givens." You are confronted with politicians or bosses, teachers or nurses, schools or courts, and you may feel you have had nothing to do with creating them. In San society, it is clear that statuses and roles emerge as the result of repeated interaction between individuals. We can see the building of social structure very clearly, because San society is limited to the family and the band. The Ju/'hoansi are distinctive (though typical of hunting and gathering societies) in that they have an extremely limited selection of statuses, roles, groups, and institutions. There are no chiefs or officials, priests, managers, employees, doctors, or servants, or any of a long list of specialized statuses and roles that may be found in your society. There are no committees, gangs, classes, clans, teams, parliaments, or clubs. Neither are there churches, courts, prisons, hospitals, schools, armies, governments, markets, or businesses.

San society is a social system based on kinship: The band, the family, and kin statuses comprise all social structure and must serve all needs. It is most helpful to think of San society not as socially impoverished by its lack of varied social structure, but as focused with extraordinary intensity on family relationships. Because social structure is created and maintained through interaction, it is easy to understand that the San are constantly involved in forming and elaborating family relations.

The Individual

Here's another important point to think about: There are no authorities in San society. No one person has any more power than another. There are no police officers, no bosses, no teachers, no generals, no presidents, no kings. No one can tell you what to do—not even your parents! Kalahari San have a tremendous amount of individual freedom. They are not in the habit of taking orders from anyone, and if a person doesn't like what others are doing, their most usual response is to pick up and leave—go off visiting, or join another band. Some modern societies pride themselves on individuality and freedom of choice, but compared to hunters and gatherers, people in modern societies are totally hedged about with bosses. Anthropologist Mathias Guenther explains that there is a tension in San life between the independence of individuals and the pressing importance of sharing. San life requires constant interaction, as autonomous individuals must continually discuss, persuade, negotiate, and plead to organize daily life. They appeal to values of reciprocity and equality, which bridge the distance between individualism and sharing (Guenther, 1999, pp. 55–56).

The Family: Putting Flexibility First

The small **nuclear family** (the reproductive unit of parents and children) is the basic unit of San society. Families are "modular" and flexible. Nuclear family modules may link together to form larger **extended families,** and extended families may also break up into their constituent nuclear units. A series of nuclear and extended families links together to form a **band,** but bands are not necessarily permanent arrangements: Some families may leave and others join, and sometimes a band will break up entirely. At certain seasons, bands come together in larger encampments forming more or less defined **band clusters** (Guenther, 1996, pp. 79–80). The modular structure of Ju/'hoan families and bands may readily be seen as a form of **cultural adaptation,** permitting flexible adjustment of group size to available resources.

Creating Nuclear Families

Whereas a couple and their children form a long-lasting, firmly bonded group in San society, nuclear families never live independently. (However, they may temporarily go off visiting on their own.) Nuclear families are small. In the 1950s, 1960s, and 1970s, anthropologists found that the average Ju/'hoan woman gave birth to only four or five children altogether, and the average family comprised only two to three living children. Marriage creates nuclear families, and also links them in larger extended families and in an even broader kinship network.

When a couple marries, the Ju/'hoansi expect the husband to move in with his new wife's family. Typically, they explain this custom in terms of food. The boy must feed his wife's parents, who are getting old, and he must feed his bride, they say, and prove he is capable and responsible (Marshall, 1976, p. 169). Members of the same band are not forbidden to marry, but such marriages are unusual. Consequently, marriages usually involve some reshuffling of band membership. This is especially so because the new husband may bring others with him to his wife's band. He remains responsible for his parents and dependents, and they may come with him. Ju/'hoan men are allowed to have more than one wife (**polygyny**), though this practice is rare, and in such a case, a man will bring his first wife, their children, and perhaps her relatives with him (in addition to his own) when he joins his new wife's family.

There is no set duration for this **bride service** with the wife's family (people say it should last long enough for three children to be born), but afterward a man has the right to return to his own people, taking his wife and dependents. He may or may not do this, depending on how well he gets along with his wife's band and what kinds of resources are available to each band. The couple and their dependents may in fact move back and forth between his relatives and hers (Marshall, 1976, p. 170). One way of understanding this is to say that Ju/'hoan society is **ambilocal:** People live with either the husband's or the wife's relatives. It is also **bilateral:** They reckon kinship on both their mother's and their father's sides.

The Band: Linking Families

There is no rigid pattern for band formation. Band members are always related to each other in some fashion (through ties of blood or marriage), but the actual linkages vary. The band grows like a chain, as in-marrying spouses bring their parents, siblings, and spouses, who in turn bring theirs. But band members are not mandated by kinship ties to remain together. People choose to stay in a band because they get along well living and working together. If they don't get along, families are free to leave the band, affiliating themselves with relatives in some other band. This is a real option, frequently exercised. Often families break off from their band to visit others—to exchange gifts, or news, or arrange a marriage, or attend a ceremony. Because bands are flexible, people can adjust the size of their group to environmental conditions and resources. Most people, Lorna Marshall found, have relatives who are parents, offspring, or siblings in 5 to 13 other bands (Marshall, 1976, pp. 180–181, 195, 200). But everyone belongs to a family and a band; there are no unattached people in San society.

Dabe's Story: The Visitors

Dabe saw the straggling line first. A dozen people approached slowly through the bush. Dabe broke into a smile as he recognized his mother's favorite brother /Gao at the head of the line. /Gao had once lived for 2 years with Dabe's band and had taught Dabe to track and hunt. Dabe rushed to meet his uncle and shouted to attract his attention. /Gao embraced Dabe and croaked out a sad and weary tale. /Gao's band's water hole had run dry and they had walked north for 6 days, searching the area for Dabe's band. /Gao's infant daughter had died 3 days ago when her mother's milk dried up. As /Gao spoke, Dabe's mother Karu rushed forward and embraced her brother.

Then /Gao's wife limped up, and her mother and brother and his family, and his wife's widowed sister and her sons. Karu brought water that had been stored in ostrich eggshells; soon the travelers had their first deep drink of good water in days. An hour later, Dabe's father Kwi and several other men of the band appeared, returning from a hunt. Kwi greeted his relatives warmly and invited them to make their camp next to his. Later, he gave them a share of the eland he had killed, but his heart was full of anxiety. There was not enough water here for even two small bands. How would they all survive?

The next day it was decided: /Gao and his band would stay with Dabe and Karu and Kwi. They were too worn to go farther. But the other people in Dabe's band decided to go to stay with their relatives at Nyae Nyae, where there was a permanent water hole and the rains usually began first.

Kinship: Elaborating Connections

Kinship systems vary from one San people to another. The Ju/'hoan system has been carefully described. You will no doubt find it surprising and interesting. Ju/'hoan kinship is rudimentary in some ways; extraordinarily complex in others. The Ju/'hoansi are not much interested in keeping track of relatives more than two generations back in time, or beyond second cousins. But they have developed several interesting devices for creating extra kinship bonds, weaving additional threads into the net of family that unites all Ju/'hoansi.

The K'ausi and the N'ore

An important part of Ju/'hoan kinship has to do with the relationship of bands to their territories. Every band is attached to a territory—a water hole and the land and resources surrounding it, called a *n'ore*. It would be impossible for a band to exist without a n'ore (and because the number of water holes is limited, this limits the number of bands). Each band is identified with a group of related older people, who have lived in the band a long time—usually siblings or cousins, who are considered to be the "owners" or *k'ausi* of the n'ore. Visitors traveling through a territory would ask the k'ausi for permission to gather plant foods and use the water hole.

The k'ausi are not formal leaders. They "own" the resources, but can't give them away or sell them; neither can they decide who joins the band or tell people what to do. They may not necessarily be the informal leaders of the band either; they may be too old or lacking in the personal qualities needed for leadership. Leadership is then likely to be exercised by someone else who has a strong personality (but is not arrogant or selfish) and who has qualities of wisdom and judgment (Lee, 1979, pp. 61–67; 1984, p. 88).

Generations and the Joking Relationship

Another kinship principle profoundly shapes life in Ju/'hoan society: the principle of alternating generations (Lee, 1984, pp. 63–66). Ju/'hoan kinship terms pair up alternating generations. You, your grandparents, and your grandchildren share a special kin relationship; so do your parents and your children. Special reciprocal kin terms are used by the alternating pairs.

Just to make all this more complicated, there is another principle related to alternating generations: the joking relationship. All of a Ju/'hoansi's kin are either people they joke with or people they avoid. The "joking relationship" is relaxed, affectionate, and familiar; the "avoidance relationship" is respectful and formal. Generally speaking, you joke with relatives in your generation, your grandparents' generation, and your grandchildren's generation, and you avoid relatives in your parents' and your children's generations. An important rule is that you may never marry someone in the avoidance relationship.

Xama's Story: The Joking Relationship

At the end of the long dry season, when everyone was waiting impatiently for the rains to begin, five bands gathered at the large permanent water hole at Nyae Nyae. They had to—it was practically the only water left—but it was also a wonderful distraction from worries about the rain. Xama thought this was the best time of the year. She saw her married older brother and her best friend who had gone to live with her husband's band. Almost every night there was a trance dance at one camp or another. Xama was 16 and knew she was ready now to get married.

At the water hole, Xama met her mother's uncle /'Ase, who had long ago left Xama's band to do his bride service in his wife's band. "Come walk with me," he laughed, "I am so old that I need help from my grandchildren." Xama laughed also. In his mid-30s, /'Ase was muscular and smooth-faced. He stood half a head taller than Xama; he was known as "Tall /'Ase." "Here is someone who makes me feel small," /'Ase said, as a hazel-eyed young man walked into view. As tall as /'Ase, Tu was in his early 20s, and, in Xama's eyes, very handsome.

"This is Tu," /'Ase introduced the young man, "he is your cousin's cousin." This made Tu a marriageable partner for Xama, and after a few comments, /'Ase left the couple alone. In a few days Xama had decided that the future would offer few better opportunities than the tall young man with the hazel eyes. But there were problems. Xama's aunt confronted her and said, "You must not joke with Tu; people are talking. Tu is the brother of your uncle's second wife. You cannot marry him; he is of your parents' generation."

Xama was stunned and frightened, but Tu reassured her. "I am your cousin's cousin; that's what's most important. People will see that." Tu's father and brother argued openly with Xama's mother. Tu and Xama, they said, could marry. No one could agree and Tu and Xama were miserable. Tu's father said he would take them to his cousin's band. They wouldn't see any problem with the marriage. The young couple waited anxiously for the rains to come and make travel possible.

Fictive Kin: Making Kinship Really Complicated

Here is the tricky part: The Ju/'hoansi take the whole kinship structure—relationships by blood and marriage, alternating generations, joking and avoidance relationships—and apply it to fictive (imaginary) kin. The system is based on names. Anyone who has your name addresses your kin as his: He calls your wife "wife," your father "father," and so on. And you can do the same: Anyone with your mother's name you can address as "mother," anyone with your son's name you may call "son," and so on. Anyone with your sibling's name or your grandparent's name stands in a joking relationship to you. Those with your father's name or your child's, you treat with avoidance. Also, and very importantly, you may not marry anyone who shares the name of a relative you are forbidden to marry (your sibling, or parent, or child, or sibling's child).

Fictive kinship extends the benefits of kinship to everyone who bears a Ju/'hoan name. With it, no one among the whole people need be a stranger or an outsider. In the very few cases in which people have no blood relatives, they live in a band with fictive kin. It also makes kinship a complex intellectual challenge, because there are very few Ju/'hoan names (only about 35 first names for each sex, and no last names) (Lee, 1984, pp. 68–71).

Why do the Ju/'hoansi bother to maintain such an elaborate kinship system? You may find the **functionalist perspective** very helpful in understanding Ju/'hoan kinship. In a society without specialized roles kinship finds places for all people. It helps the society function smoothly by ensuring that any two members of Ju/'hoan society will always know where they stand in relation to each other and what roles they should play. Depending on their actual kinship, their ages, and their names, individuals will quickly establish kinship status and determine whether they have a joking or an avoidance relationship.

Roles: Focusing on Gender

In addition to kinship and age, the other **master status** for San is sex. More than anything else, who you are and what you do in life is determined by your status as male or female. Male and female are the basic "specialties"; there are no other specialized occupations. One way of putting this is to say that the San, like other hunting and gathering societies, have only the most basic **division of labor,** for there are only two jobs, two economic roles. And because these roles are gender roles, they are part of family life. In effect, there is no economy separate from the family and the band.

Is There a "Breadwinner" Role?

San women and men both "commute" to work (Fisher, 1992, p. 103). The work roles of men and women are different, but there is no sense in which women do "housework" and men "go to work."

N!uhka's Story: The Gatherers

N!uhka is hungry, but happy. Her brother found a field of tsin beans while hunting and she is off to harvest them. Tsin beans have been scarce, so many women are eager to come along. Even N!uhka's mother, who is less active than she once was, comes along. Gathering tsin beans is work, but it's also a social occasion, a break in routine. Twikwe, N!uhka's best friend, plays a tune on her thumb piano as they walk along, and the women join in, singing a rhythmic chorus. Even though N!uhka is burdened with her heavy toddler, whom she carries in her leather kaross, her step is light and her face is smiling.

Everyone seems lifted by the prospect of the beans. Even Dasina, whose running fight with her husband has made her sullen for weeks, is smiling and singing. Suddenly, as the women enter the bean field, a duiker, a tiny antelope, breaks from its hiding place and dashes away. The women take up the chase with enthusiastic shouts. Although the duiker can race faster than any Ju/'hoansi, it is young and confused and runs in circles. N!uhka and Twikwe pelt it with stones, knocking it over, but the duiker recovers and bounds off. All the women are disappointed. On other harvesting trips they have run down small game and feasted on the meat.

Soon the women turn to the work of harvesting beans and by afternoon have collected a huge pile, which they roll in their karosses. With her kaross tied around her waist, each woman will carry 15–30 pounds of beans, the babies perched on top. Weary and joking, the women return home, knowing they can rest in camp for 3 or 4 days without further gathering.

These young women have walked out from camp for the day, to a place where they know grewia berries are ripe. Behind them stretches the Kalahari Desert—rolling grasslands, punctuated with clusters of trees and bushes.

Women's Work

Anthropologists calculate that the food women collect constitutes about 75% of the Ju/'hoan diet. Gathering is not random; the women have a plan and a clear objective. They know where fruits are ripe or roots and tubers may be found. When the band moves camp, women carry all their belongings and their young children. Lee estimates that each year the average Ju/'hoan woman carries her child 1,500 miles. Women also gather wood, and tend fires and cook vegetable foods. They build shelters and repair them and keep the family's living area clear of ash and grasses. They make household objects like ostrich eggshell water holders, tortoise shell bowls, and personal ornaments. Women don't use bows and arrows or spears to hunt, but they do kill snakes and tortoises and birds and occasionally even small animals (Lee, 1979, pp. 310–312; Marshall, 1976, pp. 92, 97, 102).

Men's Work

Hunting is the focus of male activity and talk. Men hunt small game with spears, clubs, or snares, and they hunt big game with bow and poisoned arrow. They hunt on an irregular basis, sometimes alone, but by preference in groups of two to four.

They may stay around camp for weeks at a time, then hunt for several days in a row, but averaged out, they hunt around 2 or 3 days a week.

Debe's Story: The Hunters

Debe and N!eisi were very tired. They had followed kudu tracks all day, without sighting the animals. "Let's go back to camp," sighed Debe; "I'm tired; my back hurts. Sa//gai will rub my back." "Your wife will rub her belly in hunger if we return without meat," N!eisi protested. "Let's go on just a little longer." Debe and N!eisi were lucky. They suddenly came upon the kudu in the slanting light of late afternoon, grazing as they settled for the night. Crawling to a clump of bushes only a few feet from the kudu, Debe used his bow. The poisoned arrow hit a young male kudu in the flank and it fled. By morning, the poison would weaken and then paralyze the 300-pound animal. Debe and N!eisi hurried back to the camp. They would need help to carry the meat.

The next morning they returned to the hunt with four more men from their band. They soon found the wounded kudu, but it was closely watched by a pair of lions. N!eisi tried to chase the lions: "Go lions; this is our meat, not yours!" he commanded, tossing a clod of earth in the big cats' direction. The lions would not move and growled alarmingly as N!eisi tossed another clod.

Debe raised his bow, but only in frustration. The lions would devour the foolish hunters long before the weak Ju/'hoan poison could do its work. Debe turned toward camp and shouted at N!eisi: "Now we can all rub our bellies!" "There are other kudu to hunt," N!eisi called out, but Debe kept walking toward camp.

Game is used for many purposes besides food; almost nothing is wasted. Men make animal hides into clothing and bags, bone and horn are used for tools, sinews for bowstrings and nets. Men craft all their hunting gear—bows, arrows, quivers, spears, clubs, and implements for trapping. They collect the beetle larvae from which arrow poison is distilled and carefully prepare and spread the poison. Men also butcher and cook meat, especially the meat of large animals. They light fires, by twirling sticks, or in recent decades, by use of a flint and tinder. At a Ju/'hoan campground, both men and women are engaged in domestic tasks. Men know how to gather and sometimes do so—when they return empty-handed from a hunt, or when they go with women on overnight gathering trips (Lee, 1979, pp. 216–226; Marshall, 1976, pp. 124, 132–137).

SOCIAL INEQUALITY

Everyone who has studied San societies has been struck by their lack of inequality. As we have seen, there are no economic or **class** inequalities: sharing and gift-giving ensure that food and material objects are distributed equally in families and bands. Visiting evens out resources between bands and *n'ore*. There are not inequalities of **power** either. There are no official chiefs. Informal leaders do develop in bands, but they don't have the power to give orders or make people do things against their wills. They lead by example and by their interpersonal skills. The only kind of inequality discernable in San societies is **status** inequality. Some people enjoy more prestige and respect than others, perhaps because of their skill as hunters or musicians or healers, or perhaps because of their pleasant personalities. But their prestige doesn't result in increased wealth or power. They may be sought out in marriages or as band members. But take note: These status inequalities are personal, not social; they result from individuals' personal traits, not from their membership in social groups, like classes or races. The only status inequality in San societies that is social in nature is inequality between men and women. Gender inequality does exist, but it is minimal.

Gender Inequality

Women and men are not perfectly equal in Ju/'hoan society, but they come pretty close. Women work longer hours than men, in gathering, child care, and household work, but their enormous contribution to subsistence is recognized, and the food they gather is considered theirs. Men don't scorn women's work, and they do sometimes go gathering. Women have a great deal of autonomy and power. They are not expected to obey men; they don't wait on men, and they don't eat less or inferior food than men. Women are seldom physically assaulted or coerced by men, and in fact, women hit men about as frequently as they are struck by them. Women have a voice in group discussions and a say in making arrangements. There are no formal statuses or laws that give power to men (Marshall, 1876, p. 177).

In marriage too, women are not disadvantaged. Mothers and fathers share authority over children, and divorces are as likely to be initiated by women as by men. Because of bride service, young women don't end up as powerless newcomers in their husbands' families. And finally, though there is polygyny (multiple wives), its rarity seems to be the result of women's firm opposition. Polyandry (multiple husbands) is even rarer, but not impossible; anthropologists have documented a couple of cases of women with two husbands (Guenther, 1999, p. 31; Thomas, 2006, p. 179).

Gender and Personality

In societies where men and women are very unequal, they are often socialized to develop personality traits that reinforce their inequality. In such societies, boys are taught to be aggressive and domineering and girls to be passive and dependent. Personality differences between Ju/'hoan men and women are minimal. The Ju/'hoansi find conflict and violence abhorrent (as we will soon see) and they disapprove of men who are aggressive, boastful, or dominating. It is no compliment to say that a man is a fighter, and in Ju/'hoan culture boys are never urged or taught to fight. Men who are easygoing and skillful and who help ease tensions in the group are preferred. Self-assertion, demandingness, and boldness are also discouraged in women, but perhaps slightly more so than in men. Women are expected to be gentle, modest, and gracious, and to comply with the wishes of others (Marshall, 1976, p. 176).

Gender Segregation

In many societies, women's lower status is reflected in their extensive segregation from men and from public life in general. Among the Ju/'hoansi, women and men are segregated in some of their roles, but overall, the degree of segregation is not great. Most of the time, women and men work separately, each going into the bush with friends and relatives of their own gender. But this separation is not rigid. Parties of men and women do go gathering together, especially in major expeditions to the mangetti groves, or the tsin bean fields, and these are usually rather festive occasions. Women are sometimes part of the party that returns to track down and carry home big game fatally wounded in a hunt. Within the camp, men and women sit on opposite sides of the fire, but beyond this, there is a great deal of mixing of men and women, and boys and girls. Children of both sexes play together, and spouses are commonly real companions, sitting and talking by their fire and even arranging "getaways" to visit relatives or go gathering together in the bush.

The "Masters of Meat"

Anthropologists disagree about just how equal San men and women are. Lorna Marshall argued that Ju/'hoan men did enjoy an advantage over women, an advantage in influence and prestige, which stemmed from the glamour of hunting. As she explained it, "There is no splendid excitement in returning home with vegetables." People crave meat and they call men the "masters of meat" and "the owners of hunting" (Marshall, 1876, p. 178). News of success in a hunt, particularly of big game, spreads rapidly even beyond the camp. Visitors arrive and everyone feasts and parties. Hunting confers not only prestige, however, but also concrete influence. Women distribute their plant food within their own families, but men distribute the enticing meat widely, and their gifts are a kind of investment, which gathers in honor and obligations, and grows into influence (Fisher, 1992, p. 215).

DEVIANCE AND SOCIAL CONTROL

Do you think that there is more deviance in your society or in San societies? If you think about this you will see that it is puzzling. The San have no laws or police or courts, no authority figures to make rules or mete out punishments. There are no **formal sanctions**—positive or negative—to make people conform: no diplomas to work for, no scholarships for merit, no promotions, no jobs to win or lose, no jail sentences, parole, or court-martials. The San rely entirely on the **informal sanctions** of small group life. Negative sanctions include the mocking song heard in the darkness, gossip and ridicule, teasing and avoidance, and sometimes open criticism. Though people seldom explicitly articulate approval of others' behavior, loving attention, companionship, and inclusion in group life are so emotionally essential that these informal sanctions are highly effective (Weissner, 2005, pp. 117–122).

Although there certainly is deviance in San society, there are no **deviant roles** or **deviant careers.** There are no gang members, or burglars, no confidence men, no punk rockers, no cross-dressers who inhabit subcultures condemned as deviant by the rest of their society. Most of the time, members of San societies accept group norms and act and talk and think in ways that are expected of them. But they sometimes commit deviant acts, like failing to share food, or fighting, or boasting, or engaging in adultery, or even killing another person.

Deviance and Social Interaction

In the San small bands, many norms concern how people are expected to interact with each other, and much of San deviance involves disapproved modes of inter-action. Sociologists distinguish four types of interaction, found in all societies: **social exchange, cooperation, competition,** and **conflict.** In every society, peo-ple value some of these forms of interaction and they disapprove of others. For the San, exchange and cooperation are desired, competition and conflict feared and avoided.

Social Exchange and Cooperation

Many sociologists see exchange as a universally important interaction process, and the San would agree. They tend to see the world in terms of exchanges (you give me a gift and then I'll give you one; you give me meat when you are successful hunt-ing, and then I return the favor; you extend hospitality to my family or band when we are in your territory, and later we will do the same for you). Note, however, that the San give gifts; they don't engage in trade. **Norms of reciprocity** tell people what to give as gifts, to whom, how, and when.

People usually can find some way to reciprocate a gift. Those who are too old or disabled to hunt or gather can stay in camp with the children, or shell nuts or make music. People who fail to reciprocate are teased or reproached or avoided. Some people work harder than others at reciprocal gift-giving, spend-ing many hours making ostrich shell beads and jewelry, for example. They are rewarded with an extensive network of social connections from whom they can expect gifts, perhaps help in matchmaking, or a place they will be welcome to visit.

For the San, exchange often takes the form of cooperation, when people pitch in together and pool their resources to achieve a common goal. We see this in the dry-season sharing of permanent water holes, in the help people give each other in carrying home large kills or persuading lions to move away from the camp. Most games illustrate and teach cooperation, as the whole group works together to keep the ball aloft, or the rhythm going. In one popular game, girls make a circle, each girl crooking one leg around her neighbor's, then hop in unison. When one falls, the circle collapses and the game is over.

Competition

Like cooperation, competition requires agreed-upon social rules, but competition is repugnant to the San, and they work constantly to squelch competitive tendencies in individuals and suppress arrogance in those more talented or successful. Acting competitive or acting like a big shot is a form of deviance.

Ju/'hoan norms call for extreme modesty in presenting one's accomplishments. A man whose arrow badly wounds an antelope will return to his hearth silent and dejected. Asked about the hunt, he will doubtfully admit that he just might have grazed his quarry. Then the camp will celebrate, for they know this means the hunter has scored a certain hit and there will probably be meat tomorrow. As one

Xai/Xai man, /Gaugo, explained to Richard Lee, when the carrying party finds the kill, they will loudly disparage the meat:

> You mean you have dragged us all the way out here to make us cart home your pile of bones? Oh, if I had known it was this thin, I wouldn't have come.

The Ju/'hoansi call this "insulting the meat." Anyone who shows open pride is relentlessly teased, and the object of their pride disparaged. Tomazho, a famous healer, explained:

> When a young man kills much meat, he comes to think of himself as a chief or a big man, and he thinks of the rest of us as his servants or inferiors. We can't accept this. We refuse one who boasts, for someday his pride will make him kill somebody. So we always speak of his meat as worthless. In this way we cool his heart and make him gentle. (Lee, 1984, pp. 151–57)

Conflict

Conflict occurs when normative consensus breaks down, but actually, in most cases, the events of a conflict follow an accepted script, escalating through stages recognizable to all. In conflict, people try to meet their goals by destroying an opponent. The Ju/'hoansi are horrified and frightened by conflict, especially violent conflict, and make every effort to prevent disagreements from escalating into physical fighting. Elizabeth Marshall Thomas points out that every man is armed with lethal poisoned arrows. The merest scratch results in certain death. That certainly would make conflict very dangerous and frightening (Thomas, 2006, pp. 228–233). Much as they oppose conflict, the Ju/'hoansi are only moderately successful in preventing it. In the worst case, arguments progress to insults and then into wrestling and hitting, followed by a general melee in which many people may be wounded or killed (Lee, 1979, pp. 396–399; 1984, pp. 93–95).

> ### Kushe's Story: The Fight
>
> *It seems like it has gone on all day. As Kushe sits shelling mangetti nuts, she carries on an endless shrill monologue, complaining about her husband. "He is so stingy; too stingy," goes the refrain. "He doesn't give me presents. He doesn't bring home enough meat." The whole band ignores her, and her husband's parents, who are visiting, tactfully disappear into the bush. By the time Ukwane and his brother-in-law return from hunting, the tension is so high you can practically see it. Ukwane begins to butcher the kudu and hands the first share to his mother. Kushe jumps between them, furious: "You're not going to give me any, are you?" she demands. Taken aback, Ukwane tries to deflect her with kidding: "No, of course not; I never give you anything." Kushe is beside herself. "That's right," she screams, "you don't; no food and no babies," as she hits and claws at him. Amazed by the suddenness of this emotional storm, Ukwane grabs Kushe and literally throws her out of his way. Kushe runs back and assaults him again. Ukwane's mother and Kushe's mother are now pushing and shouting at each other. Momentarily shocked, the rest of the group finds its feet and leaps into action, separating and holding the combatants. Everyone is talking and shouting and milling about.*
>
> *Tempers have cooled by the following morning, but Ukwane wants no part of Kushe or her family. "They are like warthogs, not people!" Ukwane's mother spits out. "They all look like warthogs," grunts his father. Ukwane rises, declaring, "I want to go to hunt kudu, not to live among beasts!" Having said this in a voice loud enough to carry across the camp, Ukwane leads his parents off on the long trek to his brother's camp near the Herero village.*

Managing Conflict.   How do the Ju/'hoansi ensure that most conflicts do not escalate to the point of violence? After all, they cannot call the police or campus security. Although there are no separate political or legal institutions, the Ju/'hoansi do have norms and procedures for handling conflict—within the band and the family.

One way the Ju/'hoansi manage conflict is by providing plentiful opportunity for harmless venting of complaints. The Ju/'hoansi are an exceptionally verbal people, and feelings like grief, envy, resentment, anger, or alarm are readily expressed in conversation. When anger and disagreement threaten, people use humor, jokes, and laughter to dispel the tension (Guenther, 1999, pp. 35–36). A great deal of the constant interchange in groups takes the form of semiserious argument, called "a talk," in which real discontents are jokingly aired. In such sessions, people complain about others' laziness or stinginess, about people who don't distribute meat properly or don't reciprocate gifts generously. (Though complaints like these are common, the underlying problem in uncontrolled, fatal fights is usually adultery, or anger over a previous homicide.)

A "Fight."   If "talking" fails, then people lose their good nature and begin angry argument. When they begin to make sexual insults (*za*) against each other, then you know that anger will mount and actual physical violence is likely. Women are as likely as men to be involved in hand-to-hand violence, with men or with other women. In most cases, once people separate the combatants, they are usually able to use joking to calm everyone down.

Conflict Control.   Separation in fact is one of the most effective means of limiting conflict available to the San. It is relatively easy for one party or the other in a dispute to pick up and leave the group temporarily, and people often do so. Conflict avoidance and flexible group composition are closely intertwined, with conflict-induced separations keeping groups small, and flexible group composition making conflict-avoidance possible.

The most extreme form of conflict-management practiced by the Ju/'hoansi (and the one that comes closest to the exercise of political authority) is group execution. It is a last resort to even the score when people hold a grudge for a previous murder, or to put an end to fighting caused by a single, dangerously violent individual. Richard B. Lee has recorded several such cases, in one of which a whole community joined in shooting and stabbing a probably psychotic killer (Lee, 1979, pp. 393–395; 1984, p. 6).

SOCIALIZATION

One reason why there is relatively little deviance in Ju/'hoan society is that socialization is quite successful. San learn to play new roles all through life, as they move from childhood through adulthood to old age. These age-specific roles are in fact the major roles in Ju/'hoan society. Like the rest of life, socialization takes place in the family and the band and people are socialized by their friends and relatives. Socialization for San is **implicit** and informal. There is very little direct instruction.

Observation, imitation, and play are important socializing processes. There is no formal socialization because there are no schools or other formal institutions. However, there are formal ceremonies that mark important life transitions.

Ju/'hoan socialization has a special quality because children can rely on their adult roles being just like their parents'. Adults have valuable knowledge and skills to transmit to children, and older people's long experience with the conditions of bush life makes them respected advisors. Life is filled with difficulties, but has a reliable consistency from generation to generation. Ju/'hoan children need not worry about what they will be when they grow up; but they don't have very many choices either. Everyone has to accommodate their talents to the small number of gender and kinship roles that exist.

Childhood Socialization

The Ju/'hoansi begin their lives with an immensely secure early childhood. Babies sleep beside their mothers at night and are carried all day in slings that permit constant skin-to-skin contact. They have free access to the breast, and nurse on demand, several times an hour. The Ju/'hoansi believe babies need no training or discipline. Young children are carried and nursed up to the age of 3 or even 4, but once out of infancy, they spend more time out of their mothers' arms—in affectionate play with their fathers, held by the various aunts and uncles, grandparents and cousins who surround them in the band, and often carried, like dolls, by the older siblings. Child-rearing is indulgent, and parents make few demands for obedience. Though they threaten physical punishment, they seldom follow through, and rely more on reward. Parents allow children to bargain with them, believing that it is important for children to develop assertiveness and resourcefulness (Guenther, 1999, pp. 51–52).

Children Socialize Each Other

Children from about ages 7 to 12 spend almost all their time in one another's company, playing in mixed-age and often mixed-sex groups. They play in the cleared central "plaza" of the camp, or, even more often, in a nearby "children's village," out of sight, but not out of hearing of the adults. Children play traditional games, give their smaller siblings rides on an old *kaross*, or on their backs, and endlessly "play house." Girls build rough shelters and pair off with boys or with each other as "mommies and daddies." Children gather berries or roots in the nearby bush, snare small birds or collect caterpillars, or pretend to kill and butcher an animal. Girls and boys hold their own "pretend" trance dances. Away from disapproving parents, children also experiment with sex, imitating parents glimpsed in the dark, looking and touching, but not initiating actual intercourse (Lee, 1979, p. 236; Marshall, 1976, pp. 318–319; Shostak, 1981, p. 83). A great deal of childrens' play is obviously **anticipatory socialization,** in which they learn by observing and imitating the roles they will play as adults.

Gai's Story: Learning to Be a Man
"We are masters of the meat," shouts 9-year-old Gai, as he leads two younger boys in a mock hunt through the tall grass. Gai and //Oma use their toy bows to shoot at the grasshoppers they disturb as they run. Suddenly a shout from the youngest boy, Gao,

reveals a 3-foot-long grass snake. The three boys chase the snake, shooting at it, tossing rocks, and finally killing it with a branch used as a club. "We must cook our meat!" exclaims Gai, as they build a fire and roast the unfortunate snake.

Gai enjoys his new role as "hunter" and distributes meat to the younger boys. Four girls, including Karu, an 8-year-old who often plays "house" with Gai, look on hungrily, but no food comes their way. Finally Karu shouts, "Where is my food? I am your wife; you have to give me some!"

Gai's pals are beside themselves with laughter. Karu, nearly a head shorter than Gai, chases him around the clearing. What starts as a game soon becomes a tug of war, as Karu grabs the charred snake and Gai pulls back on the other end. The snake splits and the pair are dumped on the ground. Karu and Gai scream at each other until Karu's older sister arrives and shouts at both of them, "You're acting like a bunch of babies! Grown-ups share their food, especially husbands and wives!"

Actually, children learn a great deal from each other. Older children are patient with younger ones who try to join their games and instruct them in the proper way to play. Older children act as peacemakers and mediators in the frequent minor conflicts of the informal playgroup. They often intervene when one child teases another, grabs someone's melon or toy, or when disagreements turn to physical fighting. They punish aggression—generally with ridicule—and give comfort to the victims. Also, they sometimes make fun of children who don't participate in games, or who play badly (Eibl-Eibesfeldt, 1978, p. 135). As children grow up, they gradually move from freely expressing aggression to controlling aggression in others, then to an adulthood in which suppressing their own aggressive, competitive impulses will be expected.

Adults Socialize Children

Children spend a great deal of time with adults of all ages and learn from them by imitation and informal instruction. They learn to control their tempers and avoid offending others. When young children fight, mothers' most common response is to separate or distract them. Mothers may scold and compel the return of a grabbed object. Though threats of beatings are common, actual physical punishment is rare (Eibl-Eibesfeldt, 1978, pp. 132–133, 135).

Children also learn the many norms of daily life. They learn to receive food in outstretched hands, not to grab, to wait until asked to share food, to take a modest serving from a passed bowl, and to eat with restraint, not revealing eagerness. They are scolded for greed or stealing. Girls and boys also learn the norms of sexual modesty. They learn that adults do not hug or kiss each other in public. Girls learn to sit modestly, so their genitals are not visible (Marshall, 1976, pp. 244, 249, 293–294, 311).

In adolescence children begin to go gathering or hunting with adults, in order to learn these vital skills. Girls begin to gather in earnest as soon as they marry, which could be as young as 10 or 12, but is more probably about age 16. But even then, the young wife gathers in the company of her mother, or perhaps her aunt or sisters. The transition to adult responsibilities is gradual. At about the age of 12, boys' fathers give them their first small bows and arrows and quivers, and they begin to hunt birds and rabbits. This is a time when they may also accompany an older man, perhaps a grandfather, in setting snares and tending a trapline. Finally comes the big step of going with their fathers, uncles, and older brothers on a hunt (Shostak, 1981, pp. 83–84).

Rites of Passage to Adulthood

In traditional Ju/'hoan society, major events mark the passage to adulthood: for boys, the first kill of a large animal, and *choma,* initiation into manhood, and for girls, first menstruation and marriage. All four of these events are marked by public ceremonies; they are the **rites of passage** that mark and celebrate a person's change in status before the whole community.

The First Buck Ceremony

A boy becomes a fully adult hunter when he kills his first big antelope with a poisoned arrow. Killing the first big animal is the result of hard work on hunting, and this is recognized with two important ceremonies—for the first male and first female animals killed. These ceremonies are male business, performed while the women are out of camp. The young man is given small cuts and tattoos on his chest, back, and arms; these mark him as a hunter in the eyes of the world. Further cuts are rituals to strengthen his vision, stamina, aim, and determination. Then the men gather to cook and eat some of the young hunter's meat. The ritual ends with the dramatic tale of a hunt (Lee, 1979, pp. 236–240). After killing his first buck, a young man is considered eligible for marriage.

Choma

Sometime between the ages of 15 and 20, boys participate in *choma,* a sacred 6-week-long initiation rite. Choma is an elaborate rite, in which sacred male knowledge is passed on to a new generation. It is usually held every few years during the winter dry season when several bands gather at a permanent water hole, bringing together a large enough group of boys. Choma is a challenging experience of hunger, cold, and thirst. The boys sing the men's songs and dance to exhaustion. Like the first buck ceremony, choma is performed away from women (Lee, 1979, p. 365; Shostak, 1981, p. 239).

Marriage

Marriage and first menstruation are two important transitions in the life of a Ju/'hoan girl that are marked by formal ceremony. It will probably seem quite strange to you that of the two events, a traditional Ju/'hoan girl would be likely to experience marriage first. Neither event signals an abrupt transition to adulthood, and marriage especially should be thought of more as a process—beginning with marriage negotiations and ending with the birth of a child—than as a sudden change of status.

Marriage is a stormy period in a girl's socialization. First marriages are usually arranged by parents or other close relatives (who will also arrange subsequent marriages if the spouses are still young). Arranging a marriage involves a lot of visiting, discussions, and gift-giving, and it may actually be difficult to find a suitable mate within the restrictions of actual and fictive kinship. The marriage ceremony itself is an almost casual, hearthside occasion, attended mostly by children.

But learning to play the role of a wife is a very difficult, and often long transition. Girls are expected to resist marriage. They are usually preadolescent, and the disparity in ages and sexual maturity of the bride and groom is a source of real difficulties. The groom is sexually mature, but he is expected to marry a child and wait, often as long as 5 years, before he has sex with her. During that time he must sleep by her side, live with and help her family, and probably put up with her rejection, fear, and anger. Young men find this situation very frustrating, but they usually accept it, because marriageable girls are scarce. Polygyny, though uncommon, unbalances sex ratios, and young men know that if they reject a marriage, they may have to wait for another potential bride to grow up (Shostak, 1981, pp. 129–130, 148, 150).

Khoana's Story: The Bride

When she wakes up, Kai doesn't see her daughter in her usual place, sleeping next to her fire. Could it be, she wonders happily, that Khoana has relented and agreed to sleep beside her new husband in their hut? But Khoana isn't in the hut and Kai's pleasure turns to panic. That girl has surely run away again! Hours later, they find her sleeping beneath a mangetti tree, hidden by sand dunes. "Are you crazy, girl," shouts Kai, "a lion could have eaten you!" Khoana bursts into tears and begins ripping the bracelets off her arms. "I won't go back to him. I'm afraid. I'm still a child; I'm not old enough yet for marriage."

Ju/'hoan society tolerates a girl's free expression of her objection to marriage. She may rage and storm and may even threaten or attempt suicide. Basically, if she insists, a girl can force an end to her marriage, either by driving her husband away with unpleasantness or by enrolling family members on her side. Divorce is very common in the early years of marriage, before children are born, and it is usually initiated by the wife. It is common for a girl to enter several such "trial marriages" before finally having children and settling down to a stable marriage (Shostak, 1981, pp. 130–131, 148).

First Menstruation

The onset of menstruation is celebrated in a more public, ceremonial manner than is marriage. The girl, elaborately ornamented, stays in a special hut, while the women of the band dance and sing in a sometimes suggestive fashion. Men must not see the girl, but they watch the dancing women from a distance, making bawdy comments. The rite marks sexual maturity, but not full adulthood. Girls are unlikely to conceive a baby for about 2 years after menstruation begins, and in this period, their relatives still help them with gathering, cooking and other household tasks, while they continue to play with their friends (Shostak, 1981, p. 149).

After her first menstruation, a girl usually begins to settle down, with her original or a new husband. She may come to love her husband and enjoy a period of romance before the first child is born. The married couple grow into an easy, relatively equal relationship, in which they go about together, exchange opinions, and make decisions jointly. Fear of her husband usually eases into acceptance and even enjoyment of sex. Also, the girl may come to enjoy the status of married woman, the presents given her by her husband and his family, and the meat he brings to her fire (Shostak, 1981, p. 150).

With the birth of a first child, a woman becomes fully adult. She and her husband are now referred to as the parents of their children ("/Toma's father" or "Nisa's mother") rather than by their childhood names, and they settle down to their major life roles in rearing children and provisioning their household. The Ju/'hoansi love and enjoy children and wish to have many, though not too closely spaced.

New Roles in Maturity

Growing into mature adulthood and then old age, Ju/'hoan adults must adjust to new roles. Both men and women in maturity find opportunities to express their talents, as hunters, storytellers, craftspeople, musicians, healers, and informal leaders. Because of relatively high death rates, almost every adult has experienced the death of at least one child, and many the death of a spouse. Family roles change as the result of deaths.

The Ju/'hoansi are adequately nourished, in good physical condition, and suffer little from stress or diet-related diseases. But lacking modern antibiotics and other medicines, infectious and parasitic diseases like influenza, pneumonia, gastro-enteritis, tuberculosis, and malaria take a high toll of children and adults. Close-knit nuclear and extended households are repeatedly disrupted by death. The Ju/'hoansi support each other in deeply felt mourning. People travel to attend funerals; women publicly cry and wail and men sometimes also cry. After death, people are buried with care, with their bodies facing their birthplace. A man's bow and quiver are hung on a stick near the grave and his arrows broken. Mourners mark the grave with a few stones. People are especially careful in burying a child that has died, constructing a little shelter over the grave. After the burial, the band moves its campsite away from grave. After a relatively short time, relatives and friends encourage the bereaved to stop mourning so the spirit of the dead is not tempted to stay around and make others sick. People believe the dead will be found by a god and brought to his home in the West (Marshall, 1999, pp. 179–181; Suzman, 2000, pp. 123–124; Thomas, 2006, p. 209).

Death often causes the reorganization of families. After the death of the head of an extended family, the group may split up, with some of its constituent nuclear families leaving the band. There are many more widows than widowers, and they almost always marry again. Some remarriages also take place after divorce, which is relatively infrequent among adults, but readily accomplished by mutual consent, or as the result of one spouse leaving the other. No formal grounds of divorce are necessary, and there is no property to divide. Children remain with their mother, except for teenage boys who may choose to stay with their father or visit with both parents.

The Roles of the Older Ju/'hoansi

Few of the Ju/'hoansi live to old age: Barely 20% of those born reach age 60, but those who do will, on the average, live another 10 years. The older people are relatively free of high blood pressure, heart disease, and deafness, and many are still vigorous. Older widows (over 40% of the women over 60) may marry again, or live with children or grandchildren. These people are treated with respect and often have an influential voice in the group. The older they are, the more likely they are to be the *k'ausi* of their band. Older people are consulted because their experience is valuable. They know how people are related, who married whom, and who is comparatively older or younger. They have seen so many seasons go by that they know where to find food under unusual conditions. They know the recent history of the people and the region and the folktales, songs, and legends. As long as the group continues to live the traditional hunting and gathering life, older people play an important role in the band.

Healthy older people continue to forage, but on a reduced scale. Older women may gather closer to home; older men may set snares and gather along with their wives. But most older people contribute little food; they are supported by sharing with their relatives. Old age may be a time of intense religious exploration, especially for women, who often wait until their children are grown before learning trance dancing and curing. For some people, spiritual powers strengthen with age; they achieve great control over their ability to enter trance and become valued healers and teach apprentices how to enter trance and cure.

For some people, old age is a satisfying time. If they are surrounded by children willing to provide for them, and grandchildren to be loved and cared for, they may enjoy inclusion in the life of the band: sharing the feasts and dances, telling and hearing the stories, sharing gossip, debating the merits of marriages. But for those who outlive their children and spouses (20% of all women, but relatively few men) and become a burden on those with less affection for them, old age may be far less pleasant (Shostak, 1981, pp. 324–325).

PART II: SOCIAL CHANGE AND THE FUTURE— THE POSTCOLONIAL ERA

For the San, life in modern Namibia has been tragic. They have been pushed off their land, caught in a brutal war, and treated with racist contempt by other Namibian peoples. So wise in the ways of the desert, the San have been unprepared to succeed in a modern society. They are illiterate and uneducated, stranded in the most remote, unpromising areas. And there have been terrible losses to alcoholism, depression, violence, and disease. But the San have responded to their misfortunes with their usual resiliency and ingenuity. They have found a variety of different ways to survive. To tell their story properly, we must go back to the Ju/'hoansi and introduce you to other San peoples, following different paths.

Tsumkwe, Nyae Nyae, 2008

The billboard at the entrance to Tsumkwe, the town that is the administrative center of the Nyae Nyae Conservancy, displays the Pepsi logo and the motto "Ask For More!" A shop at the entrance has sparse displays of Ju/'hoansi-made crafts for sale to tourists. We see one Ju/'hoan man who works for the conservancy washing his car in the driveway of his solid bungalow, while his children dance to radio music. Nearby, however, are shanty dwellings built by Ju/'hoansi who have left the bush because of hunger. Some San are lined up at the church mission, waiting for free cornmeal to be distributed. "We used to be owners of hunting," says old Di!ai, but now we are owners of asking." (Wiessner, 2003, p. 149)

/Gomais, 2008

The roads are poor going north from Tsumkwe to /Gomais, and we arrive dusty and tired. At first glance, the Hai//om settlement at the edge of /Gomais looks like nothing has changed in 20 years. There are three circles of grass huts (and a few pole houses), but no cattle kraals, no gardens, no permanent buildings. But by evening you can see that much has changed. Old Naberos happily climbs down from her ride on a government ranch truck with three sacks of mangetti fruits she has picked at a distant grove. She bustles off to sell the fruits to a couple in the nearby Ovambo settlement who brew alcohol from mangetti. She returns pleased with the bottle of liquor and sack of millet they have given her in exchange. Naberos is a lucky woman; her son is one of the few who have jobs at the government ranch. He is often away checking fences. !Gamekhas and her two daughters have spent the day cultivating corn at an Ovambo garden. The girls are not in school. Her brother and three other men are gathered under a tree working at a portable forge. They are using a pile of scrap metal to repair pots, forge and sharpen knives, and make arrowheads. When another man comes by with a sack of cornmeal from the church mission, several of the ironworkers break away from their work to try their luck at the mission. The Hai//om live on the margins, but they resourcefully look to the government ranch, the mission, the Ovambo farms, and the bush as they piece together a living.

Skoonheid Resettlement Camp, Omaheke Region, 2008

South of Tsumkwe we visit the Ju/'hoansi at the Skoonheid Resettlement Camp, a former White-owned farm that the government has bought and set aside as a place where landless Ju/'hoansi and Damara San can live. The farm is huge, more than 20 square miles, but much of it has been occupied illegally by Herero herders, whose cattle have taken over six of the seven borehole wells on the farm. We talk with Gao, who is known here as Thomas Chupman. He says he is trying to raise a few cows and goats, but the Herero cattle leave little grass for them to eat and several of his animals have been stolen. Thomas grew up on a nearby White-owned farm, but because of a drought, he's no longer wanted there. In a way, he is glad to escape the farm. The baas (the farmer) was harsh and arbitrary, even beating his Ju/'hoan workers. But life at Skoonheid is depressing, he says. There is no work and many people are sick with tuberculosis. Many people spend what little money they have on alcohol, and angry confrontations erupt frequently. Thomas is thinking of traveling around the White-owned farms in the commercial sector to look for some temporary work, but his wife won't be able to come with him and he is worried about how she will manage at Skoonheid. (This description draws on Suzman, 2000. See, for example, pp. 112–177)

The days are long gone when the San lived in the Kalahari Desert and moved freely over borders, careless of national boundaries and uninterested in colonial powers. Now the San are keenly aware that they live in Namibia or Botswana, Angola, or South Africa. To survive, they must deal with government officials, foreign-aid organizations, Bantu herders, and Boer commercial farmers. They have learned from their experience in the liberation struggle and in the new post-colonial Namibia.

The Liberation Struggle

We left off our history in the first part of this chapter with South Africa in control of Namibia, having just formalized a system of ethnic homelands, an apartheid system. Under South African rule in the second half of the 20th century, it became harder and harder for the San to maintain the traditional culture you have just read about.

Namibia's other ethnic groups also suffered under South Africa's repression, and they began to resist. As early as 1946, Namibian tribal chiefs had petitioned the United Nations to stop South Africa from absorbing Namibia. Later the chiefs asked the UN to declare South Africa's occupation illegal and to start the process of achieving independence (Leys & Saul, 1995, p. 10). The formation of the Southwest African People's Organization (SWAPO) in 1960 was a big step forward to seeking independence. In 1966, after repeated petitions, the UN finally declared South Africa's mandate to govern Namibia at an end. That sounds like a triumph, but in fact South Africa continued to rule illegally and the struggle for independence went on for 23 years more! It is important to understand Namibia's fight for independence in its proper context. First of all, it was part of what Leys and Saul call "The Thirty Years War in Southern Africa" (1960–1990), the anticolonial struggles and wars of liberation that at long last resulted in the replacement of White regimes by Black self-rule in South Africa, Namibia, Zimbabwe, Angola, and Mozambique (Leys & Saul, 1995, pp. 2–3). In Africa and elsewhere, this was the era of **decolonization,** the end of European and American colonies abroad and the birth of many new nations.

The San and the War for Namibia

It wasn't long before the San were drawn into the protracted warfare between the South African army SWAPO guerillas and Angolan troops. San were recruited by the South African army as scouts and infantrymen because they were such skilled trackers. South Africa located its "Bushman battalion" headquarters in the desert of western Bushmanland. San who had been dispossessed of their land were particularly attracted to the army, perhaps because they had nowhere else to go, perhaps because the wages were good, perhaps because the Ovambo and other Black Namibian peoples had been their historic enemies. By the end of the war, 9,000 San (a quarter of the San population in Namibia) were dependent on army pay and services. They were also out of work, without land, and on the losing side (Biesele, 1978, pp. 1–2; Slotten, 1995, p. 228).

Independent Namibia

After many years of warfare and repeated UN interventions, elections for an independent government were finally held in 1989, with more than 95% of the people voting. Competing with nine other parties, SWAPO won 57% of all the votes and emerged with a majority in the constituent assembly. In February 1990 the assembly elected Sam Nujoma, SWAPO's leader, to be president, and in March 1990 Namibia finally became independent (Saunders, 1999, pp. 755–757). Almost two decades have passed since independence and Namibia is now one of southern Africa's most successful democracies. It has avoided two major pitfalls for democracy in Africa: personalized, autocratic rule, like that of Robert Mugabe in Zimbabwe, and ethnic breakdown in which competing politicians arouse ethnic tensions in order to further their political careers. In its worst form, as in Rwanda, or Yugoslavia, states dissolve in ethnic warfare, hundreds of thousands or even millions are killed. The fate of democracy in Namibia matters intensely for the San. They are a tiny minority, likely to survive and prosper only in a democracy that grants rights to all ethnic groups. Luckily, Namibia is clearly a democracy.

Democracy in Namibia

A recent UN report ranked Namibia as the most democratic of seven nations in southern Africa. The nation has a thoroughly democratic constitution and system of government. Citizens are guaranteed free speech, freedom of the press, and the right to join organizations, including political parties and trade unions. The right to strike and the right to a living wage are guaranteed in the constitution, too. There are mechanisms for removal of cabinet members and even the president by the Assembly (Good, 1997, pp. 67–71). See Table 3.1.

Since independence there have been three elections, in 1994, 1999, and 2004, and all clearly were free and fair elections. Also, there has been a peaceful electoral change of leadership, when Sam Nujoma, the first president, handed over power to a new president in 2004. That's a very real democratic accomplishment, a standard many countries with "democratic" constitutions fail to reach on all continents. There are active, vociferous opposition parties and a genuine free press, which is ever critical of the government and of SWAPO. Radio call-in shows feature lively, sometimes offensive political critique as well (Good, 1997, pp. 73–74).

Problems with Poverty and Land

For the San, and for Namibia's other peoples, the need for land was the country's most serious problem at independence. Most people made their living from the land and many were without land. This was so despite the fact that Namibia is rather sparsely populated. Land is plentiful; good land, land that can be farmed, is scarce. Rapidly growing population makes the problem worse (Leys & Saul, 1995, pp. 196–197).

TABLE 3.1 Corruption (2007)

In the Corruptions Perception Index, a high score means that a country is seen as honest and lacking in corruption by businesspeople, academics, and risk analysts. Namibia scores higher than two thirds of the 179 nations ranked, above Mexico and Egypt.

	Rank 2007	CPI Score
Germany	16	7.8
Japan	17	7.5
United States	20	7.2
Namibia	57	4.5
Mexico	72	3.5
Egypt	105	2.9

Source: Transparency International, *Corruption Perceptions Index,* 2007, http://www.transparency.org/policy_research/surveys_indices/cpi.

Today, about 4,000 White farmers still own just about half the land that can be farmed. Their enormous commercial farms, many producing beef for export to Europe, are found all over Namibia, but especially in the southern half of the country. The other half of the land is shared by roughly 800,000 Black farmers of various ethnic groups, mostly Ovambo and also Herero and Kavango, living in "communal areas" (also known as "native reserves"), some of them the original apartheid ethnic homelands. They are called communal areas because land in them is not private property, but rather belongs to the whole ethnic group or tribe. The Ovambo and Herero use their land mostly for raising cattle for their own food and sometimes for game farming for hunters and tourists. Bushmanland is one of these communal areas and we will have to examine how that land is used. At independence, the government promised to purchase land from White farmers to distribute to Black Namibians, but it has never had the money to buy very much land. Most of the farms the government has purchased are used as "resettlement camps" where landless people are allowed to live. Other landless people have migrated to shanty settlements around all the major cities of Namibia, or they live on former army bases. Some live in dependent relationships with White or Black farmers on their private or communal land (Odendaal & Harring, 2006, p. 2; Suzman, 2000, pp. 12–15).

The San in Modern Namibia

For the San, as for other Namibians, land is the key to their fate. Those who have land struggle to hold it and to produce enough to feed themselves. Those without land must scrounge a living, working on White-owned farms, or for Ovambo farmers, or gathering on other people's land. None of them live any longer by hunting and gathering in the traditional way. They may live on government aid, sell crafts to tourists, work odd jobs, collect scrap, or combine all of these strategies. Things have worked out differently for various San peoples in Namibia, with some more unlucky than others. We will tell the stories of three of these groups: the Ju/'hoansi of Nyae Nyae, the Hai//om of Mangetti West, and the Ju/'hoansi of Omaheke. Their situations and problems differ, but they all have in common the struggle to preserve their culture and independence in a society that treats them with contempt.

The Lucky Ones: The Ju/'hoansi of Bushmanland

San all over southern Africa see the Bushmen of Nyae Nyae as the lucky ones because they alone have been able to hold onto some of their traditional land. They alone are not landless, though they succeeded in keeping only 10% of their original land back in 1970 when the South African government established Bushmanland. Only one permanent waterhole was located in the land they were allotted. They didn't get enough land to support themselves by hunting and gathering. In the 1960s only a few hundred Ju/'hoansi lived in Nyae Nyae, but 3,350 San live there now. Since then, the Nyae Nyae Ju/'hoansi have struggled for the right to govern themselves and they have tried to preserve some valued elements of their culture, but they have had to depend on a lot of help from outsiders. They are lucky to have the help, but they resent the dependency that results from it.

The 1970s: Tsumkwe

In 1970 when the South African government established Bushmanland it made the town of Tsumkwe into an administrative center and collected the Ju/'hoansi to live permanently there. Tsumkwe sounded promising, but it was a disaster. There was a school, a health clinic, a church, a prison, and a store, but there was no work for the San. Government promises to help with gardening and animal raising came to nothing. The government gave people "welfare"—free cornmeal. It helped an outside entrepreneur set up a store that sold canned goods and gasoline and also, disastrously, alcohol. If you had visited Tsumkwe in the 1970s you would have seen a slum, with all the chaos and pathology that word implies. On paydays, San soldiers crowded the town, pushing to be served in the bottle store, lying drunk by the side of the road, or fighting behind the store. Transistor radios blared South African pop music and trash piled up behind buildings. Prostitutes patrolled the street in front of the store. The Ju/'hoansi called Tsumkwe "the place of death" (Weinberg, 1997, pp. 8, 10–11).

The 1980s: Return to the Bush

Remarkably, the Ju/'hoansi did not succumb to despair and alcoholism. Group by group they organized themselves to leave Tsumkwe and return to the bush. And this is where luck comes in again. At least 25 groups made settlements in their families' old *n'ores,* all depending on wells with pumps. Outside help made the return to the bush possible. The Ju/'hoansi found a savvy and energetic advocate in John Marshall, who had lived at /Aotcha as a boy and felt a deep attachment to the Ju/'hoansi. When Marshall visited Tsumkwe in the 1970s he was horrified by the squalid settlement and wasted lives. He started the Bushman Development Foundation which facilitated the return to the bush. The Ju/'hoansi didn't expect to return to hunting and gathering; there wasn't enough land for that and the younger men had never learned to hunt. They wanted to support themselves in the same way their Black neighbors did, by grazing cattle and growing a few simple crops in gardens. For the San, subsistence farming represented modern life. But they needed help getting started. The foundation gave settlers a few head of cattle, seeds, and tools and help making gardens. It raised money abroad to pay for drilling the new boreholes and building windmills to pump the water (Butler, 1997, p. 2; Weinberg, 1997, p. 8). In the village settlements people could not raise enough food to live by farming alone, but they supplemented farming with some hunting and gathering, sale of crafts, salaries earned by family members in the army, and government food welfare. The key advantage was that everyone had work and could contribute, so the fundamental Ju/'hoan practices of sharing and equality and respect for individuals were upheld (Wiessner, 2003, p. 150).

Since the 1990s: The Nyae Nyae Conservancy

Things were going well until the 1990s, when new problems arose. Boreholes attracted refugee elephants, which had not previously lived in Nyae Nyae. As many as 1,000 elephants live there today, driven from their homes by poaching and loss of habitat. The elephants raid the farmers' gardens and trample the old bush foods.

Meet =Oma N!oa, the San who led the band John
Marshall's family studied in the 1950s. In the 1970s and
1980s Marshall found him still leading the band under very
changed circumstances. It was =Oma who led the
Ju/'hoansi San out of Tschumkwe to return to the
traditional n'ore at /Aotcha. In this photo =Oma is telling a
story, revealing some of the wisdom and personal charisma
that made Bushmen turn to him for leadership.

Most seriously, they destroy boreholes and windmills in their efforts to get at the
water (Thomas, 2006, pp. 297–298).

While the San struggled to make a go of farming, outside agents involved
themselves in Bushmanland, using their superior power to impose strategies they
thought would be best for the Ju/'hoansi. In the early 1990s, the government and
the foundations began to establish a community-based conservancy in Nyae Nyae.
A conservancy is a new strategy for Namibia. It is a form of cooperative "owned"
by the San, but administered by the World Wildlife Fund and the United States
Agency for International Development (USAID). Its purpose is to restore the wild
game of Nyae Nyae. The San are to protect the game rather than hunt it so tourists

can buy licenses for trophy hunting, stay at lodges, and pay to observe San reenacting the trance dances and hunts of their former life. Bushmen are allowed to hunt in the conservancy area only with bows and arrows. Conservancy administrators judge that this strategy has a better chance of success than small farming; that their expertise allows them to know what is best for the Ju/'hoansi. Today, the conservancy has 27 employees in Tsumkwe and the Ministry of Environment and Tourism maintains an office there. Experts judge Nyae Nyae to be "a model of a successful conservancy" and conservancy and government staff have been able to prevent further encroachment into Nyae Nyae by non-San cattle herders (Odendaal & Harring, 2006, p. 40). San in other parts of Namibia envy the approximately $83 per year that the conservancy pays out to each of its 770 San members. And the conservancy and the local safari company employ a few dozen part-time, and a handful of full-time Ju/'hoan workers. The problem is that many San feel that their wish to be small farmers has been ignored. The conservancy is "theirs," but they feel they have no voice (Wiessner, 2003, pp. 150–154).

Until recently, elephants were rarely seen in the Kalahari. But drought, loss of habitat, and poaching are driving elephants to seek new territory. At the same time, efforts by wildlife foundations and governments to protect elephants have had unintended consequences. Elephant populations are now growing and in many parts of southern Africa elephants and indigenous people have become competitors for land and resources. Elephants are formidable competition: They are so huge that their need for water is enormous and they can strip and trample scarce greenery when they feed. They are dangerous, too. San have been known to chase away lions, but they cannot chase away elephants when they trample their farms, destroy expensive water pumps, and trash their crops.

Cultural Adaptation and Cultural Loss in Nyae Nyae

Life in Nyae Nyae has forced the Ju/'hoansi to give up some of their traditional culture. They are no longer a nomadic hunting and gathering people. Knowledge of hunting is fading as time goes by. The first buck ceremonies for young men are no longer held now that young men don't hunt. Trance dances are less frequent and serve more for entertainment and social bonding than as ceremonies for curing disease. But in the tiny villages, where small groups of people are trying to live by herding and farming, San practices of sharing and equality still prevail. For example, villagers are very dependent on the pensions the Namibia government gives to older people (N\$250 per month, or about US\$36). Those pensions are shared with relatives. But in Tsumkwe, where Ju/'hoansi still hold to the old ideals of sharing, participation, and equality, the reality is quite different.

Inequality in Tsumkwe. Most Ju/'hoansi government employees live in Tsumkwe, the administrative center for Bushmanland. Wiessner reports that the 47 Ju/'hoan men and 7 women who worked for the government in 2003 received 36% of all the cash income in Nyae Nyae. Another 26 people worked full-time for a local mining company, and together they earned another 27% of Ju/'hoansi cash income (Wiessner, 2003, p. 153). This small San elite lives much better than other Ju/'hoansi, in solid, multiroom houses. Some drive cars and use computers. These employees tend to be younger men who have had some experience of life outside Bushmanland, facility speaking multiple languages, and more knowledge of how to deal with government bureaucracy. They have gained this experience at government-run boarding schools, in the army, or working on White-owned farms outside Nyae Nyae (Felton & Becker, 2001, p. 34).

For most Ju/'hoansi residents, Tsumkwe is a demoralized slum, where they have no employment and barely enough food to survive. Although those with good jobs give a lot of their cash income to kin, their relative affluence still violates Ju/'hoansi norms for sharing and still stimulates resentment and anger. All this plays into the high levels of violence and alcohol consumption in Tsumkwe. Drinking is one way employed people get some pleasure out of their earnings before their relatives extract the rest of it from them. Drinking is entertainment for bored, unemployed people, and it is a way to relieve the social tension that results from inequality. Weissner estimates that as much as a third of all income at Tsumkwe is spent on alcohol (Wiessner, 2003, p. 154).

Building on Ju/'hoan Cultural Strengths

Sometimes when people in rich industrial societies think about what it must be like for indigenous peoples to enter the modern world, they think first of modern products—sneakers and sunglasses, canned soda, TV, cars, and computers. But cultural adaptation is actually much more subtle and interesting. It is a two-way street in many ways. People draw upon their traditional cultures as much as they abandon them. For example, you might think that electing leaders and participating in political organizations is something totally new and strange for the San. After all, the Ju/'hoansi told Richard Lee in the 1970s that "we have no headman, each one of us is headman over himself." But actually, democracy calls up many themes deeply embedded in traditional San culture. The Ju/'hoansi have long called themselves "the owners of argument," meaning that they believed themselves to be particularly skilled in talk and debate. They also believe it is very important for issues to be openly discussed by everyone together so no one will feel excluded or resentful. If you think about it, you can see how democracy would make sense to an egalitarian people (Biesele, 1978, p. 17). At one meeting Tsamkxao, a leader, said:

> "I thank the old people who have spoken, but we also need to begin to hear from the young people about their *n'ores*. Everyone must work together. Do you see these sticks in my hand? If you pick up lots of sticks, you can't break them. But one stick alone breaks easily. So we want things from now on to be done on paper, legally, beginning with meetings where everyone comes together to listen. We don't want a Ju/'hoan representative who just stuffs news into his own ears and doesn't speak to us. If you speak for a group of people to a government, and if you speak badly, it doesn't just affect one person. It affects everyone. When you do something, all your people should have a way of learning about it. Political parties are for letting people know things." (Biesele, 1978, p. 18)

The Ju/'hoansi of Nyae Nyae have adapted their traditional culture to create democratic political organization, starting with the Nyae Nyae Farmers' Cooperative in the 1980s. The Farmers' Coop wrote a Ju/'hoan constitution. The document was written by a committee of Ju/'hoansi and then transcribed into both English and !Kung by hired scribes. Representatives from all the villages traveled through Eastern Bushmanland explaining the document. It is an inspiring constitution, formulating the traditional laws of the n'ore and explaining the need for formal political organization. Biesele quotes the constitution as follows:

> "Our Ju/'hoan land of Nyae Nyae is now small and we are many. We need the strength of unity under law to keep the land that remains to us. We need the strength of thought under written law to use the resources of our land for our individual well-being and our common good. . . .
> "Today Ju/'hoansi are people dispossessed of land and the right to own land. Without land on which to produce food to eat and without work, too many Ju/'hoansi die of hunger and disease. The Council of the cooperative must become the mothers and the fathers of the dispossessed, and give them *n'ores* on which to live." (Biesele, 1978, pp. 8–9)

In 1988 and 1989, as Namibia prepared for the end of South African rule and the first free elections, a Farmers' Coop team traveled around the settlements of Eastern Bushmanland, explaining what elections are and why the 1989 election mattered and listening to the issues Ju/'hoansi villagers raised.

In the 1990s, the Farmers' Coop evolved into a government-recognized traditional authority, with a chief, and into the Nyae Nyae Conservancy. We must, however, qualify the success of democracy in Nyae Nyae. Many Ju/'hoansi, especially those in the villages and those who are poor and jobless, complain that the foreigners brought in by NGOs and even the Ju/'hoansi elite, ignore the majority's wish to farm. The World Wildlife Fund has spent over $35 million developing trophy hunting and tourism in Nyae Nyae, but is unwilling to spend any money to protect small farmers from elephants (Marshall, 2006, Part 5). The San members of the conservancy feel ignored and marginalized, despite their political activism and democratic organization.

Landless San: The Hai//om of Mangetti West

It will be useful for us to compare the Nyae Nyae Ju/'hoansi with other San groups. None of these groups lives any longer by hunting and gathering, but patterns of adaptation differ depending on local circumstances.

There are about 11,000 Hai//om San altogether. Many live in northern Namibia between the deserts of Bushmanland and the densely populated farms of Ovamboland. Unlike the Ju/'hoansi, the Hai//om have been little studied by anthropologists. This account will rely primarily on recent work done by Thomas Widlok in the area he calls "Mangetti."

Hai//om San have lived in the Mangetti area as long as anyone can recall, but they own none of the land there, having been dispossessed during the colonial period (Widlok, 1999, pp. 3–4). South Africa gave much of their land to White settlers and later made part of it into Ovamboland, the homeland for the Ovambo people under apartheid. Elsewhere the Hai//om were evicted from Etosha, which was made into Etosha Game Park. The Hai//om did not receive any land of their own after Namibia became independent. They are illiterate and unschooled. Unlike the Ju/'hoansi of Eastern Bushmanland, they have formed no political organizations and have developed no self-leadership. No international foundation has stepped forward to take them under its wing. Nevertheless, the Hai//om have found ingenious ways to survive and to preserve some aspects of their culture, in a setting where they are geographically displaced and socially despised.

Vilho's Story: Surviving on Mangetti

Vilho (see Widlok, 1999, p. 40) is living with his family at Botos in the communal Ovambo area of Mangetti. He lives in a settlement built on Ovambo communal land, just a short distance from an Ovambo homestead. The settlement consists of two circles of Ovambo-style huts, with a fence around it. Vilho's circle includes huts for his wife and children, his widowed mother, and his younger sister and her husband. Another widowed woman also lives in their circle. Vilho, his wife, and his sister and brother-in-law all work on the Ovambo homestead during the growing season, from December through June, planting, cultivating, harvesting, and threshing millet and sorghum. They are paid in food or beer, which they bring home and share with their whole settlement. The Ovambo don't mind if their farmworkers bring their families and friends to live with them and share their food. In fact, during busy times the Ovambo feed all the local Hai//om on their homestead. (Barnard & Widlok, 1996, pp. 95–98)

Occasionally Vilho and his brother-in-law go off hunting and sometimes bring back a duiker or a springhare, but larger animals are rarely seen and it is illegal for Hai//om to kill them (Widlok, 1999, pp. 67–68). Sometimes the women of the settlement go out and gather mangetti nuts in the nearby groves, often bringing back other wild fruits and roots too. The Ovambo don't mind if the resident Hai//om gather on their land.

So what sort of life is this? It appears that the Hai//om have accommodated themselves to the agricultural economy of the Ovambo, who own the land. They combine work as agricultural laborers with hunting (a little) and gathering (quite a bit). They also combine Hai//om and Ovambo customs. They have built Ovambo-style houses and established separate hearths for men and women, according to Ovambo custom. At the same time, they continue to share gathered foods and perform trance dances (Widlok, 1999, p. 97).

Seasonal Migration

Widlok noted that the Hai//om even preserve some of their old nomadic existence. When the harvest is finished and the dry season begins, they pick up and leave Botos and move to !Gai nas, an area they consider their original *n'ore* where they stay near another band of close relatives who remain at !Gai nas year-round. This too is on Ovambo land, but there is little work on the homestead at this time of year and the Hai//om depend primarily on hunting and gathering. When he stays at !Gai nas, Vilho (an Ovambo name) is known as Xareb, his Hai//om name, and the band builds small grass huts arranged in a circle without a fence, San style (Barnard & Widlok, 1996, p. 98; Widlok, 1999, p. 40).

Sometimes the Hai//om make shorter trips into the bush. They may stay for as long as 2 weeks at distant mangetti groves, building temporary shelters and gathering nuts. Men are sometimes hired by commercial cattle ranches to hunt lost cattle in the bush, with the understanding that if they find the cattle dead, they may keep the meat (Widlok, 1999, p. 129).

Other Living Situations

There are even more ways that the Hai//om manage to make a living. /Gomais is a central town like Tsumkwe in Eastern Bushmanland and many Hai//om live permanently there. During the war, the South African army cleared Hai//om from the combat zones to the north and gathered them at /Gomais. There is a large resettlement farm there, and wild food is available there as well as a church that runs a school and sometimes gives out free food. When Vilho/Xareb visits /Gomais he is known as "Samuel," his Christian name. Also, some Hai//om gather mangetti fruits to sell to some local Ovambo who use the fruits to brew liquor. Sometimes they are paid in liquor (Barnard & Widlok, 1996, pp. 99–100).

Hai//om also works on White-owned commercial farms, where they have less freedom to practice their traditional culture. Farmers sometimes provide stone houses or provide poles and sheet metal for square houses and each house is fenced separately, so nuclear families are more separated from each other. White farmers don't allow Hai//om to bring their bands with them onto the farm; they allow only immediate relatives. At private farms Hai//om workers are more likely to own things like bicycles or even bank accounts and they may write their initials or, if they can't write, mark their possessions with symbols (Barnard & Widlok, 1996, pp. 100–101).

Wherever they live, Hai//om men collect scrap iron and do blacksmithing work, making tools such as spades, screwdrivers, knives, and arrowheads. They produce these items for themselves and also on order for the Ovambo. That is, they will forge an adze to order, usually in exchange for other useful items, like clothing, but they don't do blacksmith work as a business—they don't produce a stock of goods for sale (Widlok, 1999, pp. 120–122).

Change and Continuity: Foraging and Sharing

The Hai//om have no land of their own, so they lack even the minimal independence of the Ju/'hoansi of Nyae Nyae. They are always living on land that belongs to someone else: the Ovambo, the White commercial farmers, or the government. Consequently, they are always in dependent relationships with others who have more property and power than they do. But be careful how you think about the changes in their culture. You may assume that change will mean adopting the customs of modern industrial nations. Actually for the Hai//om change has meant adopting some of the customs of their Ovambo neighbors—making separate hearths for men and women, using Ovambo names, making Ovambo-style houses. Only a few Hai//om who work on commercial ranches have done anything so modern as having bank accounts, and their employers handle these for them.

Widlok points out that in the most fundamental way the Hai//om have not changed; they remain foragers. They are no longer living as traditional hunters and gatherers, but instead they "forage" their new environment, moving about from one resource to another, one day foraging the bush for wild food, another day foraging the church mission for free food, or the dump in /Gomais foraging for iron scrap, old tires to make into shoes, plastic pipes for bracelets, wire for snares, bottle tops for dance rattles, and old bottles and used engine oil for lamps (Widlok, 1999, p. 127). It turns out that there is a substantial niche for foragers in a commercialized setting. Hai//om work for the Ovambo in exchange for food, and then when the season changes and that resource is at an end, they move on to another setting, the bush, the town, the resettlement camp. This really isn't so different from traditional hunting and gathering.

Moreover, as Widlok points out, foraging is intimately linked to sharing. In this respect, the Hai//om have been able to maintain an essential part of their traditional culture: the sharing that supports equality. At the same time, however, as Widlok makes clear, sharing (he calls it "demand sharing") prevents the Hai//om from saving, investing, and planning. Take the distilling business, for example. The Hai//om often gather mangetti fruits and sell them to the Ovambo for use in making liquor for sale. Returns to the Hai//om are meager—a sack of millet, or perhaps a bottle of liquor. Why don't the Hai//om themselves go into distilling? They can make or borrow the simple apparatus and they have already gathered the fruits. Liquor sells for much more than mangetti. Widlok realizes what the problem is as he observes a Hai//om couple distilling. By the end of the day, all their relatives and friends have come by and each has demanded a drink. The mangettis are gone, the liquor is gone, and the enterprising couple are left with nothing (Widlok, 1999, pp. 100–105). Similarly, Hai//om who make their own gardens and herd their own cattle find themselves socially excluded. They cannot allow friends and relatives to take food from their gardens and they cannot slaughter a cow whenever people are hungry.

So the practice of sharing both supports the Hai//om in foraging and also restricts them to foraging. In a way, you could say that the Hai//om have strongly and successfully resisted changing their culture. They have resisted the influence of people and cultures more powerful than they. Their resistance has taken the form of clinging to foraging and sharing. But as so often happens, their resistance has had a downside: It has contributed to keeping the Hai//om dependent and poor in modern Namibia.

Environmental Change

Namibia is quite sparsely populated and up until now Namibians have always had a sense that there is unlimited "bush," wild land, out there somewhere. In the north, although the Ovambo are relatively crowded on the arable portions of their land, they have been quite willing to allow the Hai//om to live in the mangetti groves and dry hinterlands of their homeland. San have also lived on government-administered land and on the more remote edges of commercial ranches. But now the way people use land in Namibia is changing. Land is becoming commercialized. "Unoccupied" communal land in the southeast of Ovamboland where the Hai//om live has been taken over and fenced by wealthy Ovambos and thus effectively turned into private commercial ranches. Widlok counts 97 of these new ranches. The same thing has happened further east on Kavango communal land. Land that is used for subsistence, either by subsistence farmers or by foragers, is coming to be seen as "under-used," in contrast to land that produces crops for sale, or profits (Widlok, 1999, pp. 33–36). As land is commercialized, there is less space for the landless San.

Commercialization of land, particularly of the marginal, uninhabited land, poses an environmental threat in Namibia. Especially in periods of drought, cattle over-graze the land, stripping away vegetation. Africans call this process **desertification,** because the denuded land becomes a real desert, in which trees and grasses do not grow back and the wind erodes the soil. When rain falls, the ground doesn't hold it, and the water table gradually drops. Ranchers must then move on to less desirable, drier land, which is all the sooner exhausted. As a growing human population tries to graze more and more cattle, the process of desertification accelerates. Population growth, displacement, and desertification feed each other in a destructive cycle. Desertification is a real problem in many parts of Africa. It may be Namibia's future, but so far, sparse population and incomplete commercialization have shielded the bush.

Farm San: The Ju/'hoansi of Omaheke

There is another large group of Ju/'hoansi who live, not in Nyae Nyae, but in the Omaheke region south of Nyae Nyae. These Ju/'hoansi are unlike San further north in that they have not lived by hunting and gathering for many decades. Their land was invaded by White commercial farmers and Black herders many generations ago and most of the 6,000 or so Ju/'hoansi there were born on White-owned farms, some of them to San families that had lived and worked on the same farm for several generations. Most Namibian San are now farm laborers like them. Few anthropologists have studied "farm Bushmen." Most have wanted to study "pure" or "traditional" Bushmen, looking for small remnant groups in remote locations. James Suzman's study of the Omaheke San is an unusual source of information about the majority, and we have relied on it here.

The Ju/'hoansi in the Omaheke region are a minority population among Afrikaans-speaking White farmers, Herero farmers living on their communal land, and Damara people who speak a click language like the Ju/'hoansi. Suzman met Ju/'hoansi people at a resettlement camp purchased by the government and set aside for Ju/'hoansi and Damara farm workers. Even there, however, Herero cattle farmers had illegally taken over most of the land for their cattle. Most Ju/'hoansi living on the resettlement farm were trying to get away from being dependent on farmers, or had been laid off because of drought, or were too old to work any longer on the farms (Suzman, 2000, pp. 13–14).

Dependent, Despised, and Powerless

The Omaheke Ju/'hoansi are much worse off than the Ju/'hoansi of Nyae Nyae and the Hai//om, not so much because they are hungrier or poorer, but because they are dependent on people who have contempt for them and see them as an inferior race, more like animals than humans. Farmers described the San to Suzman as "wild," "ungodly," oversexed, unreliable, irresponsible, and also childlike. They concluded it was their role to discipline the San, often with harsh beatings and whippings. One farmer laughingly explained to Suzman, "you can take the Bushman out of the bush, but you can't take the bush out of the Bushman" (Suzman, 2000, pp. 49–52). Many White farmers believed that San gods and ceremonies, like trance dances, were "satanic." They felt responsible to make the San into Christians by giving them Afrikaans names and bible lessons and by banning Ju/'hoansi ceremonies like initiation rites and trance dances.

The experience of the Ju/'hoansi on the Omaheke farms and in the resettlement camps highlights some of the saddest changes that have affected all San in Namibia, to a greater or lesser extent. First of all, relationships between people have changed. We have seen that sharing has diminished and inequality has grown among the Ju/'hoansi. There is also growing inequality between men and women in all San groups. Furthermore, people not only have different attitudes toward each other, they think of themselves in a different and more negative way.

Gender Inequalities.   Several anthropologists have also found that inequalities between men and women have grown among the San living in villages and towns, leaving women in a more dependent, subordinate position. In their old hunting and gathering days, all life was family life, but modern society draws a line between "public" and "private" life. In most cases, San men are more able than women to get paid work, so their work takes them out more into the public realm. They learn more about dealing with other ethnic groups, with ranchers and farmers and the government. Men control the money or goods they bring home and the possessions they buy with it. Women become more tied to the home by doing housework, carrying water and wood, repairing houses and cooking food. The work they do is devalued because it is unpaid; it no longer appears to be work. Tied down by babies, no longer the main providers of food, women become more dependent on men (Draper, 1975, p. 85; Draper & Cashdan, 1988, p. 361).

Felton and Becker (2001) have found recently that where gathering remains important, as among the Hai//om, women still retain influence. But, patterning themselves on neighboring Ovambo and Herero, San have learned to see cattle as male possessions. The NGOs and the government make the same assumption. Those who own cattle, and they are always men, enjoy the accompanying prestige and influence.

On White-owned farms in the Omaheke region, women are mostly treated as dependents of the employed men. When women are employed on farms it is as domestic servants, earning especially low wages. This makes it harder for women to leave marriages or relationships in which they are unhappy (Renee Sylvain, cited in Felton & Becker, 2001, p. 6). Women are better off when they live in groups of extended kin, especially when their own relatives are nearby (p. 22).

Girls now drop out of school at a higher rate than boys, and earlier too. They have sex at a younger age and bear children younger, with a shorter period between births. This, too, makes them more dependent on men. Some men in the Omaheke resettlement camps migrate for temporary work, leaving women behind with their children. Women complain that their husbands don't send money and may have mistresses while they are away. At the same time, women increasingly get involved in exploitative relationships with men who are not San, in which the women hope to be given money, food, or alcohol, and the men seek out San women because they are known to be less likely to have HIV/AIDS than women of other ethnic groups. In this way, HIV/AIDS is beginning to spread into the San population (Felton & Becker, 2001, pp. x–xi, 18, 22).

A Damaged Sense of Self.   For the San, as for people everywhere, dependence on charity saps self-esteem. The Nyae Nyae Ju/'hoansi, who once prided themselves on their independence, are lucky, in one sense, to be the recipients of attention and aid from NGOs, but, in another sense, they are unlucky to have been made so dependent on the charity of others. That's especially true because those who run the charities are Westerners who believe that their society, their way of life, and their religion are more developed and superior to that of the San.

The Nyae Nyae Ju/'hoansi also find themselves the beneficiaries and objects of tourism, and this too is a mixed blessing. If tourists, dressed in gaily colored sports clothes, pay to look at you, dressed in skins and almost naked, as if you were an animal in a zoo, you begin to feel less than fully human. You begin to feel inferior. To protect their self-esteem, San in Namibia have begun changing their relationship to trance dancing, turning dances into performances carried out for pay. "Professionalized" trance dancers see their performances as work, conducted for tourists, government officials, or local Bantu. These dancers have adapted to the new commercial setting, simulating trance, performing in the daytime, and creating exotic paraphernalia and costumes for their dance. They gain a niche in the modern, capitalist economy of Namibia, but lose the authenticity of their culture (Guenther, 2005, pp. 211–219).

The Hai//om compare themselves with their Ovambo neighbors and feel poor and inferior. The Ovambo have cows and permanent houses with dried mud walls and tin roofs. Many San admire the Ovambo, respect their chiefs, and wish to adopt their system of farming and herding, their norms for relationships between men and women. But the San are seen as inferior by the Ovambo neighbors. When you want to be like people who reject you, that is psychologically wounding.

In the Omaheke region, the Ju/'hoansi must deal constantly with farmers who look down on them and stereotype them as subhuman and childlike. If you think about Charles Horton Cooley's concept of the **looking-glass self** you will understand that it is hard to maintain your self-respect and self-esteem when you see yourself reflected in such a negative way in the eyes of people who have power over you. The Ju/'hoansi understand themselves as victims, and the White farmers as oppressors, but they also see themselves as passive and *dom* (Afrikaans for ignorant or stupid). This refers partly to the disadvantages of illiteracy. (For example, if you can't read the farmer's record book, you must accept his word for how much he has paid you.) However, as Suzman (2000) points out, for most Ju/'hoansi, "dom-ness" is "a general metaphor through which they articulated their powerlessness and perceived inferiority to others as well as a means to legitimate their apparent defeatism" (109–111).

For all the San, and especially for the Omaheke San, alcohol is the antidote for low self-esteem. "If you are drunk," one young Ju/'hoansi told Suzman, "then you don't feel scared. Listen man, if you are finished drunk, then you won't take shit from anyone, because you feel strong" (Suzman, 2000, p. 23). But, as Felton and Becker (2001) point out, those feelings make people boastful, which then leads to fighting (p. 53).

Sociology offers some powerful concepts to help you understand the psychological state of the San. One is the concept of **marginality,** associated with two famous American sociologists, Louis Wirth and Robert E. Park. The "marginal man," said Park, "lives in two worlds in both of which he is more or less a stranger" (Park, 1950, p. 356; Wirth, 1956, p. 73). Marginality is an important American concept because it describes so well the situation of many immigrants, who find they are changed by the American experience. They no longer fit into the society they came from, while at the same time they are not fully accepted in the dominant American society. The San experience marginality when they can no longer hunt and gather, but they are still rejected by Bantus and Whites in modern Namibia.

Anomie.   The most famous sociological concept that can help you understand the Bushmen is Emile Durkheim's concept of **anomie.** Anomie means literally a state of normlessness, a social condition in which shared norms no longer effectively regulate individual desires. Durkheim saw anomie occurring in times of rapid social change, when old norms fail to apply to new conditions, and people are no longer sure what they can expect in life (Durkheim, 1951, pp. 248–250). Anomie is a condition of society, not a psychological state, but it is regularly associated with certain individual symptoms like depression and feelings of meaninglessness and aimlessness. When societies suffer from anomie, Durkheim said, rates of suicide rise, and we notice nowadays that rates of alcohol and drug abuse rise too.

The Future: Resistance and Adaptation

Commercialization, dependency, breakdown of band solidarity, feelings of inferiority, and anomie: This is a really depressing catalog of what can go wrong for the Bushmen. It's important to emphasize that although some San have been overwhelmed by their experiences in modern Namibia, others have kept their strength and pride. For the Ju/'hoansi of Nyae Nyae, land of their own and some government recognition of their rights have made a difference. They have adapted one of the strengths of their culture—egalitarianism—to develop new democratic institutions. The Hai//om of Mangetti have had no outside help, but nonetheless they have kept their forager ethic, finding niches in the mixed economy of the north and continuing to share.

Thinking Sociologically

1. Can you use the functionalist perspective to explain why the San, in their lives as hunters and gatherers, emphasized sharing, were nomadic, and had small families?
2. When the San lived as hunters and gatherers, what were their most important social groups?
3. Compare the status and roles of women in San hunter-gatherer society and in Japanese society. Is the status of women in your society more similar to that of San women or that of Japanese women?
4. Which of the four types of social interaction (social exchange, cooperation, competition, and conflict) predominated in San hunter-gatherer society? How about in your society?
5. What social changes in Namibia changed the lives of the San?
6. In what ways have foreign anthropologists and aid organizations helped the San? Have they harmed them?
7. Compare and contrast the ways that the Nyae Nyae Ju/'hoansi, the Omaheke Ju/'hoansi, and the Hai//om have managed to adapt to life in modern Namibia.
8. Which of the traditional San values helps the San adapt to modern society? Which present obstacles?

For Further Reading

Guenther, M. (1999). *Tricksters and trancers: Bushman religion and society.* Bloomington: Indiana University Press.
Lee, R. B. (1993). *The Dobe Ju/'hoansi* (2nd ed.). New York: Harcourt Brace.
Leys, C., & Saul, J. S. (Eds.). (1995). *Namibia's liberation struggle: The two-edged sword.* London: James Currey.
Shostak, M. (1981). *Nisa.* Cambridge, MA: Harvard University Press.
Suzman, J. (2000). *Things from the bush: A contemporary history of the Omaheke Bushmen.* Basil, Switzerland: P. Schlettwein.
Thomas, E. M. (1959). *The harmless people.* New York: Knopf.
Thomas, E. M. (2006). *The old way: A story of the first people.* New York: Farrar, Straus and Giroux.
Widlok, T. (1999). *Living on Mangetti: "Bushman" autonomy and Namibian independence.* Oxford, England: Oxford University Press.

Bibliography

Barnard, A. (1992). *Hunters and herders of southern Africa.* Cambridge, England: Cambridge University Press.
Barnard, A., & Widlok, T. (1996). Nharo and Hai//om settlement patterns in comparative perspective. In Susan Kent (Ed.), *Cultural diversity among twentieth-century foragers: An African perspective* (pp. 87–107). Cambridge, England: Cambridge University Press.

Biesele, M. (1978). Religion and folklore. In Phillip V. Tobias (Ed.), *The Bushmen: San hunters and herders of southern Africa* (pp. 162, 165–168). Cape Town: Human & Rousseau.

Butler, V. (1997, July–August). Bushmen at a crossroads. *International Wildlife, 27*(4), 20–27.

The Corruption Perceptions Index. (2004). Retrieved from http://www.transparency.org/documents/cpi/2004/cpi2004.html

Draper, P. (1975). Kung women: Contrasts in sexual egalitarianism in foraging and sedentary contexts. In R. Reiter (Ed.), *Towards an anthropology of women.* New York: Monthly Review Press.

Draper, P., & Cashdan, E. (1988). Technological change and child behavior among the !Kung. *Ethnology, 27,* 339–365.

Durkheim, E. (1965). *The elementary forms of the religious life* (J. W. Swain, Trans.). New York: Free Press. (Original work published 1915.)

Eibl-Eibensfeldt, I. (1978). Early socialization in the !Xo Bushmen. In P. V. Tobias (Ed.), *The Bushmen: San hunters and herders of southern Africa* (pp. 132–135). Cape Town: Human & Rousseau.

Felton, S., & Becker, H. (2001). *A gender perspective on the status of the San in southern Africa* (Regional Assessment of the Status of the San in Southern Africa Report Series, Report No. 5). Windhoek, Namibia: Legal Assistance Center.

Fisher, H. E. (1992). *The anatomy of love.* New York: Norton.

Good, K. (1997). *Realizing democracy in Botswana, Namibia and South Africa.* Cape Town: Africa Institute of South Africa.

Gordon, R. J. (1992). *The Bushman myth: The making of a Namibian underclass.* Boulder, CO: Westview Press.

Guenther, M. (1996). Diversity and flexibility: The case of the Bushmen of southern Africa. In S. Kent (Ed.), *Cultural diversity among twentieth-century foragers: An African perspective* (pp. 65–86). Cambridge, England: Cambridge University Press.

Guenther, M. (1999). *Tricksters and trancers: Bushman religion and society.* Bloomington: Indiana University Press.

Guenther, M. (2005). The professionalisation and commoditisation of the contemporary Bushman trance dancer and trance dance, and the decline of sharing. In T. Widlok & W. Gossa Tadesse (Eds.), *Property and equality: Encapsulation, commercialization, discrimination* (pp. 208–230). New York and Oxford, England: Berghahn Books.

Kelso, C. (1993, March–April). The landless Bushmen. *Africa Report, 38*(2), 51–53.

Kent, S. (1996a). Cultural diversity among African foragers: Causes and implications. In S. Kent (Ed.), *Cultural diversity among twentieth-century African foragers: An African perspective* (pp. 1–18). Cambridge, England: Cambridge University Press.

Kent, S. (Ed.). (1996b). *Cultural diversity among twentieth-century foragers: An African perspective.* Cambridge, England: Cambridge University Press.

Kluckholm, C. (1949). *Mirror for man.* New York: McGraw-Hill.

Lee, R. B. (1979). *The !Kung San.* Cambridge, England: Cambridge University Press.

Lee, R. B. (1984). *The Dobe !Kung.* New York: Holt.

Lenski, G., Nolan, P., & Lenski, J. (1991). *Human societies: An introduction to macrosociology* (6th ed.). New York: McGraw-Hill.

Leys, C., & Saul, J. S. (Eds.). (1995). *Namibia's liberation struggle: The two-edged sword.* London: James Currey.

Marshall, J. (2006). *A Kalahari family* [DVD]. Retrieved from the Documentary Educational Resources. Web site: http://www.der.org

Marshall, L. (1976). *The !Kung of Nyae Nyae.* Cambridge, MA: Harvard University Press.

Marshall, L. (1999). *Nyae Nyae !Kung beliefs and rites.* Cambridge, MA: Peabody Museum Monographs, Harvard University.

Odendaal, W., & Harring, S. (2006). *Our land they took: San rights under threat in Namibia.* Namibia Legal Assistance Centre.

Park, R. E. (1950). *Race and culture.* New York: Free Press.

Roue, M. (1998, January). An economy of sharing: There is no place for selfish individualism in nomadic hunter-gatherer societies. *UNESCO Courier,* 23–25.

Saunders, C. (1999). Recent history. In *Africa south of the Sahara.* (pp. 755–759). Old Woking, Surrey, England: Europa.

Shostak, M., (1981). *Nisa.* Cambridge, MA: Harvard University Press.

Silberbauer, G. (1978). The future of the Bushmen. In P. Tobias (Ed.), *The Bushmen: San hunters and herders of southern Africa.* Cape Town: Human & Rousseau.

Slotten, R. A. (1995). AIDS in Namibia. *Social Science Medicine, 41*(2), 277–284.

Suzman, J. (2000). *Things from the bush: A contemporary history of the Omaheke Bushmen.* Basil, Switzerland: P. Schlettwein.

Thomas, E. M. (1959). *The harmless people.* New York: Knopf.

Thomas, E. M. (2006). *The old way: A story of the first people.* New York: Farrar, Straus and Giroux.

Tobias, P. V. (Ed.). (1978). *The Bushmen: San hunters and herders of southern Africa.* Cape Town: Human & Rousseau.

Transparency International. (2007). *Corruption perceptions index.* Retrieved from http://www.transparency.org/policy_research/surveys_indices/cpi

Weinberg, P. (1997). *In search of the San.* Johannesburg, South Africa: Porcupine Press.

Widlok, T. (1999). *Living on Mangetti: "Bushman" autonomy and Namibian independence.* Oxford, England: Oxford University Press.

Wiessner, P. (2003, Spring/Summer). Owners of the future: Calories, cash, casualties and self-sufficiency in the Nyae Nyae area between 1996 and 2003. *Visual Anthropology Review, 19* (1 & 2), 149–159.

Wiessner, P. (2005, Summer). Norm enforcement among the Ju/'hoansi Bushmen: A case of strong reciprocity? *Human Nature, 16*(2), 115–145.

Wilmsen, E. N. (1989). *Land filled with flies: A political economy of the Kalahari.* Chicago: University of Chicago Press.

Wirth, L. (1956). *The ghetto.* Chicago: University of Chicago Press. (Original work published 1928)

World Bank. (n.d.). *World development indicators data query.* Retrieved November 12, 2004, from http://devdata.worldbank.org/data-query/

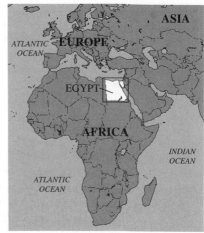

You can reach Cairo, Egypt's capital, in a short flight from anywhere in the Middle East or the Mediterranean. Athens, Rome, Damascus, and Jerusalem are only hours (or minutes) away. You will set down in one of the oldest human civilizations. Thirty centuries before Christ there were cities, scholars, and kings in Egypt.

LOCATION: Egypt rests in Africa's northeast corner bordered by Israel and the Red Sea on the east, the Sudan on the south, Libya to the west, and the Mediterranean Sea to the north.

AREA: Egypt covers 384,000 square miles. It is as large as Texas and New Mexico combined or about the size of Ontario.

LAND: Egypt is mostly desert. Population is concentrated in the Nile Valley and on the Delta—one of the world's most densely settled areas.

CLIMATE: Hot and dry. The coast gets 8 inches of rain per year, while south of Cairo there is almost none. Egypt is hot from May to October (up to 107 °F) and cooler from November to April (55 to 70 °F).

POPULATION: In 2007 there were 80 million people; 35% were under the age of 15. By 2050 population is projected to reach 113 million.

INCOME: In equivalent U.S. purchasing power, average per person GDP was $4,900 in 2005. Forty-four percent of Egyptians live on less than what $2.00 a day would buy in the United States.

EDUCATION: Fifty-nine percent of Egyptian women are literate, as are 83% of Egyptian men.

RELIGION: Ninety-one percent of Egyptians are Sunni Muslims; at least 5% are Coptic Christians.

MINORITIES: Coptic Christians and Saidis—people from the southern part of Egypt.

CHAPTER FOUR

Egypt: Faith, Gender, and Class

INTRODUCTION

It would be a good idea to start this chapter by thinking about what you already know about Egypt. When you think of Egypt, do pyramids, palm trees, and mummies come to mind? Do you think of veiled women and Muslims kneeling in prayer? Does your mind turn to terrorism and militant Islamic fundamentalists? For many people, Egypt is a faraway place with an exotic past and a frightening present. Why should you learn more about it?

Nowadays, more than ever, studying Egypt will help you understand the world. Egypt will be your key to understanding the Muslim world, the Arab world, and the Middle East. The next time there is a war or an invasion in the Middle East, you will be much better able to make sense of events. You will know something about Islam, the religion, and about the political movements that take Islam as their focus. Also, you will be acquainted with the conditions of life in the Arab world, the dilemmas young people face, and the discontents that seek political expression.

Egypt is at once an Islamic society, an Arab society, and a Middle Eastern society, but the first thing you need to understand is that these terms are not synonymous. Islam is one of the world's great religions, practiced by more than 1.2 billion people worldwide. Followers of Islam are known as Muslims. But Muslims live in many countries and belong to many different ethnic groups. All of the Arab countries have large Muslim populations. Several (like Egypt and Iraq) also have Christian minorities. The Arab countries (including Saudi Arabia, Egypt, Iraq, Yemen, Syria, Lebanon, and Morocco) are inhabited by only 12% of the world's Muslims. The three nations with the largest Muslim populations (Indonesia, Pakistan, and Bangladesh) are Asian, not Arab and not Middle Eastern. There are millions of Muslims in Central Asia too (including Iran, Afghanistan, Kazakhstan, Uzbekistan, and western China), and also in Africa (including Nigeria and Sudan). Also, Muslim population is now growing in Europe and the United States as the result of immigration. If you study only one Muslim society, Egypt would be a good choice. Politically and culturally, Egypt has played a leading role in the Arab and Muslim worlds. From President Nasser's Pan-Arabism, to early-20th-century feminism, and on to early-20th-century radical Islamism, Egypt has set the trend. Egypt's sensitive geographic location makes it important too—in the Arab oil-producing region, adjacent to Israel, in North Africa, and not far from Europe. Conflict in Egypt makes the news and reverberates around the world.

Egypt and its African, Middle Eastern, and Asian neighbors have something important in common: They are all former European colonies, struggling to define their place in the modern world and cope with poverty, economic development, and rapid population growth. But in one way, Egypt is very different from some of its neighbors. Egypt has an unambiguous national identity and stable national boundaries. Egypt was a nation long before it was a colony. The kinds of deep divisions that exist in Iraq between Sunni and Shia and Kurdish Muslims, or between Pashtun and Dari tribes in Afghanistan have no real place in Egypt. There are some tribal identities: Bedouins in the northern deserts and Nubians in the south. But people think of themselves as Egyptians first and foremost and there are no separatist movements. Everyone speaks Arabic.

We expect that if you come from a Western nation, you will find Egypt very different from your own society. You will learn a lot from contrasting the two. Three aspects of Egyptian society are absolutely central: faith, gender, and class. In Egypt the Islamic faith imbues all aspects of life: People understand the values they cherish and the norms they follow in religious terms. They debate politics, personal morality, and fashion in the light of their religion.

Another aspect of Egyptian society that may make a great impression on you is the contrasting roles played by men and women. Egyptian men and women have different religious obligations, different family responsibilities, and different legal rights. In public and private, Egyptian men and women usually carry on their lives separately from each other.

We would like you to meet Saad and Lima. They lead very different lives, and it is unlikely that they would ever meet. Islam is very important to both of them, but they understand and live it differently.

Two Egyptians: Their Stories

Saad is tired. At 14 he rises very early each morning to study for his high school classes. His father is a small shopkeeper, but Saad badly wants to be a professional with a good salary and a house in a fashionable part of the city. He interrupts his studies only for a cup of tea, a roll, and morning prayers. As busy as he might be, Saad, like his father Ibrahim, prays five times a day. Ibrahim has a "raisin" on his forehead: a small dark bruise raised by touching his forehead to the ground thousands of times in a long lifetime of prayer. Although the future that Saad dreams of may be very different from his father's, Saad cannot imagine a life outside Islam. It is as much a part of him as his family, his friends, and his hopes. Every morning Saad spends the long walk to school listening to the Quran (the holy book of Islam) recited on his Walkman.

Lima is a professor of legal studies. She was raised in a secular family of teachers and doctors and her interest in Islam developed only when Islamic marriage norms became a focus of controversy in Egypt. Lima soon found that the problems of interpreting Islamic law were at least as fascinating as the business law she studied and taught. Some of the Islamic issues were even closer to her life: Could a woman sue for divorce? Could a marriage contract forbid a man to take a second spouse? Lima soon joined a study circle of educated women who met at a mosque on the college grounds to study Islam. "I never learned much about Islam at home," she told a friend. "We considered religion not at all interesting for educated people. We observed the fasts but not much else. My father wasn't happy when he learned I was studying Sharia (Islamic law) and could cite passages and precedents from the Quran." "I never thought I'd live to see the day," he said, "when I had a son who never reads the Quran and a daughter who quotes it." After several years of study, Lima and her circle challenged a ruling by a leading cleric forbidding young couples to take out mortgages to buy apartments. The cleric responded harshly to Lima's group. Writing to a leading Cairo newspaper he argued that the circle's interpretation ignored important points of Sharia. Lima was not dismayed by his response. "When you have the country's leading clerics arguing Sharia with you in the daily papers," she told her fiance, "you've moved women into a role they haven't had in this country for a long time."

Class contrasts are unavoidable in Egypt. There are sophisticated young men and women who live in luxury apartments in Cairo's modern high-rise towers who would not be out of place in New York, Paris, or London. Their clothing comes from Milan and Paris, their luxury cars from Germany, their electronics from Japan, and their income from high-level jobs in Egypt's banking and legal establishments. Not far from the apartments of such wealthy Egyptians, poor people fill the narrow alleys of Cairo's oldest quarters. Many are recent migrants from villages in southern Egypt, where life still revolves around fields and family.

To understand why Islam is fundamental to Egyptian culture, how class inequalities have come to divide Egyptian society so deeply, and why the position of women is the subject of such passionate debate in contemporary Egypt, you need information about Egypt's long and fascinating history.

EGYPT'S HISTORY

In some countries, people look to the future and pay little attention to the past. "That's history," people say dismissively. For Egyptians, however, the past counts for a good deal in the way people look at themselves and their lives. Evidence of a glorious past surrounds Egyptians, a past in which Egypt dominated or led the world. The pyramids are a visible reminder of the advanced civilization that flourished in Egypt before the classical cultures of Greece and Rome emerged. Cairo's mosques and Al Azhar University (established in the 10th century and considered the oldest university in the world) remind Egyptians that they were once in the center of an Islamic civilization that overshadowed Christian Europe.

When Egyptians see that Egypt today is politically and economically dominated by the Christian West, that Egypt is no longer a center of scientific, economic, and artistic innovation, they feel weak and humiliated. But they take courage from the testimony of their history. They know that in the course of its history Egypt suffered conquest after conquest by other societies that successively imposed their cultures and social structures. Egypt embraced some of the invading societies and absorbed their cultures, but resisted others. In its long history Egypt has changed its language and religion three times. After the ancient pharaonic period (c. 3100 BC–671 BC), Egypt was conquered and became part of the Greek and Roman empires (333 BC–AD 641). Next came the Arab-Islamic conquest of Egypt, and the long period of Islamic civilization (641–1798) that followed. In recent centuries, Egypt was conquered once again, this time by Europeans, and subjected to European colonialism (1798–1952). Then, in the mid-20th century, Egypt entered its present era of postcolonial independence (1952–present). Throughout its history, Egypt has been an intellectual and cultural center. The great library at Alexandria brought together all the knowledge of the ancient world. Later, Cairo became an important focus for Islamic scholarship. And in the 19th and 20th centuries, Cairo was the literary and cultural leader of the Arab world, a magnet for novelists, filmmakers, journalists, and political activists, who argued and inspired one another in the literary coffeehouses and shaped cultural life in the whole Arab world.

The Pharaonic Period

One of the world's first great civilizations developed in Egypt. Egyptians began farming as early as 9,000 years ago, and by 4,000 years ago they had built towns, and wealthy people lived in elaborate houses, adorned with gold and glass ornaments, musical instruments, pottery, and cloth. Merchants traveled and traded with other societies in Africa and the Middle East. By 3000 BC the reign of the pharaohs began, which lasted nearly 3,000 years. Pharaonic Egypt created some of the first government bureaucracies, complete with record keepers and tax collectors. The power of the pharaohs and the energy and knowledge they commanded is still visible today in their surviving monuments: the pyramids, temples, deserted cities, and tombs of the Egyptian desert.

Greek and Roman Empires

Pharaonic Egypt lasted until 332 BC, when Alexander the Great conquered Egypt—one step in a stunning series of victories over all of Greece and then over the armies of Asia and Africa. Alexander was the young ruler of Macedonia, a small, poor country in the Balkans, but he put together a historic empire. After Alexander's death, one of his generals, Ptolemy, took over rule of Egypt. Ptolemy and his successors drew Egypt into the Greek world. Greek replaced Coptic, the ancient language of Egypt. Egyptian decorative arts began to follow Greek artistic ideas, and depictions of Egyptian gods began to resemble Greek gods. Ptolemy and his successors built a new capital city, Alexandria, on the shore of the Mediterranean, facing toward Europe.

Greek conquest brought great changes to the lives of Egyptian men and especially Egyptian women. Women had been respected in pharaonic Egypt. There were important female deities and priestesses, and women and men were equal before the law. Women could own property and sue for divorce and they could socialize freely in public with men (Ahmed, 1992, pp. 31–33). All this changed with the Greek conquest. In Greek civilization, free women (as opposed to slaves) were **secluded** (that is, they were kept separate from men and out of public view). They could not be seen by any men except close relatives (Ahmed, 1992, pp. 28–31).

The Roman Conquest and Christianity

Not long after Alexander's conquests, the city of Rome came to dominate much of Mediterranean Europe. Then, in the 1st century BC, Rome defeated the Ptolemies and added Egypt to the expanding Roman Empire, which now ringed the Mediterranean Sea. International trade led to a burst of economic and intellectual productivity in Egypt. Egypt grew the wheat for Rome's bread, and Alexandria became the intellectual center of the entire Roman world.

In the years after Christ's birth, Christianity came to Alexandria and found a receptive audience. For several centuries, Christianity spread throughout Egypt, gradually replacing the worship of the ancient gods of the Nile. Christian ideas about women were similar to Greek ideas. Early Christian women were frequently covered from head to toe in voluminous gowns and veils and they were strictly segregated in order to protect men from temptation (Ahmed, 1992, pp. 35–36).

But while Christianity blossomed in Egypt, the Roman Empire declined. The empire had grown so large, stretching from the Atlantic Ocean to the Red Sea, that Rome could not effectively rule it. In the 4th century AD, Rome divided itself into an Eastern and a Western Empire. The Eastern Empire, which included Egypt, was to be ruled from the ancient city of Byzantium (today Istanbul, in Turkey). Byzantium proved to be a less friendly ruler than Rome. The Byzantine rulers objected to the way Egyptians practiced Christianity and persecuted Coptic (Egyptian) Christians. By the 7th century, Egyptians regarded the Byzantines less as brothers in Christ and more as hated tyrants.

The Arab/Islamic Conquest

When the 7th century began, Egypt was a Christian country; its language was Greek and it identified with the cultural traditions of Greece, Rome, and Jerusalem. All this was to change forever with the explosive growth of a new religion: Islam. Islam originated in the Arabian city of Mecca (now in Saudi Arabia), at that time a crossroads of trade between India and the Byzantine Empire. In the 7th century, Muhammad, a 42-year-old merchant, had a revelation from God and announced a new faith—Islam—that built upon Arab culture, Christianity, and Judaism. Within a century Muhammad's followers had moved out of Arabia to conquer Egypt, Syria, and Palestine. In the centuries that followed, they swept beyond Egypt, west through North Africa, and on to Spain and east to the borders of China.

Although the Arabs came as conquerors, they were not entirely unwelcome in Egypt. The bitterness that Egyptians felt toward the Byzantines led them to stand aside as the Arabs crushed the Byzantine forces. The Arabs, for their part, demanded much less than had the Byzantines: Only obedience and taxes were required. Although the Arabs devoutly wished for converts to their new faith, they did not forcibly convert Egyptians—whether Christians or Jews or worshipers of the ancient gods.

Islam gradually transformed Egyptian society. Arabic became the common language of Egypt, replacing Coptic, the language of ancient Egypt, and the Greek of the Greco-Roman period. Cairo, a new Islamic city, replaced Alexandria in importance and became a world center of Islamic learning. By the 14th century, most Egyptians had embraced Islam, and Islamic beliefs and practices became a fundamental part of Egyptian culture.

Islam didn't much change the status of women in Egypt. It shared Christian gender norms and attitudes toward women. Islam did give Egyptian women limited rights to sue for divorce and a limited right to inherit, but it also introduced into Egypt the Arab practice of **polygyny** (which allowed men to marry more than one wife) (Ahmed, 1992, p. 33).

Islamic Civilization

People in the Islamic world remember something that Westerners forget. For many centuries after the foundation of Islam, the Islamic world was the center of civilization and progress. At the same time that Europe declined into its "Dark Ages," a period when government disintegrated, knowledge was lost, and trade withered, the Islamic world flourished. Old knowledge of science was preserved in Egypt and elsewhere in the Middle East and new scientific and mathematical knowledge was created. The great library at Alexandria preserved all the books and knowledge of the ancient world. Much of the heritage of classical Greece and Rome was preserved and passed on to the modern world by Muslim scholars. In the 11th and 12th centuries the Fatamid dynasty ruled North Africa, Sicily, Syria, and Palestine from its center in Cairo (Donner, 1999, pp. 44–49). Manufacturing and commerce expanded so that the Islamic world became the hub of the world's economy. The most desired products, like coffee, sugar, and paper, were available only from Muslim merchants. Islamic governments offered unprecedented freedom of thought and tolerance of minorities, so much so that groups like the Jews, persecuted in Europe, fled to Islamic countries for refuge (Lewis, 2002, p. 45). Islamic civilization was creative and energetic, spreading through Asia and into Europe and establishing empires like the Turkish caliphate.

European Colonialism

In the 14th and 15th centuries no one could have imagined that Europe would someday replace the Islamic world in dominance. But in fact Europe began to develop and expand, gradually pushing aside the Islamic world. Europeans forced Arab rulers out of Spain in 1492. They took over trade with India in the 16th century, and in 1798, a French army, led by Napoleon, conquered Egypt itself. The French were soon expelled by the British and Turks, with whom they were at war, but European political and economic domination of Egypt continued.

Some Egyptians prospered during this colonial period of European domination. An elite of landowners, government officials, and professionals, who cooperated with the Europeans, came under the influence of European culture and ideas. They adopted French (rather than Arabic) as their everyday language and sent their sons to schools where they were taught in French and read European books. Egypt's elite also absorbed European ideas about democracy, the right of nations to self-rule, and the need for equality between women and men. During the colonial period, some affluent Egyptian women publicly removed their veils and participated in the political struggle for independence. However, for most Egyptians life became much harder during the colonial period. Many peasants lost their land; weavers, tailors, and other skilled workers could not compete against machine-made European goods; and the growing ranks of industrial workers labored long hours for very low wages. Poor Egyptians had little contact with European culture: They spoke Arabic and took consolation in Islam. Both the economic and the cultural distance between rich and poor widened.

The European powers made increasingly restrictive demands on the Egyptian government, and in 1882 a revolt against these restrictions by the Egyptian army led to the occupation of Egypt by the British. From 1882 through 1954, the object of modern Egyptian politics was the end of the British occupation. Although a popular revolt in 1919 led the British to proclaim Egypt independent in 1921, the British army remained in occupation and the newly created king and parliament were dominated by the British ambassador. In 1952, following a humiliating defeat of the Egyptian army by the forces of Israel, the newly independent Jewish state, a group of junior officers deposed King Farouk and took control of the government. In 1954 these officers, led by Gamal Abdul Nasser, expelled the British army and created real independence for Egypt for the first time in 100 years.

An Independent Egypt

It is ironic that Western ideas played so large a role in Egypt's revolt against European domination. Nasser, Egypt's greatest 20th-century figure, transformed Egypt's government and economy and greatly improved the lives of the poorest Egyptians. While he respected Islam, Nasser looked to the West, to the United States, the Soviet Union, and Europe for political values and institutional models. Nasser moved his country in the direction of a **secular** (that is, not religious) authority: a system of business law separate from Islamic family law, a school system separate from religious education, and Western-style parliamentary government separate from religious authority. Nasser established a public school system that was open to all but the poorest Egyptians and open to women as well as men. He chose to build a **socialist** economy, in which most enterprises were government owned and the government was the society's largest employer.

Nasser also challenged Egypt's deep economic inequalities, particularly in the countryside. His first target was the great landowning families who owned more than a third of Egypt's land. Nasser seized the land belonging to the royal family and required the other rich families to sell more than half their land. He redistributed this land to hundreds of thousands of poor peasant families. Egypt's peasants benefited in a limited way from Nasser's land reform. But Nasser's attack against the great landowners transformed the rural middle class. They bought much of the land the elite was forced to sell and turned themselves into prosperous commercial farmers (Hooglund, 1991, pp. 122–123; Mitchell, 1991, pp. 22–23; Vatikiotis, 1991, pp. 396–399).

Politics in Independent Egypt

Nasser won wide support from Egyptians because he helped many people become more prosperous and he succeeded in evicting the British. At the same time, however, he severely restricted democracy. The army crushed strikes and suppressed militant Islamic groups and jailed their leaders.

In 1956 the British, French, and Israeli armies once again invaded Egypt. Britain and France wanted to reassert their control over the region, and Israel wanted to end Nasser's support of the Palestinians who attacked Israel. Although Egypt's armies were defeated in the fighting with Israel, Nasser persuaded the United States and the Soviet Union to force the invaders to withdraw. Nasser emerged as the hero, not only of Egypt, but of the Arab world as a whole. Strengthened by political and economic support from the Soviet Union, Nasser led Egypt into a period of prosperity and international leadership. But much of Egypt's progress was brought to a halt by the 1967 war with Israel. Israel defeated Egypt's armed forces so completely that it humiliated both the Egyptian leadership and ordinary Egyptians. Egypt never recovered its leadership of the Arab world after the 1967 defeat and the 1979 Camp David treaty with Israel. Both Anwar Sadat, Nasser's successor, and Hosni Mubarak, the president after Sadat, sought peace with Israel and alliance with the United States. They were rewarded with huge sums of U.S. foreign aid, but earned the contempt of many Arab nations.

When Anwar Sadat became president, he reversed many of Nasser's policies. Sadat tried to move Egypt away from socialism and toward a capitalist economy by encouraging private enterprise. He repressed the socialist political organization that Nasser had supported. Sadat permitted Islamist parties to operate openly, because he saw them as a counterweight to the socialists. But Sadat's economic policy of *infitah* (or "opening the door") failed to bring substantial benefits to most Egyptians. Many people came to believe that Sadat's regime created benefits only for a few rich businesspeople. Despite his foreign policy successes, Sadat faced growing hostility in the streets. In October 1981, during a celebration of the 1973 war against Israel, Anwar Sadat was assassinated by one of the Islamist groups he had encouraged that was operating as a secret cell within the military.

Egypt Today

Sadat's successor, Hosni Mubarak, still ruled Egypt when this book was written. In 1981 he was an airforce general, unknown to most Egyptians. Mubarak stepped to the controls of a society increasingly torn by economic inequality and political conflict. As time went on, and the government proved unable to deliver benefits to all Egyptians, Mubarak focused more and more single-mindedly on staying in power. He resorted increasingly to police repression, eliminating free speech and political choice and suppressing any possible source of opposition to his government, from socialists, from Islamists, and from those who want Egypt to be a democracy. Growing numbers of Egyptians, alienated from a corrupt and repressive government and distressed by the subordinate position of Muslim countries in the world economy and in world politics, have been looking for answers in religion. Some join Islamist social movements that hope to replace the Mubarak regime with an

Islamic state. But far more Egyptians have become part of a broader religious revival that has brought Islam much more into the foreground of Egyptian culture.

EGYPTIAN CULTURE

How important is religion in the culture of your society? Max Weber, a classical sociologist of the early 20th century, saw European societies in his day becoming less religious. He used a pair of contrasting terms to capture the change. In **sacred societies,** said Weber, religion permeates life. People treasure their religious rituals and ceremonies. They apply religious values and ideas to every aspect of life. Science, law, education, and government are all ruled by religion. When people make decisions, religious considerations trump any other factors. In **secular societies,** religion exists, but it exists in its own separate, sharply delineated space. The rest of life is, as Weber said, "disenchanted," it loses spiritual meaning and people assume that religion has no place there. In secular societies church and state are separated. People accept the idea that some aspects of life are ruled by government and law and other parts of life are ruled by religion. They are used to disagreements between religion and science. When individuals make personal or business decisions, they may think about religious values, but they often think about personal happiness, getting ahead, profit and loss, patriotism, or other nonreligious goals.

We can understand the concepts of sacred and secular societies best as what Weber called **ideal types,** constructed ideals that don't exist anywhere in pure form, but that help us understand some aspects of the real world. In some ways, Egypt seems to be a sacred society. In Egypt even people who are not devout Muslims (and even those who are Christians) live in a world filled with Islamic values and norms. Phrases such as *insha'Allah* (God willing) and *alhamdu lillah* (thanks be to God) fill everyday conversation. Egyptians use these expressions easily and sincerely. People pray and talk about religion every day. When they get dressed, go out, go shopping, or buy a CD, religion is involved. When they need advice they often turn to a local religious authority or an Islamic Web site or advice column.

But Egypt is not ruled by religious authorities and most of its law is secular law. People study engineering or medicine or computers and the principles of those disciplines are completely separate from religion. Business life is capitalist and secular. There is plenty of secular culture available in Egypt too. You can go to the movies and see the latest American action thriller, or watch *Survivor* on satellite television. Egyptian society is becoming both more secular and more sacred at the same time. You have probably experienced a secular culture yourself. But to fully understand Egyptian society, you need to know more about its sacred culture, Islam.

Egypt's Islamic Beliefs, Values, and Norms

Any Muslim will tell you that it is easy to get to know Islam; you need to begin with the five pillars of Islam: declaring belief in God, prayer, charity, fasting during the holy month of Ramadan, and pilgrimage. Each of these fundamentals reveals important Islamic beliefs and each has major implications for the conduct of everyday life.

Declaring Belief: The First Pillar of Faith

Five times a day, in the largest cities and the smallest villages, the voice of the *muezzin* (the prayer caller) cries out from the *minaret* (the highest tower) of the *mosque* (the Islamic house of worship). Nowadays the voice is likely to be recorded and broadcast over a public address system.

> God is great (Allahu Akbar), God is great, God is great. I witness that there is no god but God. I witness that there is no God but God. I witness that Muhammad is his messenger. I witness that Muhammad is his messenger. Come to prayer, come to prayer. Come to prosperity, come to prosperity. God is great. God is great. There is no God but God. (Esposito, 1991, p. 89)

The call is echoed by Muslims indoors and out, who all join in affirming their belief. They thus daily and repeatedly declare their faith: their faith in God and their belief in one single god ("there is no god but God"). You may take **monotheism** (the belief that there is only one god) for granted, but in the history of the world's religions, monotheism is relatively unusual. Most of the world's religions recognize many gods, major and minor. For example, when you read about Japan in Chapter 1, you learned that all the major religions of Asia—Buddhism, Hinduism, Taoism, and Shinto—honor multiple gods. Islam, Christianity, and Judaism all believe in a single god, and he is the same god, the god of Moses and Abraham. Islam recognizes Jesus as one of the four messengers of God—Moses, David, Jesus, and Muhammad—but Jesus is not believed to be the son of God.

All that is necessary to become a Muslim is to make the affirmation of faith: "There is no god but God, and Muhammad is the messenger of God" in the presence of other believers. But professing faith in God commits you to accepting the word of God, as transmitted through his messenger Muhammad and recorded literally in the *Quran,* the holy book. The word *Islam* actually means "submission" in Arabic, meaning submission to the will of God. *Muslim* means "one who submits" (Lippman, 1990, p. 1).

Values and Norms

Muslims believe in a Judgment Day on which each person will be sent by God either to paradise or to hell. Islam tells people that God is stern, and on Judgment Day terrible agonies await the sinner, while paradise is filled with delights. Pious Muslims fear the wrath of God if they do not live by Islamic values and norms. For example, Islam values honesty, modesty, and chastity, charity toward the less fortunate, and religious faith. To be virtuous and win paradise, the good man or woman must strive to submit to God, to make life a spiritual exercise so that in every situation he or she struggles to act virtuously, not for worldly benefit, but to honor God. It is important to follow detailed norms, but they must be obeyed in the spirit of faith.

The good Muslim does not drink alcohol, or profit from lending money, or gamble, gossip, or seek revenge. The good Muslim does not have sex outside marriage, gives to charity, helps orphans, and of course carries out the prescribed religious obligations of prayer, charity, fasting, and pilgrimage. Many of these norms are described in the Quran, which is so important that many Egyptians try to memorize it in its entirety.

Over one third of the millions of cassette tapes sold in Egypt yearly are Quran readings, and the most popular readers are treated with the acclaim of rock stars. One public performance by a Quranic star attracted 600,000 people. Tapes of sermons by popular preachers are also best-sellers (Jehl, 1996, p. A4). Other Islamic norms are recorded in the *hadith,* the collection of Muhammad's words as interpreted by religious scholars. *Sharia* is the code of Islamic law derived from the Quran and hadith. In Egypt Sharia law holds for cases involving family and marriage, but the rest of civil and business law is secular (Campo, 1991, p. 105; Lippman, 1990, pp. 30–32; Rodenbeck, 1992, p. 105).

Religious Status Symbols.   Now that religion has become such an important part of Egyptian culture and of individual identity, people embrace status symbols that show the world their piety. Women adopt the *hijab* to cover their hair, ears, and neck. Many men are proud of their *zebibah,* their "raisin," a dark bruise on the forehead acquired from touching the head to the floor repeatedly in prayer. Oddly, Muslims in other countries don't acquire zebibah; it seems to be a distinctly Egyptian symbol (Slackman, 2007g, p. A4).

Prayer: The Second Pillar of Faith

Prayer is the second of the five pillars of faith. Muslims are required to pray five times a day: at sunrise, noon, midafternoon, sunset, and night, in response to the call to prayer. Daily prayers may be recited alone or in company, in a mosque or at one's place of work. In rural areas, men may keep clear a small spot in their fields for daily prayer. In busy cities, traffic may be blocked by rows of men kneeling on mats and rugs for the noon prayer. Some people, who are not religious, or not Muslims, do not pray, but these days, more and more people pray. Increasingly, banks, shops, even government offices shut down during the hours of prayer (Abdo, 2000, p. 4; Jehl, 1996, p. A4).

Many norms prescribe the proper way to pray. People take off their shoes before entering a mosque and they ritually wash themselves before prayer. All believers face in the direction of Mecca (the city, today in Saudi Arabia, where Muhammad first heard the word of God) when they pray, so if there are many praying together, you will see them lined up in orderly rows. In daily prayer people recite standard texts; they don't make individual appeals to God. Recitation is accompanied by sequences of bows and prostrations, when people kneel, then lower their foreheads to the ground. Women generally pray separately from men because the postures of prayer might prove immodest (Bassiouni, 1989, pp. 30–31).

Prayer Structures Time.   How is time ordinarily divided in your society? Do you think in terms of the week and the weekend? The hours of classes? The time the coffee cart comes around in the office, lunchtime, and the end of the workday? In Muslim countries like Egypt, the hours of prayer divide the day, marking the passage of time as clearly as the clock. Businesses open after the morning prayer and the best bargains may be found before the call to noon prayer (Rodenbeck, 1992, p. 105).

In Egypt, Friday is the day of special religious observance. The week hurries toward Friday, when schools and government offices are closed. Women who work in private businesses, as typists or engineers, struggle to finish work early so they can go home and clean their houses by Friday afternoon, when the eye of God will be upon them. In towns and villages, the Friday market is the largest, since people flock into town for Friday prayers (Campo, 1991, pp. 126–127; Fakhouri, 1972, pp. 51–52).

On Fridays, Islamic tradition requires that Muslim men pray together in the mosque. Women may attend too, to pray in a separate part of the mosque, but it is not required. The prayer leader or *imam* leads Friday prayers and also delivers a sermon. He is not a priest, but rather an ordinary worshiper, normally someone with extra religious training. In a city, the imam is probably a person who has done a great deal of special study, but in a village he would likely be an artisan who has studied for a few years at a village religious school (Lippman, 1990, p. 14).

Finally, in Egypt religious holidays punctuate the year. The most important of these is *Ramadan,* which lasts for a whole month. Because the Islamic calendar is a lunar calendar, Ramadan begins on a different date in each year and it is not associated with a particular season. Observance of Ramadan is so demanding that people must structure their year around it.

Ramadan: The Third Pillar of Faith

Observance of Ramadan is another of the pillars of Islam. Ramadan is the Arabic name of the month in which God began to reveal the Quran to Muhammad. During Ramadan all Muslim adults must fast from dawn until dark (neither eating nor drinking anything) unless they are pregnant, nursing, traveling, or ill, and refrain from smoking and sex. Fasting teaches self-restraint and it reminds people of how the poor suffer. You can imagine how these obligations disrupt normal life during Ramadan. Especially when the fast occurs during hot weather, life slows to a crawl, with people working shorter hours and resting indoors as much as possible away from the desiccating sun. Families rise before dawn to eat the leftovers from the previous night's dinner and to take their last long drinks of water before the sun rises. Then, after dark, everyone celebrates, with a feast called the *iftar* ("breakfast"). Even the poorest Egyptians, who rarely see meat on their tables, will scrimp and save to eat meat during Ramadan. Egyptians are much more observant of Ramadan now than they were 20 or 30 years ago. Restaurants in Cairo now close during daylight hours in Ramadan, and if there is anyone who smokes or eats before sundown, you will not see them do so in public (Murphy, 2002, p. 26).

Ramadan and the Value of Unity.   Like daily prayers, Ramadan vividly demonstrates the cultural and religious unity of Muslims. The rigors of fasting are shared and people feel linked in common endeavor with their community, their nation, and the worldwide community of Islam. In cities and towns all over the country, people who have fasted will sit before tables piled high with food and drink, waiting for the broadcast cannon shot with which Radio Cairo announces sunset prayers and the end of the fast. Radio and television, which often act as instruments of secularization, work in this case to reinforce the culture of a sacred society (Esposito, 1991, pp. 91–92).

Charity: The Fourth Pillar of Faith

Charity (or *zakat*) is a major Islamic value and it is one of the five pillars of Islam. All Muslims are obliged, as an act of worship of God, to support Muslims in need and the Islamic faith. Some Muslims interpret zakat as requiring them to give a fixed percentage of their income and wealth to charity every year; or to leave money to charity in their wills. Others donate money to help build mosques. During Ramadan, charity-givers spend hundreds of dollars a day provisioning free iftar meals on the streets for the poor, feeding as many as 2,000 people a day. Egyptians also give money to the homeless on the streets or outside mosques (Bassiouni, 1989, pp. 30–31; Campo, 1991, pp. 122–124; Lippman, 1990, p. 19).

Charity and the Value of Equality. Consideration for the needy is part of Islam's traditional emphasis on equality. In the mosque, all are equal; there are no preferred pews for the rich or influential—all kneel together. Anyone can lead prayers and give the sermon; there is no church hierarchy, no official priests or sacraments, no recognized saints, no monks or nuns. Islam also requires that the rich respect the poor, even though they may be ragged and hungry. Kindness and compassion are the essence of what Egyptians refer to as *saddaqa*. The Quran warns, "A kind word with forgiveness is better than charity followed by insult" (Bassiouni, 1989, p. 30). Much of the moral energy and appeal of the current Islamic revival comes from a sense that the rich and powerful have long since ceased to care about the needs of ordinary Muslims. Even when help does come from government agencies, it often comes with a kind of contempt that is especially resented because it violates the sacred norms of Islam. In the absence of government services Islamist groups have organized clinics, built housing, and provided loans for the poor, and this dedication to charity earns them the respect of other Muslims and attracts many followers (Campo, 1991, pp. 130–137; Hedges, 1993, p. A8; Lippman, 1990, pp. 78–90).

Pilgrimage: The Fifth Pillar of Faith

The final pillar of faith and the last major obligation of all Muslims is to make the pilgrimage or *hajj* to Mecca at least once in their lifetime. Both personally and socially the pilgrimage sums up the meaning of Islamic faith. To make the journey to Mecca is certainly an affirmation of faith. In the past, when pilgrims journeyed overland, it was a grueling trip. Today, airplanes ease the journey, but it is still challenging, especially in summer. Also, for many Egyptians, the hajj represents an enormous expense, the fruit of many years' savings, and perhaps a person's single trip ever away from his or her village. As prayer and holy days structure the Islamic day and year, planning and making the pilgrimage are key events in a lifetime. In many villages you will see "pilgrimage murals," depicting the airplane and Mecca and the crowds, painted on the outside walls of their houses by those who have made the hajj.

Finally, the pilgrimage expresses with special emphasis the Islamic values of community and equality. The pilgrimage is a yearly event, taking place only on specified days. During that short time, hundreds of thousands, even millions of pilgrims pour into Mecca from all over the world. In the huge crowds that walk through the required rites of the pilgrimage—trekking to the Sacred Mosque and back and forth to other holy places—you will see people of many races, speaking dozens of languages, visibly united by their Islamic faith. Symbolically, they all put on the special clothing of the pilgrimage, white wraps for the men and loose white dresses, without facial veils, for the women, reminding them that in Islam differences of race and class are surmounted (Lippman, 1990, pp. 22–27).

The Question of Jihad

Nowadays we often hear the term *jihad,* and the Islamists who commit terrorist attacks are often called *jihadis.* This is a good place to explain the meaning of *jihad.* The term translates from Arabic as "holy struggle" or "striving," and historically it has been understood in two ways. The "greater jihad" is the struggle inside you, the internal struggle each Muslim should engage in to improve himself or herself, to submit to God and restrain sinful impulses. The "lesser jihad" is the external struggle to defend Islam against its enemies, to protect and perhaps extend the faith. In external jihad violence is sometimes permitted, but only under strict conditions. Most Muslims would say that it is never permissible to kill other Muslims and it is never permissible to kill women and children who are not soldiers. In Egypt, in the 1990s, when Islamist groups staged violent attacks within Egypt, public disapproval was overwhelming. But today an Egyptian who went off to participate in jihad on behalf of the Palestinians, or against the Americans in Iraq, would probably be congratulated.

Do They "Hate Freedom"?

In 2004 George W. Bush said that Islamic terrorists attack the United States because "they hate freedom." Was he right? Do the terrorists hate freedom? Do other Egyptians and other Muslims hate freedom? This is a really helpful question because it allows us to clarify Egyptian political values and understand something about the range of opinion about values in Egypt.

The great majority of Egyptians value freedom and very much want to have it. They want freedom of speech, freedom of the press, fair trial and the rule of law, freedom to join political parties and to freely elect the government of their choice. Is this what you mean by freedom? Egyptians, whatever their political opinions, feel deprived of these freedoms because Egypt has an authoritarian government determined to stay in power by squelching all opposition, Islamist or secular. One of the biggest complaints Egyptians have about the United States is that despite America's devotion to freedom, it has supported the Mubarak government, never criticizing its suppression of opposition parties, detention of political prisoners, and use of torture. The U.S. contribution of $2 billion per year helps keep Mubarak in power.

Islamist groups, of course, want political freedom as much as any other Egyptians, because if free elections were allowed, they would probably be elected to positions of power. Would they still permit political freedom once elected? The Islamist regime in Iran permits a limited parliamentary system, but forbids many critics of the regime from running for office. In Turkey the Islamist governing party is committed to democratic elections and secular law.

Personal Freedom.   But perhaps to you the word *freedom* has less to do with political freedom and more to do with personal, individual freedom, the freedom to make choices and express yourself. Do Egyptians value personal freedom? The answer would have to be yes, but within a religious context. If you live in Europe or Canada, this answer may seem strange, but if you are American, it will probably be familiar. Many young women in Egypt want more freedom to go out with their friends, to have a life outside their homes. Many young men would like the freedom to socialize with young women. But American-style personal freedom doesn't appeal to them. They see the American lifestyle as "debauchery," and it would be hard to find someone who would defend alcohol and drug use, homosexuality, or promiscuous sex, and no one likes to identify themselves as a feminist. Furthermore, the personal freedom Egyptians value is in many cases the freedom to explore religious ideas, hear different preachers (not just the official, government-appointed ones), go to Quran study groups, and experiment with just how pious they wish to be. Media coverage of glamorous, newsworthy young actresses in Egypt often focuses on their religious conversions, their decisions to leave acting, stop dressing provocatively and put on the veil (Kamel & Mashour, 2002).

Democracy and Justice.   We have established that Egyptians very much want political freedom and democracy, but to clarify, we'd really have to say that neither of these is the most important political value in Islamic societies. Justice is the preeminent value. A just government impartially applies the rule of law, without favoritism, bribery, or nepotism. A just government is not corrupt. Justice, for Muslims, is closely associated with equality, not only with legal equality, but economic equality. When Egyptians look at their society, they see the children of high government officials enriching themselves through government contracts, while the government does nothing to help the poor. And this state of affairs seems to them to violate the essential spirit of Islam.

The Value of Community in Egyptian Culture

As you can see, much of Egypt's culture is religious culture, derived from the sacred values and norms of Islam. But there are other important values in Egypt, values like community, generosity, and honor, which are traditionally Egyptian but are not specifically religious.

   In every situation, Egyptians would rather be with others than alone. It is easy for them to establish a sense of community within a crowd of strangers. Sociologist Andrea Rugh describes how affluent Egyptians pitch their umbrellas close to one another on the beach, rather than seeking privacy. Expensive movie theaters and cheap buses fill up in the same way: People sit next to others already seated, rather than spreading out. In the mosque, people stand as close as possible to each other to pray. If you leave a space, they believe, the devil can get in. Ordinary Egyptians find the empty streets of rich neighborhoods frightening. They like the cheerful noise of a narrow street full of people, with its constant footsteps, overheard conversations, radio music and television dialogue. It is revealing that Arabic doesn't have a specific word that means "privacy" in the positive English sense of the word. Ghannam reports that no one would say "I need some privacy" (Ghannam, 2002, pp. 13, 81, 92). Even in illness, Egyptians prefer company. A man who has a headache, or a fever, will be surrounded by a stream of friends and relatives who bring him soda, food, aspirin, and advice. Hospitals are crowded with relatives and friends visiting patients. A sly joke about the unsophisticated Saidis of southern Egypt reveals not only how Egyptians from the big cities of Cairo and Alexandria feel about Saidis, but also the comfort that all Egyptians take in the presence of the people around them:

> An Alexandrian, a Cairene, and a Saidi are stranded in the desert with no transportation and no water. Suddenly a genie appears and offers each of them one wish. The young man from Alexandria wishes that he was back on that city's beautiful beach—and in a flash he is gone. The Cairene wishes to be returned to the Hussein Mosque in Cairo—and in an instant he too vanishes. The genie then approaches the Saidi and asks, "what is your wish?" "I'm so lonely," cries the Saidi, "can't you bring my friends back?" (Rodenbeck, 1992, p. 100)

In the countryside, people live in a village, not spread out in farmsteads in the fields. Houses are tightly clustered, along narrow alleys, filled with children, water buffalo, and the bustle of everyday life. A village teacher asks children to find what's missing in a chalked outline of a peasant home, and their immediate reply is "the neighbors" (Fakhouri, 1972, pp. 17–21). According to a familiar Arabic saying, "the most important thing about a house is its neighbors" (Fluehr-Lobban, 1994, p. 58).

The Value of Honor

Egyptians will tell you that their family's honor is utterly precious to them. Individuals are judged by the reputations of their families and when Egyptians think about their own personal honor, they are thinking about how their actions will reflect upon their families. Carolyn Fluehr-Lobban (1994) defines honor as "the pride and dignity that a family possesses due to its longstanding good reputation in the community for producing upright men and women who behave themselves well, marry well, raise proper children, and above all adhere to the principles and practices of the religion of Islam" (p. 52). In everyday life, people try to avoid shameful behavior so they won't dishonor themselves and their families. Even future generations of their family would have to live with the dishonor. Use of foul language is shameful, so is losing one's temper, or gossiping in a way that harms others; failing to help a relative or neighbor when one could really do so is shameful, as is failing in one's obligation to support family members (p. 53).

To fully understand the meaning of honor we must discuss gender roles in Egyptian society, because norms for both male and female behavior are closely linked to honor.

CULTURE AND GENDER ROLES

Male and female roles in Egypt are distinctively different from each other, but people like to think of them as complementary, rather than unequal. For both women and men, roles in the family, as daughters or sons, sisters or brothers, wives or husbands, mothers or fathers, take priority in their lives. Family events like marriage or the birth of children are centrally important. Gender roles are also changing in response to changes in Egyptian society: migration from rural villages to cities, increasing religiosity, and the impact of globalization, which brings new ideas to Egypt, both from Western countries and from the oil states in the Gulf.

Beliefs About Women and Men

Students from Western societies often bring to the study of Muslim women some cultural assumptions about women that they don't even know they have. In the West, feminism has fought the assumption that women are "the weaker sex," passive, inferior, submissive. Students often assume that women in Islamic societies must fight these same stereotypes. But Islamic culture has never imagined women like this. Islamic culture sees women as active and powerful, both sexually and personally. Traditional Egyptian culture views women as dangerously distracting and tempting to men, who cannot be trusted to control themselves. If anything, women are seen as so dangerously powerful that men must impose limits on them to keep order in society (Abdo, 2000, p. 57; Mernissi, 2001). This way of thinking dates far back in Egyptian history, to the Greek and early Christian eras. If women are dangerously tempting to men, then they should act in such a way as to avoid attracting male desire, and men should protect their female relatives from unrelated men.

Gender Segregation

Separate social spheres for women and men protect women from the attentions of men and protect men from sexual impulses. We call this separation **gender segregation.** After dinner at a family party, men and women gravitate into separate rooms. In the mosque, women and men pray in separate sections and attend different study groups. They use space differently in urban neighborhoods. Men occupy public space assertively. They stroll, sit in restaurants with friends, watch people on the street, make comments to passing women, and maintain a stance of physical alertness, ready, if necessary, to intervene in public disputes. Young men especially gravitate to local "coffeehouses" where they meet their friends, play dominoes or chess, drink tea, and sometimes smoke flavored tobacco in water pipes.

Women never go to coffeehouses. They visit each other in their homes, or in densely settled urban areas, they talk across adjacent flat rooftops, or in the area by the water pump. Roofs are heavily used female areas: women hang out laundry there; they keep poultry, and prepare food. Women go out in the streets, but they generally stick close to home, fetching water or food from a local market, or calling children in for meals. Young unmarried women need permission from their parents or even their brothers to go farther from home—to the zoo, or a downtown movie, or to hear a favorite preacher, and they always go with a female friend or relative or in a noisy group. Out on the streets, women link arms and walk fast, and keep their eyes from meeting the eyes of men. They ignore any comments men might make. Traditionally, women should be accompanied in public by a male relative, often a brother, but in modern Egypt, where women go to school and work, this isn't always possible. There are female-only sections on trains and buses and many women prefer them. Swimming pools at private clubs have separate swim hours for women and men.

Chastity

Gender segregation helps men and women conform to the norms of chastity. Chastity has a broader meaning in Egypt than it generally does in Western societies. Of course it means, first of all, that women should be virgins when they marry and after marriage should have sex with no one but their husbands. Virginity is a special treasure, which a girl and her family carefully preserve and guard until marriage. Egyptian journalist Abeer Allam remembers that his high school biology teacher sketched the female reproductive system, pointed to the entry to the vagina and declared, "This is where the family honor lies" (Jehl, 1999, p. A1).

Lost virginity is a disaster for a young woman, for whom marriage will likely become impossible, and for her shamed family. Consider this incident: A 10-year-old daughter of an affluent family crashed her bicycle into a wall and tore her hymen. Her family rushed her to the doctor, who wrote an affidavit describing the injury. This document preserved the girl's marriageability.

But chastity goes beyond merely avoiding sex. Women shouldn't start conversations with strange men, or smile at them, or make direct eye contact with them. Such behavior seems flirtatious and endangers a woman's reputation. A wife, alone in the house, or with other women only, would not open the door to her husband's friend, nor would he wish to enter because it might appear improper (Wilson, 1998, p. 91).

Chastity in Men's Lives

Don't make the mistake of thinking that chastity matters only for women. It has a huge impact on men's lives too. First of all, men are also expected to be chaste, to wait for marriage before having sex. More allowances are made for men, but really, there is little opportunity for sex. Unmarried men and women may get to know each other at school or at work, but it is unlikely they will be able to spend any time alone. At a wedding or family birthday party, in the presence of their relatives and neighbors, young women will be allowed to dance and sing, to act sexy. Men can watch, but they can't get close. There is no such thing as dating in Egypt. The closest thing to dating is the time a young couple spend engaged to be married. This lasts from the time they sign the marriage contract until the actual wedding, which cannot take place until they have a home of their own. They may wait years, seeing each other in the company of family members. Except for the rich, people don't have cars. Apartments are tiny and crowded day and night with family members. The neighbors are watching and listening.

Not only is marriage the only way to have any kind of sex life, young men also face constant pressure from relatives, neighbors, and friends to get married. Marriage is a religious obligation too. While they wait for marriage, men must behave properly so potential in-laws will not reject them. Drinking, chasing women, swearing, getting into trouble with the police all dishonor a man and his family and make marriage problematical. Expectations like these are not so burdensome when men marry young, but if a man must wait years or decades to marry, he may readily run into trouble.

Obstacles to Marriage

When it comes to marriage, Egyptian men are caught between rising expectations and falling resources. Egyptian norms require that in order to marry a man must be able to pay for certain customary expenses. He must purchase the engagement gift (usually a gold ring and several gold bracelets), though his parents and even the bride and her family may help with this. He must pay for the wedding celebration and pay the "key money" for a rented apartment or pay for the purchase of an apartment. And he must buy an expensive bedroom set and other furnishings for the apartment. People in Cairo estimate the whole sum needed for a lower-middle-class college graduate at between 6,000 and 15,000 Egyptian pounds. With an entry-level government job paying about 60 to 80 pounds a month, you can imagine how hard it is for a young man to accumulate such a sum. In 38% of the marriages that took place in 1999, the groom was over the age of 30 (United Nations, 1990, 2004a). See Table 4.1.

Defending Male Honor

Beyond marrying and supporting his family, a man's most important obligation is defending the honor of his family. He does this, first of all, by personally leading a morally upright life. But honor is not personal, it is family-based and based especially on the behavior of female relatives. To avoid shame, men must protect their mothers, sisters, wives, and daughters, keeping track of their activities, accompanying them in public when possible, and watching to make sure no man compromises their reputation. A teenage boy, or a new husband, looking to step into adult roles, may tightly restrict his sister or wife, even refusing her permission to leave the house, or beating her if she returns home late. If a family is convinced that a wife has committed adultery, custom allows her husband to kill her, to "wash away the shame with blood" and restore the family honor. Such murders, considered "crimes

TABLE 4.1 Marriages

Marriage rates for each country have declined since 1971. Egypt's marriage rates have declined more than 20%.

	Number of Marriages for Each 10,000 Persons	
	1971	2003/2004
Egypt	103	79
Germany	70	48
Japan	104	56
Mexico	72	56
United States	105	78

Sources: United Nations, *Demographic Yearbook,* 1990, 2004a,
http://unstats.un.org/unsd/demographic/products/dyb/dyb2.htm.

of honor," are punished with prison terms of only 1 to 3 years, rather than the usual death penalty. In 1995, Egypt last reported relevant statistics, and 52 murders were reported as honor killings out of a total of 819 for the whole country (Daniszewski, 1997, p. A9; Fluehr-Loban, 1994, p. 55; Jehl, 1999, p. 8).

A man's obligations go beyond avoiding shame. Every man must also defend his family against disrespect and insult. The young men of a neighborhood don't make comments to one another's sisters in the street, because it will inevitably lead to assaults. In a campaign against Islamist activists, the government made mass arrests in the village of Fayoum, taking family members as well as male activists. Several men took revenge, killing a police officer. They admitted the crime, knowing they would be executed. One of them explained in court, "I killed him because he came and arrested my wife and dragged her into the street in her nightclothes in front of all the men to see. I did it to defend my honor" (quoted in Kassem, 2000, p. 153). You can see that women must be careful to maintain their reputations, not only to avoid punishment by their relatives, but also to avoid involving their male relatives in deadly reprisals and vendettas.

Modesty

Modesty in dress is expected of both men and women in Egyptian society. It shields them from shame and helps protect their reputations. Men don't wear shorts, and don't go bare-chested or in sleeveless shirts. Often they wear their shirts outside their pants instead of tucking them in. Many men still wear the traditional *galibiyya,* a long, loose robe or shirt that conceals their bodies. There isn't much talk in Egypt about modest dress for men, but what women should wear is a subject of enormous concern and constant discussion. The Quran, in a passage often cited as the source of modesty norms for women, required the wives of the prophet to cover themselves:

> And say to the believing women that they should lower their gaze and guard their modesty; that they should not display their beauty and charms except what (normally) appears of them; that they should draw their veils over their bosoms and display their beauty only to their husbands. (Quoted in Esposito, 1991, p. 99)

This passage from the Quran is rather vague, and the requirements of modest dress have varied widely in different periods in Egyptian history. Let's see what modesty means to women in Egypt today.

The Meaning of Modest Dress

Think about your society for a moment. Does the way people dress have symbolic meaning? Do people use their clothes to tell the world who they are and what they believe? A business suit or jeans, loose pants or fitted ones, expensive watches, nose rings, briefcases and backpacks all convey social messages. The same thing is true in Egypt. On the street in Cairo, just about all of the Egyptian women who pass by are wearing some version of "modest dress" or "Islamic dress." This always includes the hijab. *Hijab* translates literally as "veil," but actually it is a scarf, pinned or tied under the chin to completely conceal the neck and pulled forward at the forehead to cover the hair.

If you ask young women in Cairo why they wear the hijab, they will all tell you that they wear it because Islam requires it. They dispute whether or not modest dress protects you from attention from men. Wearing the hijab shows that piety matters to you. More, it says that you value Islam; that you are proud of your culture and Muslim heritage. Westerners tend to see the hijab as a sign of the oppression of women, the suppression of their identity. But for Egyptian women, wearing the hijab is an assertion of identity. Sometimes putting on hijab is even an act of rebellion, when girls are more religious than their parents.

Hijab and Identity.   The hijab asserts religious identity, but it expresses other identities too. There are many different styles of "modest dress" and the style you adopt says more about who you are (Menezes, 2003). Many educated working women   teachers, engineers, bureaucrats—adopt a professional style of modest dress, wearing the hijab over a long skirt with a blazer and turtleneck or a full tunic with long sleeves. Affluent teenagers, pushing the boundaries, wear their hijab with tight jeans and a long, loose tunic. More pious than the hijab is the *khimar,* a surplice that covers the hair, neck, and shoulders, hanging down and concealing the breasts. Women who have made a very deep commitment to religiosity sometimes adopt the *niqab,* a long unfitted gown in a solid color, often black, with waist-length khimar, face-veil, and even gloves, concealing all but their eyes.

Remember that for all women, the hijab is a garment worn in public, or in the presence of men who are not relatives. In their homes, women remove their scarves and put on lighter, less enveloping dresses. The hijab has been around long enough now that it is a fashion accessory as well as a statement of identity. There is an active, lively debate among women, and men too, about the hijab. Are men fooled into thinking that every woman who wears the hijab is a decent woman? Do men prefer veiled women when they choose a wife? Are women who wear niqab extremists who go too far? Is it alright to wear a hijab made of patterned cloth? How about fringe? Is it acceptable to let the hijab slide back and reveal a little hair? Egyptian women are pleased to have a fashion that is completely Muslim and not a creation of Western style. More and more now, young women modify the classic black or white hijab, wearing patterned and bright-colored scarves, tying them in unusual ways. You could say that wearing the hijab says you value Islam, but modifying the hijab says individual expression is also important to you (Menezes, 2003, El-Rashidi, 2002).

Purity.   There is a traditional custom in Egypt, practiced today by both Muslim and Christian Egyptians, which is linked to norms about modesty and chastity. Its proponents call the custom **female circumcision,** but Egyptian feminists who have campaigned against it call the custom **female genital cutting.** In female circumcision, the clitoris and sometimes the inner labia are wholly or partially removed. It is an ancient North African custom that has nothing to do with Islam.[1]

---

[1]Unicef (the United Nations Children's Fund) estimates that 130 million women, most of them in Africa, have undergone genital cutting. Seven nations account for 75% of the cases of female genital cutting in Africa: Egypt, Ethiopia, Kenya, Nigeria, Somalia, and Sudan. The mutilation is banned in eight countries: Burkina Faso, the Central African Republic, Djibouti, Egypt, Ghana, Guinea, Senegal, and Togo (Crossette, 1999, p. A10).

This is what many young women look like in Cairo. They are out in public, wearing colorful hijab and the trendiest clothing available to lower-middle-class girls. Note their jeans and their fashionable knit tops. In Cairo you can see some women wearing loose, peasant-style gowns with their hijab, and others carefully covered in head-to-toe niqab. But the only women you can see on the street with uncovered hair are tourists.

The mutilation, usually performed on preadolescent girls, is painful and risky and may result in hemorrhage, infections, incontinence, or later difficulty in childbirth. At least 95% of Egyptian women have been circumcised and most plan to have their daughters circumcised as well. Egyptian feminists and human rights groups have been fighting female genital cutting since the 1970s, when the famous writer Nawal al-Saadawi (who was also a medical doctor and the Minister of Public Health) was first imprisoned for her opposition to it. Egypt's highest court ruled female genital cutting illegal in 1997, but the ban was not enforced.

At this point you are probably asking "why would they do such a painful and risky thing?" It's a good question. We can make the answer clearer by distinguishing between two sociological concepts: **manifest functions** and **latent functions.** The manifest functions of any practice are the purposes or effects that people recognize. In Egypt, most mothers believe that genital cutting is "purifying" and that a girl who is uncircumcised would be abnormal, unclean, unhealthy, unfeminine. She might have health problems or problems with fertility or be oversexed (Yount, 2004, pp. 1079–1081). If you are from a Western country you are probably now thinking about a latent function of female circumcision, an effect that Egyptians don't acknowledge: It has got to make sex less enjoyable for women. Another latent function of circumcision that may be recognized, but isn't discussed is that circumcision is believed to make it easier for a girl to find a husband because men prefer to marry circumcised women.

A recent study for the first time provides data that shows how very risky female genital mutiliation is. Circumcized women are more than 50% more likely to die in childbirth or deliver a baby that dies. These data have pushed Egyptian authorities to try harder to end the practice and popular support for female circumcision has fallen, especially among women in urban areas. In 2007 the government tightened a decade-old ban on the female circumcision and Egypt's Grand Mufti, a religious figure appointed by the government, declared it *haram,* or forbidden by Islam. For the first time, television and radio talk shows are discussing circumcision and newspapers have reported genital cutting operations in which girls died. Activists have reached out to the villages, where support for traditional practices is especially strong. Women active in the movement against genital cutting say they have learned that lecturing people and calling the custom barbaric just makes people angry. They have to convince others that their daughters will be able to marry even if they are not circumcised (Slackman, 2007e, pp. A1, A8).

Women's Roles in Private and Public

The idea of a woman being "just" a housewife is foreign to Egyptian culture. *Housewife* is a respected, honored status in Egypt. Especially among poor Egyptians, a woman who is a good housekeeper, who can always stretch the budget to feed the family, arrange good marriages for her children, and solve their medical problems, is admired by all her neighbors and relatives. People recognize her wisdom and hard work and go to her for advice. Many poor women who must work outside their homes—in factories, as servants, as peddlers, or market women—would prefer not to. Such jobs put women under a cloud of moral suspicion. They are out in public and often under the authority of men, who, it is understood, might try to take advantage of them. And the work is menial, heavy, and poorly paid, so the role, as well as the status, is unrewarding.

Many forces encourage Egyptian women to seek education and jobs. Parents want their daughters to go to high school, if they can possibly afford it. An educated girl is more likely to find an educated husband, perhaps with a good job, from a better-off family. As you can see in Table 4.2, in 1988 60% of Egyptian women had no education, but by 2005, two thirds of women had at least a couple of years of schooling. In urban areas, a majority of women got as far as secondary school (though they didn't necessarily graduate), but in rural Egypt, only a third achieved any schooling at all after age 11. Many lower-middle-class girls aspire to go to university and get higher-status professional jobs. Girls who go to high school typically work for at least a couple of years before marriage and perhaps afterward as well. If they are lucky or well connected they may get a job in a government office as a clerical worker or secretary. These jobs are not particularly challenging or well paid (they file papers and run copy machines and keep simple

TABLE 4.2 School Attendance by Egyptian Women

Between 1988 and 2005 the percentage of Egyptian women attending school increased. More women completed at least some education, but substantial numbers remained unschooled. Many of those who attend primary and secondary schools do not graduate. Secondary school attendance starts at age 11.

Year	Women 15–19 Who Have Never Attended School (%)	Women 15–19 Who Have Attended Primary School Only (%)	Women 15–19 Who Have Attended Secondary School (%)
1988	60	31	9
1992	53	19	27
1995	44	22	34
2000	38	19	43
2005	32	12	56

Source: Demographic and Health Surveys, n.d., STATcompiler database, http://www.statcompiler.com.

accounts). Government offices are overstaffed and everyone spends a lot of time drinking tea and chatting. Nevertheless, women employees greatly enjoy office life, with its bustle of visitors and links to a larger world (*Demographic and Health Surveys,* n.d.).

College-educated women can become teachers, doctors, lawyers, and engineers, but jobs are scarce and they often find themselves working in employment far below their level of training. Uneducated women sometimes work in factories; they sell produce or cooked food in the streets; or they even own and manage coffeehouses. Overall, about 35% of Egyptian women work for wages outside their homes—in offices, factories, stores, and on farms. Almost 40% of them work on farms, and 54% work in professional or service jobs. Egypt's industrial economy is rather small, and only 7% of working women are employed in factories (United Nations, 2004b). It is mostly younger women who work; their mothers' generation was much less likely to venture away from home. That means working women can often rely on their mothers-in-law or other female relatives for help with child care. See Table 4.3.

Egyptian women portray themselves as under the authority of their male relatives. "I'll have to ask my husband's permission and let you know if I can come to the sermon with you," a woman will say. It makes it clear that she is a decent, proper wife. But we don't want you to make the mistake of picturing Egyptian women as cowed, subservient creatures. They may keep their eyes down in the street, but even women who don't work have assertive roles to play in public. In the market, women bargain aggressively. They examine all the produce, keep their eyes on the scale, and protest any attempt to cheat them. It often falls to women to deal with the powerful—with police officers, government officials, teachers, merchants, and even their husbands and brothers. Women pride themselves on their knowledge of how to manipulate, to "trick" those in power: to bribe the police, for example, so they will overlook an illegal addition to a house (Ghannam, 2002, p. 15).

TABLE 4.3 Women in Politics and the Economy

Egyptian and Japanese women play a substantial role in the economy, but are largely excluded from politics. Fewer than one in every five political leaders is a woman.

	Seats in Congress/ Parliament held by Women (% of total)	Women in Government at Cabinet Level (% of total)	Female Professional and Technical Workers (% of total)
Egypt	3.8	5.9	30
Japan	10.7	12.5	46
United States	15	14.3	55
Germany	30.5	46.2	50
Mexico	25	9.4	42
Namibia	26.9	19	55

Source: United Nations, *Human Development Indicators 2006/2007,* 2006/2007, http://hdr.undp.org/en/statistics/.

Changing Roles for Women

Egyptian women find themselves caught between two potentially conflicting trends. Many women are becoming more pious and more influenced by new Islamist preachers. They want to be good Muslims and follow religious norms for modesty, chastity, and gender segregation. But at the same time, as Egypt's economy modernizes, women are drawn more and more into public roles, and they find new opportunities for self-expression. Egyptian women are debating how they can reconcile piety with public life, and they are creating very interesting new norms and customs.

The changes began with education for women. When Nasser urged families to send their daughters to school, and then permitted women to attend high school and university, he set in motion a series of changes that are still being played out today. Girls who go to school become accustomed to going out in public, and they form friendships outside the family. Don't assume this has a Westernizing or secularizing effect. Girls may shop for makeup together, but they may equally well listen to tapes of the latest preacher and experiment with how to wear the veil.

Egyptian women today must deal with new **role conflicts.** In role conflicts people must navigate the incompatible role expectations that go with different statuses. More than ever, women want to have rewarding careers, be good Muslims and be good wives. But how can they follow norms of modesty and still go out into a world of strangers?

Solving Role Conflicts. Egyptian women don't talk about it this way, but as sociologists, we'd like to suggest that as a latent function wearing the hijab helps solve role conflicts. Modest dress declares that a woman respects Islam even though she works. It gives her respectability and thus allows her to move about more freely in public (Wickham, 2002, p. 170). Modest dress declares that a woman is a professional, not a sex object. It reassures her father, or brother, or husband. It is likely that modest dress also reduces sexual harassment in public places.

Men who annoy a woman wearing Western dress break only a poorly defined secular norm, but men who harass a woman in Islamic dress profane Islam.

Several sociologists have even argued that women in Islamic dress find it easier to interact with men, because their dress defines the situation as nonsexual, as this university student explained:

> Before I wore the veil, I always worried what people might think when they saw me speak to a man in the cafeteria or outside the class. I even wondered what the man himself thought of me. Since I wore the veil, I don't worry anymore. No one is going to accuse me of immorality. (Quoted in Mule & Barthel, 1992, p. 330; see also Ahmed, 1992, p. 224; Fernea, 1998, p. 244)

Zaynab's Story: A Good Wife

Zaynab met her future husband, Kamal, an engineer, at the government office where she still works. Zaynab's father Mamduh, a mechanic for Egyptair, the national airline, was delighted. He had begun to despair that Zaynab, already 24, would ever marry, but now she would—and an engineer at that. What a catch for an uneducated man's daughter! Mamduh hoped Zaynab would leave her job and stay home where a wife and mother should be. When Mamduh was a boy in a tiny village in Upper Egypt, no woman left her home. But after the birth of her children, Zaynab returned to her office. "It's my life," she said, "my friends are there. Besides, no family can live on one income; Kamal, the children, and I would starve!"

Mamduh was not entirely surprised. Zaynab had turned down a previous offer of marriage from a young man who had demanded that she leave her work. But Zaynab astonished her entire family in 1997 by announcing that from then on she would wear "Islamic dress," the hijab over a loose dress. Zaynab, her parents, and her husband were not especially religious. Kamal thought it was ridiculous that the wife of an educated man should "cover herself," but Zaynab persisted. "Men do not respect a woman on Cairo's streets," she argued, "only a 'covered woman' will be left alone. Besides, even women at the university are 'covered.'" (Ahmed, 1992, pp. 222–225; MacLeod, 1993, pp. 110–124; Mule & Barthel, 1992, pp. 328–331)

Women's Rights.   While Westerners (and secular Egyptians) tend to see Islam as an obstacle to women's rights, it doesn't look that way to most Egyptian women. They reject Western feminism, which they see as fomenting unnecessary hostility between women and men. Instead, they look to the Quran for a genuinely Islamic legitimation of changing women's roles. Young women find the Islamic norms embodied in Sharia an important protection against the difficulties of life in a poor and male-dominated society. Sharia, for example, provides that a woman retains the right to the property she owns at the time of marriage. She also has sole ownership of any new property she acquires in the course of her marriage. Her wages or her inheritance are hers, not her husband's (Hoodfar, 1997, pp. 5–7, 12–14). It was well into the 19th century before even a few European societies gave women such rights. People don't always fully comply with Islamic law, but a claim made under it is not easily denied. In Egypt Sharia is taken far more seriously than western principles of human or women's rights. Some educated women go to Quranic study groups that reinterpret the Quran, stressing passages that address men and women as spiritual equals (El-Gawhary, 1994, pp. 26–27; Fernea, 1998, pp. 241–245). Some women even dispute the interpretation of the Quran with male clerics.

Changing Roles for Men

For Egyptian men, the changing economy has led to tremendous frustration and strain, as they try to satisfy role expectations. In the past, in rural Egypt, most men could achieve respect in their communities. Land was the foundation of life and men controlled the land. They took pride in the masculine tone of their world. And they could afford to marry young and carry out their Islamic duties as husbands and fathers. But today, in the countryside, many men are marginalized. They are losing their land as the result of new land laws, or because their parents' landholding are simply too small to support all the children and their families.

In the city, government bureaucracies cannot grow fast enough to keep up with the rising number of high school and college graduates. Factory workforces are slashed as enterprises pass from the state into private hands. Migration abroad has become more difficult. Men feel they cannot control their futures and cannot even control their families! Clans and networks of male kin have less power in the city. Women increasingly go to school or work outside their homes. Worst of all, in Egypt today, men face barriers in carrying out their obligation to marry as soon as possible and to remain chaste until marriage.

At the same time, as Egypt modernizes, Egyptians' social ambitions are rising higher. University graduates don't want to do manual work. They want white-collar salaried jobs, preferably in management and in government. Sales jobs are looked down upon as rather humiliating or shady, and service-sector jobs, where you would actually be serving someone, are seen as demeaning. So parents want a salaried government employee as a husband for their daughter. But when they find out he makes only 80 pounds a month, that's not good enough either. Young men find they need a government job in the daytime, supplemented by a private-sector job, waiting tables or driving a taxi, at night. At the same time, a young man can see an ad in the newspaper placed by foreigners who advertise jobs for maids or nannies at $500 to $800 a month! Imagine the blow to a young man's self-esteem.

Role Conflicts and Islam

All of these conflicting expectations cause problems for Egyptian men, especially the growing number with university education. The help they find in solving their dilemmas comes mostly from within Islam. First of all, conventional Islamic authorities, the *ulamas* appointed by the government, have looked to Islamic law, Sharia, for solutions to the marriage problem. For example, some jurists at Al Azhar, Egypt's leading Islamic university, have ruled that with the agreement of the bride's family, a man may pay a smaller dowry and accept help from the bride's family in buying a home.

Islamic jurists have tried in another way to adapt the law to help men purchase apartments. In most Western countries today, the use of mortgages, long-term loans to buy houses, is common. But Islamic law forbids lending money at interest and this would seem to place mortgage loans beyond the reach of Muslims. There is hardly a consensus on this issue, but some prominent Muslim authorities have reluctantly approved mortgages for certain purposes. The Grand Sheik of Al Azhar, Mohammed Sayyed Tantawi, commented that in general no one should take a loan, except for life's necessities. Necessities, the sheik indicated, could include buying an apartment, car, or air conditioner (El Fiqi, 1999).

Legal solutions can go only so far in solving men's role conflicts. More and more men are now looking to Islamic activist groups for help in understanding the causes of their problems and in recovering their dignity. Through involvement in neighborhood mosques and Islamic networks, men find a sense of belonging and purpose. Carrie Wickham (2002), reporting on her study of lower-middle-class university graduates, puts it very clearly: Participation in Islamic activist movements transformed "poorly skilled graduates with bleak economic prospects into fellow soldiers in the noble task of Islamic reform" (p. 153). Islamist movements speak to

The mosque is the most spacious, dignified setting available to most Egyptian men. A man can escape his crowded apartment, find quiet, meet his friends, join a study group, pray, rest, even sleep. No Muslim man, no matter how poor or poorly dressed, is turned away from even the grandest mosques, like this one in Cairo. Note in this photo that the mosque is a refuge for people who are disabled, and that it attracts men in both traditional and modern dress. The carpet pattern is common to most mosques. Because each arch in the pattern is a place for a person to pray, it is easy for worshippers to line up in orderly rows, all facing the correct direction.

the bitterness of graduates who believe they should be part of society's elite, but instead find no work or only demeaning work. The Islamist movement tells discontented young men that they can join in working for a true Islamic society in which "merit—both moral/spiritual and practical/professional would be justly acknowledged and rewarded" (p. 160).

Abdel's Story: A Life in Islam

"I was dead," Abdel told his cousin. "When Fatima's family announced her engagement to the banker, I died. 'You are a good man, Abdel,' her brother told me, 'but Fatima is 27 and she cannot wait forever. You're a government clerk. On your salary you can never marry Fatima.' When I heard that, it destroyed me. I wandered the streets and all the hopes I had in college died. I wasn't an engineer; the only job I could find was filing papers. I wasn't a husband. I wasn't a father. I wasn't a man.

"One day I stopped to rest at the mosque. I had no religious feeling, but I had no money for a coffee shop either. The sheik saw me and gave me a cup of tea and something to read. I began to tell him all my troubles and he was kind. He gave me books to read and answered my questions about Islam. Although I didn't know it then, I had entered jihad. I struggled with my ignorance and doubt. By now, thanks be to God, I've found my way. When the sheik offered me a job as a tutor, I took it. By helping the children I was building my life and building the community of Islam.

"The sheik has a niece, Nadia. She's from his village in the delta. We'll marry after Ramadan. Nadia doesn't need a car or cable television. A room in the sheik's house is enough. I was dead, but now I have found life and faith in Islam."

SOCIAL GROUPS IN EGYPTIAN LIFE

One of the most interesting aspects of Egyptian society is its robust group life. The government is very suspicious of formal organizations, seeing in them a potential for political opposition, and consequently relatively few people join organizations like unions or political parties. But at the local level Egyptians create a rich variety of informal social groups that play essential roles in individuals' lives. These groups include families, clans, informal alliances of neighbors, friendship groups, savings clubs, and the religious study groups, training classes, and athletic clubs found at mosques. There are also formal student organizations, professional associations, NGOS (nongovernmental organizations, often human rights organizations or charitable organizations) and Islamist groups.

The Egyptian Family

Families are the basic unit of Egyptian social structure. They are also key to understanding the day-to-day life of most Egyptians. In many Western societies, whom you spend time with and whom you marry are individual decisions. Contemporary Americans and Europeans hold their families dear, but these families must often adapt to choices individual members make. A person may choose to marry someone of a different religion than his or her relatives or a different ethnic background.

An individual may choose to move far away from his or her family. Individual Egyptians, in contrast, must adapt to the values and needs of their families. Families are demanding and they care deeply about the behavior of family members.

In rural areas many people live in **extended families.** Such a family might include an older married couple, their two adult sons and their wives and children, and perhaps, if one of those children is old enough, a grandson and his wife and children. The constituent **nuclear families** may all live in one building or in separate houses. Either way, they operate as a single household. Extended family members carry out household tasks, work in the fields, and take care of the very young and the very old. When a father with married sons dies, the extended household formed by his sons' families dissolves. Each son then creates his own extended family including his sons, their wives, and children (Fakhouri, 1972, pp. 55–63).

Marriage and Divorce

Marriage and divorce are family matters, not individual concerns. Everyone is expected to marry and in most cases the choice of a spouse is a family decision. In rural areas, where a newly married couple becomes part of the husband's parents' household, the bride and her relatives must be acceptable to the groom's whole family, and especially to his mother, who is often the one who actually searches for and selects the bride. The bride's family, if they are wise, must concern themselves not only with the groom, but with the whole extended family with whom their daughter will live. Consequently, village marriages are a matter of careful negotiation between families. Even in urban areas, families want their child to marry someone from a family they know. Remember that the couple will not date before they get engaged. They won't know each other very well. People rely on a family's reputation to reassure them that a potential groom or bride will be trustworthy and moral.

Cousin Marriage.   There is an important custom in Egypt that has grown out of the need to choose a spouse the whole family can accept: cousin marriage. Both rural and urban Egyptians agree that the ideal marriage partner for a man is a paternal first cousin—a daughter of his father's brother. A more distant cousin on his father's side would also be preferable to a nonrelative. Marrying someone who is not kin is called "stranger marriage" (Fluehr-Lobban, 1994, pp. 65–67). The ideal cousin marriage is not often attainable in practice; only one marriage in five is actually between first cousins. But as recently as 1995, more than 40% of Egyptian women married men who were relatives of some kind (Fakhouri, 1972, pp. 63–64; Kishor, 1998, pp. 52–56). Inheritance in Egypt is patrilineal, that is, the family name and most of the land are inherited through the male line. When cousins marry, the dowry paid by the husband also stays in the family, as does any property the wife inherits. Also, because the families know and trust each other, it is also easier to negotiate the marriage, and the bride's family can have confidence she will be well treated by her in-laws, who are her own kin.

In fact, if two brothers marry their children to each other, the young bride may be able to remain in the same household as her mother. This is because rural marriages are **patrilocal,** that is, once married a bride moves to her husband's home and joins the household there, which includes his parents, his brothers, and their wives and children.

The Marriage Contract.   Arranging a marriage is a complex process, culminating in the signing of a marriage contract. Although people have a religious obligation to marry, marriage itself is a contract between two families, almost like a corporate merger. It is not a religious sacrament. The contract is a detailed document that includes an agreement about what the groom and his family will give to the couple's new household—the apartment, the bedroom set—and what sum of money they will give the bride. This money becomes the bride's own property. The bride may require that the contract include a promise by her husband never to take any additional wives, or to permit her to work. While **polygyny** (the practice of a man marrying more than one wife) is legal in Egypt, as in most Islamic societies, it is actually quite rare. Definitive data are hard to find, but experts estimate that throughout the Middle East only 3 to 4% of women are wives in polygynous marriages (Omran & Roudi, 1993, p. 31). Few men can afford polygyny and few would attempt it against a wife's objections, so it is most common when a first marriage has produced no children.

Divorce.   Divorce is permitted in Egypt, but divorce rates are rather low. For every 100,000 people, there are 117 divorces yearly in Egypt. (Compare this to the United States, where there are 419 divorces yearly for every 100,000 people. See Table 2.1, pp. 89.) According to Islamic law, an Egyptian man may divorce his wife easily, just by stating three times "I divorce thee." It is not that easy in reality; he must file legal papers and relatives often try to arrange a reconciliation. Women are now legally permitted to divorce their husbands and they needn't cite any grounds for divorce, although they do lose any claim to their dowry. But men regard being divorced by their wives as so humiliating that they will go to any lengths to avoid it, including suing for divorce themselves, thereby forfeiting the dowry. However, a woman's family may pressure her to stay with her husband because if she is divorced they will be responsible for supporting her. Also, in cases of divorce, the woman may keep her daughters until they are 10 years old and her sons until they are 8, but after that the father may legally take over their custody. These problems of course discourage women from trying to divorce. Another interesting Egyptian custom has helped hold down divorce rates. The marriage contract specifies the sum of money the groom must give the bride at marriage. The sum has grown to be very large, and it is usually divided into two parts: the "prompt" and the "deferred." The deferred part must be paid only at the time of a divorce, so it is kind of an insurance policy against divorce (Fluehr-Lobban, 1994, pp. 64, 69, 116–117, 124–130; Wilson, 1998, pp. 132–134).

Village and Clan in the Countryside

Today, half of all Egyptians live in rural areas. Roads, buses, radio and television, schools, and health clinics link villages to modern cities, and villagers themselves move to the city or abroad to find work; but villages remain a distinctive social environment. Think for a moment of the geography of Egypt: Life hugs the Nile. Green fields line its banks, interspersed with villages; but not far from the river, the barren sand begins. As a result, the countryside is crowded. People use as much of the good, irrigated land as possible for growing crops; so families never build houses in the midst of their farmland. They all live in houses clustered together in villages, along narrow, winding lanes. Poor families may have just a couple of rooms, built around a courtyard; rich families occupy a walled compound, with offices, storerooms, kitchen, and living quarters. In Egypt's heat, where rain may not fall for years at a time, much of daily life takes place out of doors in the court-yards where women prepare food and bake in outdoor ovens, on the rooftops, in the streets, and in the village center, where the mosque, the market, the coffeehouse, and the school are located (Early, 1993, pp. 41–48; Fakhouri, 1972, pp. 119–123; Rugh, 1984, pp. 1–4).

Egyptian peasants must cooperate with one another in order to prosper. Without rain, agriculture is entirely dependent on irrigation from the Nile's water. A village's land may be miles from the river and channels must be dug and maintained to sustain the flow of water to each field. Groups of men, tied together by common interests, cemented by kinship, work together to cultivate, irrigate, and harvest the land. No single farmer and no single family could do it alone.

Male Networks in the Countryside: The Clan

In villages related extended families are linked together in **clans,** theoretically descended from a long-ago common male ancestor. The men of a clan, especially the elders, usually form a tight-knit social group. They are brothers, cousins, brothers-in-law, neighbors, and lifelong friends, who have played and gone to school together as children. They have spent their lives helping each other in the fields, sitting together in the coffeehouse, attending the same weddings and funerals. In practical terms, clans are political alliances of men. Village politics often consists of the maneuverings of rival clans (Fakhouri, 1972, pp. 56–57).

Female Networks in the Countryside

Women too live in a world filled with relatives. One of the greatest sources of satisfaction that countrywomen have is the community of women who share an extended household. These women share **primary** ties, bonds that are close, personal, and intimate (Sadat, 1987, pp. 181–190). Sisters-in-law and the unmarried daughters of their household work together to prepare food, store crops, make clothing, and do the housekeeping. Village festivals, weddings, and funerals bring together large groups of women. After a funeral, a bereaved woman's home fills with her female relatives and neighbors. Day after day they bring cooked dishes and sit together crying and wailing and praising and telling stories about the deceased individual. Women visit each other on ordinary days too, and sit chatting over coffee and snacks, surrounded by their children. They exchange news of the village, analyze other people's problems and personalities, and give each other advice. The importance of the community of women in Egyptian life is marked by the many jokes men tell about the power of gossiping women.

Neighborhood Life in the City

Egyptians have been city dwellers for thousands of years, so urban life is very much a part of Egyptian culture. In the past century, Egypt's urban population has expanded rapidly. Migrants from the countryside have poured into Cairo, Alexandria, and other cities, so that today nearly half of all Egyptians live in urban areas. Cairo is an exceptionally crowded city, it packs in almost 100,000 people per square mile. See Table 4.4. Its growth has taken over surrounding villages and pushed out into the desert. Though migrants keep up ties with their villages for many decades, city dwellers develop a rich social life of their own.

Many former peasants who came to Cairo in past decades live in densely settled and colorful old downtown districts like Bulaq, which are well known in Egyptian literature and folklore. There, in crowded poor neighborhoods old four- and five-story apartment buildings face each other across unpaved, rutted alleys, many no more than six feet wide. Lines of laundry hang criss-cross overhead, and in front of shops racks of merchandise encroach on the street. Coffeehouses place benches and tables out in front of the café. Peddlers sell clothing, sweets, vegetables, and prepared foods like beans in various sauces. Storefront workshops produce furniture, shoes, jewelry, and even industrial machinery, spilling some of their operations out into the alleys. Cars can pass through these crowded streets only with great difficulty; goats, sheep, and buffalos stand in muddy corners chewing grain, and donkey carts clog the intersections. People live crowded in small apartments, so shared public space is very important to them. All the families who live on one alley negotiate its use in outdoor weddings, parties, and funerals, and to celebrate holidays. They watch over the alley to keep it safe, often take turns feeding and clothing a beggar who sleeps there. They arrange the use of shared space in courtyards and rooftops for keeping poultry and animals (Ghannam, 2002, pp. 46, 62–65, 83).

TABLE 4.4 Urban Population Growth (1950–2004)

Egypt's urban population is four times as large as it was half a century ago, but most people in Egypt still live in rural areas. In Mexico, urban population grew even faster and by 2004 most people lived in urban areas.

	Urban Population, 1950	Urban Population as Percentage of Total Population, 1950	Urban Population, 2004	Urban Population as Percentage of Total Population, 2004
Egypt	6,800,000	31	30,902,000	42
Germany	49,200,000	72	72,814,000	88
Japan	42,100,000	50	83,671,000	65
Mexico	11,800,000	43	79,428,000	76
Namibia	48,000	9	663,000	33
United States	101,200,000	64	239,196,000	81

Source: Food and Agriculture Organization, *Statistical Yearbook,* 2005/2006, http://www.fao.org/statistics/yearbook.

There is no place for millions of Egyptians in the country's factories, farms, offices, or stores. So people survive through the informal economy. They create jobs for themselves such as setting up a simple food cart. The most poorly educated Egyptians or their wives can cook the foods popular with Egyptians, such as fuul (fava beans) or the falafel (made with chickpeas) sold at this stand. These cheap foods are essential to the millions of Egyptians who live on less than $2 a day. Tens of thousands of migrants from the countryside to Cairo arrive without family, friends, or even a place to stay. Carts selling cheap food help make their lives possible.

People act like their neighborhood is a village and their neighbors are relatives. Residents emphasize their closeness, even to strangers, by addressing each other by kin terms. A younger woman calls an older, unrelated man "uncle." Women the same age call each other "sister." Egypt is a "touch" society (but only in same-gender interaction). Men greet their friends and relatives by kissing first on one cheek, then the other. Men may hold hands as they walk, and women walk down the streets together arm in arm. Egyptians of the same gender are comfortable standing quite close to one another when they talk, and they smile a lot and look intensely into one another's eyes.

Recent migrants to the city often cannot afford to live in the old city neighborhoods. They live in squatter settlements, like Cairo's Imbaba and Zawya on the outskirts of the city, in tiny houses constructed of packing crates, tin sheets, pallets, or, at best, concrete blocks. Many have settled in Cairo's large graveyards, making their homes in tombs and memorial buildings. Squatter neighborhoods lack running water, electricity or sewers, mail delivery, police patrols, fire stations, and public schools. In some neighborhoods, people work together to install sewer pipes, which run to cesspools in the street. Other migrants move to government-constructed housing projects in outlying areas. There, people who are not relatives, and who have not known each other for a long time, organize tenants associations to control shared space like stairwells and courtyards, and to arrange additions to the buildings.

Men and Women in the City

In the city, the clan is no longer the center of men's social life. Instead, men look to social groups called *shilla*. These are small groups bound by friendship or family ties—friends from the village or from school, a group of brothers and their friends, and some of their friends' brothers. Often the members of a shilla have a regular table in the coffeehouse or a regular weekly get-together, and they are also mutual-aid networks. A group member who has prospered and moved high in the government bureaucracy will expect to help his friends and relatives.

Urban women have many more opportunities than rural women to make new friends. At work in factories or offices women create new social networks and share information about health care, or dealing with government bureaucrats. They hear one another's experiences with husbands or brothers. They meet other women in their buildings or alleys or in local mosques and in the clinics, training classes, and study groups provided by mosques. Women choose those they trust most to form savings associations, with each woman contributing a set amount each month, the whole sum going to a single individual at set intervals (Ghannam, 2002, pp. 80–81).

The Mosque and Group Life

Egyptian cities and villages are full of mosques, some of them tiny one-room affairs indistinguishable from apartments, others grand structures with domes and minarets. For many Egyptians (though not all) the mosque is increasingly a focus of their lives. Jobless young men can pass their time in the mosque without loss of dignity and without spending any money. Women find it easier to get out of the house if their purpose is to attend prayers or study groups at the mosque. Going to the mosque is considered virtuous, while standing around gossiping seems sinful. Ghannam describes one pious woman who goes to six different mosques within a few blocks of her home, to perform prayers, attend literacy classes, and participate in Quran recitation sessions. Women form friendships at the mosque and increasingly, marriages are arranged through mosque-based networks. Mosques offer after-school tutoring for children, diet clinics for women, lending libraries of religious books and tapes of sermons. Male and also female sheiks help families resolve disputes. Female sheiks run weekly lessons for women discussing topics like menstruation, circumcision, abortion, sexual relationships, domestic abuse, and relations between neighbors (Ghannam, 2002, pp. 127–130).

Islamist Community Organizations.   Since the Egyptian government provides little in the way of social services, in many communities mosques, Islamist organizations, and community-based development associations linked to mosques have stepped into the gap. Some village groups consist of just a few people, while in middle-class areas of Cairo there are large "societies" that employ whole staffs of hospital workers, teachers, and clerical workers. These groups supply day-care services, health care clinics for mothers and children, and training in sewing for women or carpentry for men. Islamic hospitals, connected to mosques or Islamic organizations, are often preferred by patients over government or private hospitals. People believe they help the poor and also offer better quality care than other hospitals (Sullivan & Abed-Kotob, 1999, pp. 24–26, 33).

DEVIANCE AND SOCIAL CONTROL

Now that you know something about Egyptian culture and about Egyptian social structure, we can take up the interesting topic of deviance and social control. You learned that people in Egypt are expected to follow quite demanding norms, many of them religious in origin. It makes sense to ask, do people actually follow the norms of their society? What forces in their society produce conformity or deviance? We are worried that your images of social control in the Muslim world have been shaped by news coverage of the Taliban in Afghanistan. Are you picturing religious police beating women who show a bit of wrist or ankle? Are you picturing beheadings or the stoning of adulterers? The first thing you need to know is that these extreme forms of social control are not common in the Islamic world and they do not exist in Egypt.

Formal and Informal Controls

Egypt is interesting because it has high rates of social conformity without very effective institutions of criminal justice. Many neighborhoods go unpoliced. Police can be bribed and the court system is notoriously slow. It will help us understand the situation if we distinguish between two kinds of social controls: **formal controls** and **informal controls. Formal controls** are used by institutions: governments, the police, the courts, or even schools, churches, and businesses. Typically, formal controls are **institutionalized.** They are codified in rules and procedures, and the penalties or sanctions for deviance are formalized too. For example, the government of the state of Minnesota says that if convicted of vehicular assault, you can be sentenced to a certain number of years in jail, or your college will put you on probation if you accumulate a certain number of Ds, Fs, and Ws. **Informal controls** are different. They take place in different social contexts, and they consist of different sorts of penalties. The members of small groups bring informal sanctions to bear on one another. The sanctions are not codified and they are typically interpersonal in nature, involving the way others see and respond to you. So, for example, if you steal your friend's girlfriend or boyfriend, the other members of your social circle will—well, what? Shun you? Stop including you in the group? Regard you as dishonorable? Gossip about you to others? These are all informal sanctions. Which do you think are more effective in getting people to conform—formal or informal sanctions? Would you be more likely to refuse to drink alcohol because your government says you are too young or because your friends disapprove of drinking?

Egypt's Government and Formal Sanctions

Egyptians will tell you that the Hosni Mubarak regime devotes all its efforts to protecting itself from the people, rather than protecting the people. The government sees political dissent of any kind as deviant and uses all its police and judicial power in harsh repression of dissent. It is rather uninterested in dealing with ordinary kinds of deviance and crime. You could say that in Egypt the people have a disagreement with the government about how to define deviance: The people think the government is engaged in deviant acts and the government sees deviant opposition and political activism on all sides. But merely to say this doesn't capture the degree of cynicism, fury, and despair that Egyptians feel about their government. Here are some of the government actions that make people so angry: In 2005 a fire in a government-constructed theater in a small town killed 32 people. After the bodies were removed, police in riot gear stood guard outside and kept people waiting for hours to find out if their relatives were alive. When the crowd became angry, police beat them (Slackman, 2005, p. A3). In 2007, an accidental fire burned down the Cairo slum of Qalaat el-Kabash. It took 3 hours for fire trucks to arrive. The police arrived a day later to clear out residents, so the residents threw rocks and the police threw tear gas. Then Islamists showed up with food and money. After that, aides to the local

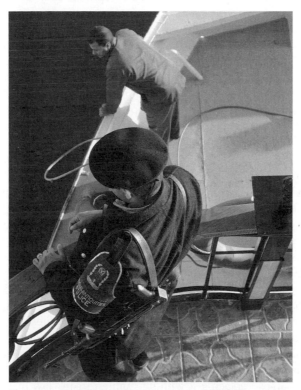

Egypt's government offers intensive and effective police protection to only one group: foreign tourists. Tourism is so important to the Egyptian economy that there is a special force: the Tourism and Antiquities Police. This officer is accompanying a tour group on a Nile cruise. A tourist invited to dinner with a Cairo family has to surrender his passport to the police and accept police escort to his host's apartment, where a plainclothes officer is stationed outside during the entire evening. What is the government afraid of? In 1992, 70 German tourists were killed in a terrorist attack at the tombs at Luxor. Afterward tourism plummeted for several years.

parliamentary representative arrived in turn with frozen chickens which they threw into the crowd from behind a locked gate (Slackman, 2007b, p. A11).

Human Rights Violations

Egypt's interior ministry, the government branch in charge of law enforcement, employs an estimated 1.4 million people, including uniformed police as well as plain-clothes officers of the State Security Investigations department. These officers routinely use torture, not just on Islamic militants, but on ordinary citizens who fall into the hands of the police. The Egyptian Organization for Human Rights, a secular lobby, can document 567 cases of police torture in the past 14 years, with 167 of them resulting in the victim's death. They say these are the exceptional cases that can be fully documented. There are many more, since torture is used systematically whenever people are detained by the police. Within the past year a new phenomenon in Egypt has publicized some of these cases. Bloggers have been posting video footage embarrassing to the government. In one case cell phone video of a man being sodomized with a stick in a Cairo police station spread around the internet to YouTube and Egyptian blogs. Public outrage forced authorities to convict and imprison the two police officers shown on the video. The government now is trying to suppress political bloggers, sentencing one young Egyptian to 4 years in jail after he criticized Mubarak on his personal blog (*The Economist*, 2007b, p. 54; 2007e, p. 38; *The New York Times*, 2007, p. A17).

Election Fraud

The government rigs elections to make its candidates win. Riot police surround polling stations on election day, letting in busloads of government supporters to vote, but barring anyone they suspect might vote for opposition parties. Ayman Nour, the brave opposition candidate in the last presidential election, won just 7% of the votes, but he was nevertheless jailed afterward, on trumped-up charges. When Egyptians get so frustrated that they protest in Cairo streets, even tiny demonstrations of a couple of hundred people are greeted by thousands of police and undercover agents, who beat and then jail them. The government has postponed local elections, tried to punish judges who reported fraud at the polls, and denied requests to form new political parties (Slackman, 2006b, p. A3). In 2007, a rigged vote approved constitutional changes that limit what judges can do to monitor elections. The changes also affect the emergency law that for 25 years allowed the government to detain prisoners indefinitely without charges, replacing it with an "antiterrorism" law that constitutionally gives the government the same powers (*The Economist*, 2007a, p. 57; Slackman, 2007c, p. A8). And there's more, but you get the idea.

But when it comes to nonpolitical deviance, the Egyptian government and criminal justice system are relatively lax. You could say that Egypt is an authoritarian state, but not a police state. There is quite a lot of personal freedom. It is easy to buy alcohol. Some young men smoke hashish. There is no official policy on whether women must or must not be veiled. In most cases, the government is uninterested in what people do in their private lives. While tourist sites and tourist hotels are conspicuously surrounded by armed police, poor Cairo settlements and rural towns have little police presence, except when raids on Islamists take place. And then the police may well sweep up everyone they find, jailing many innocent people.

Corruption

Very significantly, Egypt's government does nothing to control corruption, bribery, and favoritism, which Egyptians consider the most troubling form of deviance in their society. They call corruption *kossa* ("zucchini") probably because wealth from corruption grows suspiciously fast. Corruption of those at the top is particularly resented. Egyptians complain about the "Gang of Sons," the children of a number of important officials in the government, including the sons of President Mubarak, who are believed to collect bribes and use their fathers' positions for business advantage (Weaver, 1995, p. 56). They are also angered by bureaucrats who give business licenses, property deeds, or visas to those who can afford to give the biggest bribes, and by officials who give no-bid contracts to their relatives and friends.

> Egyptians find this joke very funny; it rings true to them. "U.S. President George W. Bush visits Cairo and gets to talking with the waiter who serves him in his hotel there. The waiter pours out his heart and tells Bush about his sick wife and his son who can't afford to marry. President Bush is very moved and tells the waiter he will pray for him. He puts his arm around him and gives him a nickname. When he gets back to Washington, Bush calls President Mubarak and tells him, 'I've sent you $5,000. Please give it to Ibrahim Sayed, who works in the Hilton Hotel in Cairo.' Mubarak calls in an aide. 'Here's $2,500 from George W. Bush. Find Ibrahim Sayed at the Hilton and give it to him.' The aide calls his assistant. 'Go to the Hilton and find Ibrahim Sayed and give him this $1,000 from President Bush.' The assistant calls his assistant. 'This $500 is from George Bush. Find Ibrahim Sayed and give it to him.' The assistant calls his secretary. 'I want you to find Ibrahim Sayed and tell him George Bush prayed for him and God will provide.'"

Working your connections to get rich is called *wasta,* and it reminds Egyptians of the old proverb, "How great is the luck of one whose uncle is chairman" (Murphy, 2002, pp. 18–19). But corruption is not restricted to the rich. Egyptians also see consumer fraud and scams all around them in everyday life. Construction companies charge for the best materials, buy the worst, and pocket the difference. A parking lot in downtown Cairo parks your car and asks when you will return, then rents your car out as a taxi in the interim.

Homosexuality

Until recently, one sign of permissiveness in Cairo was the existence of a substantial gay scene, underground in a sense, but hidden in plain sight. Men were never openly gay, in fact, most participants in the gay scene were married with children. But it was common knowledge that gay men gathered on certain nightclub boats on the Nile. Online, there were Web sites and chat rooms where gay men talked and arranged meetings.

Then, in 2001, the government began an all-out assault on gay people, raiding a nightclub called The Queen Boat (the name is said to refer to the wife of the former king, Farouk) and arresting 52 men on charges of "debauchery." (There is no law against homosexuality in Egypt or in Sharia.) That began a continuing crackdown on gays in which the police even ran sting operations online, with officers who posed as gay men. Human Rights Watch said that 17 people died in police custody in 2003 because of torture, used against gays and militants. Egyptians speculate that the government suddenly launched this operation in response to the growth of religiosity in Cairo. Mubarak wanted people to believe he cared about religious norms without, however, letting up in his attacks on Islamists. Gay people were simply an easy target (Goldberg, 2001, p. 55; Kersaw, 2003, p. A3; *The New York Times,* 2004; Sherif, 2004).

Social Integration and Informal Social Controls

What is most significant, however, is that despite the government's mixed record in applying formal social controls, there is actually relatively little deviance in Egypt, other than corruption. Rates of violent crime are very low. In Cairo, 84% of residents say they feel safe walking in their neighborhoods after dark. Less than 1% report having been assaulted in the previous year. Rates of robbery are similarly low. There are few stories about crime in Egypt's newspapers, and those that do appear are funny human interest stories about bumbling thieves (Del Frate, 1998; United Nations, 1994). Why is Egypt such a safe place?

From a sociological point of view, the answer lies in strong informal social controls. We have seen that ordinary Egyptians belong to a variety of social groups, including the family, the clan, the neighborhood, and the village, that are very important in their lives. These groups exercise robust informal social controls. Groups discipline their members, and group members also monitor and restrain their own conduct to maintain their reputations—their honor—and the reputations of their groups. "In the village," one woman reported to Farha Ghannam, "no matter where you go, you will find someone who knows either you or a member of your family. If you do something that violates the norms, someone is prone to report what you did to your relatives and neighbors." Men and women must act with propriety so as not to shame themselves and their families (Ghannam, 2002, p. 85).

Social Controls in the City

In the city, most people live in crowded neighborhoods. Shopkeepers stand in their doorways; men sit in coffee shops and at tables in the street. Women look out of their windows and stand on the rooftops to talk to friends in adjoining buildings. Many people live in small apartments or houses at street level. You can look in the windows and watch their televisions and they can watch the street. Egyptians don't hesitate to intervene with neighbors or even strangers if there is a problem. An argument on the street between a vendor and a customer or between two young men brings all the merchants out of their stores and gathers a crowd of passersby. Those nearby willingly jump in and take sides or calm down the antagonists. At the end of Ramadan in 2006 there was a shocking incident on the street in Cairo, reported by blogs and independent media. Crowds of young men attacked women, tearing their clothes and touching them. Police on the streets failed to take action, so store owners came out with sticks to drive off the men. (Predictably, the government denied the attacks had taken place, and Cairo residents accused the government of not caring about the people.) But people who saw the attacks took matters into their own hands as a matter of course (Abdelhadi, 2006; Slackman, 2006, p. A4). In a way, the propensity of Egyptians to get involved permits people to dramatize disagreements. Antagonists shout, pound on tables, make threatening gestures, and wave their arms. People rely on others, even strangers, to stop their conflict before it escalates too far (Wilson, 1998, pp. 108–109).

In the narrow, crowded streets of Cairo it is not unusual for a car to hit a pedestrian. Then the driver of the car will leap out and begin bewailing the accident and beseeching God's help. He will probably load the victim into the car to drive off to the hospital. The driver may act out of genuine contrition; we'll never know, because as soon as they hear a thump, the crowd gathers and buzzes with anger at the careless driver. The watching crowd also doesn't hesitate to chase down a thief, or even a murderer, and they will hold the suspect for the police.

Islam and Social Controls

Egypt today is in a ferment of moral discussion. Egyptians have always understood their values and norms in terms of Islam, but now, with a religious revival in full swing, talk about Islam is ubiquitous. Many norms of behavior are being redefined, and there is a continual debate about what the appropriate Islamic norms are in a given situation. People struggle to become better Muslims, and this struggle plays a very powerful role in social control.

Geneive Abdo describes visiting a barbershop where a local, unofficial *sheik* (one who has no special religious education, but who is respected for his piety) is explaining to the customers why women should be veiled. She visits the *dars,* or religious lesson of a sheik who answers questions from a crowd of several hundred, "ranging from whether using facial cream was against Islam to whether children were allowed to take revenge against a father who killed their mother." When one young man confesses that he yelled at his wife until she cried, the sheik berates him: "This is an example of how men can be jerks" (Abdo, 2000, pp. 31–32).

In cases of moral uncertainty more and more Egyptians seek a *fatwa,* a religious ruling from a scholar who bases his or her edict on the Koran and the hadith (the teachings of the prophet). Thousands of fatwas are issued every month, mostly on dilemmas of daily life. There are two government-approved, official sources of fatwas, the Fatwa Committee at Al Azhar University and the House of Fatwa (Dar Al-Ifta), formally part of the Ministry of Justice. But many people don't trust these government institutions and seek their fatwas from other sheiks, from Islamist organizations, from Web sites, and from satellite television shows. Technically, you can reject a fatwa and look for one more agreeable to you from another source. May I divorce my husband if he takes another wife and spends more nights with her than with me? (Yes.) Is buying a car on the installment plan allowed by Islam? May I keep money I found in the street? May a woman drive a car without her husband's permission? (Slackman, 2007d, pp. A1, A10). On issues large and small, Egyptians seek religious advice. In an atmosphere of intensified piety, people are actively trying to decide what their religion requires of them and to live by it.

SOCIAL INEQUALITY IN EGYPT

It is remarkable that there is so little deviance in Egyptian society, because there is no shortage of frustration and strain. Egyptians live in a society deeply divided by economic inequalities, with shrinking opportunities and increasing competition. Many people feel worn out with struggle. The Egyptian economy, as of 2007, looked from the outside like a huge success story. Growth was rapid; gross national product (GNP) grew almost 7% a year between 2005 and 2007. That's one of the highest rates of growth in the world. Exports grew 20% a year and the Cairo stock exchange made tremendous gains. Some people got much richer. Real estate speculators, for example, profited from a Cairo building boom. But at the same time, the gap between rich and poor widened. Rising real estate prices pushed housing farther out of the reach of the poor. Wages still average only about $75 a month for unskilled workers, while prices continue to rise. Egypt was one of 30 countries where there were food riots in 2008. In the first half of that year alone the world price of wheat rose 55%. Many basic Egyptian foods once subsidized by the government are now sold at market prices. But bread is so essential to Egyptians that it is still subsidized to keep it very cheap. People wait for hours and fights break out in the bread line (*The Economist,* 2007d, p. 40; *The New York Times,* 2008).

In Egyptian Arabic bread is called aish, which means "life." For poor Egyptians bread really is life; it is their basic food. These people are waiting in line to buy cheap, government-subsidized bread. The bakery behind the window has been able to buy flour from the government at a price way below market value. It is supposed to sell the bread at the government's fixed price, but the temptations to cheat are great. The baker could sell the flour or the bread on the black market, bribing the inspector who is supposed to keep him honest. Some customers try to buy lots of bread and resell it at a higher price (Slackman, 2008, p. A4).

Class Inequality

Sociologists use the term **class inequality** in discussing several related matters. They use it to talk about inequalities in the distribution of economic resources like income and wealth and to ask how broadly or narrowly these resources are spread through the society. They also use it to discuss **social classes,** groups of people whose economic resources and lifestyles are similar, and which may form real, self-identified social groups. Finally, sociologists use the term *class inequality* in discussing **social mobility,** the extent to which people in different social classes have a chance to move up or down in the social stratification system.

The class stratification system in Egypt is quite distinctive. It bears the imprint of Egypt's history as a socialist society, when the government took control of land and capital and strove to distribute resources more equally. It also shows the effects of Egypt's recent "opening" to capitalism and global business. Today, most Egyptians are quite poor. Egypt's yearly GNP averages only U.S. $1,354 per person, which is equivalent in purchasing power to $3,810 per person in the United States. About one fifth of all Egyptians live on less than what $2 a day per person could buy in the United States (El-laity, Lokshin, & Banerji, 2003, pp. 21–22; United Nations, 2004b). At the top of the stratification hierarchy there is a very small class of very wealthy Egyptians—probably no more than 1% of the population. A good way to understand Egyptian class inequality is to say that the top and the bottom of the Egyptian hierarchy are very far apart, but most people cluster near the bottom. As a result, if you examine distribution of income by quintiles (see Table 1.6, p. 49) you will find that Egypt has a relatively equal distribution of incomes—much more equal than Mexico, for example. In 1997, the most recent year for which income distribution data are available, the richest 20% of all Egyptians received almost 7 times as much total income as the poorest 20%. (The poorest 20% of Egyptians received 6.7% of all income and the richest 20% received 46.6%.) Data on earnings by occupation reveal a similar level of inequality: Skilled workers earn 6 times as much as unskilled workers, and supervisory and professional employees earn 12 times more than laborers (World Bank, 2004).

Economic Resources and Social Class

For any society, knowing about income and wealth distribution gives us only half the picture of class inequality. We also want to know who these people are: Who are the Egyptians in the top income fifth? Who are the poorest Egyptians? Where do they live and what is the source of their earnings? Egypt is making a transition out of its socialist experiment. That means it is official government policy to encourage private enterprise, but, so far, only one third of Egyptian workers are employed in the private sector—in industry or manufacturing, retail sales or services. People with connections to the private sector operate in a different world than do people in public-sector jobs. They earn much more money. This discrepancy in pay is one of many sources of frustration and anger for Egyptians (Wickham, 2002, pp. 61–62).

One third of all workers are government employees, working either in the government bureaucracy, the army, in the civil service (as postal clerks, teachers, bus drivers, mail carriers, etc.), or in government-owned companies like the Helman Steelworks, the state-owned oil industry, or the Suez Canal Company (American

University in Cairo, Social Research Center, 2001; *The Economist,* 1998, p. 4). A very large number of Egyptians can get no regular employment at all. They make their way as best they can in the **informal sector** or else they migrate abroad to find work. Because relatively few people own or work for private businesses, "ownership of the means of production," in Karl Marx's sense, isn't the most important source of income or class position in Egyptian society. Much more important is a person's **power** or access to government-controlled resources. In Egypt, unequal access to government power results in unequal rewards. People who can get jobs as government employees (as skilled factory workers, clerical workers, or professionals) enjoy an enviable job security, even though their pay is usually low. They are likely to treat their jobs as economic resources—a way to get medical insurance, or a way to find jobs, or contracts or connections, for relatives and friends. They may supplement their wages by accepting bribes for ordinary services or by skimming government funds that come through their hands. They don't hesitate to skip work when their family needs them, and they may even leave work early every day to go to a better paid, but less secure second job.

Even for those who are not government employees, access to government resources is critical to prosperity. Owners of private businesses operate in an economy that is largely government owned. Banks are government owned, as is transportation, and many industrial supplies must be purchased from government factories. Import and export licenses must be granted by the government and paperwork must find its way through the vast government bureaucracy. Business owners can't use their property profitably without government permission.

The same is true in agriculture. Ninety-five percent of Egyptian farms are tiny—below five acres. Many of these landowners have the government to thank for their holdings, having received them in the post-1952 land redistribution. But new landowners didn't receive outright ownership of their land. They were required to join farm cooperatives that decide what crops should be grown, and supply seeds and fertilizer, storage, transportation, and marketing. Farmers are given credit by government banks and sell their crops to the government at prices the government sets. Egyptians look upon their government officials very differently than do the Japanese. In their eyes the bureaucracy certainly is not a rational, dispassionate agency committed to the public good. Ministries and bureaucrats operate in their own self-interest and they are open to influence and bribery. To get ahead, Egyptians need good connections, through family or shilla networks.

Social Classes in Rural Egypt

Many Egyptians are desperately poor, without enough resources to buy sufficient food for their families. According to the World Bank, 17% of Egyptians lived in poverty this severe in 2000. They had incomes equivalent to less than what $2 a day could buy in the United States. Poverty rates are especially high for the 25 million Egyptians who depend on agriculture for their livelihood. The poorest rural people are landless agricultural workers who must find work on other people's farms, seasonally or by the day (El-laithy et al., 2003, pp. 11, 21–22; Food and Agriculture Organization, 2004). About 1 million Egyptians (occupying 62% of all farms) are sharecroppers, farming land for which they must pay rent in the form of a percentage of their crop. A smaller number of tenant farmers pay their rent in cash. The rest of the farmers own their own land, but almost all of them (95%) have very small farms—under five acres (Koran, 1992, p. 568). They are better off than the landless, but are still poor and, as we have seen, dependent on the support and goodwill of the government (see Table 2.4, p. 111).

Mina's Story: Life on the Land

Mina is in her early 40s. All her life she has lived in Bisat, a rural community at the edge of Egypt's western desert. Her family and her husband's family have farmed the land here as long as anyone can remember. At 15 she married her cousin Yussef, her father's brother's son. They farm less than a feddan (an acre) of land. To make ends meet, Yussef has had to find employment for part of the year at a factory in a nearby town. Mina works in the fields at planting and harvest times, along with her sisters and sisters-in-law, her cousins and her aunts. The rest of the year they do their household chores in each other's company, baking bread, cooking, raising children, and going to the local market where Mina sometimes sells her cheese. Life is not so placid for Mina and Yussef's son Hassan, who is 23. There is no land in Bisat for him to farm, so last year he went to Cairo, hoping his cousin there could help him find work. "Here I am," he says, "sharing a miserable room and looking for work every day. Sometimes a builder hires me and I get 7 to 10 pounds (about $3) for a day's work. Some days I get nothing. Often I live on fuul (boiled beans) and nothing else for days. How will I ever be able to marry and raise a family?"

Because such an overwhelming percentage of rural Egyptians are poor, it is easy to miss the rural elite. As a result of the land redistributions, there are relatively few large farms. Only 5% of farms are larger than five acres—but these farmers own 49% of the land! Egyptian soil is so fertile that 5 to 20 acres is a good size for a commercial farm and the owner will be quite prosperous. Such farmers usually live locally and farm their land with hired labor. They are part of a rural upper class, together with village professionals like the town lawyer and doctor and perhaps a successful storekeeper. They live in comfortable houses, with gardens and shaded courtyards, and employ servants. Villagers look up to them, and they are able to send their children to university in the city.

But while these landowners are the elite of village society, in national terms they are not part of the upper class. This distinction belongs only to the largest landowners—one tenth of 1% of farmers who own more than 50 acres of land. These farmers don't live locally; they let their land out to tenant farmers, hire a manager, and live in the city. Many of them are actually foreign corporations from Saudi Arabia, Europe, or the United States that buy Egyptian land and employ landless laborers to produce crops like cotton and sugar for export.

Social Classes in Urban Egypt

Class differences are highly visible in Egyptian cities too, and city residents are aware of the hierarchy of classes and where they stand in it. In Cairo people of different classes live in distinctively different neighborhoods. Nearly three quarters of the population of Cairo lives in **informal communities** without any government services, like schools, fire departments, or sewers. Some of these are shanty settlements, but others have brick apartment buildings that people build themselves, sometimes squatting on desert land (Slackman, 2007a, pp. A1, A4). Those who are luckier or slightly better off live in old crowded downtown slums like Bulaq or in the concrete high-rise towers of government-built "satellite cities" on the outskirts of town. More prosperous people live in spacious neighborhoods with solid apartment houses and paved streets. The wealthy elite are found in downtown luxury apartment towers or in gracious, tree-lined enclaves of private homes. Only the rich own cars; everyone else must ride the slow, sputtering buses, jammed with people, or else walk. People of different classes dress differently too. Lower-class men are likely to wear the traditional *gallibiyya,* a long, loose cotton shirt while middle-class men generally wear Western-style clothing. The upper classes are easily identified by their fashionable clothes, imported from Europe (MacLeod, 1993, p. 34).

The Lower Class.   Those most likely to be poor are people who live in households headed by someone who is illiterate. You should probably picture an illiterate family from a rural part of Upper Egypt, that moves to a city, perhaps Cairo, and then has a very hard time making a life for themselves. They probably live in a squatter settlement, on the desert outskirts of the city. There is no safe drinking water and health problems are rampant. Some of these squatter settlements are built in the city's cemeteries, where poor people have moved into the stone tombs in which rich Egyptians inter family members' remains. See Table 2.3, p. 109 and Table 4.5.

Imagine that our poor urban family doesn't have many connections in the city. Without *wasta,* and without the ability to read and write, family members haven't a prayer of getting a secure government job. It is much more likely that they will work in the informal sector, which employs an estimated 26% of all Egyptian workers. *Informal sector* is often a polite way of saying that people scrounge for work. They work off-the-books, often as temporary laborers, or they work as unlicensed street vendors, outside the regular markets, outside the tax system, sometimes selling "pirate" goods—illegal copies of cassette tapes or foreign designer clothes. More than 200,000 street vendors flood Cairo's downtown. Thousands of people work the garbage dumps of big cities, picking through the trash for recyclable materials to sell. Others buy and sell old clothes from door to door, collect and sell used cigarette butts, shine shoes, and hawk used newspapers on the street. Organized groups illegally control the streets of a quarter, where they park and protect cars for

TABLE 4.5   Illiterate Men and Women

Despite substantial gains in literacy, more than one Egyptian in every four cannot read or write. Women are far more likely to be illiterate than men.

	Illiterate Women (%)		Illiterate Men (%)	
	1970	2004	1970	2004
Egypt	83	41	54	17
Namibia	49	17	36	13
Mexico	30	10	20	8

Source: United Nations, *Human Development Report 2007,* 2007, http://hdr.undp.org/en/reports/.

a fee. Some informal-sector workers are not poor. They are educated, recent graduates unable to find work, or government workers who need second jobs. They make use of their literacy and bureaucratic know-how by writing letters for illiterate Egyptians or taking sidewalk passport photos. Hundreds work as "facilitators," freelance guides to the bureaucracy, who for a fee will help people find their way through the bewildering corridors of Mugamma, Cairo's huge government building (Bayat, 1997, p. 4; Hedges, 1994, p. A4; Rodenbeck, 1992, p. 80).

Rasha's Story: Life in Mottakam

Rasha worked nimbly at the rug. Her family's rising income depended more and more on her ability to turn recycled rags into colorful rugs. For years, times had been very good for her father, Isak. Twenty years ago he left the desperately hard life of a tenant farmer near Asyut, in the south, to join his brothers in Mottakam, Cairo's Garbage City. Coptic Christians, like Isak and his family, cluster together in Mottakam. When Isak arrived in Mottakam, his brothers were making a meager living for themselves by raising pigs and goats on the garbage they collected from Cairo's wealthier neighborhoods. Then the Zabeleen, *as these Coptic communities are called, discovered that there was money to be made in recycling. They took over the garbage dumps and garbage collection, selling plastic, aluminum, and rags as scrap or for recycling. With seed money from international agencies the Zabeleen turned garbage into money.*

Rasha's family did well enough that their children were able to go to school through 6th grade. Rasha can read and write. Rasha's brother, Wali, is an accomplished businessman at 13 years of age. "Even when I was a child," he says, "I helped sort garbage. I made a few pounds by putting aside the shampoo bottles and reselling them to dealers. Now Proctor and Gamble pays us to shred their bottles into scrap so no one can reuse them. Then I thought, why should I spend all my time looking for these bottles when my friends can help me? I promised to buy any bottles my friends could find. Then I resell them to the Proctor and Gamble people. Now I am learning to read so that I can be sure I am not cheated when I sign a contract."

"Everything would be wonderful," Wali and Rasha say, "if it were not for our governor and his afrangi *(foreign) friends. They'll leave nothing for us." In an effort to clean up Cairo's legendary dirty streets, Cairo's governor has signed contracts with waste disposal companies from Italy. Block by block they are taking over the collection of the garbage that the Zabeleen depend on. "The government doesn't really care about us," complained Isak. "If we starve so that tourists can take pretty pictures, that's fine with them. I think they were surprised when we took to the streets to protest, but we won't give up our livelihoods without a struggle."*

The Middle Class.   When thinking about Egyptian social class, you must remember the sociological concept of **relative poverty.** Many Egyptians consider themselves middle class, even though their incomes are barely above poverty line, because their family has two rooms to live in rather than one, or owns a television. In the same situation, you would consider yourself desperately poor. About half of all Egyptians (and about three quarters of urban Egyptians) identify with the middle class, but actually their circumstances vary greatly. Saad Edin Ibrahim divides the Cairo middle class into three **strata** (or layers): the lower middle stratum (including 26.5% of Cairenes), the middle stratum (36.1%), and the upper middle stratum (15.3%) (cited in MacLeod, 1993, pp. 34–35). The lower middle class includes manual workers who, in many other societies, would consider themselves "working class."

Egypt's industrial workforce is small, only about 10% of the whole labor force, mostly in government-owned enterprises. Relatively skilled industrial workers, who are literate and secure in their jobs, tend to think of themselves as middle class, dress like middle-class people, and have middle-class aspirations for their children. They see themselves as socially equal to other government employees, like clerks or lower civil service workers, whose wages are indeed similar. In fact, their wives and daughters very well may be clerical workers. The bottom of the lower middle class lives barely above the poverty line and they live in the same neighborhoods as the poor.

Those who are better off may have a larger apartment, with perhaps as many as four rooms, a TV, refrigerator, and maybe a few other appliances. In cases in which the husband has a skilled job in a private company the family will be better off, since pay is much higher in private companies than in the public sector, though jobs are less secure. Many lower-middle-class families would be poor were it not for income earned by the wife, who works in a regular job in the formal economy (MacLeod, 1993, p. 36). Women are steadily entering the labor force, with about 35% of women aged 15 and above in paid work (United Nations, 2004b).

The middle stratum of the middle class has a more secure hold on its class position. They are university educated and many are young professionals or senior clerical workers in the government bureaucracy. They are self-employed workers in the skilled trades, like plumbers and electricians, or they are shopkeepers or small merchants. Many live in the modest neighborhoods where their businesses are located, but they are actually quite prosperous (Barakat, 1993, pp. 89–90; Rodenbeck, 1992, p. 82). They expect their children to go to a university.

The upper middle class shades off into the upper class. These people are much more secure than the rest of the middle class. They are established professionals, government bureaucrats, army officers, and prosperous owners of private businesses. Upper-middle-class Egyptians live in air-conditioned modern apartment houses, or in large apartments in old-fashioned middle-class districts. Their homes may be lavishly furnished with inherited antiques or modern European furniture. They can afford servants and even perhaps to send their children to a university abroad.

The Upper Class.   The Egyptian upper class is very small, but it is growing. Ibrahim estimates the upper class in Cairo, the national center of business and government, as not more than 1% of the population (Ibrahim, cited in MacLeod, 1993, p. 35). The upper class includes the elites of the government bureaucracy and the top managers of government-owned industries. It includes the most successful owners of private capital—entrepreneurs, big wholesale merchants who engage in international trade, and the owners of big construction firms favored by government contracts. The most successful professionals who work for the public and private elites are members of this class, too. Upper-class people are dependent on each other to maintain their wealth. After all, exporters need government licenses and permissions; lawyers need clients, and bureaucrats, no matter how powerful, earn relatively low wages; they use their official positions and their contacts in the private sector to earn upper-class incomes, often through private commissions. For example, in recent years President Mubarak's sons have become very wealthy acting as business agents in the airline industry. They earned commissions from foreign airplane manufacturers when they negotiated contracts to supply planes to Egypt's government-owned airline.

Old and New Wealth.   In Egypt today there is an old upper class and a new upper class. The old upper class was formed in colonial era Egypt, though many of its members were able to preserve their wealth and connections in socialist Egypt. This elite formed a small, self-conscious group in Cairo and Alexandria. They lived amid family antiques in a few exclusive, guarded villa neighborhoods, spoke French, and supported Egyptian literature and theater. Their children attended exclusive private schools together and they socialized together at English-style country clubs. This elite still prospers in Egypt, but because it always sought to live privately and conceal its wealth, the old elite is overshadowed today by the newly rich.

Egypt's new millionaires have made their money since Sadat's *infitah,* the opening to global capitalism. Some are the sons of old elite families, but others are enterprising operators, some of modest background, who parlayed a nest egg earned abroad or a gift for speculation into tremendous wealth. Some of the newly rich have made their money in industrial production—steel, appliances, aircraft— but others have profited from currency speculation or from skimming business loans from international banks. Ex-officials and their sons grew rich from bribes paid by Western multinational corporations eager to break into Egypt's markets for arms, aircraft, communications systems, and so on. Others made their fortunes investing in the oil-rich Gulf states and have brought back both their new wealth and Islamist styles of dress, architecture, and piety. As new money flows into Egypt, a whole secondary layer of businesspeople has grown wealthy selling con- sumer goods to the newly rich. They are architects and developers, interior decora- tors, advertising consultants, dealers in cars, jacuzzis, and cell phones. Entertainers, lawyers, and doctors who serve the rich have also prospered (*The Economist,* 1998, p. 6).

The newly rich have not hesitated to show off their wealth, making the contrast between rich and poor more obvious to everyone. A huge apartment tower in the suburb of Giza boasts "villas" of 17,000 square feet each, selling for up to $15 mil- lion. A new golf course, constructed in the desert on the road to Suez, has carefully watered and manicured green fairways and 300 villas, advertised as "a lifestyle for the privileged few." It sits right next to a bleak, rundown group of concrete public housing blocks, surrounded by eroded sand and blowing trash, home to 20,000 (Ajami, 1998, pp. 235–237; Ibrahim, 1995, p. A4).

Ahmad's Story: The Developer

Ahmad Moustafa looked out over the Nile from the balcony of his Zemalek apartment. At 54 he wished his country had done as well as he had in these turbulent times. He marvelled at his own capacity to find a way to profit in every circumstance. A Mercedes, a luxury apartment in Cairo's most fashionable quarter, hand-tailored suits made in Italy, a glamorous wife, and a son to follow in his footsteps—not bad!

When the monarchy ended in 1952 and the estates of large landowners were broken up, Ahmad's father took the family to live quietly at one of their country properties. But

Ahmad went to university, did his army service, and finished his degree in engineering. A classmate helped him get a job in the Ministry of Construction and then he married the daughter of his commanding officer.

In the 1980s, Ahmad saw the opportunities in luxury construction. He went into partnership with his old classmate and they pooled their resources. His father-in-law helped him get a bank loan and with 10 million pounds in hand they were able to buy an old colonial mansion in Garden City from the squabbling heirs who had just inherited it. The house cleared away, they planned 16 apartments, sold for 2,400,000 pounds each, and a well-timed "gift" to a crucial colleague in the ministry and others at the city council made it possible to build two extra floors, another four apartments. In the end, accounting for construction costs and bribes, net profits amounted to 24,000,000 pounds. Ahmad never looked back: three more apartment complexes, a golf course, and now the condo development in the resort at Sharm el Sheikh. Ahmad's son manages land acquisition and is soon to marry the daughter of one of the top bureaucrats of a major bank. They may well fly all the guests to Sharm for the wedding.

Social Mobility in Egypt

For ordinary Egyptians today opportunities for upward mobility are shrinking. Population growth outpaces job growth and young people face high rates of unemployment. This situation is particularly upsetting to Egyptians because their expectations were formed during several decades of rapid economic growth after the 1952 revolution, when living standards rose and opportunities for upward mobility expanded rapidly.

Closed and Open Systems.   Sociologists make a theoretical distinction between two kinds of societies: **closed stratification systems** and **open stratification systems.** In closed systems, people must remain in the social class into which they were born and no amount of talent or effort can have any effect. In contrast, in open systems, parents are unable to pass any advantage on to their children. All children have an equal chance to prosper or fail, based only on their ability and hard work. In real life, no stratification system is completely closed or completely open, but it is useful to think about the two theoretical extremes in order to understand the situation in Egypt today. Before Nasser and the revolution of 1952, Egypt's stratification system was based primarily on inherited land and wealth. It was very difficult for people who didn't have these to acquire any. After 1952, Egypt changed from a rather closed system to a more open one, and opportunities for social mobility increased.

The Revolution and Social Mobility.   Nasser created vastly more opportunities for Egyptians in two ways. First, he expelled the existing upper class, by ending colonialism and nationalizing almost all Egyptian businesses. European managers, Greek, Christian, and Jewish merchants, and even wealthy Muslim business owners fled the country. Their departure deprived Egypt of their skills, but created many new openings for those loyal to the revolution (Kurian, 1992, p. 550). A new class of Egyptian managers grew. Second, Nasser quickly moved to create a modern economy under state ownership. Economic expansion laid the foundation for a new middle class, and Nasser deliberately poured the nation's resources into training Egyptians for modern industrial jobs. He opened schools and universities and made education available to ordinary Egyptians. He created a modern health care system as well. Suddenly teachers, doctors, nurses, engineers, architects, accountants, managers, and industrial workers were required in great numbers. To encourage young people to go to school, Nasser promised each college graduate a job in the bureaucracy or in government-owned industry. In Nasser's time, the sons of postal workers became doctors, and the sons of peasants became skilled workers (Fakhouri, 1972, pp. 40–45; MacLeod, 1993, pp. 31–34; Vatikiotis, 1991, pp. 390–396, 457–458).

Aspirations and Realities.   Every year 1.2 million people enter the labor force for the first time and half of them cannot find jobs. The official unemployment rate stands at 10% (unofficially it is 20%) and that isn't counting the 3 million workers (one quarter of the total labor force) who cannot find regular jobs but work in the informal sector (*The Economist,* 2007, p. 48).

However, Egyptians still look to education as the route out of poverty, and even quite modest jobs as clerks or semiskilled workers require a high school degree. Many educated young people find their expectations disappointed. Nearly one quarter of those unemployed in Cairo today hold university degrees (Rodenbeck, 1992, p. 82). Intensified competition and unsatisfied aspirations fuel social unrest.

Migration.   The most common response to shrinking opportunities is migration. About 1.9 million Egyptian men—out of a labor force of 22 million—work outside Egypt today. Men don't take their families abroad with them and women never become migrant workers. Migrant work pays well; that is its great attraction. Those working abroad send home an average of $1,600 apiece yearly.

In total, the money migrants send home, called **remittances,** amounted to almost $3 billion in 2003–2004. About half of Egyptian migrants go to Saudi Arabia and most of the rest to Libya, Jordan, and Kuwait. Smaller numbers go to the United States, Germany, and the United Arab Emirates, but they send the most money home, probably because they are the most educated and skilled. But in the post–September 11 world, it is becoming more difficult for Egyptians to use migration as a route out of poverty. The number of Egyptians migrating reached its peak in 1997, and since then migration is down 12% (El-laithy et al., 2003, p. 232; International Labor Organization, *International Labor Migration Statistics, 1970–2000,* n.d.; *Middle East and North African Business Report, Newsletter,* 2004). See Table 2.5, p. 113.

Don't think of migrant work as something done only by the poor and unskilled. Men of every class work abroad, especially the insecure children of the rural and urban middle classes—the sons of small landowners, shopkeepers, and government bureaucrats. They often work as engineers, teachers, and doctors. Egyptian universities graduate a great many students with degrees in education—more than 17,000 per year—but 80% of them go abroad to teach (Kurian, 1992, p. 569).

Idris's Story: The Teacher
Idris had always thought of himself as a man with a bright future. His parents had been born in the countryside, but in the flush times of the early 1960s they came to Cairo. Idris was a bright child and did well in school, and his parents believed his intelligence and hard work would bring success. But this was not to be. By the time Idris left teachers' college in

the early 1980s, there were no jobs for teachers in Egypt. For 2 miserable years he searched desperately for any job, but only found work tutoring neighborhood children to pass their exams. Idris was rescued by the offer of a job as a teacher's assistant in a private school in Kuwait. A college friend was teaching there and had some small influence. Idris was delighted, even though working in Kuwait meant leaving his family. He arrived in Kuwait penniless; the bribe he paid for his exit visa took the last of his cash.

But then Idris hated Kuwait. Even though he was an educated man, an Arab, and a Muslim, he was treated with contempt. And he thought Kuwait was a wasteland—no culture, no night life, no nothing. Idris lived with other Egyptians, rarely going out and sending most of his money home to his family. They needed it too. His father's wages as a factory worker failed to keep pace with rising prices.

On one of his infrequent visits home, Idris married Aisha, whom he had known since childhood, and in the middle of the Kuwaiti school year he became the father of twins. He couldn't even return home for their birth; it was either a hospital room for Aisha or an airline ticket for him. What, thought Idris, had become of his life? What hope could there be for the future? Even in 8 or 10 years, when his name finally came up on the waiting list for a teaching job in Egypt, the salary would never be enough to support his wife and family and also help his parents.

Compared to the tremendous class and gender inequalities in Egyptian society, other status inequalities seem minor. There are racial and religious inequalities in Egypt, but they are of lesser importance.

Racial Inequality

Egypt is a racially mixed society. Its people come from Africa, the Middle East, Central Asia, and Europe, but they have been mixing and intermarrying for thousands of years. As a result, Egyptians vary in their skin colors and facial features. There is no doubt that light skin is a source of prestige. Before the 1952 revolution, many families in the landowning elite were aristocrats descended from Egypt's earlier rulers (including Greeks, Turks, and Macedonians). They were conscious of their lighter skin and sought similar spouses for their children (Hooglund, 1991, p. 119). Today light skin is still associated with elite status, with wealth and power. Movie stars and women in advertisements have light skin. On the other hand, skin color is only one of many sources of prestige in Egypt, including gender, education, occupation, family background, and city origins. Furthermore, while Egyptians are aware of skin color, they are not race conscious. That is, they do not classify people by race: "she is black," or "he is white." They might note that among a family of siblings, some have lighter skin and others darker skin, but they would not feel a need to decide if the family was "white" or "black." Another way of putting this is to say that race is not a **master status** in Egypt even though color is associated with prestige.

Religious Inequality

Now that Egyptians are so conscious of being Muslims, living in an Islamic society, we need to ask: What does this mean about their attitudes toward people who are not Muslims? The evidence is not particularly reassuring. Probably the most conspicuous case of hostility to non-Muslims is the treatment of Jews in Egypt. Once there was a diverse and flourishing community of more than 80,000 Egyptian Jews. Some had lived in Egypt since ancient times and others had come to Egypt as refugees from persecution in Europe all through the medieval and modern periods. Jews were always second-class citizens in Egypt, whose rights were not the same as the rights of Muslims, but they were tolerated, and in a sense welcomed for their contributions to business and government. But over the course of the second half of the 20th century almost all Egyptian Jews left Egypt in response to escalating anti-Semitism.

Modern anti-Semitism first emerged in Egypt in the 1930s, through the activities of Egypt's largest and oldest Islamist group, the Muslim Brotherhood. The Brotherhood attacked Egyptian Jews in response to the growing conflict between Arabs and Jews in Palestine, then a British colony where Jews were settling and pressing for the creation of a Jewish state. The Brotherhood did not distinguish between Egyptian Jews who supported the idea of a Jewish state and those who opposed it or were indifferent to it. This pattern persisted through the rest of the 20th century and remains today: Anti-Semitism in Egypt grows out of hostility to Israel. It is not restricted to Islamists; secular Egyptians are also anti-Semitic (Benin, 1998, pp. 241–267).

Today, with intensified conflict between Israel and the Palestinians, and with the U.S. invasion of Iraq, anti-Semitism has grown stronger in Egypt. Many Egyptians attribute their country's misfortunes to Jewish conspiracies. Anti-Semitic scenes and plot twists turn up often in popular films, and even *Al-Ahram,* the moderate, semiofficial Cairo newspaper often carries anti-Semitic articles and cartoons.

The Coptic Christians

Prejudice is greatest against Jews in Egypt, but they are an absent minority. What about Coptic Christians, Egypt's largest minority? Their treatment is more contradictory. Copts make up somewhere between 5 and 20% of the population. The true total is a matter is dispute, because the government does not enumerate Copts. Some people say the government is afraid to know how large the Coptic minority has grown. Sociologically speaking, Copts are a **religious minority group,** not just in numbers, but in terms of their lack of power. Arabic-speaking Muslims are the social **majority** in Egypt, and were so even when their numbers were small because they controlled the military, the government, and the laws. At many points in Egyptian history, the Muslim majority permitted Copts to maintain their own communities and religious institutions, as long as they accepted their subordination to Muslim authority. At other times, Coptic institutions and property were attacked despite their official protection under Islamic law (Nisan, 1991, pp. 115–121).

For example, in the early 1990s, before the militant Islamic groups Gama'a and Islamic Jihad were defeated by the government, they carried out anti-Christian actions. Militants attacked and killed as many as 200 Copts and vandalized and burned churches. The government's response was contradictory. For several years, before it succeeded in destroying the Islamic groups, the government stationed police guards outside churches. In 2003, President Mubarak surprised Egyptians by declaring the Coptic Christmas (January 7) a national holiday, like the Prophet Muhammad's birthday. But at the same time, in their efforts to co-opt Islamist sentiment, government officials sometimes made statements that reflected deep hostility toward the Coptic minority. Since then, many Copts who can afford it have emigrated, mostly to the United States (Ajami, 1998, pp. 206–209; Friedman, 2003; Jehl, 1997, p. A3; Nabeel & Shryock, 2000, pp. 30, 229; Nisan, 1991, pp. 127–133).

The Life of a Religious Minority

In some ways, Copts can be considered a highly **assimilated** minority, one which has taken on the culture of the dominant group. Copts cannot easily be distinguished from their Muslim neighbors. Centuries ago, Copts adopted Arabic as their daily language; the ancient Coptic language is rarely used. Copts wear the same clothing as other Egyptians and eat the same foods too. In daily life, only a visible cross or a Christian name distinguishes Copt from Muslim (Hooglund, 1991, pp. 141–142). Before the 20th century, Copts often served as clerks and administrators for Egypt's Muslim rulers. When the British colonial administration forced them out of government positions, they turned to the professions and many become doctors and pharmacists (Nisan, 1991, pp. 122–127). Copts have held a few positions in Mubarak's cabinet, and there are many important Coptic businessmen (*The Economist,* 2000, p. 41).

Socially, however, Muslims and Copts have drawn apart. As Egypt's Muslims become more focused on their religious identity so, too, have Christians. In the past, in poor neighborhoods, Christian and Muslim women knew each other as neighbors, watched one another's children, and attended one another's weddings and funerals. Christians worry that their children will want to marry Muslims. (Early, 1993, p. 73). This kind of relaxed socializing is less common now. Just as Muslim life has come to revolve more around the mosque, so have Christian churches become more active, running their own voluntary organizations, schools, and health facilities (Yount, 2004, p. 1069). Copts and Muslims are more likely to settle in separate parts of new communities and to avoid each other. Disputes between individual Muslims and Christians spiral into community-wide conflict, even violence (Slackman, 2008b, p. A5).

SOCIAL CHANGE

Egypt today is in an unstable situation. The society is simmering with problems and pressures for change, but so far, as of 2008, the government has managed to keep the lid on. Everyone wants to know: How long can this go on? Power is concentrated in the hands of President Mubarak, and he is getting old. Economic change is raising expectations that go unsatisfied for many people. Population growth is outpacing the ability of the economy to create jobs. Intensified interest in Islam is reshaping Egyptian culture. Movements for social change express all the discontents and aspirations in Egyptian society. And all of this is taking place within the context of globalization.

Globalization and Social Change

As we assess the impact of globalization and Egyptians' responses to it, let's start with two words of caution: Don't assume that globalization is something new in Egypt, and don't assume that globalization always involves Western influence.

You learned earlier in this chapter that Egypt was never isolated from the world. Since the 10th century, trade, diplomacy, and pilgrimage have connected Egypt with North Africa, southern Europe, Central Asia, and India. But it is certain that modern transportation and communications have strengthened connections to other countries. Egyptians are more aware of Western cultures, but they are also more connected to the Muslim world and especially to the oil-producing countries like Saudi Arabia, Kuwait, and Libya (Ghannam, 2002, pp. 17–18).

Globalization and Daily Life

Ordinary Egyptians are more exposed than ever to influences from abroad. They interact with foreigners who are tourists or perhaps their employers. They see American movies and ads for Western products. But they also enjoy consumer goods brought home by their male relatives who work in Kuwait. Satellite television lets people watch Al Jazeera, instead of the old state-controlled Egyptian television stations. And Al Jazeera shows Egyptians events in Iraq and Palestine,

In this old quarter of Alexandria small apartments are stacked up the hillside. Residents have no clothes dryers so they hang their clothes out the windows to dry, but almost every apartment has a satellite dish. Television connects Egyptians to the world. They get their news from Al Jazeera (the Arab world's most popular TV news network) and their films from Hollywood. Even small Egyptian kids know Mel Gibson's name.

stimulating a closer identification with Muslims in other countries. When they watch the soccer World Cup, Egyptians support African and Arab teams, then any third-world team, then European teams with African players (*The Economist,* 2005, p. 54; Ghannam, 2002, pp. 18–20).

As Farha Ghannam (2002) argues, for Egyptians globalization is not "Americanization" or "McDonaldization" (p. 19). Egyptians don't feel they have to choose between Western products and activities that they prize and their Muslim identities. Instead, they create new identities and practices that fuse the two. For example, a new genre of children's magazines, published in Egypt, Kuwait, Saudi Arabia, and other Middle Eastern countries, has grown very popular with middle-class parents and those who aspire to the middle class. These magazines help children construct a broader Islamic identity, with articles about Islamic values and Islamic history around the world. But they also teach familiarity with Western taste, technology, and knowledge of the status brand names that is part of middle-class culture in Egypt (Peterson, 2005, pp. 184–185). Here's another example: Even as more and more people in Egypt observe the Ramadan fast, the holiday is changing from a purely religious celebration to more of a commercialized event. Ramadan is an advertising blockbuster on television, with some brands spending half their advertising budget during the month. Shopping malls close during the afternoon when people nap during Ramadan, but they stay open until 2:00 a.m. when they are thronged with celebrating shoppers (Fattah, 2005, pp. A1, A10).

Global Economic Change and Government Policy

For years now, the Mubarak government has been working to make Egypt more connected to the global economy. In the 1990s, under pressure from the International Monetary Fund, and with the help of U.S. foreign aid and debt relief, the government began to privatize the economy. There are now privately owned steel companies, appliance manufacturers, telecommunications companies, aircraft manufacturers, and lots of construction businesses. To attract more tourists and increase exports, the government devalued Egypt's currency in 2003. That helped the economy grow, but it made imported goods more expensive for Egyptians. The price of basic foods went up between 33 and 109% (*The Economist,* 2004a, pp. 47–48; 2004b, p. 92).

Globalization and Agriculture

The government wants to connect Egypt's agriculture with the global economy too. That means modern mechanized cultivation of commercial crops like fruit, cotton, and rice for export. But modernizing agriculture requires phasing out **subsistence agriculture,** in which peasant families grow food for their own consumption, usually on tiny plots of land, using lots of labor but little machinery. To do this, the government has substantially weakened the land reform laws instituted by Nasser and allowed foreign businesses to buy up huge tracts of fertile land (Mitchell, 1991, pp. 22–23).

Changes in agriculture have created a **food gap** in Egypt. Production is up: Egypt's farmers produce more and more grain. Production is even running ahead of population growth. Nevertheless, the government must import grain to feed the poor. In fact, half of all wheat sold in Egypt is now imported. Increasingly, wheat and corn

TABLE 4.6 Dependence on Food Imports

Despite substantial agricultural production, Egypt and Mexico import very large amounts of basic grains to feed their populations. Even so, millions are undernourished.

	Mexico: Tons of Corn Imported	Egypt: Tons of Wheat Imported
1970	760,900	1,185,860
2003	5,858,070	4,064,660
Increase	770%	343%
Number undernourished	5,300,000	2,600,000

Sources: Food and Agriculture Organization, *Food Balance Sheets,* n.d., http://faostat.fao.org/site/502/default.aspx; Food and Agriculture Organization, *Food Security Statistics,* n.d., http://www.fao.org/faostat/foodsecurity/index_en.htm.

are used as animal feeds to raise cattle for beef sold to those affluent Egyptians who have benefited from the globalizing economy. Also, foreign companies grow thousands of acres of cotton and sugar for export. Obviously, this also reduces domestic food production in Egypt (Metz, 1991, p. 358; Mitchell, 1991, p. 21). See Table 4.6.

Population Change

Why does Egypt need to become more connected to the global economy? Egypt faces a **demographic** problem: Population is increasing and there are more and more young people. How can Egypt feed, house, and find jobs for its growing numbers? Mubarak has gambled on economic globalization as the solution. In 1947 there were 19 million Egyptians; by 1976 there were nearly 37 million; and by 2000 there were 68 million. Although Egypt's population is not expected to increase as rapidly in the future, substantial growth is still expected. By some estimates, Egypt will have nearly 105 million people by 2025 (Omran & Roudi, 1993, p. 4).

The Demographic Transition

Egypt, like many other developing countries, is in the midst of very important changes in population patterns. **Demographers** (the scientists who study population) call these changes a **demographic transition.** Before 1950, Egypt had a high birthrate, but there was a high death rate too. Many babies failed to survive to adulthood and consequently population growth was slow. Then, after 1950, there was a big change. Death rates fell rapidly: In 1950, 24 people out of every 1,000 Egyptians died every year; by 1990, only 8 out of every 1,000 died yearly. This striking drop in death rates started when the Nasser government embarked on a huge campaign to make free or low-cost health care available to all Egyptians. Between 1952 and 1976 government expenditure on public health increased 500%. At the same time, however, birthrates stayed high, so in consequence, population soared. Recently Egypt has entered another stage in the demographic transition: Birthrates are falling, while death rates remain low. As a result, the rate at which its population is growing has slowed. In 1950 the birthrate in Egypt was 48 births yearly for every

1,000 Egyptians, but by 1990 the birthrate had fallen to 33 per 1,000 yearly. Birthrates continue to fall, but so far the rates are still high enough to keep population expanding (Hooglund, 1991, pp. 124, 148–152; Omran & Roudi, 1993, p. 4). Also, there is the **momentum factor.** Each family is having fewer children, but there are already so many more families that population growth continues at a rapid rate. See Table 4.7.

Urbanization and Population Growth

Better health care brought down death rates. What changes made birthrates fall? One critical change has been the migration of people from the countryside to the cities and their involvement in an urban economy. In 1950 only one Egyptian in three lived in an urban area, but by 1990 half of all Egyptians lived in cities. In 1992 rural women had an average of five children each, but urban women had only three. In the cities, women in the paid labor force are likely to have fewer children. Also, city families see that educated children earn more than those who are barely literate. If families think it likely that they will be able to send their children to school, then it pays to have fewer children so they will be able to afford to educate them. Conversely, poor families that know education is out of the question will find it more rational to have many children, all of whom can work and bring in some income to help the families.

Population Policy

Since 1966 Egypt's government has encouraged family planning and the use of contraceptives to limit population increase. The government has created a national network of family planning clinics, conducted an extensive media campaign in

TABLE 4.7 Population Momentum

Births—and the total population—rise despite a fall in the number of births per woman. The rising number of births reflects the growing number of women in the childbearing years.

	Number of Women in the Childbearing Years 15–49	Number of Births	Average Number of Births to a Woman in Her Childbearing Years[*]	Total Population
Egypt				
1960	6,200,000	1,200,000	6.6	27,000,000
1980	9,800,000	1,700,000	5.5	43,000,000
2000	15,800,000	1,800,000	3.2	68,000,000
Mexico				
1960	13,900,000	1,800,000	6.7	56,000,000
1980	16,000,000	2,400,000	4.7	69,000,000
2000	20,800,000	2,500,000	3.5	85,000,000

[*]Total fertility rate.

Source: International Data Base, United States Census, http://www.census.gov/ipc/www/idbsprd.html.

favor of small families, and made contraceptives widely available. These efforts have not been as successful as the government hoped: Egyptians tend to distrust anything that their government promotes. Nevertheless, it is clear that programs to reduce family size have met with some success. By 1992 almost half of all married Egyptian women reported that they used a modern contraceptive method such as the diaphragm or the intrauterine device. The same survey also reported that 67% of married women wanted no more children (Omran & Roudi, 1993, p. 13).

Cultural Change

You probably observe in your own society that young people are the source of new trends, new fashions, and new ideas in art and music. Egypt is plentifully supplied with young people. What kind of culture are they creating? Cultural trends in Egypt are varied and interesting, but it is important that you recognize that almost all cultural innovation takes place within the context of Islam. Fashion makes this clear. Some young women have moved from the hijab to the khimar and then on to the black niqab. Some add gloves and even a veil that hides their eyes. But at the same time, others sew sequins on their colorful hijabs and along with the hijab they wear skinny jeans and fitted blouses.

Some young Egyptians have become involved with conservative Wahabi Islam. They want to purify Islam of modern influences and return it to an imagined past golden age of the Prophet and the early caliphs, when society was governed entirely by Sharia. They want to resegregate men and women, put everyone in more conservative Muslim dress, get rid of suggestive ads, television, movies, pop music, and elaborate weddings. They are very willing, however, to use modern media to spread their message via Web sites, cassette tapes, and DVDs.

But Islam is a broad movement; it encompasses a wide range of innovation. It also includes the privileged young woman who adopts a fashionable hijab and watches the sermons of Amr Khaled, the most popular televangelist in Egypt and beyond. Khaled sells more cassette tapes than Egypt's top pop singers (*The Economist*, 2002, pp. 44–46). Khaled, a former accountant, preaches a moderate, personal form of Islam. He has no beard and wears a suit. According to sociologist Asef Bayat, Khaled "articulates a marriage of faith and fun." He is compassionate and colloquial, not grim and moralizing like traditional preachers, and he talks about the ethics of everyday life: wearing hijab, dressing neatly, not smoking, improving relationships. When he preaches, his audience cries and laughs and feels an emotional release (Bayat, 2003).

Movements for Social Change

You may think of the Egyptian government, like many other Middle Eastern governments, as the still eye of the storm. In 2007, after 26 years in power, Hosni Mubarak, at age 76, remained president, keeping his authoritarian regime frozen in place, and crushing any real opposition. Mubarak has ruled the whole time under emergency decrees that suspend the constitution and allow the government to ban opposition parties, restrict freedom of the press and freedom of speech, and try political prisoners before harsh emergency security courts. Complex election rules make vote-rigging easy, and in a pinch the government just calls in the police and shuts down the polls.

But demands for democracy in Egypt are growing, not least because the government functions so badly, unable to provide even clean water and sewers to its people. Banks, schools, health care, and legal systems are all in a state of neglect. In 2005 the government made some gestures in the direction of permitting contested elections, but rapidly reversed course when opponents were elected to parliament.

The Islamist Movement

The largest and most influential **social movement** in Egypt today is the Muslim Brotherhood. It was first organized in 1928 by Hassan al-Banna, a schoolteacher who dreamed of bringing back the golden age of the caliphate. The early Brotherhood had a secret paramilitary wing that tried unsuccessfully to assassinate President Nasser. Nasser executed the Brotherhood leadership, jailed thousands of members, and banned the organization in 1954. In the 1970s, Sadat released many Brotherhood leaders and allowed the organization to operate and recruit. The Brotherhood found many new members among university students and young professionals in the 1980s. It organized within professional associations and universities, taking over many groups in internal elections. Islamists gained important positions in mass media, education, and community social services. As Saad Edin Ibrahim puts it, the Islamists "steadily infiltrate(d) Egypt's public space" (Ibrahim, 2002, p. 71). Now the Muslim Brotherhood insists it has renounced violence and will work for an Islamic state by peaceful, legal means in Egypt, though it approves violence against Israel in Palestine. The leadership includes many respectable professional men who are willing to work with secular groups to achieve democracy and who seem to have no wish to institute the most repressive parts of Sharia, like stoning of adulterers. One leader, Abdul Fotouh, is a doctor and university professor. "In general," he says, "I don't find the western way of life at odds with Islam. At the end of the day, we have a common set of humanist values: justice, freedom, human rights and democracy" (*The Economist,* 2003, p. 7; Traub, 2007, p. 48).

In Egypt, the Muslim Brotherhood is the leading organization of **political Islam.** Its goal is to bring about an Islamist state, a just society based on Sharia. Under Islamic rule, the Islamists promise there will be an end to corruption, a more equal society, and a society that will prosper because it is god fearing and moral. Islamic rule also promises to moderate the harsh inequalities of capitalism, by forbidding speculation and loan sharking, enforcing charity, and requiring the wealthy to invest their money productively, creating jobs for others and services for the community. Many Muslims see in Islamic fundamentalism the hope of "something uniquely Islamic between capitalism and socialism that will marry private enterprise with social justice and a sense of family and community" (Smith, 1994, pp. 85–88).

It is important to understand that the appeal of political Islam is not solely ideo-logical. Islamist ideas are communicated in a rewarding social context. Particularly in the newly settled neighborhoods on the outskirts of Cairo, the Brotherhood has established a network of social groups that anchors residents' lives and institutions that give people concrete help. It sees Islamic reform proceeding from the bottom up: the individual, then the family, the neighborhood, and finally the whole society, rather than through a direct attack on the government. One of Carrie Wickham's informants told her that the problem with jihadis "is that they are in a rush. They have their eyes on the end, but they don't attempt to find the proper means. While they are prepared to use force, we stress the means of upbringing and persuasion" (Wickham, 2002, pp. 127, 129–130).

A very important benefit of Islamist life is that people help each other through networks formed in the mosque. If you need to find an apartment, find a job, get a visa, or find a spouse, mosque contacts are a wonderful resource. Also, the mosque provides access to Islamic institutions that parallel government institutions. There are jobs in Islamist publishing houses and Islamist-run health clinics. The mosque has charitable funds to distribute to the needy and provides subsidized day care and health care services. When a woman decides to adopt modest dress, the local Islamic circle provides the veil and dresses as a gift (Wickham, 2002, pp. 125, 153, 155).

Islamist groups run health clinics, schools, day care centers, and furniture factories to provide jobs to the unemployed. They sell meat at discount prices to the poor and give free books and tutoring to poor children. They help young pro-fessionals like doctors, dentists, and lawyers by giving them loans to set up clin-ics and offices and by underwriting health and life insurance policies. Members of the Muslim Brotherhood seem earnest and dedicated, and above all, honest, especially in contrast to Egypt's corrupt government (Hasan, 1995, pp. 60–63; Weaver, 1993, p. 82).

Nabeel's Story: The Sympathizer

Ever since he was a small boy, Nabeel had loved cars, trucks, tanks, planes—things that moved. His parents despaired when he failed the high school entrance examination, but he thrived in the local technical and vocational school, learning to be a mechanic. On graduation, Nabeel looked for a job in Asyut, the city in Upper Egypt where he was raised, but there was little work to be found, only unskilled and poorly paid labor. Unhappy, but resigned to the need, Nabeel left to join one of his uncles in Cairo who promised to help him find work. Nabeel's uncle found a job for him repairing postal vans, but the pay was low and he had to make a large payment to the garage manager "for his help." After 3 years, Nabeel, now 22, owned only his clothes and a few books. His wages fed him, but let him save little. When his mother was ill, Nabeel sent most of his small savings to pay for doctors and medicines.

Cairo was not the bright promise it had once seemed. He was poor, had no future, and every day rich men and women drove past him in expensive cars and foreign clothes. Nabeel was shocked by the women in Cairo; they walked the street uncovered and immodest. Bared bosoms were displayed on every movie poster! It was all part of the influence of the afrangi—the Westernized Egyptians who thought and acted as foreigners, not Egyptians, and not Muslims.

Later that year, Nabeel's mother came to visit him in Cairo and he took her to a free health clinic run by the Muslim Brotherhood. There were dedicated young doctors there who took their work seriously. The doctor really listened to Nabeel's mother and she was able to diagnose her breathing problems and get the asthma under control. Nabeel was overjoyed, but he was also furious at the government clinics that had made his mother wait and wait, then hadn't helped her. Nabeel listened to sermons by imams who sympathized with al Jihad. They called for an Islamic Egypt where the government would care about ordinary Egyptians and there would be jobs and decent wages for all. "Perhaps," thought Nabeel, "this is the path we need to follow."

Electoral Gains and Losses.   Officially, the Muslim Brotherhood is still an illegal organization in Egypt, not a legal political party, and it is not permitted to run candidates in elections. Instead, the Brotherhood runs its candidates as independents. In the freer-than-usual 2005 parliamentary election, 88 of these independents were elected (out of 454 seats total), despite government efforts to shut down the polls and beat up and arrest activists. The Brotherhood did not run candidates in all districts, fearing that if it swept the election the government would retaliate with mass jailings and killings. The Brotherhood block afterward impressed Egyptians by taking their parliamentary role seriously (unlike ruling party representatives). Its members showed up, formed coalitions with other opposition parties, and created committees and seminars to make parliament into "a real legislative body." Frightened, Mubarak's government launched a campaign of mass arrests of Brotherhood leaders and financiers, also freezing $2 billion in Brotherhood assets (Traub, 2007, pp. 46–47).

Jihadi Islam

Jihadi social movements are groups willing to use terrorism and revolution to achieve an Islamic state. Of course, jihadi Islam gets the most attention in the West, but in Egypt today, jihadi movements are just about nonexistent. This wasn't always so. Sayyid Qtub, one of the intellectual founders of Islamic terrorism, was Egyptian, and during the 1980s and 1990s some Egyptian students came under the influence of his ideas. They were drawn into two radical offshoots of the Muslim Brotherhood, Gama'a al-Islamiyya and Islamic Jihad. In the 1990s, these groups also attracted followers in the poor squatter settlements of Cairo and in rural towns. Jihad and Gama'a were antimodern in philosophy and jihadist in strategy. They were willing to use violence and terrorism to challenge the government and redefine the norms of Egyptian society (Ibrahim, S., 2002, p. 69).

In the 1990s, Gama'a and Jihad began to assert their power. In poor neighborhoods dominated by Gama'a, groups of young male militants armed with knives and guns went about enforcing Sharia (Islamic law), as their religious leaders, their *sheiks* defined it. They burned video shops selling tapes they considered immoral—tapes that showed men and women touching or that seemed insulting to Islam. They burned the office of the biggest billboard manufacturing company, which puts up revealing pictures of popular Egyptian actresses (Dawoud, 1999, p. 1). They burned churches and attacked Copts and tourists.

The militants also mounted a powerful attack on Egypt's secular intellectuals, accusing certain writers of heresy and apostasy, crimes punishable by death under Sharia. It began in 1992 with the assassination of Farag Foda, a well-known author who wrote as a Muslim, but criticized the fundamentalists and rebutted their claim to know the only true Islam. Then in 1997 came the infamous massacre of tourists visiting the temples at Luxor (Ajami, 1998, pp. 205–221; Miller, 1998, pp. B7, B9).

Starting in 1992, the Mubarak government responded by ruthlessly hunting down members of Gama'a and Jihad. Every terrorist attack was followed by immediate arrests, summary convictions, and executions. The government shut down mosques where radicals preached, arrested preachers, jailed and tortured Islamists, invaded activist neighborhoods, and threatened or arrested Islamists' relatives. The repression was bloody and thorough. By the end of the 1990s, revolutionary Islam had been militarily defeated in Egypt. Egyptian terrorists decided that they could only conduct their warfare abroad, where some individuals helped organize Al Qaeda.

Movements for Democracy

Secular opposition parties have a long history in Egypt, but have never held power. Recently, several new secular pro-democracy parties have been organized. They are small and brutally repressed by the Mubarak government, but they are significant as a secular opposition. These parties contribute to the general atmosphere of public frustration and anger with Mubarak and his ruling National Democratic Party (NDP). In 2005, Ayman Nour, the leader of the Tommorow Party, was allowed to challenge Hosni Mubarak for the presidency. He received 7% of the vote and was promptly jailed on trumped-up charges. Another pro-democracy party, called Kifaya (Enough!), boldly risks street demonstrations.

What will happen to Egypt in the near future? Most people are increasingly pious, but against terrorism. However, they find life harder and harder and their personal situations more precarious. The government is controlled by an aging autocrat and his bureaucracy. It appears that Mubarak is grooming his son Gamal to eventually succeed him. Gamal is younger and more modern. He certainly has no commitment to Islamism, and probably not to democracy either. The United States is responsible in large part for keeping the Mubarak government in power by giving it $2 billion a year in foreign aid and selling it arms, fearing that a successor government would not tolerate Israel as Mubarak has (Slackman, 2007f, p. A4). If democratic elections were ever held in Egypt, it is clear that Mubarak would be replaced by the Muslim Brotherhood. What would it mean to Egypt to have an Islamist government? Would it be like Turkey, where an Islamist government has remained resolutely democratic and secular? Or like Afghanistan, where the Taliban instituted a puritanical, backward-looking regime? Your authors would guess Turkey, simply because the followers of the Muslim Brotherhood are so heavily educated, middle class, and professional. Do you think it would be worth the risk to allow real democratic elections? Or is any regime, however autocratic, better than an Islamist regime?

Thinking Sociologically

1. How do Islamic norms shape daily life in Egypt?
2. What are the norms for "modest dress" in your society?
3. How has modernization in the Egyptian education system and economy changed the roles women play? How has the religious revival changed Egyptian women's roles?
4. Is it ethnocentric to condemn female genital cutting?
5. What role conflicts do men in your society experience? What strategies do men pursue to resolve them?
6. Compare the power of women and men in Egyptian families. What power and influence do women have? How about in your own society?
7. Discuss the importance of work in the informal sector and work abroad for Egyptians and Mexicans. Is there an informal sector in your society? Who works in it?
8. Is the social stratification system in Egypt becoming more open or more closed? How about the stratification system in your society?
9. Based on what you have read in this chapter, do you think the Islamist movement in Egypt will become stronger or weaker in the next few years?
10. In what ways has the experience of colonization shaped the cultures of Egypt and Mexico? How has it affected attitudes toward the West?

For Further Reading

Abdo, G. (2000). *No God but God: Egypt and the triumph of Islam.* New York: Oxford University Press.

Ahmed, L. (1992). *Women and gender in Islam.* New Haven, CT: Yale University Press.

Armstrong, K. (2000). *Islam: A short history.* New York: Modern Library.

Fernea, E. W. (1998). *In Search of Islamic feminism.* New York: Doubleday, 1998.

Fernea, E. W., & Fernea, R. A. (1997). *The Arab world, forty years of change.* New York: Anchor.

Fluehr-Lobban, C. (1994). *Islamic society in practice.* Gainesville: University Press of Florida.

Ghannam, F. (2002). *Remaking the modern: Space, relocation, and the politics of identity in a global Cairo.* Berkeley: University of California Press.

Haddad, Y. Y., & Esposito, J. (Eds.). (1998). *Islam, gender and social change.* New York: Oxford University Press.

Ibrahim, S. E. (2002). *Egypt, Islam and democracy: Critical essays.* Cairo, Egypt: American University in Cairo Press.

Lippman, T. (1990). *Understanding Islam: An introduction to the Muslim world.* New York: Penguin.

Murphy, C., (2002). *Passion for Islam: The Egyptian experience.* New York: Scribner.

Singerman, D., & Hoodfar, H. (Eds.). (1996). *Development, change, and gender in Cairo: A view from the household.* Bloomington: Indiana University Press.

Wickham, C. R. (2002). *Mobilizing Islam: Religion, activism and political change in Egypt.* New York: Columbia University Press.

Bibliography

Abdelhadi, M. (2006, November 1). Cairo street crowds target women. *BBC News.* Retrieved from http://news.bbc.co.uk/2/hi/middle_east/6106500.stm

Abdo, G. (2000). *No God but God: Egypt and the triumph of Islam.* New York: Oxford University Press.

Ahmed, L. (1992). *Women and gender in Islam.* New Haven, CT: Yale University Press.

Ajami, F. (1998). *The dream palace of the Arabs: A generation's odyssey.* New York: Pantheon Books.

American University in Cairo Social Research Center. (2001). *Economic participation of women in Egypt.* Retrieved from http://www.aucegypt.edu/src/wsite1/index.htm

Barakat, H. (1993). *The Arab world: Society, culture and state.* Berkeley: University of California Press.

Bassiouni, M. (1989). *An introduction to Islam.* Chicago: Rand McNally.

Bayat, A. (1997, June). Cairo's poor: Dilemmas of survival and solidarity. *Middle East Research and Information Project.* Retrieved from http://www.merip.org

Bayat, A. (2003, May 22–28). Faith and fun: Can one have it all? *Al-Ahram Weekly On-Line.* Retrieved from http://weekly.ahram.org.eg/2003/639/fel.htm

Benin, J. (1998). *The dispersion of Egyptian Jewry: Culture, politics and the formation of the modern diaspora.* Berkeley: University of California Press.

Campo, J. E. (1991). *The other side of paradise: Explorations into the religious meanings of domestic space in Islam.* Columbia: University of South Carolina Press.

Crossette, B. (1999, January 18). Senegal bans genital cutting of girls. *The New York Times,* p. A10.

Daniszewski, J. (1997, June 1). Disabling acid attacks on women are on the rise in Egypt. *Los Angeles Times,* p. A09.

Dawoud, K. (1999, March 11–17). Militant video burners get 5 to 15. *Al-Ahram Weekly On-line,* no. 420. Retrieved from http://www.ahram.org.eg/weekly/1999/420/eg11.htm

Del Frate, A. A. (1998). Victims of crimes in developing countries (Publication No. 57). United Nations Retrieved from the Interregional Crime and Justice Research Institute Web site: http://www.unicri.it/cvs/publications/index_pub.htm

Demographic and health surveys. (n.d.). Retrieved from the STATcompiler database, http://www.statcompiler.com

Donner, F. (1999). Muhammad and the caliphate. In J. Esposito (Ed.), *The Oxford history of Islam* (pp. 1–62). New York: Oxford University Press.

Early, E. (1993). *Baladi women of Cairo: Playing with an egg and a stone.* Boulder, CO: Lynne Rienner.

The Economist. (1998, March 20). A survey of Egypt: New and old, pp. 1–18.

The Economist. (2000, January 8). Egypt's vulnerable Copts, p. 41.

The Economist. (2002, June 29). Egypt's Islamists: Kinder, gentler Islam, pp. 44, 46.

The Economist. (2003, September 13). In the name of Islam (special survey), pp. 3–16.

The Economist. (2004a, July 17). Egypt: New surgeon, same old scalpels, pp. 47–48.

The Economist. (2004b, July 24). Emerging market indicators, p. 92.

The Economist. (2005, December 10). Not yet a democracy, p. 54

The Economist. (2007a, March 31). Reform to preserve, p. 57.

The Economist. (2007b, April 14). Egypt: Bloggers may be the real opposition, p. 54.

The Economist. (2007c, July 7). A little less purity goes a long way, p. 47.

The Economist. (2007d, August 11). A summer of discontents, p. 40.

The Economist. (2007e, September 1). Bashing the Muslim brothers, pp. 38, 44.

El Fiqi, M. (1999, November 11–17). Borrowing in the balance. *Al-Ahram Weekly On-Line.* Retrieved from http://web1.ahram.org.eg/weekly/1999/455/ec3.htm

El-Gawhary, K. (1994, November–December). An interview with Heba Ra'uf Ezzat. *Middle East report.*

El-Laithy, H. Lokshin, M., Banerji, A. (2003, June). *Poverty and economic growth in Egypt, 1995–2000* (World Bank Policy Research Working Paper 3068).

El-Rashidi, Y. (2002, October 3–9). Young and hip, veil optional. *Al-Ahram Weekly On-Line.* Retrieved from http://www.ahram.org.eg/weekly/2002/606/li2htm

Esposito, J. (1991). *Islam: The straight path.* New York: Oxford University Press.

Fakhouri, H. (1972). *Kafr El-Elow: An Egyptian Village in Transition.* New York: Henry Holt.

Fattah, H. M. (2005, October 12). Ramadan ritual: Fast daily, pray, head to the mall. *The New York Times,* pp. A1, A10.

Fernea, E. W. (1998). *In search of Islamic feminism.* New York: Doubleday.

Fluehr-Lobban, C. (1994). *Islamic society in practice.* Gainesville: University Press of Florida.

Food and Agriculture Organization. (2004). *FAO statistical databases.* Retrieved from http://www.apps.fao.org/

Food and Agriculture Organization. (n.d.). *Food balance sheets.* Retrieved from http://faostat.fao.org/site/502/default.aspx

Food and Agriculture Organization. (n.d.). *Food security statistics.* Retrieved from http://www.fao.org/faostat/foodsecurity/index_en.htm

Food and Agriculture Organization. (2005/2006). *Statistical yearbook.* Retrieved from http://www.fao.org/statistics/yearbook

Friedman, T. (2003, January 8). After the storm. *The New York Times,* p. A23.

Ghannam, F. (2002). *Remaking the modern: Space, relocation, and the politics of identity in a global Cairo.* Berkeley: University of California Press.

Goldberg, J. (2001, October 8). Behind Mubarak. *The New Yorker,* pp. 48–55.

Hasan, S. (1995, October 25). My lost Egypt. *The New York Times Magazine,* pp. 60–63.

Hedges, C. (1993, October 4). As Egypt votes on Mubarak, he faces rising peril. *The New York Times,* p. A8.

Hedges, C. (1994, June 7). In bureaucrats' castle, everyone else is a beggar. *The New York Times,* p. A4.

Hoodfar, H. (1997, Summer). The impact of male migration on domestic budgeting: Egyptian women striving for an Islamic budgeting pattern. *Journal of Comparative Family Studies, 28*(2), 73–99.

Hooglund, E. (1991). The society and its environment. In H. Chapin Metz (Ed.), *Egypt: A country study* (5th ed.). Washington, DC: Federal Research Division, Library of Congress.

Ibrahim, S. E. (2002). *Egypt, Islam and Democracy: Critical Essays.* Cairo, Egypt: American University in Cairo Press.

Ibrahim, Y. (1995, August 17). The "tower of power:" Something to babble about. *The New York Times,* p. A4.

International Labor Organization. (n.d.). *Economically active population estimates and projections: 1950–2010.* Retrieved from http://laborsta.ilo.org/

International Labor Organization. (n.d.). *International labor migration statistics: 1970–2000.* Retrieved from http://laborsta.ilo.org

Jehl, D. (1996, March 6). Above the city's din, always the voice of Allah. *The New York Times,* p. A4.

Jehl, D. (1997, March 15). Killings erode Cairo's claim to "control" militants. *The New York Times,* p. A3.

Jehl, D. (1999, June 20). Arab honor's price: A woman's blood. *The New York Times,* pp. 1, 8.

Kamel, Y. & Mashhour, S. (2002, November 14–20). Jumping on the bandwagon more and more stars take the veil. *Cairo Times.*

Kassem, M. (2000). *In the guise of democracy: Governance in contemporary Egypt.* Ithaca, NY: Ithaca Press.

Kershaw, S. (2003, April 3). Cairo, once "the scene," cracks down on gays. *The New York Times,* p. A3.

Kishor, S. (1998). Women's empowerment and contraceptive use. In M. Mahran, F. H. El-Zanaty, & A. A. Way (Eds.), *Perspectives on the population and health situation in Egypt.* Cairo, Egypt, and Calverton, MD: National Population Council and Macro International.

Kurian, G. (Ed.). (1992). *Encyclopedia of the Third World* (Vol. 1). New York: Facts on File.

Lewis, B. (2002, January). What went wrong? *The Atlantic Monthly, 289*(1), 43–48.

Lippman, T. (1990). *Understanding Islam: An introduction to the Muslim world.* New York: Penguin.

MacLeod, A. (1993). *Accommodating protest: Working women, the new veiling and change in Cairo.* New York: Columbia University Press.

Menezes, G. (2003, September 25–October 1). Religious chic between beauty and modesty, fashion for hijabs multiplies. *Cairo Times.* Retrieved from http://cairotimes.com/

Mernissi, F. (2001). *Scheherazade goes west: Difference cultures, different harems.* New York: Pocket Books.

Metz, H. C. (1991). *Egypt: A Country Study* (5th ed.). Washington, DC: Federal Research Division, Library of Congress.

Middle East and North Africa Business Report Newsletter. (2004, October 31). Egyptian expatriates' remittances amount to almost $3 billion. Retrieved from http://www .menareport.com/story/TheNews.php3?sid=288013&lang=e&dir=mena

Miller, J. (1998, January 31). With freedom, Cairo intellectuals find new stress. *The New York Times,* pp. B7, B9.

Mitchell, T. (1991, March/April). America's Egypt: Discourse of the development industry. *Middle East Report,* 18–34.

Mule, P. & Barthel, D. (1992). The return to the veil: Individual autonomy versus social esteem. *Sociological Forum, 7*(2), 323–332.

Murphy, C. (2002). *Passion for Islam: The Egyptian experience.* New York: Scribner.

Nabeel, A., & Shryock, A. (Eds.). (2000). *Arab Detroit: From margin to mainstream.* Detroit: Wayne State University Press.

The New York Times. (2004, March 2). Egypt: Torture charged, p. A6.

The New York Times, (2007, November 6). Egypt: Police officers guilty of torture, p. A17.

The New York Times. (2008, July 6). Man-made hunger, p. WK9.

Nisan, M. (1991). *Minorities in the Middle East.* London: McFarland.

Omran, A., & Roudi, F. (1993, July). The Middle East population puzzle. *Population Bulletin, 48*(1), 1–39.

Peterson, M. A. (2005). The *Jinn* and the computer: Consumption and identity in Arabic children's magazines. *Childhood, 12*(2), 177–200.

Rodenbeck, M. (1992). Religion. In J. Rodenbeck (Ed.), *Cairo.* Singapore: APA Publications.

Rugh, A. (1984). *Family in contemporary Egypt.* Syracuse, NY: Syracuse University Press.

Sadat, J. (1987). *A woman of Egypt.* New York: Simon & Schuster.

Sherif, Y. (2004, March 12). Gays under attack in Egypt. *Middle East Times.* Retrieved from http://metimes.com/2K4/issue2004-11/eg/gays_under_attack.htm

Slackman, M. (2005, September 7). Lethal fire heightens Egyptians' anger at government. *The New York Times,* p. A3.

Slackman, M. (2006a, April 28). Melee in Cairo reveals stress in government. *The New York Times,* p. A4.

Slackman, M. (2006b, May 1). Egypt renews emergency detention law. *The New York Times,* p. A3.

Slackman, M. (2007a, March 1). In Arab hub, the poor are left to their fate. *The New York Times,* pp. A1, A4.

Slackman, M. (2007b, March 26). As Egypt votes on laws, cynicism rules the street. *The New York Times,* p. A11.

Slackman, M. (2007c, March 28). Charges of vote rigging as Egypt approves constitution changes. *The New York Times,* p. A8.

Slackman, M. (2007d, June 12). A compass that can clash with modern life. *The New York Times,* pp. A1, A10.

Slackman, M. (2007e, September 20). In Egypt, shielding girls from an old practice. *The New York Times,* pp. A1, A8.

Slackman, M. (2007f, October 16). On human rights, U.S. seems to give Egypt a pass. *The New York Times,* p. A4.

Slackman, M. (2007g, December 18). Fashion and faith meet, on foreheads of the pious. *The New York Times,* p. A4.

Slackman, M. (2008a, January 17). Egypt's problem and Its challenge: Bread corrupts. *The New York Times,* p. A4.

Slackman, M. (2008b, August 2). As tensions rise for Egypt's Christians, officials call clashes secular. *The New York Times,* p. A5.

Smith, P. A. (1994, March/April). Where capitalism is shaped by Islam. *Utne Reader,* 85–88.

Sullivan, D., & Abed-Kotob, S. (1999). *Islam in contemporary Egypt: Civil society versus the state.* Boulder, CO: Boulder Press.

Traub, J. (2007, April 29). Islamic democrats? *The New York Times Magazine,* pp. 44–49.

United Nations. (1990). *Demographic yearbook.* Retrieved from the UN Web site: http://unstats.un.org

United Nations. (1994). *United Nations surveys on crime trends and the operations of criminal justice systems* (Fourth Survey). Retrieved from http://www.unodc.org/unodc/en/crime_cicp_ surveys.html

United Nations. (2004a). *Demographic yearbook.* Retrieved from http://unstats.un.org/unsd/demographic/products/dyb/dyb2004.htm

United Nations. (2006/2007). *Human development indicators 2006/2007.* Retrieved from http://hdr.undp.org/en/statistics

United Nations. (2004b). *Human development report 2004.* Retrieved from http://hdr.undp.org/en/reports/global/hdr2004/

United Nations. (2007). *Human development report 2007.* Retrieved from http://hdr.undp.org/en/reports/

Vatikiotis, P. J. (1991). *The history of Egypt* (3rd ed.) Baltimore: Johns Hopkins University Press.

Weaver, M. A. (1993, April 12). The trail of the Sheikh. *The New Yorker,* 71–88.

Weaver, M. (1995, January 30). The novelist and the sheik. *The New Yorker,* pp. 52–69.

Wickham, C. R. (2002). *Mobilizing Islam: Religion, activism and political change in Egypt.* New York: Columbia University Press.

Wilson, S. (1998). *Culture shock: Egypt.* Portland, OR: Graphic Arts Center.

World Bank. (2004). *World development indicators 2004.* Retrieved from http://econ.worldbank.org/external/default/main?pagePK=64165259&theSitePK=469372&piPK=64165421&menuPK=64166093&entityID=000160016_20040608153404

Yount, K. M. (2004, March). Symbolic gender politics, religious group identity, and the decline in female genital cutting in Minya, Egypt. *Social Forces, 82*(3), 1063–1090.

Five hours east of Montreal and New York by air, less than an hour from London and Paris lies Berlin, the capital of a reunited Germany, one of the most prosperous countries on earth and the birthplace of Albert Einstein, Ludwig van Beethoven, and other figures who shaped Western civilization.

LOCATION: In the center of Europe. France, Belgium, and the Netherlands border Germany to the west; Denmark and the North Sea to the north; Poland and the Czech Republic to the east; and Austria and Switzerland to the south.

AREA: Germany covers 135,000 square miles—the size of California or Japan.

LAND: Lowlands in the north, highlands in the center, and a mountainous region in the south bordering the Alps.

CLIMATE: Temperate similar to the northeastern United States, Canada, or Japan.

POPULATION: In 2007 there were 82 million people; expected to decline to 79 million in 2050. Germany's population is aging: 17% are 65 or over.

INCOME: Germany is a wealthy industrial nation. In equivalent U.S. purchasing power per person GDP averaged $31, 390 in 2006.

EDUCATION: The average adult (25+) has completed almost 12 years of school.

RELIGION: Forty-two percent Protestant; 35% Catholic.

MINORITIES: Germany has a large immigrant population. In 2007 there were 10.6 million foreign residents in Germany—12.6% of the population. As many as 2.7 million Germans are of Turkish origin and more than 1 million are from the Balkans. Jewish population has grown to over 200,000.

CHAPTER FIVE

Germany: Diversity in a Modern Nation-State

INTRODUCTION

You probably take for granted that around the world people live in **nation-states**— "countries," like Germany, or Mexico, or Egypt, or Japan. Actually, however, nation-states are relatively new in the world's history. They are distinctly modern. **States** are territories ruled by some kind of government, based on a legal system, and some capacity to use force to back up government decisions. Think about the traditional San for a moment. Like other hunter-gatherers, they had a society, but not a state. They moved around a large area and didn't have clear boundaries separating themselves from others. They didn't have a government or a legal system, or a special group responsible for using physical compulsion to enforce the society's decisions. Before modern times, many states had unclear boundaries. Where in the desert did Egypt end and Sudan begin? For centuries, that wasn't clear and no one particularly cared.

It was not until the 18th century that real nation-states developed in Europe. States like Britain or France established fixed borders. Eventually, people living within the state began to identify with it, to see themselves as members of a national community, often as **citizens.** That was the beginning of **nationalism**—a sense of membership in a state, of pride, often expressed by national symbols and ideologies (Giddens, 1991, pp. 379–382).

If you think about the world today, you will see that nation-states are not something to take for granted. In the world's trouble-spots, nation-states are often fragile. You may hear talk about **failed states,** like Congo or Somalia, where there is nominally a government, but it lacks the power to enforce its laws and chaos reigns. Then there are weak states. Think of Pakistan: Does the government there really rule the "tribal areas" on the border of Afghanistan? Think of Iraq: The government sits in Baghdad, but it's not clear that it really has the power to govern the entire country. Also, it is questionable whether Iraq is really a nation. Do people there identify themselves with the nation of Iraq, or with their ethnic group, or their tribe, or their religious sect? In extreme cases, nations fragment bloodily into separate states along ethnic lines, as the former Yugoslavia split and is still splitting into Bosnia, Serbia, Croatia, Kosovo, and Montenegro.

GERMAN HISTORY: BORDERS AND PEOPLES

First of all, Germany was late becoming a nation-state, so its national history is briefer than that of Egypt or Japan. Germany didn't even exist as a separate nation until modern times. Nevertheless, Germany's history has been very eventful. It is studded with wars, treaties, monarchs, changes of borders, and successive governments and policies. We cannot begin to tell you the whole involved story in a sociology text. Instead we will focus on the nation-state and nationalism in German history, tracing changes in Germany's borders, major migrations that reshaped Germany's population, and the story of how nationalism developed in Germany.

Ingrid's Story: A Life in Germany

Ingrid H., a retired nurse, gave this description of her life in an oral history interview. In many ways Ingrid's life mirrors the changes that have transformed Germany and the Germans since 1945.

"I'm an immigrant. I've immigrated twice although I never left Germany. I fled my childhood home in Stettin in fear of the Red Army in 1945 and found myself in East Germany—the German Democratic Republic. In 1989 East Germany collapsed and I found myself in an entirely new country—the Federal Republic of Germany. Unlike immigrants from Turkey or Bosnia I can't go home again, even to visit. Stettin is now part of Poland, not Germany. The language in the streets is different; even the streets are different. The buildings and places I knew were destroyed during the war. My old home is buried under an apartment building. It's even more difficult to return to East Germany. It's not there anymore. It ceased to exist over a decade ago. When I walk the streets near my old home in East Berlin I see that even the physical remains of the past are being destroyed and replaced by new museums, fast-food restaurants, and stores.

"We fled Stettin on foot in fear for our lives and when order was restored we found ourselves in a culture so different from the one we had lived in that we might as well have moved to the moon. My father was a very prosperous businessman. We had a huge home and servants. People looked up to us. In East Germany all the values we had lived by were turned upside down. No one was better than anyone else. Capitalists like my father were exploiters—the enemy of the workers. In East Germany they spoke German, but that was about the only thing they had in common with prewar Germany. I started cleaning bedpans in 1947 and I eventually was admitted to a nursing program and became a skilled pediatric nurse in East Berlin. I enjoyed my work. I married, had a son and a daughter, and looked forward to the future. Things didn't turn out, though. In 1991 our clinic was closed and I was offered a position in a West German clinic. At first I thought, 'this is too much. . . . I'll retire,' but then I thought, 'you're just 61; what will you do for the rest of your life?' So I took the job.

"Again I found myself in a world I didn't know and didn't like. When my West German colleagues saw my East German car, my Trabant, they said, 'Why don't you get rid of that dreck and buy a German car.' My clinic boss told me, 'Now you'll have to learn to use German medicines.' German car! German medicines! Who do you think made my Trabant? Elves? What was I doing in the clinic for 30 years if not German medicine? I was angry and disgusted and I still feel that way today. My East Berlin clinic was world famous. Before the wall fell my West German boss worked in a dinky clinic in some tiny village. Now he thinks he knows everything and I know nothing.

"My grandson reads a lot of science fiction. Sometimes the stories are about time machines. A time machine would be the only way to go back home for me."

Changing Borders: What Is Germany?

Germany was not fully united as a nation-state until 1871. Before that, Germany experienced many centuries when periods of national unification alternated with fragmentation into small kingdoms. In the 1st and 2nd centuries BC, Germanic tribes settled the area that is now modern Germany, battling the Romans, and after the collapse of the Roman Empire they spread over northern Italy, Britain, and France. In early medieval times (AD 800) Charlemagne unified these peoples in an empire known in Germany as the First *Reich* (or empire) and elsewhere as the Holy Roman Empire. Charlemagne's empire was much larger than modern Germany, including much of present-day Europe. Its people did not think of themselves as "Germans." The word didn't even exist until the 15th century and wasn't widely used until a century after that. People thought of themselves as Thuringians, Bavarians, Alemanni, Saxons, and so on—"peoples" who were not ethnic groups, but simply the inhabitants of Charlemagne's old administrative districts. There was no common German language. When people from different regions needed to talk they spoke Latin or West Frankish, the language that later became French (Schulze, 1998, pp. 15–17).

During the Middle Ages, as the Holy Roman Empire disintegrated, it broke down into a variety of political entities: principalities, duchies, bishoprics, counties, imperial cities, and land controlled by religious orders. There were 1,600 separate territories and cities in all in the land that was to become Germany, including large states such as the duchies of Bavaria and Wurtemberg, principalities like Saxon and Hesse, free cities like Nuremburg, and bishoprics like the cities of Cologne and Trier (Schulze, 1998, pp. 25, 33, 36).

War and Boundaries

If you look at a map you will see that Germany today occupies a strategic location in the heart of Europe. You could say that Germany was geographically fated to be a battleground. Centuries of warfare shifted political boundaries back and forth. In the 17th century the Thirty Years War devastated Germany. Battles, famine, and the plague reduced German population from 17 million to 10 million. The peace treaty that ended the war established a system of nation-states, including Sweden, Great Britain, France, and Russia, that recognized one another's sovereignty. But Germany remained fragmented. Prussia emerged, unified from smaller political fragments, and West Pomerania and Bremen became part of Sweden. France took Metz, Verdun, and Alsace (Schulze, 1998, pp. 64, 67).

In the 18th century, Austria, Prussia, Bavaria, Saxony, and Wurtemberg all became independent states. People began to debate: Should all the smaller German territories form a third bloc, alongside Austria and Prussia? Or should they join Prussia? Could a "greater Germany" unite Austria, Prussia, and all the smaller states? In 1815, after Napoleon's defeat, the Congress of Vienna established the

German Confederation, a loose alliance of 39 states and cities (including Denmark) headed by Austria, under Prince Metternich as chancellor. Then, after the Franco-Prussian War, in 1871, Austria was ejected from Germany and 22 smaller and middle-sized states formed a federal state, a Second Reich, dominated by Prussia, under King Wilhelm I and his prime minister, Otto von Bismarck. Germany gained back Alsace and Lorraine from France.

The World Wars

Imperial ambitions for military might and global political power led Germany into World War I in 1914, a war the nation expected to win within months. When, after 4 grueling years of trench warfare, Germany finally conceded defeat, it was humiliated by the loss of 20% of its territory, all of its colonies, and much of its coal, iron, and agricultural production. But Germany remained one state through the Weimar Republic and Hitler's Third Reich. Hitler attempted to create a "greater Germany" by absorbing or conquering Austria, Poland, Russia, and much of the rest of Europe. When he failed, and Germany was defeated at the end of World War II in 1945, the country was divided into two separate states: West Germany (the Federal Republic of Germany, or FRG) under Allied domination, and East Germany (the German Democratic Republic, or GDR) dominated by the Soviet Union. Germany also lost territory to Poland, Czechoslovakia, and Hungary, shrinking to its smallest size since the Middle Ages.

Germany Today

There is just one final chapter in our story: In 1990, the two halves of Germany—East and West—were rejoined, the GDR merging into the Federal Republic. Or perhaps it is not a final chapter. Germany is now an important part of the European Union. Perhaps in the future "Germany" will be seen as just a brief historical phase on the way to the unification of Europe.

Changing Population: Who Is German?

Who is German? It won't surprise you to hear that when the borders of a nation keep shifting, it is difficult to define what people are part of that nation. Were Austrians German? How about Danes? How about Alsatians? In the early 19th century when German nationalism first developed, national feeling could not flow from attachment to a traditional territory, or from a shared history, language, and culture. Germans were a mixed population in the 19th century and became even more mixed in the 20th century. At the end of World War I, 10% of Germany's population was lost to the nation along with its lost territories. When Germany was defeated in World War II, millions of Germans were expelled from Poland and Czechoslovakia. Others fled from the advancing Russian army. There were 700,000 released survivors of concentration camps and 4.2 million people from all over Europe who had been forced laborers in Germany. Twelve million refugees, the largest migration in European history, joined 67 million residents of Germany (Schulze, 1998, pp. 287–288).

As Germany recovered from the devastation of World War II and became an economic power, it drew in millions of immigrants, recruited for industrial work. Fourteen million guestworkers came to Germany between 1955 and 1973, at first from Italy, from Greece, and then, during the 1960s and 1970s, mostly from Turkey. It sounds like a huge number of immigrants, but most actually returned home in the end. People claiming German ancestry continued to emigrate to Germany from the Soviet Union. In the 1990s and 2000s, refugees arrived from Bosnia and Kosovo, including about 50,000 gypsies. Amazingly, by 2007, Jewish immigrants to Germany had swelled the country's Jewish population to a size larger than it had been in 1939. And after reunification in 1990, millions of East Germans, Poles, and other eastern Europeans emigrated to western Germany (Green, 2001; Wood, 2005). Later in this chapter we will learn the stories of all these minority groups in German society. Now, however, we want to ask how Germany created a national identity in the midst of such demographic diversity. All nation-states require nationalism to hold them together, but the character of the nationalism, and their nation's symbols and myths, have great consequences for their society and history.

The Rise of Nationalism in Germany

Germany came late to nationalism. Though intellectuals began speculating about "Germanness" in the 18th century, national identity and patriotism did not spread widely until early in the 19th century. It happened quickly, between 1806 and 1815. Nationalism was the preserve of middle-class intellectuals until Napoleon invaded Germany and conquered Prussia. Spurred by the crisis, nationalism spread. From the start, German nationalism was defined in reaction to France. Everything French was condemned and Germans began to see their own national character as the opposite of the French. But Germany as a nation did not yet exist, and would not exist for another 50 years. Nationalism had to be more abstract than patriotic loyalty to a state.

Instead, people thought of the nation as the home of the German *Volk,* the people. New terms arose: *Volkgeist* (the spirit of the people), or *Nationalgeist,* which had the same meaning. Wilhelm von Humboldt wrote, "Other nations do not love their country in the same way as . . . we love Germany. Our devotion is maintained by some invisible force. . . . It is not so much affection for a particular land as a longing for German feeling and German spirit." This "German spirit" was an intellectual virtue, "a superior artistic sensibility and scientific spirit." German language and literature were superior; German culture "expressed humanity most fully," and for that reason Germany had a special destiny as the most perfect nation in the world (Greenfeld, 1993, pp. 305, 307, 363–368).

Racial Thinking

Soon German nationalists found a way to anchor these romantic ideals in something concrete. The German spirit was so superior, they argued, because it was based in pure German blood and "not bastardized by alien peoples," as Arndt wrote. Thus, very significantly, from the start, German nationalism was a racial identity, based on ideas of racial purity and racial superiority. The German Volk, the peasants, were superior because they were racially pure. The French, in contrast, were an odious "impure, shameless, undisciplined race." They were shallow and artificial chatterers. The Jews too represented "un-German" values, the values of materialism, trade and money-making; city values. Foreign invasion, in this way of thinking, threatened the sacred purity of the people, but war was desirable too; it was ennobling; it built national consciousness (Arndt, quoted in Greenfeld, 1993, pp. 368–371).

Once you know about Germany's future and the horrors of the Nazi period, reading about 19-century nationalism is chilling. We can see a glimpse of the future in it. But from a sociological point of view we can also understand its usefulness. Germany didn't exist as a nation-state. It was fragmented and inchoate. How could German people be brought to think of themselves as a group and even fight for their national identity? Sociologist William Graham Sumner (1906) first used the terms **in-group** and **out-group.** In-groups are groups individuals identify with and with which they feel at home. Out-groups stand in contrast. They are the groups to which individuals do not belong and with which they don't identify. As in-groups define others as outsiders they heighten their own members' sense of cohesion. A common enemy draws people together. In conflict, group boundaries tighten and **we-feeling** increases. Georg Simmel (1859–1918) said, "a state of conflict (with outsiders) pulls the group members . . . tightly together. . . . This is the reason why war with the outside is sometimes the last chance for a state ridden with inner antagonisms to overcome these antagonisms" (Simmel, quoted in Coser, 1956, p. 87). Germany needed Napoleon and the French invasion to become a nation-state and in future years it needed the Jews to maintain German solidarity.

GERMAN CULTURE

Because Germany was for so long divided into separate monarchies, there are still regional variations in customs and identity. The cultures of Prussia (in the north) and Bavaria (in the south) are distinct. Also, values were rather different in the former East Germany and the former West Germany. Nevertheless, we can easily single out certain enduring values and norms in German culture. Germans have long been known for their love of order, respect for authority, seriousness, hard work, and social responsibility. These are traditional German values that still animate Germans today.

Order

Germans prefer order in all aspects of their lives. Norms require promptness, tidiness, and cleanliness, careful conformity to the law, and a proper formality in relating to others. If you have a business appointment with a German executive you must get right down to business, because when your time is up, the manager will become impatient and soon send you on your way (Hall & Hall, 1990, pp. 35, 53, 83–84). Social small talk will not be appreciated. If you are late to a job interview, there is no way you can get the job, and if you are late to dinner, your hosts will be insulted and annoyed. Stores must close by 8 p.m. on Saturdays and are closed all day on Sundays. Sunday is supposed to be a day of rest. If you mow the lawn or use power tools or hang out laundry to dry, you will scandalize your neighbors (*The Economist,* 2000b, p. 44).

Germans also carefully order the space around them. Spending the day at the beach, West German families pile up sand as high as 4 feet in a wall around their blankets, defining their own private territories (Gannon, 1994, p. 75). In a business, the offices of different departments are separated by closed doors and the department chief carefully closes the door of his private office. It would be rude to pick up or move a chair in someone's home or office to make yourself more comfortable (Hall & Hall, 1990, pp. 40–41). In a German hotel, the maid arranges a foreigner's jumbled shoes in a neat row and lines up the toothbrushes.

Obedience

Germans have long seen it as their duty to obey the law and to submit to the authorities—government officials, bureaucrats, police officers, and judges who make and enforce the laws. Russian dictator Josef Stalin once said, "Revolutions can't happen in Germany, because you would have to step on the lawn." Neighborhoods have informal rules about when and where you can wash your car or put out

Impeccably engineered and maintained, the autobahn curves through the orderly, productive landscape of rural Germany. Despite Germany's deserved reputation as an advanced industrial nation, farming remains an important part of Germany's economy and culture.

the trash and when children are allowed to play noisily outdoors. People will reproach a neighbor whose windows are unwashed or whose lawn grows too high. Germany has complex recyling laws, which people patiently follow. They must sort their trash into four different color-coded bins, take wine bottles down to a special dumpster on the corner, and return jars and bottles to the supermarket (*The Economist,* 2006c, p. 51; Hall & Hall, 1990, p. 47; Landler, 2003a, p. A4).

Germans cross only when the light is green and let their dogs off the leash only in specially marked areas. Dogs, like people, are expected to obey and obedience schools for dogs are very popular. They teach dogs and their owners how to behave in public places like trains, shops, and restaurants. Dogs that complete the course successfully are given a diploma, the *Hundefuhrerschein I* (Cohen, 2000, p. A4).

While many other cultures rely on informal understandings, Germans like to make all the rules explicit. It is typically German to make thousands of detailed laws and regulations that people carefully obey to the letter. In each German state detailed laws specify how schools should operate: from the marking system to the types of punishments permitted. Businesses must conform with endless and growing legal regulations: health and safety laws, laws regulating competition, and laws specifying the structure of corporate boards and their membership.

Ulrich and Helga's Story: The Marriage Contract

Ulrich and Helga, after living together for a year, have decided to marry. Tonight they are sitting over glasses of wine with their friend Otto, a lawyer, to draw up a prenuptial agreement. "We agree to share domestic tasks equally," the document reads. "We will take turns in cooking, cleaning, and dishwashing, laundry, grocery shopping, and bill paying. We each agree to contribute 10% of our salaries monthly toward a fund for buying a house, to retain 10% for private use, and to place the rest in a joint bank account. We agree that each of us shall have the right to go out alone with male or female friends, but we pledge ourselves to sexual fidelity. We agree that if we have a child, Helga will stay at home for 6 years and, during that time, Ulrich will support her and the child." Ulrich, Helga, and Otto see nothing unusual about this document. All their married friends have done something similar and they believe it is good to discuss all these matters explicitly and reach a formal agreement.

Seriousness

Germans take life seriously. They are very concerned with ideas and principles and they insist on things being done right. Many observers have characterized German culture as "intellectual." West German TV features many earnest discussion programs in which people sit at round tables and solemnly debate current issues. The TV audience sits before them at smaller tables, sipping drinks and listening attentively (Buruma, 1994, p. 23). Germans are idealistic. They want to find the right principles and follow them, no matter what.

In the 19th century, Germany was a breeding ground for trade unionism and socialism, developing a tradition of working-class organization and an analysis of class conflict expressed most influentially by Karl Marx. German dedication to improving the condition of working people influenced societies all over the world, and particularly in the United States, where many German immigrants became involved in the antislavery movement and the trade union and socialist movements. As immigrants in America, they fought successfully for higher wages, shorter hours, limits on child labor, safer working conditions, and recognition of contracts with labor unions.

Dedication to principle has had some admirable results, but some ghastly ones too. German fascination with absolute principles facilitated Nazism. People were willing to accept a simple principle—"Aryan supremacy"—that explained everything in life and told them what to do, and they closed their eyes to its immoral consequences. But you mustn't forget that German conscientiousness also underlay resistance to Hitler by some German aristocrats, Catholics, and Communists.

Hermann's Story: The Police Officer

Hermann Schnabel is a 17-year veteran of the Hamburg police force, recently promoted to detective. He has been assigned to track down foreigners who have overstayed their visas and are now in Germany illegally. One day Hermann is called by an angry landlord to a shabby walk-up apartment building on the industrial outskirts of the city. "That woman up there never pays her rent on time, and she looks so foreign and her apartment smells funny; I want you to investigate," the landlord demands. Climbing up to the top floor, Hermann finds a terrified woman who falls weeping at his feet. "Please don't arrest me," she pleads, "it's not for me, but for my daughter. If you send us home my relatives will circumcise her. Do you know what that means? I can't let her be mutilated like that." Hermann does know what it means. He has heard this story before. And this is on top of yesterday's encounter with an Algerian journalist who wrote an exposé of a fundamentalist militia. If he is sent home, the militia will hunt him down and kill him. Mumbling with embarrassment, Hermann takes a 20-mark bill out of his wallet and gives it to the woman, then flees.

Trudging back to the station house, Hermann feels anguished and torn. "It's my assignment," says one side of his mind; "it's my duty." "I can't do this," says another side. "I can hear my history teacher telling us, 'Germans must never simply acquiesce in persecution again.'" "How can I send foreigners home to be killed or mutilated?" Back at the station house, Hermann drags himself into his captain's office. "I can't do this," he says. "I want to resign from the illegal alien detail. Please, can you transfer me to another duty?" "Well Hermann, I'm not surprised," says the captain. "You're the third officer in the last four months to ask for transfer off this duty. Maybe I'll ask for a transfer too."

Careful Work

Dedication to work is another aspect of German seriousness. Germans are renowned for their hard work and efficiency and their "insistence on precision." Germany has long excelled in industries that produce quality goods to exacting standards, like machine tools, cars, cameras, arms, and small appliances. Cars like Mercedes-Benz are built to be driven for hours on the German *Autobahnnen* (highways) at speeds over 100 miles an hour. In 2004, a proposal that goods produced in Germany be labeled "Made in E.U." (European Union) set off a roar of protest. The "Made in Germany" label had become "a pillar of postwar German identity," associated as it was with quality, fine craftsmanship, and precision engineering. Germans were embarrassed by a recent survey that ranked Mercedes behind Lexus and Infiniti in dependability—it was an assault on their national reputation

(Landler, 2004a, p. WK14). German business managers are slow to reach decisions, because they require a great deal of very detailed technical information. Slide presentations, reams of data, and long histories of background events are all carefully attended to and digested (Hamilton, 1990, p. 58; Lewis, 1987, p. 375).

Modern German Values

Germany today is an affluent Western capitalist society. In 2007, per capita income was the equivalent of about what $29,000 would buy in the United States. Smooth, carefully engineered highways allow Mercedes-Benz cars, BMWs, Audis, and Porsches to zoom along at 100 miles per hour. High-speed railroads connect cities filled with upscale shopping districts and malls, sleek apartment towers, and new housing estates. Landmark buildings destroyed in World War II have been perfectly rebuilt or restored. Germany is an individualistic consumer society.

The Value of Individualism

In Germany people see themselves as individuals, autonomous actors, free to join groups or remain separate. They value their privacy and their right to speak as individuals. Businesses and politicians address citizens through advertising and the mass media, but people are expected to make individual decisions and act on the basis of their own needs and judgments. In Germany it is not unusual or deviant behavior to belong to no group beyond the family, friendship circles, and a rather formal work group membership. When Wal-Mart opened stores in Germany it required salespeople to smile at customers. Shoppers were offended. The friendly salespeople were too intrusive, people complained, and male customers thought that female sales clerks who smiled were flirting with them (Landler & Barbaro, 2006, pp. C1, C4). In 2007 Wal-Mart failed in Germany and closed its doors.

Turkish immigrants in Germany are amazed by German individualism and not favorably impressed. One young man told ethnographer Sandra Bucerius, "Germans just deport their kids as soon as they are 18, so that they can live their lives—and eventually, when the mother is eighty, the son deports the mother to a nursing home. That's just ridiculous" (Bucerious, 2007, p. 7).

The Value of Possessions

In Germany, people are busy making money and spending it. They have many labor-saving devices but are always in a hurry. Meetings with friends are carefully scheduled on busy calendars. In many regions, the simplest single-family house cost $300,000 and people spend heavily on luxury furnishings: leather couches, oriental rugs, and original paintings. Designer clothes and upscale cars and trendy sports equipment are the means to declare one's status and express an individual identity (Rademaekers, 1992, pp. 9–10). Germans invest a great deal of money and time in their homes and they enjoy their possessions in privacy. See Table 5.1, p. 265.

The Value of Leisure

In recent decades, Germans have moved away from the traditional German dedication to work. Today they devote themselves less to duty and more to pleasure.

TABLE 5.1 Measures of Affluence

Americans, Germans, and Japanese have far more extensive connections to global communications, entertainment, and information than Egyptians and Mexicans do.

	Television Sets per 1,000 Persons	Cell Phones per 1,000 Persons	Internet Users per 1,000 Persons	Personal Computers per 1,000 Persons
United States	835	488	552	659
Japan	731	637	449	382
Germany	586	727	411	431
Mexico	283	255	99	82
Namibia	38	80	27	71
Egypt	217	67	28	17

Sources: United Nations, *Human Development Report 2004,* 2004b, http://hdr.undp.org/en/reports/global/hrd2004/; World Bank, *World Development Indicators 2004,* 2004, http://www.worldbank.org/data/dataquery.html.

Germans have achieved the highest wages, the shortest workweek, and the most paid holidays of any industrialized nation. They work an average of 37 hours per week, compared to 41 in the United States, and over 60 in Japan. Plus, they get 6 weeks of paid vacation, with an extra month's pay at vacation time, a Christmas bonus, and noncash benefits equal in value to 80% of their take-home pay (Glouchevitch, 1992, pp. 112–113). On their long vacations, Germans are dedicated travelers, filling the beaches of the Greek islands, Miami, and Cuba during the winter months and seeking the latest tropical resorts on remote Asian islands. Travel agents do a booming business in tour packages.

Conflicting Values

Many of Germany's values are interrelated and fit comfortably together. People find no problem in valuing both order and privacy, seriousness and hard work, individualism and materialism. But some German values conflict. When East and West Germany were reunified in 1990, eastern Germans found themselves uncomfortably different from their western cousins.

East German Values in the New Federal Republic

East Germany was a **socialist** society. It was poorer than West Germany, drab and slow-moving. When the Berlin Wall came down in 1989, East Germans seized the change to become part of the west. They wanted to share in the west's consumer abundance, its individual freedom. But they discovered that some of the central values of East German society were dismissed and disdained in the west. Easterners were surprised to find that it was hard to let go of their old values. They felt insulted by western disregard.

The Value of Collectivism. An important part of socialist culture in East Germany was belief in the virtue of group participation and distrust of individualism. People were expected to involve themselves in **collectives** (organized groups): to join youth organizations, women's organizations, and the Communist Party; and to attend meetings at their office or factory. Individualism was suppressed. If you avoided joining group life, and insisted on setting yourself apart, that was seen as "antisocial" and it was actually a legal offense.

East German **collectivism** was at one and the same time resented and absorbed. People became very involved with their coworkers socially and emotionally. They depended on friends and workmates for mutual aid, much more so than in West Germany. Friends helped one another find scarce goods and cope with bureaucracy. Typical friendship groups of perhaps two dozen people often linked individuals with very varied occupations, from doctors to auto mechanics, who all had contacts or skills to share with the group. After reunification easterners were happy to be free of the official party organizations, but they missed the informal collective life of the east. Life in the Federal Republic seemed cold and lonely.

The Value of Social Responsibility.   East Germany's socialist society laid great emphasis on what the individual owed to society. East German children were taught to ask themselves, "To whom can I be useful? Who needs me?" Children were expected to do good deeds for others: to help older people by carrying their packages and their coal, to perform volunteer work on Saturdays, to raise money for hungry children in Africa or war victims in Asia. They picked up trash and trimmed hedges in parks. Jana Hensel (2004), who was a child in East Germany and a teenager in reunified Germany, wrote that in her new life she learned to ask, "Who can be useful to me? Whom do I need?" (pp. 81–83, 113). Children could adapt easily, but after 1990 older people found themselves torn between the value systems of the two Germanys.

Diversity Versus Homogeneity

A serious people, Germans take their history very seriously. They worry about Germany's past susceptibility to racist ideologies, and to demagogues like Hitler. Do you come from a society with an ugly past? Is there racial oppression or genocide in your country's history? If so, you will understand some of the painful dilemmas Germans face. Young Germans long to put the Nazi horror behind them; to be part of a "normal nation." "How long do we have to keep apologizing?" they ask. But if they try to close the books on Nazism, doesn't that show insensitivity to Hitler's victims? For example, there is the issue of Germans criticizing Israel. Have they any right to do so? Recent books and a television documentary about the devastation of Dresden and other German cities by British and American firebombing in World War II broke a half-century taboo on discussing German suffering in the war. Germans ask, is it morally acceptable to portray ourselves as victims during the Nazi era?

Protecting Diversity.   In the aftermath of World War II, Germans hastened to forget the horrors of Nazism. But in the late 1960s, a new generation of young West Germans insisted on confronting the public with the truth about Nazi crimes. Germans began a serious national self-examination of their guilt, a process of *Trauerarbeit,* as they call it (the work of mourning), that continues to this day

These examples of medieval German houses are in the center of Frankfurt, one of Germany's largest cities. The buildings seem remarkably well preserved. In fact, many of them are reconstructions of buildings destroyed by American and British bombers during the Second World War. Germans are only now feeling freer to discuss the impact of wartime bombing. Some people suggest that the bombings were unjustified and some believe they were war crimes.

(Buruma, 1999, p. 21). West German schools made study of the Holocaust a required part of the curriculum.

Government policy reflects Germans' fear of repeating the past. The constitution grants draftees the right to refuse to fight on grounds of conscience (Buruma, 1994, pp. 24–25). Germany has also made it state policy to welcome refugees from political persecution and any Jews who wish to claim German citizenship. And Germany has worked to protect free speech, within the limits of a refusal to allow Nazi slogans or anti-Semitic speech. The government has moved very carefully in its efforts to root out Muslim terrorist cells in German cities because of the reluctance of politicians, spies, and police officers to be accused of Gestapo tactics or Stasi tactics (the Stasi was the East German secret police).

Longing for Homogeneity. But despite contemporary Germans' moral commitment to tolerance and diversity, the culture has a deep undertow of attraction to the old ideology of the German Volk, to the ideal of racial and cultural homogeneity. Germans would be terribly embarrassed by any reference to the "purity of German blood," but nevertheless it is commonplace to hear people say, "Germany is not an immigration country." Whatever do they mean? Almost 9% of people in Germany (7.3 million people) are citizens of some other country. Altogether, there are 15 million people who are immigrants or the children of immigrants. Among European Union countries, only Switzerland has a higher percentage of foreign-born people (Facts About Germany, n.d., Green, 2006). It has been 50 years since the guestworker program began to bring workers from Turkey to Germany. And yet, though they try to suppress it, Germans are uncomfortable with difference. This tension, between commitment to atoning for Nazi racial atrocities and a continuing wish for homogeneity, runs right through majority–minority relations in Germany today. We can see it in the experiences of every minority group.

MINORITY GROUPS IN GERMANY

This is going to be a long discussion, because the truth is that there are many minority groups in Germany, beginning with the Jews, and including ethnic German immigrants as well as several waves of immigrants from other societies.

Jews: The Original German Minority Group

Any discussion of minorities in Germany must start with the Jews. They are the original German minority group, the one treated most brutally, and the group toward whom Germans feel the most guilt and obligation.

The first thing to understand about German Jews is that they were always a tiny population. Up to the Nazi takeover Jews never exceeded 1% of the total German population (Elon, 2002, p. 5). Yet, for centuries they were regarded with tremendous enmity, and they were segregated and persecuted. Tolerated during the early Middle Ages, from the time of the Crusades in the 10th to 12th centuries, Jews were the victims of periodic massacres. They were reduced from a middle class to a population of peddlers, vagrants, rag dealers, money changers, and pawnbrokers, confined to ghettos and marginal areas, and subject to special taxes and fees. For example, in Frankfurt in the 18th century, Jews were banned from public gardens and Christian areas, except for business purposes, prohibited from walking more than two abreast, and not allowed to carry walking sticks (Elon, 2002, pp. 21–27).

Assimilation

Despite all the discrimination against them, during the 17th and 18th centuries some Jews managed to become middle class. They were needed in Germany to finance the courts of German principalities, so some favored Jewish bankers and wholesalers grew rich and privileged (Elon, 2002, pp. 27–28). Well-to-do Jews were allowed to live in cities. Some learned German and educated themselves. Many of Germany's most renowned intellectual figures—including the poet Heinrich Heine, the composer Felix Mendelsson, Sigmund Freud, Max Weber, and Albert Einstein—came from this class of cultured Jews. Educated urban Jews identified with Germany and especially with German culture. In the 19th century they worked at becoming German. They wanted to **assimilate,** to adopt the culture of the German society they lived in, to adopt German identity, and to be accepted as Germans. Tens of thousands converted to Christianity. They gave their children German names, celebrated

Christmas with Christmas trees, and abandoned traditional Jewish dress. Many married non-Jews. Thousands of German Jews served with honor in the German army in the First World War, and even in the Second World War (Elon, 2002, pp. 8–9)!

There were periods in German history when assimilation worked, when Jews were accepted and discrimination, at least against urban middle-class Jews, abated: under the protection of Napoleon after his 1806 conquest of Prussia, for several decades between 1888 and 1914. But in every period of crisis, anti-Semitism took on new life.

Scapegoating

Scapegoating is often part of the psychology of prejudice. People blame a person or group for events and problems that are not their fault. The scapegoat is usually a distinctive group that is relatively powerless—an easy target. In Germany, Jews were historically the scapegoat. Anti-Semitic riots followed the economic crisis of 1816, with its hunger and unemployment. Police and militia stood by while mobs attacked Jews. In many places old restrictions on Jews were restored (Elon, 2002, pp. 101–108). During the Revolution of 1848, peasants rioted against Jews. In 1873, after a devastating stock market crash provoked a deep recession, Jews were blamed for bringing on the crash by swindling and market manipulation. Amos Elon explains the piteous irony of the Jews' situation: "The more Jews came to resemble other Germans the more, it seemed, Germans resented them" (Elon, 2002, pp. 115–116, 211, 215). Obviously the worst scapegoating of Jews and the worst anti-Semitism occurred in the years after Germany's defeat in World War I, leading up to the Nazi takeover. Jews were blamed for Germany's military defeat and "Jewish capitalism" was blamed for the hyperinflation and economic collapse of the 1920s. The Nazi Party disparaged Weimar Germany as a *Judenrepublic* (Elon, 2002, pp. 356, 374).

Racism

Late in the 19th century, just as Jews became more assimilated, an ideology of anti-Semitism became more elaborated and entrenched. This prejudice was explicitly racist. In a way it was a reflection of rising German nationalism. Just as Germans came to associate their nationality with the German "race," so they came to see Jews as a distinct and inferior race. The "Jewish question" was not a matter of religion, Germans said. It made no difference if Jews were baptized as Christians. Jews were **stereotyped** as an "Asiatic" alien race, a "social pest" (Greenfeld, 1993, pp. 383–386). By the 1930s, Hitler's National Socialism made Jews its most important enemy. Nazism's ultimate goal was "the destruction of the Jewish race in Europe." The true Volk—"Aryans"—were to liberate Germans from the corrupt Jewish capitalism of the east (Schulze, 1998, p. 271). We know where that led: 6 million Jews dead in the concentration camps and death camps, 10 million Russians dead, 6 million Poles, 5.5 million Germans. Twelve million refuges roamed Europe at the end of the war.

Atonement

Germans take seriously their nation's responsibility for the Holocaust. In the early 1960s a "public commemorative culture" emerged in West Germany. It became awkward to discuss the many Germans who were killed, wounded, or made home-less by the war, and impossible to characterize Germans as victims of Allied fire-bombing of German cities. Any call for Germans to remember their own losses was attacked as falsely equating the suffering of Germans and Jews in order to avoid guilt and responsibility (Moeller, 2005, p. 150). Instead, Germans publicly and repeatedly commemorated Jewish victims of Nazism. They emphasized the need to remember their nation's shameful history so they would not repeat it.

Germany paid compensation to Holocaust survivors. The nation established diplomatic relations with Israel. Almost 100 German cities adopted twin cities in

This street sign in the town of Marburg has a story to tell, a story about segregation, persecution, and atonement. The street is named Schlosssteig (Castle Way), but it was formerly named Judengasse (Jews' Alley). Until the 1930s Marburg had a tiny Jewish community concentrated here. Then, in 1933, the name of the street was changed, just as Nazi persecution of Jews intensified. By the end of World War II there were no Jews left in Marburg. But now, Marburg has decided to remember its Jews and the Holocaust. The town has posted this sign and it has excavated a buried 15th-century synagogue and built a little archeological museum around it.

Israel and many thousands of young Germans and Israelis visited one another's countries in exchange programs. When Germany was reunified in 1990 the new "Berlin Republic" used the occasion to further its work of atonement. After considerable public debate, parliament voted to construct a Holocaust Memorial right in the heart of the new capital. Completed in 2005, this memorial looks like a vast, sobering cemetery. Germany is unique among nations in the way that it keeps building monuments to the victims of its national disgrace. Construction is due to begin in Berlin on two more monuments: one to Gypsies and another to gays and lesbians killed in the Holocaust. There are new exhibits and visitor centers at the sites of the Bergen-Belsen and Dachau concentration camps and two exhibits are currently running on the role of the railroads in the Nazi terror. In 2007 Germans were scandalized when a traditional parade held every year in carnival season was permitted to take place on International Holocaust Remembrance Day (Kulish, 2008b).

Other efforts at atonement have major policy effects. In the 1990s, the new German republic proclaimed that anyone in the world who would have been considered a Jew under Hitler's Nuremberg Laws was welcome to immigrate to Germany. There were many who took up this offer (mostly from parts of the former Soviet Union like Kazakhstan and Uzbekistan where anti-Semitism remains strong). Germany's Jewish population increased from 29,000 in 1990 to 200,000 in 2005, a level one third higher than it was before World War II. Germany now has the fastest-growing Jewish population in the world. Berlin and some other cities have seen a revival of Jewish culture (Bernstein, 2005a; *The Economist,* 2005, p. 48).

But Germans do express some ambivalence about continuing to atone for the Holocaust. A recent survey found 60% of Germans saying they are tired of being reminded of German crimes against the Jews. Media coverage of the 60th anniversary of the end of World War II focused a great deal on German suffering in the war. And in 2005 a new immigration law tightened the rules on admitting Jews (Bernstein, 2005a; *The Economist,* 2005, p. 48).

Gavril's Story: From Russia to Germany

"People ask 'how does it feel to be a German?' but it's the wrong question. They should really ask me how does it feel to be a Jew? When Masha and I emigrated from Russia 10 years ago, the move was an easy one as such things go. Jobs were waiting for us here at the Institute and they helped us find housing and made life easy for us in most respects. As scientists Germany wanted us. Not everyone had it so easy. Germans are not always this kind to immigrants.

"When we left Leningrad—St. Petersburg as they call it today—in the '90s Russia's economy was in chaos. We had thought about emigrating. As a Jew I knew that both Germany or Israel would be open to us, but it all remained a distant possibility. Then our department chair at the university called us in and told us that we would no longer be on salary and that the cafeteria was closing. We were stunned—we'd worked without being paid for months, but we thought we would be paid eventually. And the cafeteria was the only place we could afford to eat. As if this wasn't enough, as I left the meeting, Yuri, whom I'd worked with for 3 years, turned to me cursing and said that it was Jews like me who led Russia into this miserable state. My colleagues had to break up the fight. When I met Masha I said 'this is it; we're emigrating!' Three weeks later we were in Germany.

"It was very strange to be in Germany at first. My grandfather had died fighting the Germans and many of my family had starved in the Nazi siege of Lenningrad. But one goes where one can, one must, to survive and prosper.

"I didn't think much about being Jewish; I didn't in Russia and I didn't see why it should be different in Germany, but it was. Our first December here we bought a New Year's Tree as we did in Russia. Everybody did; we didn't think much of its religious meaning. When one of my American Jewish colleagues came to our apartment he stared at the tree and then at both of us—this was very unnerving as people in Germany don't do such things. Later he told me that the tree was very much a Christian symbol and that Jews don't have them in their homes and they don't celebrate Christmas, they celebrate Hannukah. It was the first time that I'd ever heard the word—my family in Russia was very secular.

"Gradually we learned a bit more about being Jewish—there were some things I liked: the traditions, the stories, the holidays, and some things that made no sense like not eating pork or lobster. Some things were very troubling. Our son Isaac was born in Germany. We named him for my grandfather and many young Germans are given that name. 'If your name is Isaac and your father's a Jew,' I thought, 'well then you must be Jewish.' Not so, apparently. According to Jewish law, your mother has to be Jewish and Masha is not. I want to raise Isaac as a Jew, but I don't know if Jews will accept him. Some will, but some will not. It's troubling. And then there's Masha. She hasn't said anything, but Jewish ideas and customs are more alien to her than they are to me. I don't think she'd be happy if I wanted Isaac to go for Jewish religious instruction and she's more than once had to politely decline the opportunity to join a Jewish feminist group—she's certainly a feminist, but a Jew? This is more problematical. I think this is going to be a continuing and growing difficulty for us, but if we could endure the chaos of Russia in the '90s we can sort this out."

Ethnic Germans: The Nonminority Group

The first people to come to Germany as immigrants were Germans. At the end of World War II millions of Germans who lived in Poland and Czechoslovakia fled westward as the Russian army pushed toward Germany. Then, after its defeat, Germany was forced to concede territory to Poland, the Soviet Union, and Czechoslovakia. People of German background living in those areas were expelled. By 1950 8 million of these expellees had settled in West Germany and 2 million more in East Germany and Austria. Also, between 1949 and 1961, before the Berlin Wall sealed the border between east and west, up to 3 million easterners moved to the west. German citizenship laws defined ethnic Germans as automatically entitled to citizenship. The relevant constitutional provision came from a 1913 law based on Germany's racial definition of nationality. Anyone of "German blood," any descendant of a German was considered German.

Ethnic German immigrants organized themselves politically and wanted to retain separate identities based on their countries of origin. Most hoped to reverse the 1945 border changes and return to their old homes. But German officials and the Allies wanted ethnic Germans to assimilate: to abandon their separate identities and intermarry with local Germans. Perhaps because the societies of West and East Germany were still fluid in the postwar years, or perhaps because economic growth was rapid and there was a labor shortage, ethnic Germans did assimilate relatively smoothly. It helped too that many of the ethnic Germans thought of themselves as German (Green, 2006, p. 2; Stearns, 2003, pp. 821–822).

Germans from the Soviet Union

Things did not go as smoothly for a third group of ethnic German immigrants. They arrived from the Soviet Union, Romania, and Poland after the end of the Cold War in 1989. Their links to Germany were weaker. Their ancestors had left Germany centuries before, many spoke no German, and they had little connection to German culture, even though some of them had experienced discrimination because of their ethnicity. By 1990, when 400,000 of these *Aussiedler* reached Germany, the government set new limits on their immigration and by 1999 new arrivals had dropped to 100,000 a year. The desire to limit ethnic German migration encouraged the government to shift away from a blood descent definition of "Germanness" (Green, 2006, p. 5).

East Germans: The Unacknowledged Immigrants

When East and West Germany rejoined in 1990, they didn't join on equal terms. Really, the Federal Republic, the west, absorbed the east, the former GDR. Many easterners, especially young, educated, skilled people moved west, but even those people who stayed where they were felt like they were in a new country. The old socialist industries shut down and eastern Germany was flooded with western products. The government changed, the school curriculum changed, the old state-run peoples' organizations disbanded, and the values of the society changed. Many easterners, *Ossis* as they are called, felt that their whole way of life had been dismissed as inferior and wiped out. They called the westerners *Besserwessis,* meaning "know-it-alls." As Jana Hensel (2004) explained in her best-selling memoir:

> The problem is that my parents are fluent in the language. If they spoke broken German, everyone would understand what they are: refugees from a country that no longer exists, who don't know how to get on in their adopted homeland. And people would also understand that people like me have to negotiate the same situation as the kids of Italian or Korean immigrants to the U.S. (p. 174)

Immigrants and Asylum-Seekers: New Minority Groups

Acceptance has not come readily to Germany's most recent immigrants. During the 1960s and 1970s, West Germany had a labor shortage and recruited male temporary workers, "guest workers" from Italy, Greece, Spain, Portugal, Morocco, Turkey, Tunisia, and Yugoslavia. Early on, the largest group of guest workers was Italian, but by the end of the period Turks predominated. Guest workers were expected to go home; they were not welcome to stay, but stay they did. First, employers got tired of constantly training new workers. Then, in 1973 when the government ended the guest worker program many foreign laborers chose to stay in Germany, bringing their families to join them. Germany acquired a permanent immigrant minority composed of people who were not of German background, many of whom were, in fact, Muslims (Green, 2006, pp. 2–3).

Asylum-Seekers

You must understand Germany's attitude to asylum migration in the context of repentance for the Holocaust. West Germany's Basic Law (its postwar constitution) established a generous right to political asylum that went beyond the obligations of the Geneva Convention. Asylum-seekers were entitled to generous welfare benefits and were allowed to work while their applications for asylum were pending. While the number of those claiming asylum remained low, the law worked smoothly. But by 1980, applications had shot up to 100,000 a year. Many asylum applicants were from Turkey where there was a military coup in 1980. Once the civil war in the former Yugoslavia began in the 1990s, applications rose still further, up to over 400,000 in 1992, including people from Yugoslavia, Poland, Romania, and Bulgaria. Applications piled up. By 1993 there were about 1.5 million people in Germany whose applications were being processed, who hadn't yet applied, who had been rejected but had not left, or who were there as temporary refugees (Green, 2006, pp. 4–5). In terms of public morality it was almost impossible for Germans to reject helping victims of political persecution, but nevertheless discomfort and opposition grew. In the early 1990s there were several fatal attacks on foreigners and eventually the offer of asylum was restricted. Fifty thousand Gypsies from Kosovo were deported (Wood, 2005).

German Responses to Immigrants

Worldwide, migration rates are high at present. In many nations immigration is a major political issue. Some people advocate closing the borders to keep out immigrants. Some people think immigrants don't try hard enough to adapt to their new country. Others think citizens are being harmed by the immigrant influx. In Germany, as elsewhere, much of the debate revolves around what should be expected of immigrants. Picture two opposing ideals: assimilation on the one hand and **multiculturalism** on the other. Assimilation means that immigrants completely adopt their new country's values and norms, putting their old culture behind them. In Germany that would mean immigrants speak German, eat German foods, celebrate German holidays, follow German marriage customs, even become Christians like other Germans. Americans used to call this ideal "the melting pot." Multiculturalism, in contrast, means that all the different ethnic/cultural groups in a society recognize and appreciate one another's cultures. Each group may follow its own norms and values. Canadians call this "the glorious mosaic."

In Germany, assimilation is not a publicly acceptable goal. It suggests the Nazi insistence on Aryan uniformity. But multiculturalism seems too radical. At bottom, Germans feel immigrants ought to adapt. The compromise goal has been *integration,* meant to be a kind of midpoint between assimilation and multiculturalism, with some mutual acceptance and adaptation, along with some agreement on basic political values. If you think that is a vague goal, you are right. It has been very hard for Germans to define which aspects of immigrant culture are acceptable and which are not. There is debate and conflict over each new issue that arises, and plenty of room for double standards (Green, 2006). Let's see how this applies to the largest and most controversial immigrant group in Germany: Turkish immigrants.

Immigrants from Turkey

There are approximately 2.7 million people in Germany who are Turkish immigrants and their descendants. Turks are the largest single ethnic group, except for ethnic Germans. Many Turkish Germans have been in Germany for more than 30 years. How have the Turks adapted to Germany and how has Germany adapted to them? Over the years Turkish immigrants have become increasingly invested in German society. Many who once planned to return to Turkey remain in Germany to be with their children and grandchildren. Turkish Germans have bought homes, started businesses, and built mosques. If the original immigrants did not always learn German, their children certainly did. There are Turkish German doctors and lawyers, architects and writers, even some representatives in parliament, women as well as men. There are Turkish television stations and newspapers. Some young Turkish people graduate university and some even marry Germans, though intermarriage rates are low.

Adnan: The German of the Future

"I'm the German of the future, no blond hair, no blue eyes, not a good Catholic or Lutheran, but a dark-haired dark-eyed Muslim . . . and of course a Turk. German citizen or no, I'm still a Turk to too many and they don't think of it as a compliment." Adnan Aygun is a second generation Turkish immigrant. Unlike many other Turkish immigrants from the rural heart of Turkey, Adnan's parents are professionals—teachers—who fled cosmopolitan Istanbul in a period of political repression. Spurred on by their high standards he entered one of Germany's most prestigious universities. "Despite my record and recommendations, I don't think my firm would have hired me if they didn't need a lawyer who felt comfortable negotiating in Turkey and Saudi Arabia. And you know it didn't really matter how many contracts I brought in, I was still 'The Turk' in the office. If the countries of the Muslim east were not our most promising market, I'd have a hard time moving ahead.

"People at the office who have worked with me for many years are still not comfortable with me. I've learned to have a very busy schedule during Ramadan so I don't have to explain why I'm not available for lunch. Germans—the ones who think of themselves as blond haired and blue eyed (who are often as dark as I am)—look at me and don't see a German lawyer for a multinational corporation: they see Osama bin Laden! They see a Turkish peasant who arrived yesterday from Anatolia in central Turkey. They talk about integration—but they don't really mean it—perhaps they wish they did. They're not in their hearts bad people. My wife has a college degree and teaches mathematics at a Gymnasium, but if she wore the headscarf that she wears outside of work when she's in the classroom she's be a former teacher of mathematics. We'll they'll just have to get used to it . . . we're as German as they are and we're not going anywhere . . . this is our home."

Segregation. One hears little about the place Turks have made for themselves in German society. Instead, there is constant complaint about how Turks keep themselves separate, apart from Germans. Turkish immigrants are concentrated in Germany's older industrial cities, like Hamburg and Frankfurt, where 40% of the population comes from an immigrant background, and even in particular neighborhoods of those cities, identifiable by their Turkish shops, tea houses, and mosques. German children do meet Turkish children in school, but Germans don't invite Turks to their homes. Unemployment rates are higher for Turks than for Germans, and graduation rates are lower. It is clear that Turks in Germany are a **minority group:** They live in social and physical isolation from the German majority; they think of themselves as a group and have created group institutions; and they suffer from disadvantages in German society.

German Reaction to Turks.   It helps to understand that integration has to be a two-way process. Turks must be willing to adapt to Germany, but Germans also must be willing to accept Turks. Yet there is much more German criticism than acceptance or appreciation. Immigrants say they do not feel welcome in Germany. Sixty percent of Germans say "there are too many foreigners living in Germany" (*The Economist,* 2006e). In Duisberg, a largely Turkish industrial city, a local nursing home has a mix of German and Turkish residents. When the staff played some Turkish music at a special dinner, German residents broke out into *"Deutschland, Deutschland uber alles,"* Germany's old national anthem (Landler, 2007b). The local government offers grants to "restore" storefronts to their original "German" appearance (Ehrkamp, 2005, p. 9).

Anti-immigrant feeling was much more openly expressed in 2008 after two immigrant youths—a Turk and a Greek—were caught on a security video beating up an elderly German man on a subway in Munich. Soon after, in state elections, Roland Koch, the premier of the state of Hesse, tried to play on anti-immigrant sentiment, calling for law and order and pointing out that half of all juvenile crimes are committed by young people who are immigrants or the descendants of immigrants. It is interesting that Koch's xenophobic campaign strategy backfired. His party lost votes and the local Social Democratic Party, which called for "social justice," increased its share of votes (*The Economist,* 2008b, p. 58; Kulish, 2008a, p. A3). See Table 5.2.

Headscarfs, Mosques, and Marriages.   Are German worries about Turks carping criticism or a recognition of serious problems? It is hard for people to find a sense of proportion. Muslim headscarfs are a magnet for controversy in Germany, where 3.2 million people, mostly Turks and Bosnians, follow Islam. In Germany, as all over the Muslim world, more and more women are adopting the headscarf. To Germans the Islamic scarf appears to be a symbol of the suppression of women, or a signal of anti-Western Muslim fundamentalism. They see it as a sign of the failure of integration. Half of Germany's 16 states have banned the wearing of headscarfs for state workers or in public buildings and many women say they feel discriminated against because they wear the scarf. They also say the scarf was not forced on them by male relatives and that they believe the sexes are equal (*Deutsche Welle,* 2006).

Mosques are another sore point for Germans. Muslim immigrants who are committed to living in Germany and who have enjoyed growing prosperity want to build real mosques in their communities to replace the makeshift, inconspicuous facilities where they have been praying. Many Germans are alarmed. In Cologne, a famous German Jewish writer said the large planned mosque there would be "an expression of the creeping Islamization of our land." A journalist added, "a mosque is more than a church or a synagogue. It is a political statement." An imam in

TABLE 5.2   Anti-Immigrant Sentiment and the Relative Size of Immigrant Populations

In some societies with relatively large immigrant populations there is a lot of hostility to immigrants, but in others negative attitudes to immigrants are much less common. For example, compare Germany and the United States. The proportions of their populations that are foreign-born are very similar, but the percentage of people opposed to immigration is twice as large in Germany as it is in the United States. In Canada, the percentage of the population that is foreign-born is even larger, but fewer people are hostile to immigrants.

	Respondents Who Say Immigration Is a Bad Thing (%)	Immigrants as a Percentage of Total Population	Millions of Immigrants
Germany	64	12.9	10.6
France	44	8.1	4.9
Britain	34	9.7	5.8
United States	32	12.9	38.3
Sweden	28	12.4	1.1
Canada	21	19.1	5.9

Sources: Pew Research Center, *47-Nation Pew Global Attitudes Survey,* October 2007, http://www.pewresearch.org; Organisation for Economic Co-operation and Development, *International Migration Outlook 2007,* 2007b, http://www.oecd.org/els/migration/imo.

Cologne replied that a mosque would be a "crowning moment for religious tolerance." In Munich, mosque opponents called plans to build a mosque opposite a Catholic church "a provocation," "a power play" unrelated to religion (Landler, 2006f, p. A3; 2007c, p. A3).

Germans' deepest misgivings center on Turkish marriage norms. Perhaps half of all Turkish men look to Turkey to find a wife. They believe the woman they marry must be "pure," in order to preserve the honor of their families. They suspect that German women and even assimilated Turkish German women are not pure. They mix with men socially, go out with men, and may even have sex before marriage. Turkish men would rather be sure by marrying a woman from home (Bucerius, 2007, p. 7). But these marriages alarm Germans for two reasons. First, they keep the Turkish immigrant population in Germany growing. Second, Germans believe these marriages slow assimilation. The wife comes from Turkey; she doesn't speak German and doesn't teach it to her children. Many binational marriages are arranged marriages, which Germans tend to regard as forced marriages, oppressive to women. They believe there is more domestic violence associated with these marriages.

There is a dilemma here about **ethnocentrism.** Are Germans being ethnocentric in condemning arranged marriage and seeking to impose the value they place on individual freedom of choice? Or are there at stake here basic human rights for women that should be universal? Some relatively assimilated, educated Turkish women agree with German critics. They find themselves rejected both by German men and by Turkish men who look for more traditional wives (Caldwell, 2007, pp. 44–49). Germans are even more alarmed by cases of "honor killings" of young

This celebration of "Turkish Day" in Berlin in 2006 reveals both the diversity of the Turkish German community and the fears and hopes of ethnic Germans. Young men who identify strongly with Turkish nationalism are waving red Turkish flags. Less visible are parade-goers whose identity is primarily Islamic, who are soliciting donations for a new mosque. Also much in evidence are German police, filming everyone. The celebration is being held in front of the Brandenburg Gate, perhaps the most prominent symbol of German national identity. The contrast of German and Turkish national symbols vividly portrays a changing Germany. Older Germans who witness scenes like these are often fearful: Are they seeing the birth of a diverse Germany or the death of the society they know?

Turkish women who have opted for a life in German culture and been killed by their families, who accuse them of disobedience and promiscuity (Schneider, 2005, pp. 66–71). Where should Germans draw the line between avoiding past sins of racism and cultural intolerance, and a positive obligation to root out unaccept-able deviant behavior? Our discussion of immigrants in Germany brings us inevitably to issues concerning deviance and social control.

DEVIANCE AND DIVERSITY

Certain kinds of behavior are universally considered deviant. All the societies described in this book condemn murder, rape, assault, and theft. But you have prob-ably noticed that beyond these criminal acts there are some behaviors considered deviant in one society that are tolerated or even accepted in another.

In Germany rates of deviance are relatively low and, with a few important exceptions, Germans feel rather secure. They think deviance is not a big problem in their society. That's the overall assessment. The details are interesting though, and distinctively German.

Criminal Deviance

If you examine Table 1.3 (p. 27) you will see that Germany's murder rate is low: 15 murders yearly per million people. It is similar to Japan's rate and far lower than the murder rate in the United States. The rate of auto thefts in Germany is higher than in Japan (where there are almost none) but much lower than in the United States. Germany's robbery rate is half that in the United States (United Nations, 2005). Also, Germany has a rather low rate of incarceration, similar to Japan's and only about a tenth that of the United States (see Table 1.4, p. 29). It is notable, though, that even with its low crime rates, Germany is heavily policed. It is quite consistent with German values that people are reluctant to use informal means of social control to monitor and sanction their neighbors. They don't want to interfere, or be nosy, so they would rather rely on formal social controls like the police and the courts to deal with deviance. There are 303 police officers for every 100,000 people in Germany, a police presence similar to that of the United States and almost three times that of Japan (United Nations, 2005). Police officers with German Shepherd police dogs patrol train stations, and city residents don't worry about street crime, even at night. Germany ranks among the safest countries in the world (*Deutsche Welle*, 2007b).

Defining Deviance

Another reason why Germans feel secure is that many acts that are considered deviant in other societies are accepted in Germany. Prostitution is legal in Germany. Recreational drug use is tolerated in many parts of Germany, though drug trafficking is illegal. Homosexuality is accepted. When we examine German society we can see that sometimes societies change their definitions of what is deviant during relatively short periods of time. We can also see that sometimes deviance as defined by law and deviance as defined by public opinion change at different rates.

Homosexuality

One of the most interesting cases in the definition of deviance in Germany may be seen in changing attitudes toward homosexuality. For most of Germany's history, homosexuality and homosexual subcultures were considered criminal activities. Even the 1920s, under the relatively liberal Weimer Republic, homosexuality remained a crime, despite the almost open existence of a flourishing gay subculture in Berlin and elsewhere. When the Nazis came to power open homosexuality was fiercely repressed. Gay men had to wear pink triangles as Jews had to wear yellow stars of David. Many German gays ended their lives in the gas chambers of the Nazi death camps. At the same time it's worth noting that homosexuality was not unknown among Nazi leaders.

To some extent today's acceptance of gay men and women may be a reaction to their vicious persecution under the Nazis. Germany and Germans take great pains to demonstrate that Germany has left the Nazi past behind. For example, Germany defines attacks on gay people and hate speech directed toward the gay communities, not only as a human rights violations but as political crimes. The constitution permits monitoring extremist individuals and even banning antidemocratic parties and organizations.

It took many years, however, for Germany to arrive at its current acceptance of homosexuality. After Germany's defeat in 1945 homosexuality remained a crime in both East and West Germany. In both countries gay people worked actively to redefine a gay lifestyle as legitimate. In East Germany homosexuality was decriminalized in 1968, but West Germany continued to define homosexual acts as crimes. It was only in 1998 that the reunified Germany decriminalized gay lifestyles (Murray, 1993, pp. 427–431).

Perhaps the most important reason that Germany made this change was the adoption of the Treaty of Amsterdam in 1997 by the European Union. Because Germany was one of the principal moving forces behind the European Union, the nation felt compelled to approve the treaty even though it required many changes in German law. One of these changes was the decriminalization of gay and lesbian relationships. Actually, the government at that time, a left-leaning coalition of Social Democrats and Greens, enthusiastically supported these changes while the former conservative government of Christian Democrats resisted them (Stefans & Wagner, 2004, pp. 137–149). A broader European definition of human rights entered into German culture.

Today Germany has open and flourishing gay subcultures. Not only are gay men and women open about their sexual preferences in areas that have been traditionally accepting, such as the worlds of theater and music, but Germans running for some of the highest political offices have come out as gay. Klaus Wowereit is the popular, recently reelected mayor of Berlin and he is openly gay, even hugging his partner at a Social Democratic Party celebration. He disclosed his homosexuality in 2001 with the now-famous line, "I'm gay and it's good that way." One mass-market newspaper recently speculated, "Will Wowie [that's his nickname] Be the First Gay Chancellor?" (Landler, 2006d, p. A4). While Berlin is the most socially liberal place in Germany, national sentiment has been moving toward acceptance of homosexuality. Younger Germans aged 18 to 39 are the most accepting of homosexuality, but even the older generation is changing its attitudes. In 2007, 91% of those 18–39, and 76% of those over 40 said that homosexuality should be accepted as a lifestyle (Pew, 2007). See Table 5.3, p. 281.

Alev's Story: Gay in Berlin

Alev is a popular music journalist who writes for several alternative papers in Berlin. Recently she was interviewed on radio:

Interviewer: You write one of the most closely followed columns on German popular music, but as your name indicates, your background is Turkish. Do your dual identities give you a different perspective on German music?

TABLE 5.3 Attitudes About Homosexuality

*Respondents to an international survey were asked about their attitudes to homo-
sexuality. There was wide variation among societies in public acceptance of
homosexual lifestyles, with Germans the most accepting and Egyptians the least.
Do you think that the large difference between Germans and Turks in their attitudes on this topic would exacerbate ethnic tensions in Germany?*

	Homosexuality Should Be Accepted as a Way of Life (%)	Homosexuality Should Be Rejected as a Way of Life (%)	Don't Know or Refused to Answer (%)
Germany	81	17	2
Mexico	60	31	9
United States	49	41	10
Japan	49	28	23
Turkey	14	57	29
Egypt	1	95	5

Source: Pew Research Center, *47-Nation Pew Global Attitudes Survey,* October 2007, http://www.pewresearch.org.

*Alev: You make identity sound as if it were a restaurant special: "Lunch of the Day: choose
either Krautbraten or Braetknoedel." Identity is much more complex. If I had to define
myself I'd say I was a German-Turkish-dyke-music-journalist!*

Interviewer: Did you always think of yourself in those terms?

*Alev: Certainly not when I was 5, but I gradually became aware of all the things in me.
When I was a kid in Frankfurt I knew I was a Turk because all the German kids called me
one. When my father sent me to high school and college in Istanbul, people called me the
German. I went to work in Istanbul after college and gradually I realized that I was not a
Turk, I was German Turkish. I missed too many things about Germany. Much to my
surprise I was homesick for Germany. I moved to Berlin and took the first job I could
find—writing promos for music companies.*

*Interviewer: Yet you retain some obvious ties to Turkey, that's a Turkish sweatshirt you're
wearing. What does it say?*

*Alev: Oh, Galatasaray, the great Turkish football (soccer) team. I'm their biggest fan in
Berlin. But, if I go to the Olympics I wear the red, gold, and black colors of German fans,
not the Turkish red.*

*Interviewer: Not everyone accepts lesbians—or dykes—as you prefer to call yourself, isn't
this particularly difficult for you? There isn't a lot of tolerance I'd guess for dykes among
Turks in Germany.*

*Alev: In some ways that's true. I'm very careful to avoid embarrassing my family. Alev
isn't the name my family gave me and I never do TV. My parents would feel utterly
shamed if their neighbors and relatives found out. My brother wouldn't kill me, but he'd
feel like it when it happened. But in other ways it's much simpler for me to be a Turkish
dyke in Berlin than it is to be for many straight Turkish women in most of Germany.*

Interviewer: I'm not sure I understand.

Alev: Well, look at it this way. My cousin is my age, she's a teacher in Frankfurt, and she's straight. Turkish men won't look at her because she's "too German" and might shame their family if she wasn't a virgin at marriage. She might be but since she works with Germans and often goes out to clubs she's suspect. There'd always be persistent doubts about her purity. On the other hand, German men consider her "too Turkish." Her mother says that if she doesn't marry soon she'll end as a spinster and my cousin has the same worries. She's thinking of emigrating to Canada or the United States.

Interviewer: And it's easier to be a dyke?

Alev: Yes, certainly, especially for a Turkish women here in Berlin. German men may not want Turkish women as permanent partners, but German women have no such problems . . . or at least most of those I meet in Berlin don't. My partner and I have lived together for 6 years and she's as German as can be—blond hair, blue eyes—everything.

Interviewer: Well this has been interesting, but let me ask one last question. If you had to choose which of your many identities was the most important to you, which would it be?

Alev: Oh, that's easy: being a Galatasaray fan. That comes first.

Drug Use

Laws on recreational drug use vary from state to state, but police efforts are focused on trafficking in hard drugs. Germans see drug trafficking as an aspect of international crime that may be related to terrorism, since Afghanistan is the major source of heroin in Europe. Drug use by individuals is often seen as a personal habit or personal affliction and may be permitted, especially when it is a matter of less serious drugs like marijuana, rather than crack cocaine or heroin.

Prostitution

The Artemis Sauna Club in Berlin is a luxury brothel. It has a nude bar, a Finnish sauna, a theater for pornographic films, 50 regular workers, and a Web site. In Hamburg and Cologne there are famous red-light districts where brothels have huge neon marquee lights. Brothels offer 50% discounts to senior citizens. Prostitution in Germany today is not just legal, it is highly regulated. Prostitutes must register with the government and pay taxes on their earnings, but they also have the same rights as workers in any other industry, including the right to health insurance (Landler, 2006a, p. A3; *Spiegel Online,* 2007).

The history of prostitution in Germany is interesting and displays Germans' deep ambivalence. Prostitution was legalized in Germany in 1927, but prostitutes remained a socially vulnerable and publicly stigmatized group. Prostitutes could not be prosecuted for the sale of sexual services, but they had no legal protections—they could not sue a customer who refused to pay or paid with a bad check. They had to pay taxes but received none of the benefits taxpayers received: They were excluded from the system of old-age pensions and the medical coverage enjoyed by most Germans. During the first days of Hitler's rule attempts were made to eliminate prostitution, but as massive numbers of German men entered years of military service these attempts were abandoned. After the Second World War the widespread revival of street prostitution led many German cities to establish legal red-light zones where prostitution could flourish legally (Jolin, 1993, pp. 129–135).

The ambiguous legal status of prostitution satisfied almost no one. Prostitutes still found themselves legally vulnerable and outside Germany's extensive social welfare network. More conservative Germans continued to be offended by any legalization of prostitution. Attempts to provide further legal and social protections for prostitutes provoked furious reaction. One conservative politician responded to reform proposals by declaring that "prostitutes are outside the moral contours of our society. . . . There is no reason for upgrading them socially. . . . It is sending a devastating signal to young women" (Boyes, 1999).

Many of the existing laws worked at cross-purposes. Prostitutes could work legally, but if you offered prostitutes a safe, clean, and even attractive place to work you were guilty of encouraging prostitution and liable to legal action. A lawsuit in 1997 brought by Felicitas Weigmann, the owner of Café Pssst—a well-known brothel in Berlin's upscale Charlottenberg neighborhood—led to a court decision declaring Germany's decency laws unconstitutional in 2000. The advent of a Social Democratic government in 1998 brought to power a government that viewed prostitutes as exploited workers rather than moral pariahs. This made possible the legal changes that took place in 2001 that placed prostitution and prostitutes in much the same situation as workers in any service industry. They had to pay taxes; they could receive social benefits; they could form unions and sue those who defrauded them. A 2002 estimate suggested that Germany had some 400,000 working prostitutes earning about $6 billion annually (Homola, 2001, p. A6; Schelzig, 2002, p. A13).

Changes in German attitudes toward prostitutes and prostitution have been shaped by a broader European trend toward greater legal protections for prostitution. The neighboring Netherlands has offered legal and social protections to prostitutes for some time. Prostitution and the rights of prostitutes also became an issue litigated before the European Court of Justice created by the European Union. In 2002, for example, the court ruled that if prostitution is legal, then prostitutes should be able to move from one member state of the European Union to another in order to practice their trade (Schelzig, 2002, p. A13).

Prostitution and Political Deviance.   It is revealing that while prostitution is legal in Germany, Germans are deeply troubled by **human trafficking,** forced prostitution, usually of women smuggled into Germany without proper visas. The distinction makes clear that Germans are much less concerned about deviant lifestyles than they are about political deviance, deviance that threatens democracy by violating human rights. Police carry out searches of brothels to ensure that no sex workers are being held illegally and against their wills (Landler, 2006a, p. A3). It is useful to consider German uneasiness with Turkish marriage norms against this background. Germans tend to think of arranged marriages as forced marriages, and marriages of Turkish German men to women brought from Turkey as a sort of human trafficking. They find it hard to imagine that any woman would freely consent to marry a man she did not know or did not choose herself.

Political Deviance

Germany's government defines political crime broadly, making hate crimes and violations of civil rights into crimes against the state. The reasoning goes like this: Germany's constitution, its "Basic Law," established a universal principle of equality for every individual and it accords ethnic, racial, and religious minorities special protection. Any political group that advocates racial superiority or racial homogeneity, even just as propaganda, violates the constitution (Federal Minister of the Interior, 2005). Politically motivated crimes make up less than 5% of all crimes, and fewer than 10% of political crimes are violent crimes, but they seem singularly threatening to Germans.

A surprising example of a group defined as politically deviant is the Church of Scientology. The German government makes Scientology the object of security surveillance. Courts claim that Scientology seeks to undermine Germany's "free democratic order" because it works toward a religiously dominated society (run by the Church of Scientology) "without general and fair elections," which would abrogate or restrict "fundamental basic and human rights, such as human dignity, the right to free development of personality and the right to equality" (Federal Minister of the Interior, 2005).

Extremist Groups

The government carefully counts and publishes data on political crimes. In 2005 it counted about 16,000 crimes classified as "right-wing," five thousand as "left-wing," and almost 800 as "politically motivated crimes by foreigners." Only some of these offenses were violent crimes and most of the violent crimes were attacks by one extremist group on another: 199 attacks by right-wing groups on left-wing groups and 449 attacks by the left on the right. Also, there were 355 attacks on foreigners by right-wing extremists and 37 anti-Semitic attacks.

Right-Wing Extremists

In the 1990s, after reunification, there was an upsurge in right-wing political deviance, particularly in the states that were part of the former East Germany. More young men were seen in the streets with shaved heads and paramilitary gear, wearing Nazi symbols. Violent underground computer games like "Aryan Test" and "Total Auschwitz" drilled antiforeigner youths in running a concentration camp or gassing Turks. "Skinzines" (underground right-wing magazines) included *Macht und Ehre* (Power and Honor) and *Schlachtruf* (Battle Cry) and brought news of neo-Nazi groups worldwide. "Hate rock" (a neo-Nazi blend of punk and heavy metal) was the most powerful part of the movement. There were at least 50 *Faschobands,* including *Volkszorn* (The People's Anger) and *Zyklon B* (the name of the poison gas used in Nazi death chambers) (Rodden, 2000, p. 199). (There are still bands like this today, including *Aryan Duo* and *Reichsfront,* with songs like "White and Full of Hate" that glorify violent attacks on immigrants.)

Neo-Nazis staged many attacks on foreigners and also firebombed synagogues and vandalized Jewish cemeteries. According to government figures, far-right groups committed 746 acts of racial violence in 1999—about six times the level of the early 1980s, but down by a third since the early 1990s (*The Economist,* 2000a, p. 18). Ultraconservative parties, like the German People's Union and the National Democratic Party, term foreigners "parasites" who feed on the "*Aryan Volk,*" and "*Zecke Verrecke*" (death to the vermin) is one of the slogans of the movement (Tzortzis, 2005, p. B7). It may seem strange that antiforeigner sentiment is so strong in the eastern part of Germany where there are in fact very few foreigners. Immigrants are only one half of 1% of the population in the east, compared to 9% in the western states. Foreigners are really scapegoats for young East Germans' problems (Rodden, 2000, p. 198).

> ### Erich's Story: The Skinhead
> *Erich Kessel (age 17) is a high school student in Bitterfeld in the eastern state of Saxony. Like his friends, Erich cuts school a lot. He lives in a cracked, water-stained apartment tower complex near the abandoned chemical plants. He wears black leather, shaves his head, and sports T-shirts with neo-Nazi slogans. Late last Saturday night, Erich's high school principal spotted him and his best friend spray-painting swastikas on the gravestones in the old Jewish cemetery. The principal was furious. "You give all Ossis a bad name," he railed. "Why don't you come to school and learn a trade? Make something of yourself so your parents could be proud of you." "What's the point," said Erich. "With the plants closed down, half this town is out of work. My father has been sitting around drinking beer for 12 years now. And they keep bringing in more and more Jews, and give them good apartments and welfare. Hitler was right: There's a tide pouring out of the East, Jews and Poles and Russians, taking all the good jobs and stealing our women, breeding a new race of Untermenschen [inferior people]. You'll see, soon you'll all thank me and my friends for trying to save Germany."*

Neo-Nazis and skinheads are oddly attracted to a new cultural phenomenon in Germany—gangsta rap, a genre popularized mostly by immigrant rappers. Their lyrics glamorize violence, especially against women. Songs like "*Dreckstuck*" ("Piece of Crap"), which encourage listeners to beat and humiliate women, have landed rappers on a federal watch list set up by the Federal Department for Media Harmful to Young Persons, an agency that usually monitors neo-Nazi music. "It is as dangerous to advocate violence against women as it is violence against immigrants," the head of the agency said (Tzortzis, 2005, p. B7).

Muslim Extremists

A great deal of attention in Germany is now focused on a new source of political deviance and violence—Muslim extremists. After the September 11, 2001, attacks in New York, it became clear that many of the terrorists had lived in Germany while planning and coordinating their attacks. Mohammed Atta, the pilot of one of the planes that struck the World Trade Center, was the leader of an Al Qaeda cell in Hamburg. His group held meetings by pretending to be an Islamic prayer group. Two other leading hijackers lived in Hamburg, too. The September 11 attacks mobilized Germans to tighten things up. The parliament repealed a provision of the constitution that gave special protection to religious groups. In December 2001 Germany banned an Islamic group called the Caliphate and carried out more than 200 raids on members. Also, the government tightened security laws, scrapping privacy protections that had made it difficult to get access to bank account and income information, computer records, even addresses and telephone numbers.

Since then, Germany has not (as of 2007) suffered a terrorist attack, but several planned bombings have been discovered by security forces and interrupted. A plot to set off bombs on trains was thwarted in 2006, and in 2007 three Muslim militants were arrested with a large stock of explosive chemicals and military-grade detonators. The three included two German converts to Islam and a Turkish resident of Germany who had trained in terrorist camps in Pakistan.

Debate continues over how far Germany should go in guarding against terrorist attacks. A 2006 government report classified some 32,000 Muslims as potential extremists, but said that only a very small number, fewer than 100, were dangerous enough to keep under regular surveillance (Landler & Kulish, 2007, p. A5). Do these small numbers and the successful actions to foil plots mean that the government is doing enough to protect its citizens? Some politicians call for more aggressive measures: closed-circuit cameras in public places, a central antiterrorist database, secret online searches of computers belonging to people suspected of terrorist sympathies. Such measures remind many Germans of the Nazi Gestapo and the East German Stasi, the secret police. Germany's constitution is set up to give priority to the rights of the individual over the rights of the state. How far should the government go in guarding against terrorism? In 2005 Germany's highest court ruled against a state law that permitted wiretapping in cases where there was no concrete evidence of plans for a crime. And in 2007 a court in Munich issued an arrest warrant for 13 CIA officers whom it accused of abducting a German citizen for "extraordinary rendition" to a prison in Afghanistan (Bernstein, 2005b, p. A3; *The Economist,* 2007a, p. 52; Landler, 2006c, p. A8).

INEQUALITY AND DIVERSITY

Germans have long shared a commitment to limiting economic inequality. Chancellor Gerhard Schroder articulated widely shared sentiments in 2005 when he said, "People are not objects. The link between economic development and social justice must be maintained." "We don't want to leave anyone behind," the next chancellor, Angela Merkel, said in 2007 (Landler, 2005a, p. 3). By the second half of the 20th century West Germany had a moderate degree of income inequality—more than its neighbor Denmark, but much less than the United States. In the mid-1980s, the percentage of total income received by the richest fifth of West Germans was 5.8 times as large as that received by the poorest fifth. East Germany, as a socialist society, had an even greater commitment to equality. There, in 1980, the share of total income that went to the richest fifth was only 2.5 times as big as the share of the poorest fifth. The average factory manager was paid only about twice as much as the average factory worker (Ardagh, 1991, pp. 174, 374).

Since reunification, class inequalities have grown in Germany, particularly since 2000. Studying class inequality in Germany reveals a lot about German culture and society as well as about globalization and the global reach of new patterns of inequality.

Child Welfare

In 2007 Germans were shocked by repeated news of crimes against children, murdered by their mothers, dead of neglect and starvation, living homeless on the streets. Overall there were more than 3,000 reported child abuse cases in 2006, quite a bit more than the 1,900 cases recorded in 1995. The problem is especially severe in Berlin, which has a child abuse rate four times the national average (Clermont, 2007; *Deutsche Welle,* 2007c; Kulish, 2007b, p. A4).

The stories prompted national self-examination and debate about how well Germany cares for its children. Politicians and social workers agree that the tragedies are connected to rising rates of child poverty. Germany has seen a steady rise in child poverty since the mid-1980s. As much as 5.9% of German children under 17 lived in poor households then. It was 10.3% by the mid-1990s, and 12.8% by 2000. That level is an embarrassment to Germany because it compares unfavorably to rates in its nearby European neighbors: 2.4% in Denmark, 7.3% in France, 9% in the Netherlands. We'd like to note, however, that child poverty levels are much higher in some other rich, industrial societies. In a United Nations survey Germany came out halfway down a ranked list of 21 industrial countries. The United States and the United Kingdom were at the bottom, with the highest child poverty rates (*Spiegel Online,* 2007). See Table 5.4.

Trends in Inequality

Let's put child poverty in context. Income inequality increased in Germany through the 1990s and 2000s. But the increase was slow and inequality in Germany remained at moderate levels. Income is neither as equally distributed as it is in Denmark or Finland, nor as unequally distributed as in the United States or the United Kingdom. (Refer back to Table 1.6 on p. 49.) But the slow increase in inequality masks many

TABLE 5.4 Child Poverty Rates

Child poverty rates show the percentage of children under the age of 17 who are living in households with income less than half the median income in their country. Income data includes both earned income and government supplements. Germany has higher rates of child poverty than its European neighbors. Also, child poverty has increased in the past decade in Germany.

	2000 (%)	Mid-1990s (%)
Germany	12.8	10.3
Denmark	2.4	1.8
Switzerland	6.8	10.4
France	7.3	7.1
Netherlands	9.0	9.1
Japan	14.3	12.0
United States	21.7	22.3
Mexico	24.8	26.0

Source: Organisation for Economic Co-operation and Development, *Society at a Glance,* 2005b, http://www.oecd.org.document/24/0,3343,en_33873108_33873402_2671576_1_1_1_1,00.html.

changes. If we look just at pay, not total income, we can see that for the lower and middle classes pay declined. In 1997, 16% of German workers earned wages considered "low pay." By 2004 it had risen to over 20% (*The Economist,* 2006f, p. 61). At the same time, pay increased for the rich and the super-rich, by up to 50% (Bach, Corneo, & Steiner, 2007, pp. 15–16). Poverty rates rose, especially after 2003.

Increasing Poverty

Germans worry now that they are seeing the development of an **underclass,** a population of low-skilled, often unemployed people who are persistently poor and have little prospect of upward mobility, who live concentrated in poor neighborhoods. A Social Democratic Party think tank estimates the size of this group at up to 8% of Germany's population. Conservatives fear that the values of the poor are growing more and more different from those of the middle class, as their isolation grows. They point to lifestyles focused on "fast food, alcohol, trash television, and large tattoos" (*The Economist,* 2006h, p. 60).

Behind the Trends

Much is changing, economically and politically in Germany, with pronounced effects on class inequality. First of all, Germany isn't going it alone; like all the societies in this book, Germany is part of a global economy and must deal with new economic pressures and global competition. That is a big shock for Germans. The government-financed safety net that Germans take for granted is under attack. And the educational system that used to be a great source of strength for German society is working badly now, blocking social mobility for poor Germans. Also, German society is less homogeneous than it used to be. Immigrants are poorer than German natives and easterners are poorer than western Germans, so that too makes for more class inequality.

Globalization and Inequality

After World War II West Germany built one of the world's most successful capitalist economies, but in characteristically German style. German capitalism is different from Japanese or American capitalism. The particular nature of German capitalism is consistent with German culture and values. Germans call their economy a "social market economy."

Valuing order and social responsibility, Germans find the workings of free-market forces unacceptably cruel and disorderly. In unregulated competition, some companies become so successful that they drive out all the others, becoming monopolies and destroying competition itself. Also, unregulated market economies often exhibit strong **business cycles,** periods of boom when profits rise, businesses grow, and more workers are hired, followed by terrible depressions when companies go bankrupt and many workers are unemployed. Workers may be forced to accept very low wages and bad working conditions, just to have a job. Even business owners in Germany want the government to step in to control free-market competition.

Germans agree that it is right for the government to set the rules for business and use its power to make sure the economy works well. Complex laws regulate business practices, the use and disposal of toxic materials, the kinds of advertisements permitted, work conditions in factories and offices, how businesses should bargain with unions, and how corporate management should be structured. For example, by law stores are permitted to have sales only twice a year, in January and July. While Germans sometimes complain about the difficulty of complying with so many regulations, they think that their society is better off because of the role government plays in the economy.

Labor–Management Cooperation.   German capitalism is distinctive in the emphasis it places on workers' security. In Germany, businesses must be profitable, but maintaining "the social peace" by recognizing the rights of labor is an equally important value. This is apparent in the organization of firms and in management goals.

Approximately one third of German workers are union members and almost all of their unions belong to a powerful central federation, the German Trade Union Federation (DBG). Employers and unions run big businesses together in a unique system known as **codetermination.** By law, all big companies have two boards of directors, a management board, and a supervisory board. Union representatives must make up half the members on the supervisory boards. Workers councils, elected by employees in medium- and large-sized firms, can actually veto some management decisions, including decisions on hiring and firing and job elimination.

Germany in the Global Economy.   Everyone sees the problem: All the benefits of the social market economy that made life good for working Germans in the past 50 years now make Germany less competitive in the global economy. The bottom line is that industrial workers in Germany are paid much, much more than their counterparts in eastern Europe and Asia. Even in Portugal, hourly wages are only about a third of German wages. If you include benefits, auto workers in Germany cost their companies $40.80 per hour. Compare that with $35.40 in Japan, and $5.40 in nearby Slovakia. German workers have 35 hour workweeks and 7 weeks of paid vacation and 10 paid holidays a year. Germans work fewer hours per year than employees anywhere else in the industrialized world. In addition, strict laws to protect jobs mean that it is very hard for companies to fire German workers and laid-off employees are entitled to generous unemployment benefits. Until 2005, those benefits could continue indefinitely (Landler, 2005b, pp. BU1, BU4).

To survive competition from companies in lower-wage countries, German manufacturing companies have been pushing back hard. They have laid off workers and threatened to move factories abroad if employees don't make concessions on wages and hours. In 2005 Siemens threatened to move 2,000 jobs assembling telephones to Hungary and won an extension of weekly hours to 40, without a wage increase. Volkswagen agreed to build a new factory in Germany rather than Portugal after the union consented to exempt the employees from its regular contract so their wages could be reduced 20%. General Motors, which owns Opel, cut 10,000 jobs in Germany in 2005 (Landler, 2005b, pp. BU1, BU4).

Industrial "restructuring" like this has had two effects: The economy has become more competitive, and by 2007 economic growth had picked up markedly. Company profits rose sharply and unemployment fell, but pay raises failed to keep up with inflation. The share of national income that goes to wages fell from 60 to 55% (*The Economist*, 2007d, pp. 80–81). In Germany, as elsewhere around the world, the pressure of global competition produced greater inequality: Corporations and business elites made more money and workers made less.

Shrinking the Welfare State

German companies have worked hard to bring down labor costs, but they have been hemmed in by all the government regulations that protect workers and unions. The next step in restoring German competitiveness was to scale back the safety net so Germans would feel more pressure to accept management terms.

Welfare Benefits.   Germany is a **welfare state.** That means the government accepts responsibility for its citizens' social welfare. Germans today will tell you that welfare benefits support the "social peace" and relieve class tensions. Though their taxes are high, they believe the benefits are worth it. The government pledges to guarantee citizens the right to certain benefits and services, like health care and housing, even if they can't afford to buy them on the free market.

The institutions of the welfare state date back long before the division of Germany. The welfare state began in the 1880s, under the rule of Kaiser Wilhelm I and his prime minister, Otto von Bismarck, as a conservative response to the trade union and socialist movements of the time. They instituted three historic components of a universal welfare system: national health insurance, accident insurance, and old age/disability insurance. Unemployment insurance was added in 1927. During the 20th century other European countries followed Germany's example, establishing similar welfare programs. In the United States, where the obligation of the state to ensure the social welfare of its citizens is not fully accepted, only two of the usual welfare programs—old-age pensions and unemployment insurance— have been enacted. See Table 5.5.

TABLE 5.5 Health Care Spending and Life Expectancy

Germany and Japan spend about half as much per person on health care as the United States, but average life expectancy is a few years longer.

	Spending on Health Care per Person Yearly ($)	Number of Years You Can Expect to Live
Germany	3,142	78.7
Japan	2,311	81.9
United States	6,031	77.3
Mexico	608	74.9
Egypt	244	69.6
Namibia	475	48.6

Source: United Nations, *Human Development Report 2006/2007,* 2006/2007, http://hdr.undp.org/en/statistics/.

Germany later added to this basic welfare package. The government gives all parents a yearly family allowance for each child, regardless of income or marital status. There is also a program of rent allowances for low-income families, to make sure they can afford market rents and prevent homelessness. Finally, there are cash allowances for people who for some reason cannot work (Nyrop, 1982, pp. 97–98). Germany's social insurance and welfare programs are expensive. Approximately one third of the country's GNP is spent on health and welfare. Social programs are paid for by high income taxes, payroll taxes, and mandatory employer contributions.

In East Germany the welfare state went even further. It added very generous family benefits: long maternity leaves, free "starter loans" for newly married couples, inexpensive day care, factory hospitals and clinics, free holidays, and subsidized low prices for basic food, theater tickets, and rent, which was kept to about 5% of average family income (Burant, 1988, pp. 88–89).

What this means in practical terms is that in 2000 22% of Germans received some kind of government support, including 1.8 million long-term unemployed people. Compare that with 11.4% in Japan and 13.7% in the United States (Jones, 2007, p. 23). Until 2005, welfare benefits were generous. A single person who lost his or her job received an average of $825 a month, plus money for housing. Families got even more, with all sorts of extra allowances for children's clothing, school supplies, Christmas gifts, and special grants to fix a washing machine or a car (Clermont, 2007; *The Economist,* 2006f, p. 61). Germany doesn't have a minimum wage, so these benefits were a kind of de facto minimum. To lure workers off welfare and into jobs employers had to pay more. They suspected that Germany's relatively high unemployment rate could be brought down and government spending could be lowered if people were cut off from government benefits.

The Hartz IV Reforms.   In 2005 the government drastically cut unemployment benefits by half and required many recipients to work in very low-paid community service jobs (so-called one-Euro jobs) in order to qualify for the much-reduced benefits. Many people previously considered unable to work were reclassified as employable (O'Brien, 2005, p. C3; Zimmerman, 2005).

Several big changes followed the Hartz reforms. First, unemployment rates fell and employment rose. The growth rate of the economy picked up. But at the same time poverty rates, and especially child poverty rates, immediately increased. That can't be surprising. In 2000, 20.5% of Germans were poor, based on their earned income alone. But after adding government help, only 8% were poor. When that help was cut, poverty rates shot up (Jones, 2007, p. 21). Many Germans were scandalized to learn that people could now work full time and still be poor. Unions demanded a national minimum wage of about $20 an hour and social work agencies demanded more government help for children (*The Economist,* 2007e, p. 60; Zimmerman, 2005).

Changes in Education

Germany has a distinctive three-tier system of education that is intended to sort children on the basis of their "calling," their innate talent for one kind of work or another, preparing each child for his or her place in the class system. At the primary level, German states try hard to give each child an equal start. There is no **tracking** (ability grouping) in elementary school. All children are taught the same lessons in heterogeneous classes. But at age 10, after only 4 years of primary school (in some states 6 years) German children face a crucial life transition. Based on their grades, their teachers' assessments, and their parents' wishes, they transfer to one of three types of secondary schools.

Three Tracks.   Students considered to have the strongest academic ability go to *Gymnasium,* an academic school that awards the *Abitur* diploma necessary to attend university. Students who go to *Realschule* prepare mostly for white-collar jobs and do not go to college. Realschule are schools that provide some academic instruction, but mostly concentrate on vocational education in commercial or technical fields. Students graduate Realschule at 16, after 10th grade, and some go on to a technical college (*Fachhochschule*) to train for careers like nursing or accountancy. Others get apprenticeships as lab technicians, precision mechanics, secretaries, or personnel managers. Finally, the least academically skilled students attend vocation high school (*Hauptschule*) until age 15. These schools prepare students for apprenticeship or work in manual, clerical, and semiskilled service jobs. They become construction workers, auto mechanics, file clerks, and salespeople in retail stores. The Hauptschule is usually a neighborhood school, often in the same building as the primary school, and its prestige is low.

Apprenticeships.   There are some very attractive features to this system. Students who don't like school, and students who prefer to work with their hands, can train for real careers without having to go to college. Apprenticeships make vocational training serious and useful. Apprentices spend 4 days a week in the workplace and 1 day in a school setting. They are paid by the companies that take them on.

Young people apprentice as auto mechanics and personnel managers, postal workers, computer programmers, graphic designers, copywriters, plumbers, railway conductors, shoe sales workers—for white-collar and blue-collar jobs in over 350 occupations. You might even think that German apprenticeships overtrain young people. Even relatively unskilled jobs are treated with the greatest seriousness. For example, shoe sales workers serve a full apprenticeship and learn about sales, sizing, cash-register operation, the process of shoe manufacture, and bookkeeping. Ordinary workers are very competent as a result, which adds to their status, and they are also qualified to advance to the next step of promotion. Every shoe salesperson has the knowledge necessary to be manager (Hamilton, 1990, pp. 35, 143–144). So there is a very clear school-to-work transition.

Georg's Story: The Apprentice

At 18, Georg Messer is in his final year of apprenticeship with the famous Konigsdorfer Shoe Company in Hamburg, training to be an Industriekaufmann, *an office worker in an industrial firm. Georg felt lucky to get this apprenticeship; it was highly competitive. One thousand graduates applied for 25 places. Konigsdorfer chose young men and women who were socially skilled and presentable and whose records attested to their ability to work hard and carefully. Having served in 12 different departments at Konigsdorfer, Georg is finishing his apprenticeship in the Cost Accounting Department, working closely with his mentor and applying new computer models to develop prices for the spring shoe line. He uses his knowledge of international exchange rates, import–export tariffs, and the costs of materials and labor, learned in the 1-day-a-week formal instruction* (Berufsschule), *which is part of his apprenticeship.*

We asked Georg if he is ever sorry he didn't go to Gymnasium (academic high school) and on to university. "No, not at all. Why should I be," he answered. "I was really getting tired of school by the time I was 15. This apprenticeship has let me out in the real world, and the 1-day-a-week formal school makes sense, because I use what I learn in Berufsschule here at the factory. Did I tell you I've been offered a job, in the Cost Accounting Department? I can begin as soon as I take my qualifying exams. My bosses seem certain I'll pass. You know I'll have a responsible job with a real adult salary and plenty of room for advancement by the time I'm 18."

Attending University.   About one third of German students go to Gymnasium and those with good grades, who pass a rigorous entrance exam can go to university. Starting in the 1970s, German universities, most of which are public institutions, admitted all qualified students, charged no tuition, and gave students allowances for living expenses, so they didn't need to work while they were in school. But because of the selection process relatively few students in Germany qualify for university. Only 22% of young Germans graduate with a university degree, compared to 31% in Britain and 39% in the United States (*The Economist*, 2006i, pp. 51–52).

Tracking and Social Mobility.   Though the German system sounds great in the abstract, there are problems with the way it actually works. At age 10 very few students know what they want to do in life. They tend to assume they will do the sort of work their parents do. Perhaps teachers make the same assumptions. The result is that middle-class children tend to get tracked into Gymnasium and children from poor families and immigrant families are steered early on into Hauptschule and manual work. International comparative studies show a tighter connection between class background and education achieved in Germany than in any other rich industrial country. The bright child of a professor is four times as likely to go to Gymnasium as the equally smart child of a manual worker. A student who begins in a Hauptschule and discovers an aptitude for academic work finds it difficult to move up to a Gymnasium. And schools don't make much tutoring or other individual help available. Parents who can afford it spend a great deal of money on private tutoring, another source of inequalities in the system (*The Economist*, 2006b, p. 7).

Problems with Apprenticeships.   Germans have been so proud of their apprenticeship system, which in the past educated young people to a high level of competence and placed them into secure, career-track jobs. The problem now is that as the economy slowed after 2000, there were fewer jobs available for young graduates, and businesses offered fewer paid apprenticeships. As many as 100,000 young people between the ages of 17 and 25 have neither jobs nor apprenticeships.

Businesses also now permanently hire fewer apprentices than they used to and of those they do hire more are put on limited contracts. Smaller firms are backing away from the expense of training apprentices. And many companies now prefer to give their apprenticeships to graduates of Fachhochschulen rather than Hauptschule students (Thelen, 2004, pp. 272–275).

Educational Quality.   German minister of education Helmut Rau recently said, "In Germany there is nothing more controversial than education." The latest trouble comes from a disturbing surprise: In 2001 a reliable international achievement evaluation ranked German students only 21st in reading and 20th in math, out of 31 countries (*The Economist,* 2006b, p. 7). Universities have also come in for criticism. The system of free university education is strained. Enrollment has increased, but because economic problems are squeezing government budgets, spending on universities has been cut. Classes are overcrowded, library acquisition budgets are cut, science research labs ill-equipped. State governments have introduced rather minimal tuition fees of about $600 a semester. Students from richer families go abroad for university to institutions where the quality of education is higher. The government has now designated three universities as elite schools and allocated $100 million to each for science and technology education, in an attempt to deal with the problem (Landler, 2006e, p. A3).

Immigrants and Inequality

Inequalities in access to education fall particularly heavily on immigrants and the children of immigrants. Fifty-seven percent of native Germans graduate from upper secondary school, but only 41% of foreign-born Germans do so. Immigrant children, especially Turkish boys, are less likely to go to Gymnasium and more likely to end up in a beat-up local Hauptschule where the majority of the children are immigrants like themselves. Forty percent of Turkish boys drop out before completing school and vocational training (*The Economist,* 2006b, p. 7; 2006e).

Teachers struggle to instruct students who don't speak German as their native language and less learning is accomplished. Remarkably, second-generation immigrant students (those born in Germany to immigrant parents) get lower scores on reading tests than first-generation students (those born in another country). In most countries second-generation children score better, sometimes, as in the United States, much better. Even when we compare children of the same social class, the second generation still scores worse than the first in Germany. These data seem to suggest cumulative disadvantages to children who live in poor, isolated, immigrant areas with inferior schools. Lower educational achievement for immigrants goes along with higher unemployment—26% for immigrants in 2006, more than twice the national average (*The Economist,* 2006e; Organisation for Economic Co-operation and Development, 2007a).

Regional Inequalities

Another group in Germany hard hit by unemployment is residents of the former East Germany. Unemployment rates there remain double the rates in the west. Although wages in the east have risen almost to the level of western wages, median income has dropped by more than one third. This is the effect of unemployment (Bach et al., 2007, pp. 4, 10). There is a lot of disguised unemployment, too. After reunification many people over 50 were encouraged to retire early. Everyone admits there is a whole generation of middle-aged people who will never work again. Especially in depressed industrial areas, east Germans feel like they are a welfare colony, maintained on the charity of the west, and it angers them very much, because in the past they took pride in their workmanship, their productivity, and their role as the leading socialist economy (Landler, 2004b, p. A4).

The New Economy of the East. In some parts of the east, economic redevelopment has been successful. Dresden, the capital of the eastern state of Saxony, has been beautifully reconstructed, its baroque historic center restored. It is now, as in the past, a popular tourist destination. Many high-tech start-ups have come to the Dresden area, bringing jobs in data processing, biotechnology, optical precision instrument manufacture, and electrical and medical engineering. The Dresden area now calls itself "Silicon Saxony" (*The Economist,* 2004, p. 58; Landler, 2003b, pp. C1–C2).

But many more towns are like Hoyerswerda, in Brandenburg, which is Germany's fastest-shrinking city. Hoyerswerda has lost 39% of its residents, and its unemployment rate is still 23.5%. Ironically, Hoyerswerda's problems actually result from modernization of its factories. The city's biggest employer, Schwarze Pumpe, employed 18,000 people before reunification, but after privatization and modernization, it employs only 1,000 (O'Brien, 2004a, pp. W1, W7). We see the same pattern in eastern Germany's old chemical industry. In Bitterfeld, a dangerously polluted old industrial town, Bayer invested 630 million euros (including a government subsidy of 100 million euros) to build a new complex. The factory, which in the past required hundreds of workers, is now run by eight chemists, who monitor the computers in the control room. As industries close down or modernize, people leave eastern towns. About one in seven eastern Germans has moved to western Germany or abroad since 1990, and population in the eastern states has dropped 10%. There are fewer working-age people and fewer children, and elderly people make up a larger and larger percentage of the eastern population (O'Brien, 2004b, pp. W1, W7; Zielbauer, 2002, p. A3).

Before unification East Germany had an unusually low level of inequality: Managers and professionals earned only a little more than twice what factory workers earned, and almost everyone was a state employee. Now there are some entrepreneurs and self-employed professionals in the east. They earn more money and so do the engineers and technicians who work for the high-tech start-ups. With some people earning more and, at the same time, more people unemployed, income inequality has increased markedly in the east. That is reflected in data showing growing inequality for Germany as a whole (Bach et al., 2007, pp. 13–14).

Let us sum up: Why has class inequality grown in Germany? Globalization, the shrinking of the welfare state, an education system that constricts opportunity, a growing immigrant population with fewer opportunities, and the growth of inequality in the former east have all contributed.

SOCIAL CHANGE

Of course we have been talking about social change all through this chapter. We've discussed the reunification of Germany, the growth of immigration, increasing inequality, and globalization, among other subjects. Now we would like to discuss two overarching social changes that form the backdrop to all other change in Germany. Both of these changes are so broad that they affect all European countries and almost all of the world's rich industrial countries.

Demographic Change

Birthrates are falling in Germany, the nation's population is actually shrinking, and it is aging. Germany has the lowest birthrate in Europe, and unlike some of its neighbors, such as France and Italy, where birthrates are low but stable, Germany's birthrate continues to fall. On average, German women have only 1.3 children each. It takes an average of 2.1 children per woman to keep the population at the stable level. In 2003 Germany's population began to get smaller, though by just 5,000 people. By 2006, population was down by 130,000 people. If birthrates don't rise, Germany will experience "negative exponential growth": Its population will shrink by greater and greater amounts each year (Kulish, 2007a, p. 4). Reiner Klingholz, director of the Berlin Institute for Population and Development, calculated that without immigration, Germany's population will fall from the current 82 million to 24 million at the end of the 21st century. Even including immigration, at current rates, Germany's population will shrink by 700,000 by 2020. And a bigger proportion of Germany's population will be old: By 2050, Klingholz predicts, one third of Germans will be over 65, twice the current proportion. That will put an enormous strain on Germany's public health care system and on the public pension system. Germans worry that there will be too many schools, too many hospitals, too many roads, and a deserted, depopulated countryside (Landler, 2004c, p. A3). See Table 5.6, p. 297.

With its low birthrate, Germany is in the vanguard of a demographic change that is happening throughout Europe, eastern Europe, and Japan. Only the United States, among rich nations, manages to keep its birthrate up to 2.1. And the rich nations are graying too: in Germany, Italy, and Japan more than a quarter of the population is over 60. This demographic change is putting a very heavy burden on pension plans and producing shortages of workers. Even if European countries were willing to accept a much higher rate of immigration than they have now, there would not be enough foreigners to fill the labor shortage. A UN report in 2007 called global aging "a process without parallel in the history of humanity" (Kulish, 2007a, p. 4; Rosenthal, 2006, p. A3).

Women and Babies

Why are German women having so few children? Women are postponing childbearing from their early 20s into their 30s. By that time grandmothers may be too old to help much, particularly for second or third children. Also, women find it difficult to combine work and motherhood. Professional women have especially low birthrates. The elementary school day ends at 1:00 p.m., with children sent home

**TABLE 5.6 Number of Young Adults 15 to 34 in 2000 and 2025
(in Millions of Persons)**

*There has been a sharp decline in the number of young adults 15 to 34 in
Germany and Japan. Germany's decline is limited by substantial immigration, but
Japan has virtually no immigration. These declines may lead to serious shortages
of labor in the future.*

*In Egypt and Mexico the number of young adults in the population is still rising,
even though the populations overall are aging. These increases may result both in
rising unemployment and increasing emigration.*

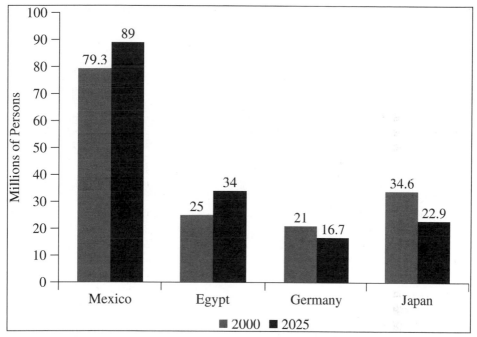

Source: U.S. Bureau of the Census, *International Data Base, Tables by Country,* http://www.census.gov/ipc/www/
idb/tables.html.

for lunch, and there is room in Germany's preschools for only 1 in 10 three-year-
olds. A study done at the Berlin Institute for Population and Development found
that the birthrate is highest in countries where men and women are more equal, and,
surprisingly, higher in countries where more women work (Pham, 2007, p. 3).

Government and Family Policy

Germany's politicians would like to see birthrates increase. They are trying to use
economic incentives to smooth the way for childbearing. One new program would
allow families with two working parents tax deductions for child care costs. Another
will triple the number of places in nursery school, at a cost of about $16 billion over
5 years. These plans will make it easier for women to combine motherhood and
work. Still another program helps mothers who want to stay home with their children, and fathers too. It pays up to two thirds of a new parent's salary, up to about

TABLE 5.7 Delayed Marriage

Women in many societies are delaying marriage. In Germany and Japan a majority of women were married by age 24 in 1972. Today only one in four marries that early. In 1972 half of all Egyptian women were married by 19, today only one in eight marries before 19. The number of Mexican women marrying by 19 also declined.

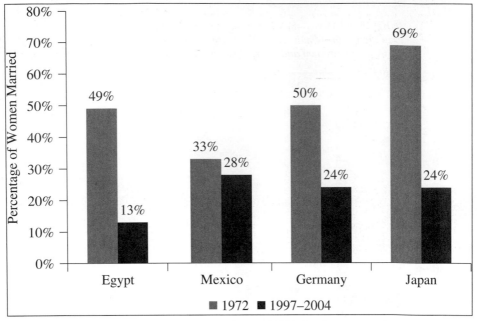

Source: United Nations, *Demographic Yearbook,* 1982, 2000, and 2004a, http://unstats.un.org/unsd/demographic/products/dyb/dyb2.htm.

$2,500 a month, for a year for one parent or 14 months if two parents share the benefit. This will cost the government about $5.6 billion a year (Kulish, 2007a, p. 4; *The Economist,* 2006a, p. 46). See Table 5.7.

But the government faces some cultural obstacles to raising birthrates. Any government policy to promote childbearing reminds people of Hitler's government which gave medals to mothers of large families. At the same time, Germans aren't quite comfortable with the idea of working mothers, who are sometimes called "raven-mothers," implying that they abandon their chicks prematurely (*The Economist,* 2007c, p. 66).

Migration

The movement of people is an important part of globalization. And, in truth, the world's people are on the move. Experts estimate that there are 200 million international migrants in the world today. Still more people migrate within their own country. Worldwide, people are leaving the countryside and moving to cities (*The Economist,* 2008a, p. 4). We can see all these patterns of migration in Germany today: migration within Germany, immigration into Germany (which we have already discussed), and emigration from Germany. These human migrations are both helpful and disruptive, and German society has had a hard time keeping up.

Internal Migration

Germans are moving from east to west and north to south and from rural to urban areas. It is the largest internal migration within the nation since World War II. A million and a half people have left the former East Germany, especially the young, women, and the highly educated. Some parts of the former East have lost a third of their population. That makes it harder for eastern communities to thrive economically, and sharpens inequalities between east and west. There are 1.3 million empty apartments in the east and communities have to close schools and raise taxes to maintain infrastructure and help the growing number of older people. That makes communities even less attractive to business and the young. It is a vicious circle. Young people are also leaving the old industrial Ruhr area in northern Germany and moving south to Bavaria and Baden-Wurtemberg, the most prosperous German states (*The Economist,* 2006d, p. 55).

Immigration and Emigration

Immigration to Germany is declining now. Although Germany has a large population of people of foreign birth, it looks like the era of massive immigration, when millions of foreigners flocked in, is over. In 2006, fewer than 200,000 immigrants arrived. Having spent several decades worrying about people coming in, Germans now have a new worry: Germans leaving, or **emigrating** out of Germany to other countries. A popular television series in 2007 was called *Goodbye Deutschland: The Emigrants.* It followed several families who left Germany for South Africa, or Spain. In 2005, 144,000 Germans left Germany, but 128,000 others returned, so there was only a small net loss. Germans are nervous because the number who leave is growing and many of the emigrants are professionals—doctors, engineers, scientists. People fear that Germany is beginning to experience a **brain drain,** a loss of educated, highly skilled people. The idea that a rich industrial society like Germany could experience a brain drain is shocking. Usually it is professionals from poor countries who move to the richer nations. No other rich country in Europe is losing professionals.

Already, some 12,000 German doctors work abroad, the largest numbers in Britain, Switzerland, and Austria. Doctors say they are leaving Germany to earn higher salaries and to advance in their fields. Medicine is a very rigid profession in Germany, with advancement slow and under the control of powerful chief doctors. Women doctors find they can work part-time abroad, but not in Germany.

To some degree, emigration is part of globalization. German university students often spend at least one semester abroad. They become fluent in English or French. Germany is part of the European Union, so the borders are open and any EU resident can live and work anywhere in Europe. Some educated young people feel more "European" than German and they look around and see more opportunities outside Germany. At the same time, Denmark is concerned that so many educated young people migrate to Germany, and young Swedes are flocking to Norway

TABLE 5.8 Emigration, Education, and Anxiety (1999–2002)

Many Germans worry about emigration as well as about immigration. Germany and Mexico face a substantial exodus of college graduates—a "brain drain" for both countries. One in every eight Mexican college graduates emigrates. College graduates are more likely to emigrate than the rest of the population.

	Emigrants for Every 1,000 Persons 15 Years Old and Older	College-Educated Emigrants for Every 1,000 College-Educated Persons	Population Saying That People Leaving the Country for Jobs Is a Significant Problem (%)
Mexico	86	133	52
Germany	36	72	33
Japan	5	15	12
United States	3	4	9

Sources: Organisation for Economic Co-operation and Development, *Beyond Borders: The OECD Database on the Foreign Born and Expatriates,* 2005a, http://www.oecd.org/0.3373,ed_2649_37415_1_1_1_37415.html; Pew Research Center, *What the World Thinks in 2002,* n.d., http://www.people-press.org.

for work. So many Romanians have migrated to Italy and Spain that Romania has to import contract workers from China to staff its factories (Brunwasser, 2007, p. C7; Dougherty, 2007, p. C7; Ekman, 2007, p. 4). See Table 5.8.

Some politicians want to make it easier for foreign professionals to immigrate to Germany. They say Germany has a shortage of professionals, technicians, and scientists. Opponents say there are still skilled Germans who need jobs and companies are just trying to hire cheaper workers. It's very hard for Germans to accept that the country could need more immigrants when there are 3.8 million people unemployed (*The Economist,* 2006g, p. 61; Landler, 2007a, p. A10; Kinast, Reiermann, & Sauga, 2007). In this respect Germans are like people all over the world, unable to comprehend that globalization results in rapid shifts of population as well as of capital.

Social Change and the Environment

We've talked a lot now about the problems caused by demographic change. But wouldn't there be an upside to shrinking population? If you drive to school or work through heavy traffic, the idea of a smaller population might sound good to you. If you are concerned about global warming, climate change, or pollution, or shortages of water or resources like oil, a shrinking population might seem to be just what is needed. Certainly a falling human population is good for animals. Along the rural eastern border of Germany, as villages empty animals are coming back. There are now lynx, even wolves, and possibly bears (*The Economist,* 2006d, p. 55).

But when it comes to the environment, it isn't just the size of the human population that matters. The environmental impact of humans is a function of the number of people combined with their level of affluence and the technology they use. One German uses about 500 times as much power as one San in Namibia.

Germans are very concerned about pollution and climate change. In some respects they have been world leaders in combating global warming, though they cling to some technologies that are really problematical.

German Environmentalism

In Germany, it started with the forests. Germans have long had a deep attachment to their forests. Two thousand years ago the Roman historian Tacitus reported that the Germanic tribes worshipped in groves of trees that they regarded as the dwellings of the gods. In the 18th and 19th centuries German romanticism revived the idea of the forests as the true soul of Germany. But starting in the 1980s, Germans noticed their forests dying, weakened by acid rain blown over from heavy industry in the Ruhr valley and in East Germany. The Rhine River was so polluted that fish could not survive in it. That inspired the start of the environmental movement in Germany. The Green Party grew in strength, attracting young people in particular, so much so that it actually became part of the coalition governing Germany between 2000 and 2005.

After reunification in 1990, Germany was stuck with the state-owned factories in the east, many of them powered by highly polluting soft coal. The factories were too outdated to be saleable, so many were shut down. Old plants also closed in the industrial cities of West Germany, victims of Chinese competition. In fact, some of those factories were actually disassembled and moved to China. These closings greatly reduced pollution and carbon emissions in Germany, but the pollution was, in effect, deported to China, which now is one of the world's most polluted countries and a growing contributor to global warming.

Germans are pleased though to be able to reduce greenhouse gas emissions. Their nation is one of only three European countries that are meeting the goals they promised in the Kyoto climate accord. Chancellor Angela Merkel entered politics in 1994 when then-chancellor Kohl appointed her minister of the environment. Now, as chancellor, Merkel has made combating global warming a focus of her foreign policy (Kahn & Landler, 2007, pp. A1, A27).

Environmental Policy. In 2000 parliament committed Germany to doubling the percentage of renewable energy it produces by 2010. And in 2007, it passed legislation to reduce Germany's carbon emissions by 40% by 2020. Other legislation has aimed to boost energy efficiency. Germany has the largest wind-power industry in Europe, supported by government subsidies. New legislation in 2004 guarantees producers of solar power a high price for their energy. Some farmers in southern Germany are converting their farms to solar parks, or using animal waste to produce biogas.

The Roadblocks. Despite its commitment to reducing greenhouse gases, Germany is still dependent on coal-fired power plants, the dirtiest way to produce energy. As Germany becomes more affluent, and people use more and more technology, electricity demand rises. There are even 20 new coal-fired plants planned for the near future. Nuclear power plants emit no greenhouse gases, but Germans had decided to phase out their nuclear industry. Now they are debating prolonging the life of the plants. Germans are attached to another technology that is directly related

The people in the photo are visiting a new sewage treatment plant in Kiel, Germany, specially designed to protect water supplies from pollution and to prevent the escape of methane gas, a major contributor to global warming. Safeguarding the environment has become a major concern for Germans today. The Green Party, Germany's environmental party, has become a big player in German politics, helping enact environmental standards that are among the world's highest.

to their affluent lifestyles: gas-guzzling, polluting luxury cars and the habit of driving them at speeds over 100 miles per hour on Germany's beautifully engineered autobahns (Blake, 2007, p. 10; *The Economist,* 2007b, p. 50; Landler, 2006b, p. A4). Germans, like citizens of other affluent societies, have a lot of decisions to make, not only about technology, but about whether their affluent way of life is sustainable in the long run.

Thinking Sociologically

1. People in Germany are aware that their society has long had problems dealing with diversity. What obstacles are there in Germany today to integrating minorities? What progress has been made?
2. Compare attitudes to immigrants in Germany and in Japan. How does your society react to immigrants?
3. Germans pride themselves on remembering and atoning for the genocide in their past. How about your society? Were there shameful episodes in your society's history? How does your society deal with them now?
4. Do you live in a capitalist society? If so, is its style of capitalism similar or different in any way from Germany's or Japan's?

5. Germany, Japan, and the United States are the world's three biggest capitalist economies. Refer back to Table 1.6 (p. 49) and compare how equally or unequally these three societies distribute income to their citizens.
6. Compare the system of higher education in Germany with the system in your society. What advantages or disadvantages do you see in each?
7. How is Germany responding to the prospect of a declining total population and an aging population?

For Further Reading

Ardagh, J. (1991). *Germany and the Germans.* New York: Penguin.

Baer, H. (1998). *Crumbling walls and tarnished ideals: An ethnography of East Germany before and after unification.* New York: University Press of America.

Elon, A. (2002). *The pity of it all: A history of Jews in Germany, 1743–1933.* New York: Henry Holt.

Fulbrook, M. (1995). *Anatomy of a dictatorship: Inside the GDR 1949–1989.* New York: Oxford University Press.

Hensel, J. (2004). *After the wall: Confessions from an East German childhood and the life that came next.* New York: Public Affairs.

Marcuse, P. (1991). *Missing Marx: A personal and political journal of a year in East Germany, 1989–1990.* New York: Monthly Review Press.

Bibliography

Ardagh, J. (1991). *Germany and the Germans.* New York: Penguin.

Bach, S., Corneo, G., Steiner, V. (2007, April). From bottom to top: The entire distribution of market income in Germany 1992–2001. *IZA Discussion Paper Series* (No. 2723). Institute for the Study of Labor. Retrieved from http://ssm.com/abstract=982113

Bernstein, R. (2005a, February 21). Germany tightens Jewish immigration rules. *International Herald Tribune,* p. 1.

Bernstein, R. (2005b, July 28). German high court rules a state's wiretap law is unlawful. *The New York Times,* p. A3.

Blake, M. (2007, December 5). In Bali, Germany takes dramatic step on climate change. *The Christian Science Monitor,* p. 10.

Boyes, R. (1999, August 29). Germany embraces oldest profession. *The Times (London).* Available from http://www.lexisnexis.com/lnacademic

Brunwasser, M. (2007, April 11). Romania, a poor land, imports poorer workers. *The New York Times,* p. C7.

Bucerius, S. M. (2007, Summer). What else should I do? Cultural influences on the drug trade of migrants in Germany. *Journal of Drug Issues, 37*(3), 673–697.

Burant, S. R. (Ed.). (1988). *East Germany: A country study* (3rd ed.), Area Handbook Series. Washington, DC: U.S. Government Printing Office.

Buruma, I. (1994). *The wages of guilt: Memories of war in Germany and Japan.* New York: Farrar, Straus & Giroux.

Caldwell, C. (2007, May 27). Where every generation is first-generation. *The New York Times Magazine,* pp. 44–49.

Clermont, R.-A. (2007, November 28). Rich Germany faces up to child poverty problem. *Spiegel Online.* Retrieved from http://www.spiegel.de/international/germany/0,1518, 520202,00.html

Cohen, R. (2000, June 20). A dog's best friend, it seems, may be a German. *The New York Times,* p. A4.

Coser, L. (1956). *The functions of social conflict.* New York: Free Press.

Coser, L. (2000, December 30). Germany's financial heart is open but wary. *The New York Times,* pp. A1, A6.

Demographic and health surveys. (n.d.). Retrieved from the STATcompiler database, http://www.statcompiler.com

Deutsche Welle. (2006, September 25). *Study challenges widely-held notions about Islamic headscarf.* Retrieved from http://www.dw-world.de/dw/article/0,2144,2179580,00.html

Deutsche Welle. (2007a, January 5). *Street children on the rise in Germany, aid agency warns.* Retrieved from http://www.dw-world.de/dw/article/0,2144,2301119,00.html

Deutsche Welle. (2007b, May 11). *German interior ministry announces progress on crime.* Retrieved from http://www.germany.info/relaunch/info/publications/week/2007/070511/politics2.html

Deutsche Welle. (2007c, December 30). *Germans increasingly concerned about wellbeing of children.* Retrieved from http://www.dw-world.de/article/0,2144,3029341,00.html

Dougherty, C. (2007, December 26). Denmark feels the pinch as young workers flee to lands of lower taxes. *The New York Times,* p. C7.

The Economist. (1999, February 6). Germany survey, pp. 1–18.

The Economist. (2000a, August 12). Germany's Neo-Nazis, pp. 18–19.

The Economist. (2000b, September 2). Germany: The church victorious, pp. 44–45.

The Economist. (2004, September 18). Eastern Germany: Getting back together is so hard, p. 58.

The Economist. (2005, May 7). Germans and Jews: Uncertain normality, p. 48.

The Economist. (2006a, February 4). Germany and the family: The martyrdom of Ursula, pp. 46–47.

The Economist. (2006b, February 11). A survey of Germany, pp. 3–16.

The Economist. (2006c, February 18). German trade unions: There's life in the old dinosaurs yet, p. 51.

The Economist. (2006d, March 18). German demography: Cradle snatching, p. 55.

The Economist. (2006e, April 22). Multicultural hysterics: New Germans, p. 66.

The Economist. (2006f, May 13). Germany's labour market: A lesson from Tony Blair, p. 61.

The Economist. (2006g, October 28). Germany: Land of emigration: Auf wiedersehen, fatherland, p. 61.

The Economist. (2006h, November 11). German inequality: Class concerns, p. 60.

The Economist. (2006i, December 10). German higher education: Jacob's ladder, pp. 51–52.

The Economist. (2007a, February 3). German anti-terrorism: A complicated business, pp. 52–53.

The Economist. (2007b, February 10). Germany's nuclear power: A policy of denial, p. 50.

The Economist. (2007c, May 5). Germany: Raving ravens, p. 66.

The Economist. (2007d, July 14). Briefing Germany's economy, pp. 80–82.

The Economist. (2007e, December 8). Pay in Germany: How low can you go? pp. 60–61.

The Economist. (2008a, January 5). Open up, pp. 3–5.

The Economist. (2008b, February 2). German state elections: Hessen lesson, p. 58.

Ehrkamp, P. (2005, March). Placing identities: Transnational practices and local attachments of Turkish immigrants in Germany. *Journal of Ethnic and Migration Studies, 31*(2), 345–365.

Ekman, I. (2007, December 30). Young Swedes flock to newly rich Norway for work. *The New York Times,* p. 4.

Elon, A. (2002). *The pity of it all: A history of Jews in Germany, 1743–1933.* New York: Henry Holt.

Facts About Germany. (n.d.). *Facts on immigration and integration in Germany.* Retrieved from http://www.germany.infor/relaunch/politics/domestic/immigration/immigration.html.

Federal Minister of the Interior of the Federal Republic of Germany. (2005). *Annual report on the protection of the Constitution.* Retrieved from http://www.verfassungsschutz.de/download/SHOW/vsbericht_2005_eng.pdf

Federal Minister of the Interior of the Federal Republic of Germany. (2007, May 11). *German interior ministry announces progress on crime.* Retrieved from http://www.germany .info/relaunch/info/publications/week/2007/070511/politics2/html

Gannon, M. J. (1994). *Understanding global cultures.* London: Sage.

Giddens, A. (1991). *Introduction to sociology.* New York: Norton.

Glouchevitch, P. (1992). *Juggernaut: The German way of business.* New York: Simon & Schuster.

Green, S. (2001, October). Immigration, asylum and citizenship in Germany: The impact of unification and the Berlin Republic. *West European Politics, 24*(4), 82–106.

Green, S. (2006, December 21). Rethinking immigrant integration in Germany. *AICGS Advisor.* Retrieved from http://www.aicgs.org/analysis/c/green122106.aspx

Greenfeld, L. (1993). *Nationalism: Five roads to modernity.* Cambridge, MA: Harvard University Press.

Hall, E. T., & Hall, M. R. (1990). *Understanding cultural differences.* Yarmouth, ME: Intercultural Press.

Hamilton, S. F. (1990). *Apprenticeship for adulthood.* New York: Free Press.

Hensel, J. (2004). *After the wall: Confessions from an East German childhood and the life that came next.* New York: Public Affairs.

Homola, V. (2001, October 20). Germany lifting status of prostitutes. *The New York Times,* p. A6.

Hughes, M. L. (2003). Vertriebene in Deutschland. *Journal of Social History, 36*(3), 821–823.

Jolin, A. (1993). Germany. In N. Davis (Ed.), *Prostitution: An international handbook on trends, problems and policies.* Westport, CT: Greenwood Press.

Jones, R. S. (2007, June). Income inequality, poverty and social spending in Japan. Organisation for Economic Co-operation and Development, Economics Department Working Papers No. 556, pp. 1–41.

Kahn, J., & Landler, M. (2007, December 21). China grabs West's smoke-spewing factories. *The New York Times,* pp. A1, A27).

Kinast, J., Reiermann, C., & Sauga, M. (2007, June 22). Where have the skilled workers gone? *Spiegel Online.* Retrieved from http://www.spiegelde/international/business/0,1518, 490031,00.html

Kulish, N. (2007a, September 23). Falling German birthrate dispels baby miracle myth. *The New York Times,* p. 4.

Kulish, N. (2007b, December 14). Crimes against children set off a debate about care. *The New York Times,* p. A4.

Kulish, N. (2008a, January 14). Attack jolts Germany into fray on immigrant crime. *The New York Times,* p. A3.

Kulish, N. (2008b, January 29). 75 years after Hitler's ascent, a Germany that won't forget. *The New York Times,* pp. A1, A4.

Landler, M. (2003a, January 1). New deposit on aluminum cans tests German sense of order. *The New York Times,* p. A4.

Landler, M. (2003b, November 21). Eastern Germany is able to prevent industrial flight to Third World. *The New York Times,* pp. W1, W2.

Landler, M. (2004a, May 9). Germans have a breakdown over quality. *The New York Times,* p. WK 14.

Landler, M. (2004b, July 21). East Germany swallows billions and still stagnates. *The New York Times,* p. A11.

Landler, M. (2004c, November 18). Empty maternity wards imperil a dwindling Germany. *The New York Times,* p. A3.

Landler, M. (2005a, September 11). Germans see pain but no gain as Schroder's star dims. *The New York Times.*

Landler, M. (2005b, October 26). German labor's new reality. *The New York Times,* pp. C1, C4.

Landler, M. (2006a, July 3). World Cup brings little pleasure to German brothels. *The New York Times,* p. A3.

Landler, M. (2006b, July 28). Hot German July doesn't faze farmer who reaps the sun. *The New York Times,* p. A4.

Landler, M. (2006c, August 22). Bomb plot shocks Germans into antiterrorism debate. *The New York Times,* p. A8.

Landler, M. (2006d, September 23). Berlin mayor, symbol of openness, has national appeal. *The New York Times,* p. A4.

Landler, M. (2006e, October 20). Seeking quality, German universities scrap equality. *The New York Times,* p. A3.

Landler, M. (2006f, December 8). In Munich, provocation in a symbol of foreign faith. *The New York Times,* p. A3.

Landler, M. (2007a, February 6). Germany agonizes over a brain drain. *The New York Times,* p. A10.

Landler, M. (2007b, March 25). After lifetime in Germany, Turks still alone and torn. *The New York Times,* p. 3.

Landler, M. (2007c, July 5). Germans split over a mosque and the role of Islam. *The New York Times,* p. A3.

Landler, M., Barbaro, M. (2006, August 6). Wal-Mart discovers that its formula doesn't fit every culture. *The New York Times,* pp. C1, C4.

Landler, M., & Kulish, N. (2007, September 8). Arrest of one Turk in Germany brings new scrutiny to a society of 2.7 million. *The New York Times,* p. A5.

Lewis, F. (1987). *Europe: A tapestry of nations.* New York: Simon & Schuster.

The New York Times. (2007a, September 11). Germany: Attack on rabbi is condemned, p. A8.

The New York Times. (2007b, October 2). Germany: Mob attacks Greeks in Berlin, p. A12.

Moeller, R. G. (2005, Spring/Summer). Germans as victims?: Thoughts on a post–Cold War history of World War II's legacies. *History and Memory, 17*(1 & 2), 147–194.

Murray, H. (1993, Winter). Gay voices from eastern Germany [Review]. *Journal of Social History, 27*(2), 427–431.

Nyrop, R. F. (Ed.). (1982). *Federal Republic of Germany: A country study* (2nd ed.), Area Handbook Series. Washington, DC: U.S. Government Printing Office.

O'Brien, K. J. (2004a, May 28). Last out, please turn off the lights. *The New York Times,* pp. W1, W7.

O'Brien, K. J. (2004b, September 8). Eastern German chemical industry stages a comeback. *The New York Times,* pp. W1, W7.

O'Brien, K. J. (2005, July 5). In Germany, the jobless work to keep their benefits. *The New York Times,* p. C3.

Organisation for Economic Co-operation and Development. (2005a, November 13). *Beyond borders: The OECD database on the foreign born and expatriates.* Retrieved from http://www.oecd.org/0.3373,ed_2649_37415_1_1_1_1_37415.html

Organisation for Economic Co-operation and Development. (2005b). *Society at a glance.* Retrieved from http://www.oecd.org.document/24/0,3343,en_33873108_33873402_2671576_1_1_1_1,00.html

Organisation for Economic Co-operation and Development. (2007a). *Factbook 2007: Economic, Environmental and Social Statistics.* http://lysander.sourceoecd.org/vl=2493990/cl=20/nw=1/rpsv/fact2007/

Organisation for Economic Co-operation and Development. (2007b). *International migration outlook, 2007.* Retrieved from http://www.oecd.org/els/migration/imo

Pew Research Center. (2007, October). *47-nation Pew global attitudes survey.* Retrieved from http://www.pewresearch.org

Pew Research Center. (n.d.). *What the world thinks in 2002.* Retrieved from http://www.people-press.org

Pham, K. (2007, March 15). Germany's neo-housewives spark debate on gender roles. *Spiegel Online.* Retrieved from http://www.spiegel.de/international/0,1518,470941,00.html

Rademaekers, W. (1992). The oh so good life. In R. E. Long (Ed), *The reunification of Germany* (pp. 8–12). New York: Wilson.

Rodden, J. G. (2000). *Repainting the little red schoolhouse: A history of eastern German education 1945–1995.* New York: Oxford University Press.

Rosenthal, E. (2006, September 4). European Union's plunging birthrates spread eastward. *The New York Times,* p. A3.

Schelzig, E. (2002, May 12). Perks for the oldest profession: German law offers prostitutes union rights, profit sharing. *The Washington Post,* p. A13.

Schneider, P. (2005, December 4). The new Berlin Wall. *The New York Times Magazine,* pp. 66–71.

Schulze, H. (1998). *Germany: A new history.* Cambridge, MA: Harvard University Press.

Spiegel Online. (2007, March 15). *German brothel offers 50-percent discount to senior citizens.* Retrieved from http://www.spiegel.de/international/zeitgeist/0,1518,471907,00.html

Stearns, P. (2003). Vertriebene in Deutschland (review). *Journal of Social History, 36*(3), 821–823.

Steffans, M. C., & Wagner, C. (2004, May). Attitudes towards lesbians, gay men, bisexual women and bisexual men in Germany. *The Journal of Sex Research, 41*(2), 137–149.

Thelen, K. A. (2004). *How institutions evolve: The political economy of skills in Germany, Britain, the United States, and Japan.* Cambridge, England: Cambridge University Press.

Tzortzis, A. (2005, August 9). Germany's rap music veers toward the violent. *The New York Times,* p. B7.

United Nations. (1982). *Demographic yearbook.* Retrieved from http://unstats.un.org/unsd/demographic/products/dyb/2000_round.htm

United Nations. (2000). *Demographic yearbook.* Retrieved from http://unstats.un.org/unsd/demographic/products/dyb/2000_round.htm

United Nations. (2004a). *Demographic yearbook.* Retrieved from http://unstats.un.org/unsd/demographic/products/dyb/2000_round.htm

United Nations. (2004b). *Human development report 2004.* Retrieved from http://hdr.undp.org/en/reports/global/hdr2004/

United Nations. (2005, March 31). *Eighth survey of crime, 2001–2002.* Retrieved from http://www.unodc.org/unodc/en/data-and-analysis/Eighth-United-Nations-Survey-on-Crime-Trends-and-the-Operations-of-Criminal-Justice-Systems.html

United Nations. (2006/2007). *Human development report 2006/2007.* Retrieved from http://hdr.undp.org/en/statistics/

U.S. Bureau of the Census. (n.d.). *International data base, tables by country.* Retrieved from http://www.census.gov/ipc/www/idb/tables.html

Wood, N. (2005, May 19). Germany sending gypsy refugees back to Kosovo. *The New York Times.* Retrieved from http://www.nytimes.com

World Bank. (2004). *World development indicators 2004.* Retrieved from http://www .worldbank.org/data/dataquery.html

Zielbauer, P. (2002, December 25). As eastern Germany rusts, young workers leave. *The New York Times,* p. A3.

Zimmerman, E. (2005, September 15). Rapid increase in child poverty in Germany. Retrieved from the *World Socialist Web Site:* http://www.wsws.org

Index